The Value of Public Service Media

The Value of
of Public Service Media

Gregory Ferrell Lowe & Fiona Martin (eds.)

NORDICOM

The Value of Public Service Media
RIPE@2013

Gregory Ferrell Lowe & Fiona Martin (eds.)

ISBN 978-91-86523-84-8

Published by:
Nordicom
University of Gothenburg
Box 713
SE 405 30 GÖTEBORG
Sweden

Cover by: Roger Palmqvist
Cover photo by: Arja Lento
Printed by: Litorapid Media AB, Göteborg, Sweden, 2014
ISO 14001

NORDIC ECOLABEL

341 834
PRODUCT GROUP

Contents

Preface

As this sixth RIPE Reader goes to press, published again by the Nordic Information Centre for Media and Communication Research (NORDICOM) at the University of Gothenburg in Sweden, the RIPE network is healthy and enjoying a new phase of international growth. This Reader offers the best fruits of the RIPE@2012 conference in Sydney, Australia, in a thoroughly mature form. The contents were peer reviewed (double blinded) and the standards were rigorous.

Building on our efforts in the RIPE@2011 Reader (edited by Lowe and Jeanette Steemers), this collection again includes non-European contributors as we pursue the effort to become a more globally inclusive initiative. The RIPE@2012 conference was titled *Value for Public Money – Money for Public Value*. In our first collective venture outside Western Europe, the historic home of public service broadcasting and the roots of the RIPE initiative, the experience was excellent and the results fruitful – as we trust this Reader will amply demonstrate. The RIPE network is keen to support the growing international interest in establishing independent public service media organisations of various types and in diverse arrangements in countries and regions where this approach has not been common in Asia, the Middle East and Africa. We are hopeful that developments will have a mutually beneficial and reinforcing role for rethinking public service media also in Europe.

The 2012 conference, hosted by the University of Sydney and sponsored by the Australian Broadcasting Corporation [ABC], owes a debt of gratitude to the collaborative work, guiding hand and enthusiasm of the late Associate Professor, Anne Dunn, who sadly passed away before the conference she had worked so hard to produce, and for so long, took place. Anne was a former television and radio broadcaster, ABC radio manager, and a founder of the University of Sydney's media studies programme. Our tribute during the conference underscored how greatly she was missed. We hope the collective efforts and results did her the honour that is merited. We are mindful, as well, of her husband, Peter Dunn, who participated fully in the conference and contributed to the results.

We wish to also thank the conference hosts and sponsors, and especially the ABC's Chairman, the Hon. James Spigelman, and its Managing Director, Mr. Mark Scott; the University's Faculty of Arts and Social Sciences and Department of Media and Communications; and key participants, including executives of the Special Broadcasting Service [SBS], Australia's multicultural broadcaster, and our RIPE@2014 conference sponsor, Japan's Nippon Hoso Kyokai [NHK]. We are all thankful to the staff and volunteers of the Art Gallery of NSW for the Indigenous art tour, and the indefatigable chef Angie Hong for the Vietnamese banquet we enjoyed at her restaurant on King Street – *Thanh Binh*.

On behalf of the 2012 conference host and sponsors, we express our gratitude to the Conference Planning Group [CPG] and the RIPE Advisory Board [RAB], together with their home institutions that provided funding and support for their involvement. The CPG members for RIPE@2012 were: Anne Dunn and Fiona Martin for the University of Sydney; Paul Chadwick for the ABC; Michael Huntsberger, for Linfield College, USA; Gregory Ferrell Lowe, for the University of Tampere, Finland; Yoshiko Nakamura, for NHK, Japan; Philip Savage, for McMaster University, Canada; Jeanette Steemers, for the University of Westminster, UK, and Hilde Van den Bulck, for the University of Antwerp, Belgium.

The CPG thanks the RAB members for their cheerful guidance and wise counsel: Minna Aslama Horowitz, for St. John's University, USA; Jo Bardoel, for the Universities of Amsterdam & of Nijmegan; Netherlands; Maureen Burns, for the University of Queensland, Australia; Taisto Hujanen, for the University of Tampere, Finland; John Jackson, for Concordia University, Canada; Per Jauert, for the University of Aarhus, Denmark and Brian McNair, for the Queensland University of Technology, Australia.

Importantly, we all wish to thank David Sutton, Head of Strategic Policy for ABC Corporate Affairs, Lisa Hresc, Head of Corporate Marketing at ABC Research & Marketing, and Jenny Sterland, Information Coordinator at ABC Editorial Policies for their organisational capacities, grace under pressure and attention to detail. Day 1 of RIPE@2012 at the ABC was a stimulating event and impressively presented, with a dedicated set design and excellent stage management. Kudos, as well, to Madeleine King, the conference assistant from the University of Sydney. Her diligence, patience and cheer throughout – especially when wrangling student volunteers and wayward academics – is much appreciated.

Finally we give special thanks to the contributors to the 6th RIPE Reader for you dedication, flexibility and patience during a rigorous year-long editorial process, and to Ulla Carlsson and her team at NORDICOM who, as usual, have made this an efficient and enjoyable creative experience. Thanks especially to Karin Poulsen who shepherded the volume through the final stages. The series of RIPE Readers continues to grow in significance and reputation thanks in no small part to the excellent editorial and publication support of NORDICOM.

The Faculty of Arts and Social Sciences at the University of Sydney, and the Graduate Studies Program in Media Management at the University of Tampere, have funded this RIPE Reader. We are grateful.

Now we all look forward to the RIPE@2014 conference, co-hosted by the Institute for Media and Communication Research at Keio University and NHK in Tokyo, Japan, that will take place from August 26th-29th. For more information about the RIPE initiative, our conference and this series of Readers, as well as useful updates, please visit our website at: www.ripeat.org.

November 2013

Gregory Ferrell Lowe
Media Management Programme
University of Tampere
Finland

Fiona R. Martin
Dept of Media & Communications
University of Sydney
Australia

Prologue

Paul Chadwick[1]

In this transitional, transformative era for media it is both daunting and exciting to consider, the implications of what RIPE stands for: Re-visionary Interpretations of the Public Enterprise[2]. RIPE is a unique network that hosts a biennial gathering of scholars from around the world who share a particular interest in public service media. The RIPE@2012 conference was the first to be held outside Europe, which marks an important development. RIPE@2014 will be another similar collaboration, this time in Japan.

What brings the academies and the public service media together in this way? Based on my own experience, I think it must surely be their shared commitment to the public interest, to the common good. Although these institutions have different histories and serve different functions in respective societies, the universities and the public broadcasters tend to share defining characteristics as well:

- Recognition under law

- Nourishment from public funds

- Service for the common good

- Custodians of collective memory

- Respect for accuracy and fairness

- Aspirations to high quality

- Expectations of accountability

- Open debate, civilly conducted

- Traditions of independence

RIPE conferences are living examples of the mutual reliance of the academies and the public service media in open, democratic societies.

Media entities routinely seek out the research and expertise of academic scholarship in all the rich variety of disciplines. Sometimes, and haphazardly, the two institutions combine as a kind of informal check on the claims and counterclaims of other powerful institutions – especially, but not exclusively, government. Academicians regularly find in public broadcasters the specialist programme-makers and prominent media platforms necessary to ensure that their work can spread beyond the universities to fuel public debate. Via such contributions, academic work reinforces the legitimacy of the role of publicly funded universities in democratic societies.

In this light it seems natural for public service media and universities to collaborate in co-hosting RIPE conferences. For the ABC, which celebrated its 80th birthday in 2012, it was a pleasure to work with colleagues at the University of Sydney. And it was equally a pleasure to welcome so many participants from right around the world. This was a good conference – productive, useful and enjoyable.

In their introductory chapter the editors introduce strands of thinking and research which this book has harvested from among the sixty (+) papers presented in Sydney from 5 to 7 September 2012. The theme, 'Value for public money – Money for public value', was conceived with the intention of encouraging multi-disciplinary analysis of two of the great recurring issues for public service media in many and diverse countries:

1. How can public media demonstrate convincingly that it represents value for the public money that sustains it?

2. In what ways can a society willingly pay to ensure public value (not only private gain) from the media?

Both questions engage significant – and significantly entrenched – political positions. And both offer rich possibilities for consideration by those who want to preserve the best of public service media but also recognise the practical challenges entailed in this for the Digital Age.

The challenges must be faced and academicians can help. Nothing about public service media can be taken for granted today as audiences fragment, as technologies proliferate and as spectrum scarcity, the organising principle of the regulation of broadcasting since the early 20th century, diminishes.

One, and only one, of the practical challenges: accountability

In this prologue I want to address one very important practical challenge: how public service media can be accountable without losing the independence, which would make them little more than mouthpieces of the State.

As the executive with responsibility for the ABC's self-regulation framework from January 2007 to November 2012, I found this issue was central to my own work as it is to many media professionals and scholars. In 2012 and 2013, the issue of media accountability gained far wider prominence than usual because of extraordinary events in the UK. The Leveson Inquiry about the phone-hacking scandal at *News of the World* focused attention on the culture, practices and ethics of the press. Few experienced practitioners in any country who are familiar with newsrooms would have failed to experience spasms of recognition as the hearings brought to light and into sharp focus attitudes and techniques that are mostly unexamined within media institutions, and certainly under-reported by them.

By coincidence, at around the same time as Leveson made his recommendations for what he regarded as a better accountability framework, one of the greatest public service media organisations in the world, the British Broadcasting Corporation, was reeling from revelations about how one of its longest-serving and best-known presenters, the late Jimmy Savile, had systematically used his fame to obtain access to children whom he sexually abused. In the UK at least, the link between trust and accountability had rarely been so starkly demonstrated.

RIPE conferences, and the books which result from them, enjoy an international audience of media professionals and specialist scholars. So, reader, let me ask you to reflect on whether in your country you have seen something like the pattern that I will describe:

A public broadcaster will usually be required by the statute that creates it to meet certain standards.

Typically, those standards will include accuracy, impartiality, independence and integrity.

The extent to which the public broadcaster maintains those standards will have a bearing on whether it remains credible and trusted.

Unless credible and trusted, a public broadcaster loses legitimacy.

Questions arise about why it should be publicly supported.

Those who covet its spectrum or its audiences grow restive.

Those who would clip its independence grow bolder.

Those who would ordinarily defend it grow doubtful.

The cry goes up for more regulation.

This broad pattern can be glimpsed in the histories of media organisations that have generally enjoyed legitimacy in the democratic societies they serve. I believe a similar pattern can be discerned from another angle. It can be seen in countries that, to varying degrees, have been undemocratic and then undergo political upheaval, one result of which is a desire to build some legal and institutional structure typically associated with democratic societies. One important element of such a structure is a free and diverse media system with, as discussed in the RIPE@2011 book, a public service media sector. We've seen this in the experiences of former state broadcasters when authoritarian regimes end. And we've seen efforts developing in the Middle East in recent years. When a Wall falls, when Spring comes, when the work of democratic reform begins across a range of old institutions, there is evident need for, and efforts to, develop *public service* in broadcasting.

The pattern I have described seems to recur regardless of technological change, although obviously with variations, and across diverse cultures. It appeared, to varying extents, after political changes came to eastern and central Europe, parts of South America, and Southeast Asia. At the outset of its new era, the former state broadcaster may have little legitimacy; it is usually handicapped by a past in which it was used an instrument of authoritarianism, a past which may be vividly, bitterly remembered and sardonically, mistrustfully recalled. In its efforts to build credibility and trust, a nascent public broadcaster will adopt, adapt and develop standards of ethical practice and pledge to uphold them. Typically those standards will include accuracy, impartiality, integrity and – crucially – independence. These are principles at the heart of public service in media. Having adopted such as standards, a public broadcaster must give attention to the framework it uses to uphold them.

Since independence is an imperative, and heavy regulation of content diminishes independence, it is necessary for a public broadcaster to make its self-regulation authentic and genuine. Mere window-dressing is worse than nothing at all because that adds hypocrisy to other, deeper failings which, in time, can cause a withering of credibility, then trust, then legitimacy.

In a media context, what are the elements of authentic self-regulation? I offer six that the ABC considers to be vital, and of course other PSM institutions as well:

1. **Set standards succinctly** – being careful to separate aspirations and principles from enforceable rules

2. **Test standards fairly** – either in response to others (complaint handling) or by developing your own tests (quality assurance processes)

3. **Provide just remedies** – recognise the benefits of swift correction and clarification where that is appropriate, especially in a digital age of big, widely cast and enduring data

4. **Encourage reflection, discussion, and training** – so that experience among colleagues is shared among colleagues

5. **Collect good data and circulate it** – close the feedback loops after opening them

6. **Review and disclose; disclose and review** – in media in this era, five years is a very long time.

The ABC undertook a major review of its self-regulation framework in 2009 (ABC 2009) and is undergoing a continuing process of reform in all six elements. Much was already being done. Much remains to be done. Authentic self-regulation is always unfinished business. In this realm, to declare completion is to reveal complacency.

Authentic self-regulation has dual aims. It is an important aspect of *accountability*. But it is also a contributor to *continuous quality improvement*. In my experience this second aim is too often neglected – by practitioners, critics and academicians. In a spirit of innovation, can we conceive these elements of authentic self-regulation as more than dour and necessary rules and processes? Can these elements contribute to what makes a public broadcaster a successful part of a healthy democratic polity and of a vibrant culture? Can self regulation – like content-making itself – vitalise creativity and collective memory, with brevity and an acute awareness of the zeitgeist, to help it fulfil its proper role within the larger endeavour that is a public service media organisation? I think the answer to all these questions is yes.

One example among many is the ABC's approach to social media. This radical change in the media environment was approached warily by many traditional media organisations. When many others adopted social media they tended to devise rules for its use that too closely resembled policies that had emerged from the cultures of older media forms. The ABC was an early and agile adopter of social media. A traditional media organisation, yes, but evolving quickly. The ABC was conscious of the risks inherent in social media for a large public institution and conscious also that something quite new was happening among, as one manifesto puts it, "the people formerly known as the audience" (Rosen 2006). And conscious, too, that social media was having its effects among ABC staff and contractors.

In response, the ABC adopted a policy on use of social media that is, in essence, four short sentences:

Do not mix the professional and the personal in ways likely to bring the ABC into disrepute.

Do not undermine your effectiveness at work.

Do not imply ABC endorsement of your personal views.

Do not disclose confidential information obtained through work.

With some effort, these standards can be compressed into 140 characters for dissemination via Twitter. I consider this authentic self-regulation with a sense of the zeitgeist. Audiences, empowered in part through social media, can detect and expose sham self-regulation.

In November 2011, the philosopher Onora O'Neill gave a lecture at the Reuters Institute for the Study of Journalism at Oxford entitled 'The Rights of Journalism and the Needs of Audiences' (O'Neill 2011). At the time the Leveson Inquiry was underway. Prescriptions for more regulation were emerging from many quarters and O'Neill reviewed the traditional philosophical bases for freedom of expression, making the case that nowadays an adequate interpretation of freedom of expression must take the needs of audiences seriously. O'Neill argued that the expression of media organisations, as with the speech of other institutions, is more powerful than the expression of individuals. That is not to say necessarily more valuable, just more powerful. She proposed a test of 'assessability': that the audience must be able to assess what powerful organisations provide.

This is a key challenge for the self-regulation frameworks of all media, but especially for those that are genuinely public service media.

Notes

1. Paul Chadwick is Former Director Editorial Policies (2007-2012) for the Australian Broadcasting Corporation and was the primary ABC representative on the RIPE@2012 planning committee. The prologue is based on his opening remarks for the conference in Sydney in September 2012.
2. For details see www.ripeat.org

References

ABC (2009) Review of the ABC's Self-Regulation Framework Report – September 2009. Accessed at: http://about.abc.net.au/reports-publications/review-of-the-abcs-self-regulation-framework-report-september-2009/

O'Neill, O. (2011) The Rights of Journalism and the Needs of Audiences. Lecture presented at Reuters Institute for the Study of Journalism, Oxford. Accessed at: http://reutersinstitute.politics.ox.ac.uk/fileadmin/documents/presentations/The_Rights_of_Journalism_and_Needs_of_Audiences.pdf

Rosen, J. (2006) The People Formerly Known as the Audience. *Pressthink* Accessed at: http://archive.pressthink.org/2006/06/27/ppl_frmr.html

Appendix

Examples methods for media self regulation and continuous quality improvement

This list was compiled as part of a submission by Paul Chadwick to an Independent Media Inquiry conducted at the request of the Australian Government by a former federal court judge, Ray Finkelstein QC, in 2011-12. Submissions and the inquiry's Report can be found at http://www.dbcde.gov.au/digital_economy/independent_media_inquiry

The selection in this appendix is illustrative only. Inclusion here does not necessarily mean endorsement by the author of the Prologue. The methods that require or imply a statutory basis are expressly not endorsed.

Examples of system overviews

A More Accountable Press Part One: The need for reform – Is self-regulation failing the press and the public? Media Standards Trust, UK, February 2009, http://mediastandardstrust.org/wp-content/uploads/downloads/2010/07/A-More-Accountable-Press-Part-1.pdf

Self-Regulation of Digital Media Converging on the Internet – Industry Codes of Conduct in Sectoral Analysis, Oxford University, Centre for Socio-Legal Studies, http://pcmlp.socleg.ox.ac.uk/sites/pcmlp.socleg.ox.ac.uk/files/IAPCODEfinal.pdf

The Media Self-Regulation Guidebook http://www.osce.org/fom/31497

Media Accountability Systems – a wide variety of techniques, from a wide range of countries, compiled by a longstanding scholar in field, Claude-Jean Bertrand.

Examples of corrections pages

Associated Press, http://hosted.ap.org/dynamic/fronts/CORRECTIONS?SITE=AP&SECTION=HOME

LA Times, http://www.latimes.com/news/custom/corrections/

Wall Street Journal, http://online.wsj.com/article/Corrections.html?mod=WSJ_footer

The Guardian, Corrections and clarifications, http://www.guardian.co.uk/theguardian/series/correctionsandclarifications?INTCMP=SRCH

NY Times, Corrections, http://www.nytimes.com/pages/corrections/index.html

Christian Science Monitor, http://www.csmonitor.com/About/Corrections

Examples of newspapers inviting readers to propose corrections

Washington Post, http://www.washingtonpost.com/wp-srv/interactivity/corrections/

LA Times, http://www.latimes.com/about/mediagroup/la-feedback-email-form-rr,0,5493970.customform

NY Times, http://publiceditor.blogs.nytimes.com/corrections/

Examples of systematic fact-checking systems

St Petersburg Times – Politifact (website) and Truth-O-Meter (mobile phone app), http://www.politifact.com/ – tracking and rating campaign promises made by presidential candidates – trialled by (USA) ABC News, http://abcnews.go.com/blogs/politics/2010/04/this-week-joins-with-politifact-to-factcheck-the-newsmakers/

Annenberg Public Policy Center & University of Pennsylvania – FactCheck, http://factcheck.org/ – monitors the factual accuracy of what is said by major U.S. political players in the form of TV ads, debates, speeches, interviews and news releases

Examples of non-media efforts online to prompt improved media accuracy

Regret the Error – http://www.regrettheerror.com/

MediaBugs – includes online form, bookmarklet, widget and plugin (http://mediabugs.org/) and online monitoring of how media errors (bugs) are being addressed, http://mediabugs.org/bugs

Examples of active encouragement of ideas for quality improvement

Building trust in the news – 101+ Good Ideas, Associated Press Managing Editors, http://web.archive.org/web/20080918030601/http:/www.apme-credibility.org/

Knight-Batten Awards for Innovations in Journalism (yearly since 2003), http://www.j-lab.org/projects/knight-batten-awards-for-innovations-in-journalism/

APME 'Great Ideas, Great Journalism' (yearly since 2007), http://www.apme.com/?page=GreatIdeas

Reynolds Journalism Institute, http://www.rjionline.org/ideas

Examples of newspaper ombudsmen/readers' editors/ public editors as in-house critics

Organization of News Ombudsmen, http://newsombudsmen.org/resources/ombudsmen

The Guardian, Readers' editor, http://www.guardian.co.uk/theguardian/page/readerseditor and 'Open door', http://www.guardian.co.uk/commentisfree/series/open-door

National Public Radio, United States, Ombudsman http://www.npr.org/blogs/ombudsman/

DR, Public Broadcaster, Denmark, Ombudsman http://www.dr.dk/OmDR/Lytternes_og_seernes_redaktoer/Klummer/2013/0918160849.htm

Chapter 1

The Value and Values
of Public Service Media

Fiona Martin & Gregory Ferrell Lowe

In the 21st century the worth of public service media [PSM] is under increasing scrutiny. In countries where public broadcasting [PSB] was established during the early to mid 1900s, governments are now considering whether the public monies spent on that institution, and its multiplatform evolution, represent a good investment in terms of their political, social and cultural outcomes – as well as their economic impact. They are assessing what its essential functions should be, whether PSM competes fairly or not in established markets, and whether it crowds out private sector investment in new media and inhibits innovation. Economic rationales – from Europe's ex-ante market impact assessments to New Zealand television's contestable funding model – play an increasingly central role in approaches to provisioning public media goods and services.

As bailout politics develops across Western Europe and PSM is targeted for cuts in that context, politicians have been reminded how strongly the institution is valued beyond instrumental or economic criteria. When the Samaris government shut down ERT in Greece on the grounds that it was wasteful and corrupt, and on that basis suggesting the license fee was an unwarranted burden to households (Nevradakis 2013), citizen protest and trade union court action saw programming resume online within hours. A new broadcaster, DT, was instated within weeks, although how that situation will turn out in the long run remains unclear (Lowen 2013). In Portugal plans to privatise RTP's channels have been postponed following fierce political lobbying, although staff cuts will go ahead and any potential future sale "will be subject to the company's ongoing restructuring process and appropriate market conditions" (Gomez et al 2013).

Such struggles over the scope and impact of government intervention are hardly new. However the task of evaluating PSMs' importance as a regulatory strategy and in its contribution to public life has taken on renewed significance in the light of global financial upheavals and austerity measures. The task has also expanded and become more complex in the past century, involving more measurements of worth, more sites of scrutiny and decidedly more critics – especially as PSB has been transformed by its incorporation of online and co-creative media technologies. The on-going debates about PSM's value to society were catalytic for the RIPE@2012 conference, which examined the concept of public value, its origins and impacts, and did so from a critical, historical and comparative perspective.

Since the 1980s with the rise of neo-liberal political agendas in the West, public service media institutions have become preoccupied with the task of valuing their worth in both presence and performance. This is notably due to the neo-classical economic prioritisation of free market competition, productivity and efficiency targets, with its accompanying 'governmentality' (Foucault 1991). This thinking is driving PSM's pursuit of strategies for constituting and measuring the preferences of what are presumed to be its rational, freely choosing economic subjects (Rose 1999) as audiences and users. In the process public service institutions have become corporatized and construed as public enterprises with their worth increasingly calculated in terms of efficiency, performance and accountability measures. In this collection, Hallvard Moe and Hilde van den Bulck provide an overview of the 'public value' concept that captures the essence and variation well, while the chapters by Peter Goodwin and by Michael Tracey provide relevant critique of economic rationality in application to PSM.

Public broadcasters in many countries have gained some boost in legitimacy by applying, and promoting, economic measurement. It has played a helpful role in securing them approval to act in various developmental pursuits. This has been especially important in their push to become more than broadcasters – to develop into PSM providers (i.e. including online and mobile platforms). But the positives are offset by tensions and contradiction as pressure for economic value assessment is, in key respects, at cross-purposes with the underlying public service ethos that is fundamental to the institution's societal legitimacy. The public sector in media isn't supposed to be a business, even if it is required to operate in a more business-like manner. The Hon. James Spigelman, Chairman of the Australian Broadcasting Corporation [ABC], offers insightful discussion about this in his published reprisal of a splendid keynote address to the RIPE@2012 conference.

PSM organisations are mandated to provide services and cater to groups that are not attractive in commercial terms, and this is entirely appropriate given their public charters and funding. In practice, however, this has meant the institution is torn between evidencing market value, a concept strongly embedded in commercial logic where success depends on achieving sufficient popularity, and embodying its mandate as a not-for-profit institution with values that are in principle contrary to that logic. PSM has become an institution caught between the contrary demands of audiences that are construed as 'sovereign' media users and meeting charter requirements that have a pronounced collective, social-welfare orientation. The institution struggles with the pressure to be both popular and to provide a comprehensive service that might not always be liked by the majority or even wanted by some. This balancing act creates significant complexity for a fair, comprehensive and robust measurement of 'public value'.

These tensions are partly contests rooted in historically different political strategies for understanding, orienting and handling the role of government in mediation. But they also arise from structural shifts in media industries that have been triggered by the advance of digitalisation and internetworking. These shifts have facilitated new and more complex flows in information and content provision, and contributed to more volatile media markets and policy ecosystems. They have encouraged platform proliferation and increasingly dynamic uses of online services that continue to grow in scope and volume. This is the context for Karen Donders' and Hilde van den Bulcks' critical analysis of the 'digital argument' supporting policy change, and their helpful focus on assessing implications for the value of PSM.

The forces of economic rationality and globalisation have undermined the original national, and national cultural, remit of PSB (Lowe & Jauert 2005). The massive expansion of the media offer and range of services in recent years, together with the explosion of rich audio-visual content distributed on the Web, facilitates new forms of competition for revenue and attention. It also sets new benchmarks for quality and innovation that are quite outside the familiar remits of traditional broadcasters and traditional broadcasting regulation. When everyone can ostensibly be a publisher, what need for PSM to represent diversity or nurture democratic debate, and how might its contribution to those historic roles be better understood? Christian Berg, Gregory F. Lowe and Anker Brink Lund address relevant issues in their chapter focused on the question of whether the market failure thesis still applies to broadcasting and the extent to which it might also apply to the broadband environment, which has been so rapidly and increasingly commercialised.

PSM scholars are investigating a comparatively radical shift in the essential understandings of PSB's value to socio-political systems, and a related struggle to re-articulate historically characteristic values and principles for renewed relevance under circumstances and conditions that are very different compared with the era in which the ethos was formulated. That is complicated enough in a particular sociocultural context, and infinitely more so in cross-country comparisons. We not only live in a more internationally connected world than most could have imagined in the 1920s and 1930s, but also in a world with shared financial and environmental problems and all the challenges that are inherent to coping with vastly more pluralistic societies.

As Castells (1998) noted some time ago, the cohesive force of public institutions such as churches, schools and media is breaking down; identity politics is triumphing as new tribal rifts emerge, and older ones are reanimated. We are increasingly working with, and dependent on, globally networked technologies and relationships. This presents extraordinary challenges for PSM's role in facilitating a sense of national identity and cultural belonging. It suggests – in line with public value theory – that new alliances are needed to achieve the social objectives once accorded to single public institutions. Tim Ratts, Karen Donders and Carolyn Pauwels consider some key implications in their chapter on the significance of partnership approaches to public service provision.

Although many traditional supporters and proponents would prefer it otherwise, it is important for PSM to demonstrate that the money invested in the enterprise and spent on production and distribution constitutes a fair deal. The resource is public money and that is increasingly scarce. Yet it is equally obvious that delivering value for money cannot legitimate PSM's overall role or functions because these are not primarily about economic criteria or industrial priorities.

Of utmost important is ensuring that its output and outcomes deliver value that is appreciated by its publics, and add value to the public sphere (Benington & Moore 2011). That is the foundational heuristic of public value theory and is reflected in the RIPE@2012 conference theme: "Value for Public Money, Money for Public Value". This book distils the main results from the conference discourse. The chapters represent a careful selection from the 60+ conference papers that were peer reviewed as proposals for presentation. Each of the papers chosen for inclusion in this book has been thoroughly updated, revised and subjected to double blind peer review prior publication.

This collection investigates diverse conceptions of public service value, which are keyed to differences in the values and ideals that legitimate the enterprise. These values and ideals are historic within nations and national across them. The BBC is ever the relevant case and possessed of iconic status. It certainly has had, and continues to exert, tremendous influence on other PSB organisations, even producing what some resent as an unwarranted and unwise 'Beebification' of PSB vision and strategy in the field. We agree that its impact has sometimes obscured sociocultural differences and political-economic distinctions that are highly significant. As the RIPE@2011 Reader (edited by Lowe & Steemers) illustrated, PSB's founding political, social and cultural ideals have not produced an array of BBC clones, but rather an alternative constellation of public media organisations.

Our chapter prepares the ground for a collection that addresses and assesses the value of public service media across a range of cases. While many studies in this volume are local and empirical, our introduction provides a broad international context, stipulating some of the crucial ways in which global trends in economics, media business and public sector management have influenced strategic thinking on PSM value creation. In this chapter we clarify the theoretical origins and practical applications of the "public value" framework, and consider its significance for the evolution of public service media. We then discuss approaches to quantifying value and emphasise the continuing importance of reinterpreting the institution's core legitimating values. Finally, we consider the challenges of a more dispersed, networked model for creating public value and achieving innovation.

Constructing 'public value'

Public value has, in the last decade, become a much-debated lens for assessing PSM. This began, in practice, after the BBC developed its public value framework as an instrumental approach to securing the 2005 Charter renewal. The original formulation of public value theory was proposed by management scholar Mark H. Moore in his seminal 1995 book titled *Creating Public Value: Strategic Management in Government*. Moore articulates an idea of public value in the pragmatist tradition of William James and Charles Sanders Pierce that hinges on the notion that truth can be found in the practical consequences of action and thought. Moore's intention was to develop a conceptual model, with tools, for developing management competence in the public sector. In the background Moore was reacting against the approach to public administration called New Public Management [NPM] that emerged as one important dimension of neo-liberal sensibilities in the UK and the USA (see Freedman 2008).

The philosophical genesis of NPM emerged in the early Clinton years as 'Third Way' politics took hold, with its characteristic emphasis on modernising and decentralising government functions. In Moore's view, public value is created through satisfying the needs and desires of citizens as politically arbitrated and authorised by their representative government (1995: 27ff), not citizens conceived as 'customers'. Public value is both "what the public most 'values' and also what adds value to the public sphere" (Benington & Moore 2011: 14). As Richard Collins argued in his dissection of the BBC's attachment to the public values concept, it is centrally:

> ...both a *practice* whereby providers work with users to produce outcomes that genuinely meet users' needs and an *aspiration* to go beyond 'hitting the target but missing the point' and so re-orientate public bodies to 'ends' (such as 'health') rather than to 'means' (Collins 2007: 6).

In the 2011 book that Moore edited with John Benington, the authors provide a concise comparison to clarify the significant differences between their public values framework, NPM and the traditional approach to public administration:

> Whereas traditional public administration assumes a context of relative political economic and social stability, and whereas new public management trusts the logic of free market competition, public value recognizes the complexity, volatility and uncertainty in the environment. [Whereas]... traditional public

administration assumes that the needs and problems to be addressed by governments are fairly straightforward, and that the solutions are known and understood, New public management assumes that needs and wants will be expressed and satisfied through the mechanism of market choice. The public value framework, however, starts with a recognition that the needs and problems now facing citizens, communities and governments are complex rather than simple, 'wicked' rather than 'tame', and diverse rather than homogeneous (ibid: 13).

Public managers found Moore's propositions timely and of strategic importance. Neo-liberals, who favour small government and see anything public as inherently less efficient and less desirable than a private sector alternative, had been restructuring the public sector across OECD countries (Touraine 2001). Moore in contrast presented the public sector as a positive, co-productive agent for change, with a necessary task of revalidating the role of government in social organisation.

Yet the public value framework also corresponded with a general political interest to strengthen the evaluation of public sector activities, and improve economic performance, in the drive to improve administrative efficiency. Unlike familiar morality-based normative objectives for market intervention, which are difficult or impossible to quantify, this approach to 'public value' could presumably be measured, tabulated, calibrated, demonstrated and, therefore, managed.

In some lights, Moore's work could itself be read as having a neo-liberal complexion, or at least one that is quasi-liberal, given its demand that public sector institutions be measurably more efficient and accountable. But Moore actually argued against adopting a purely, or even largely, economic understanding of value in public sector activity: "We should evaluate the efforts of public sector managers not in the economic marketplace but in the political marketplace of citizens and the collective decisions of representative democratic institutions" (1995: 31).

It is also significant to note that Moore advocates the supreme importance of citizen engagement rather than delivering 'customer satisfaction', and that he prioritised innovation over routine service. Excellence in public sector management is not only about meeting objectives in an efficient and effective manner, but achieving them in clever, novel ways that respond to market conditions and produce socially valuable outcomes. Further, Moore emphasised the need for collaboration and co-production between sectors, agencies and interests in order to extend the reach and impact of public sector organisations (1995: 117-118). A networked governance model for conducting policy development and ensuring service delivery became a featured aspect in his later work with John Benington.

Public value theory proposes three intersecting, interacting aspects (Figure 1), a model described by Moore (1995) as the "strategic triangle". The "authorizing environment" is a socio-political arena in which managers of public sector institutions work to build and maintain a coalition of stakeholders, considered necessary for sustaining the enterprise. The focus of production is keyed to "public value outcomes", which is distinguished from output. Public sector managers should specify not only what their institutions will do (output), but more importantly with what intended results (outcome). This is largely where measurement comes into play – assessing the extent to which the enterprise has succeeded in achieving outcome goals. The third leg of the triangle is "operational capacity", which can't be taken for granted. It must be resourced and continually developed, therefore requiring public sector managers to make convincing arguments and to demonstrate in performance that continuing, as well as additional, investment is merited.

Figure 1.   Summary of Mark H. Moore's strategic triangle

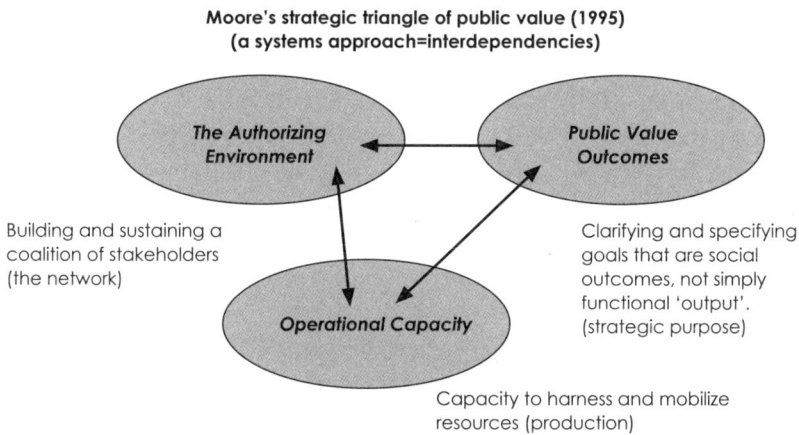

Moore's strategic triangle of public value (1995)
(a systems approach=interdependencies)

The Authorizing Environment

Public Value Outcomes

Building and sustaining a coalition of stakeholders (the network)

Clarifying and specifying goals that are social outcomes, not simply functional 'output'. (strategic purpose)

Operational Capacity

Capacity to harness and mobilize resources (production)

Public sector managers "have role in orchestrating the processes of public policy development, along with other actors and stakeholders" (p.4). This is the continual work of alignment.

Source: Benington & Moore 2011.

The public values framework found purchase in PSM first in an accountability assurance proposal developed by the BBC (2004) – a two-step process for assessing the public value of any new or radically altered service. First the BBC Trust, as the governing authority, would decide whether or not the proposed change was a service to the public. Second, the Office of Communication [Ofcom], the UK regulatory agency, would establish whether allowing it would be unfair or undesirable in terms of market impact. This proposal was accepted by the British government and applied from 2005. Its market impact assessment [MIA] process is increasingly being adopted throughout Europe as a basis for decisions about PSM developments, as part of an ex-ante evaluation or public value testing [PVT] approach.

PVT is supposed to determine the legitimate scope of public sector activity in new media markets. It claims a 'common sense' underpinning in trying to locate the appropriate limits for PSM production and distribution, ultimately with implications for innovation. Proponents also suggest that PVT ensures the value publics receive from PSM in return for their investments. However PVT has also generated long, costly and ultimately ritualistic verification processes (Collins 2011) without many actual rejections – ironically, perhaps, raising serious questions about the economic value of public value testing. For example NRK's recent bid in Norway to develop a web-based travel planner with three public sector partners took 18 months and four levels of inquiry to resolve, only to be decided on the basis of royal involvement in favour of the national broadcaster (Lilleborg 2012; van den Bulck & Moe 2012).

So Moore's legacy is of some consequence for PSM. Public value has become a media policy term 'du jour' in Europe. It is the primary lens for interpreting the BBC's public service ethos (Coyle & Woolard 2012) and is highly favoured by the European Commission (Donders & Moe 2011). The concept has been useful as a tool for rethinking institutional values, and in that regard has instrumental importance for PSM today. That is the good news.

Less positively Moore's framework has spawned bureaucratic ordeals whereby PSM organisations must justify new activities. The assessment of public value has become an industry in itself. Under the watchful eye of competition authorities, the practice often consumes considerable time, money and energies without unequivocal resolution in the public's favour. Arguably where PSM's operating boundaries are being rolled back, PVT has had more obvious benefits for the private sector than the public at large. Analysts see the influence of the commercial lobbies in ZDF's decision to pull the plug on various online activities (Woldt 2010), and more recently in the cancellation of a joint video-on-demand service with ARD (Roxborough 2013). This happened without even needing to apply Germany's version of PVT, called the 'Three Step' test, which suggests the mere possibility of its application can have a stifling effect on innovation and development.

Ever since the BBC, under Tony Blair's New Labour government, conceived public value as a blueprint for the shaping of a modern public enterprise there has been a strong critical response to the concept. Oakley, Naylor and Lee (2011), for example, argued that the term lacked both intellectual rigour and the historical importance of alternatives, especially public service, public interest and public domain. And James Crabtree observed that public value was becoming a god term which, "as an objective for public service modernization...gives motherhood and apple pie a good run for their money" (2004: 4).

In this volume Peter Goodwin argues that the rise of public value as a core concept for policy and application should be read as a political phenomenon that signals a *fin de siecle* shift to a market-based rationality that is too often insufficiently critical, and that exposes anomalies in the economic logic used to justify funding on this basis. The public value framework has been instrumental in the growth of cultural quantification, which is tricky at best and potentially harmful as well. Michael Tracey addresses this concern in his contribution, which argues that the experience of human creativity and its affect are immeasurable.

Moore conceded that politics is properly the final arbiter of what is deemed to be valuable for the public sector to produce (1995: 38). But the problem, as noted in scholarly provocation, is that governments' assessment of public value largely depends on how they think they should best respond to the changing tides of public opinion in order to secure their own career interests (Lee, Oakley & Naylor 2011). Further, it is telling, and not a little disingenuous, for Moore to declare that public managers can "proceed only by finding a way to improve politics and to make it a firmer guide as to what is publicly valuable" (1995: 38). It seems quite a stretch to think that a public institution that is supposed to be politically impartial could be a primary driver of improvements in political process, despite its otherwise democratic purpose. Even if that intervention in the political arena was possible, it would be a difficult task because the authorising environment is a place of "contestation where many different views and values struggle for acceptance and hegemony" and where there will be "conflicts of ideology, interest and emphasis" (Benington & Moore 2011: 6). Finally, it would arguably be 'the kiss of death' for PSM to be tainted as a politically partisan institution. What and where is the public value in that?

Rather than conceiving public service as a practice of giving impartial advice, as in the British tradition, Moore proposed that public sector managers need to be active in negotiating and brokering to convince all stakeholders – government, bureaucratic, corporate and civic – that there is some common set of values and objectives on which they can agree. Just how painful and complex that can be in practice is well illustrated in the case study of Belgium's VRT during its 2012 management contract negotiations. In the chapter by Karen Donders and Hilde van den Bulck, this process is characterised as a battle between parties favouring economic versus social imperatives. The case illustrates deeper conflicts at work in the definition of PSM purpose and value, a debate that goes far beyond the dualistic politics and critiques of neoliberalism that characterise earlier narratives of pervasive PSB crisis (e.g. Skene 1993; Frazer & O'Reilly 1996; Tracey 1998).

Seen more broadly, PSM's problems in building consensus are the same as for any institution that is subject to, and constitutive of, continuous social debate in an agonistic model of democratic politics (Craig 2000). Because PSM exists to represent and engage societies that are always in flux it must continually adapt to and be aligned with changing political and cultural preferences. Otherwise its mission will be out of step with what is needed and expected in a specific period, or it will fail in its efforts to fulfil in a mission that no longer has sufficient validity. This necessarily exposes the enterprise to both risk and uncertainty, hence the appearance of perpetual crisis. This is not to diminish real threats to the funding or autonomy of individual PSM broadcasters, but only to note that the on-going calculation of public value is inherently difficult and contentious, and that it is also shifting as notions of the public change and as different conceptions of value are given political priority as a consequence of evolving circumstances.

Australia's system is a case in point. There PSB has always existed in direct competition with commercial broadcasting, and has expanded and evolved with the increasing pluralisation of society. When the ABC was created in the late 1920s from a network of commercial stations, it had more of an economic than a Reithian focus. It was meant to spur the uptake of radio licenses and to connect remote rural populations with distant cities, furnishing the communicative conditions in which both political participation and agricultural markets could flourish, despite geographic isolation. It addressed a majority British and Irish immigrant population, and until the 1980s had little to say about, or to, the country's increasingly diverse post-War migrant groups (Brown & Althaus 1996; Craik & Davis 1995), let alone its Indigenous peoples.

The ABC's failure to reflect Australia's growing cultural diversity fuelled lobbies for new broadcast services, with two distinct public sector outcomes. In the early 1970s the government licensed the first 'public' radio stations, the basis of what is now one of the world's largest formal, not-for profit 'community media' networks that is comprised of at least 424 licensed radio and television stations (ACMA 2013; Forde, Meadows & Foxwell 2002). Then in 1975 a second national public broadcaster, the Special Broadcasting Service [SBS], was chartered with a specific multicultural and multilingual remit. In the decades since SBS has adapted to the changing needs of second-generation and new migrants alike, to provide appreciated services for a more cosmopolitan society and effectively responding to greater market competition.

In the process SBS has evolved from an ethnic community broadcaster into a globally focused PSM company (Ang et al. 2008) with a marked investment in digital media citizenship strategies, such as user generated content (McClean 2011) and public outreach. The chapter by Georgie McClean provides a useful overview to explain what this means for the public value of PSM in Australia today. The ABC has also developed successful diversity strategies through improved local and Indigenous programming, and most importantly via participative media. Jonathon Hutchinson fleshes this out in useful detail in his chapter on the ABC Pool project, in which he was a community manager and participant researcher.

The transformation of these organisations into multiplatform PSM entities has been the subject of on-going debate about the scope of their roles (Inglis 2006; Ang et al. 2008). But so far, at least, the PVT testing regime has not been applied in Australia. And despite various calls from conservative politicians to merge the ABC and SBS, to cut funding or privatise portions of their respective operations, the most recent government review of national broadcasting found that "Australians realise significant benefits from the existence of two vibrant national broadcasters" and that each performs "important and distinct roles" (DBCDE 2009: 15). As is *always* the case with PSM, the public value of these organisations has been *uniquely* constructed on the basis of a *distinctive* national history, attuned to social, cultural and political change over the decades, and formulated accordingly in Australian media policy. It is nonetheless true that that way that worth is demonstrated, in budgetary processes and annual reports, owes far more to internationalised economic assumptions and practices than national factors.

Measuring public value

In *Creating Public Value* (1995) Moore surveyed a variety of techniques for determining the worth of public sector activities, which include policy analysis, cost-benefit and cost-effectiveness analyses, programme evaluation, and customer satisfaction surveys. He considered cost-effectiveness and programme evaluation especially useful because they look at how well collective objectives are being met – a vital emphasis in this theory's emphasis on outcomes. Moore also emphasised the importance of time because the effects of any action or innovation can only be appreciated at some point after its introduction, often distant, with that point being difficult to nail down and with variation in repeated measurement over longer spans. Moore also acknowledged that each form of assessment has its weaknesses and "none alone is up to the task" (ibid: 22).

In Benington and Moore's recent collection (2011), Louise Horner and Will Hutton raise two primary problems that confound efforts to measure public value:

> The first is whether an absolute measure can be derived, and whether this can be translated into a monetary value. This draws on economic as well as democratic theory. The second is the adequacy of performance management frameworks and whether they fully capture what public bodies do and to what extent they involve the public in decisions (p. 123).

The first problem speaks to PSM's problem with ratings and their inability to capture the full satisfaction or knowledge impact of programme consumption. The second includes the intangibility of procedural principles like equity or inclusiveness in programme or service development, and 'externalities' that result from consumption, such as higher degrees of racial tolerance or social cohesion. Organisational capacities, such as the ability of PSM to solve problems and adapt to new challenges, are also hard to capture (Moore 1995: 34). Nevertheless as Mulgan (2011) argues, while metrics for public value may not be able to deliver actual improvement, they are nonetheless essential for rhetorical reasons:

> Better metrics do not of themselves deliver better outcomes. You can't fatten a pig by weighing it. But if you don't have some means of weighing it you may find yourself unable to persuade others that it's as fat as you believe (Mulgan 2011: 212).

Moore recognises that public and private organisations have different goals, which should suggest different emphases on what is measured and how. For PSM the objective can't be, or should not be, to simply 'satisfy audience demands', but rather must also be about ensuring that programmes and activities comply with their charters and fulfil remit obligations. In that regard it is essential to measure outcomes, not only or mainly 'performance'. It is not enough to be efficient; public service organisations must be fair, provide services for marginalised social groups, and seek to promote social justice. Being effective can mean being inefficient (i.e. sociocultural value may have little or nothing to do with economic value per se).

Moore's rejection of economics as the final arbiter of public sector worth is a welcome perspective, but PSM is fraught today with political contention. It must justify its existence and many of its efforts to governments that are sometimes quite hostile, and to special interest groups and even competitors. Measuring public value in economic terms is therefore a focus of existential importance; like it or not diverse accountability processes and assessment are a necessity.

PSM's drive to produce public forms of 'calculus as accountability' (e.g ratings, productivity and audience satisfaction indicators) has been amplified by the larger conditions of industrial modernity and rapid structural change. These have produced the need for internal measures that comprise a 'calculus as control' (e.g. risk assessments, business plans, performance indicators, environmental impact data, sales and marketing targets). Responding to technological evolution and to higher market risk encourages managers to adopt techniques with capacity to improve control of the organisation and facilitate better management across wider and more diverse information networks. This is increasingly evident throughout the public sector because expenditure must be documented for government, if not always opened to public scrutiny.

Nearly twenty years ago the growth of control technologies (Beninger 1989) and expert systems (Giddens 1990) were already inextricably linked to measurement regimes. It needs to be understood that measurement of value is a reflexive act that reinforces the authority of experts, encourages systems for quantifying, evaluating and justifying resource allocation, but can be a means for cultivating higher trust in complicated processes required for deciding on public investments. In this context 'public value' tests are about more than accountability strategies – they are a means for government to evaluate and manage the risks of governing a shifting, diversifying media environment.

From the 1990s the academic fields of media and cultural economics, and then media management, emerged in response to these conditions. Looking back at the themes for RIPE conferences and books one finds ample evidence of the growing intellectual significance of these fields for PSM. Section II of this book investigates varied managerial perspectives on valuing PSM. Some are historic and familiar, such as the thesis of market failure in broadcasting, but most are comparatively new, such as multi-stakeholder arrangements, management contract negotiations, and the evaluation of strategic 'media literacy' projects.

These phenomena have a normative centre of gravity that invokes traditional defences of PSM, based on its social role and civil society relationships, they introduce new dimensions. This is clear in the chapter by Christian Berg (et al.), which extends the potential of the market failure thesis to digital broadcasting and into broadband PSM environments, and yet ultimately acknowledges the greater importance of normative ideals as the basis for PSM legitimacy. Normative principles are equally central to an insightful discussion by Minna Aslama Horowitz and Jessica Clark about the importance of multi-stakeholder networks and hybrid arrangements to policy and operations in public media production. Josef Trappel argues that measuring public value fails if it focuses simply on modelling individual or customer benefits or satisfaction, and is largely confined to an interest in utility or exchange value. He suggests that all media firms, private as well as public, could usefully expand their interest in creating social value in order to cultivate wider and deeper appreciation for fundamental collective objectives – such as equality, liberty, solidarity, accountability and civic participation.

PSM cannot afford to be complacent about its capacity to meet a broad range of increasingly complicated social objectives. As Stoyan Radoslav demonstrates in his chapter, investigating European broadcasters' investments in the promotion and development of media literacies as part of the European Commission's knowledge society push (see European Commission 2009), many of the assumptions about public value creation are too shallow. Broadcast-oriented organisations tend to lean on idiosyncratic national definitions and instrumental, politicised approaches to producing media literacy in various projects, mostly with inadequate evaluation procedures that would convincingly validate public value claims. His findings are a good example of the need for PSM to provide richer accounts of its worth – not only to legitimate its claim on the public purse, but more importantly to distinguish itself from the many other media forms that now provide public goods and services.

In this respect public managers' 'must rely on the articulation of ethical principles that clearly distinguish, define and determine the character and importance of PSM practice. One implication of Benington and Moore's work (2011) is that PSM executives can garner the popular authority they need in order to act by putting principles before politics or business:

> There might even on some occasions be a kind of moral legitimacy created by public managers and professionals [by] reminding society and its repre-sentatives of important values that are being put at risk by actions that are politically supported, have legal sanction, and would likely work technically, but fail to protect or promote foundational moral values (p. 11).

Although putting principles before political fall-out or profits is not a con-troversial position for PSM, it is often difficult in practice because doing so involves potential conflict of values. This was illustrated recently when ABC managing director, Mark Scott, defended the publication of classified govern-ment information, leaked by whistle-blower Edward Snowden, which revealed that the Australia government had spied on Indonesian officials. Here the ABC controversially prioritised public interest and investigative independence over national political sensitivities. In the public value framework this would represent conflict within the authorising environment over what form of value is being generated.

Conceptions of public value, as Noel Whiteside (2011) notes, are historically grounded in the conventions and guidelines that define, valuate and steer col-lective co-ordination. These principles are what some majority has agreed upon as being acceptable behaviour, appropriate standards and proper duties. Thus, public value is not simply a by-product of strategic action, or measurement of an organisational outcome like multiplatform delivery or app interaction; public value is an essential ingredient of planning and executing principled action based on public expectations. Thus, public value and public *values* are inextricably intertwined.

Often public expectations change over time (Charles, de Jong & Ryan 2011) and are not as stable as many apparently assume. They are context-dependent and have cultural specificity. For example, the U.S. constitutional notion of people having 'inalienable rights' granted by nature at birth is a grand ideal but suspect in empirical observation. Institutional arrangements are the prod-uct of such beliefs even if it seems fair to argue that values don't give birth to institutions so much as institutions enable particular values to take form, enjoy preference and take precedence. That's why PSM managers need to take special care in efforts to translate schemes for generating public value outcomes from one national arena to another.

To effectively conceive what might be valuable as public service PSM must monitor, analyse and understand the expectations of the various publics it is required to serve, and what knowledge and experiences they might find valu-able to acquire. Thus one of PSMs' on-going strategic challenges is developing capacity and competence to capture, interpret and respond to the diversity of expectations for its service. In our view, that is where Moore's framework is most useful and important.

Co-producing values and value

For Horner and Hutton (2011: 113) one of Moore's great conceptual contributions is the "ethos of co-production", which he argues is critical to designing public value processes. Co-production refers to the variety of reciprocal relations between public organisations and their many stakeholders, which emphasise "downward accountability to users…as citizens as well as recipients or consumers" (ibid.). In the BBC version, co-production involves "public explanation, justification and transparent decision making," together with a degree of dialogue with stakeholders (Coyle & Woolard 2012: 8). Co-production is not specifically about consultation or participation, but rather acknowledges the range of knowledge inputs that can be applied for improving service development and delivery. The concept creates fresh challenges for audience research:

> For example, public value informed broadcasting, instead of mainly measuring audience ratings, would foster cultured and knowledgeable viewers and listeners, whose judgments would be included in assessment of performance and public value added (Horner & Hutton 2011: 113).

For PSM, co-production goes to the heart of public value outcomes in Moore's strategic triangle because it means ensuring that the public's views and values are influential in the design of public value strategies. This is not simply an altruistic principle, but as Lowe (2009) argues it has demonstrated practical utility. The practice will, for example, engender greater trust in and support for PSM sustainability. And yet this raises thorny questions for PSM: who are its publics? Numerous cultural studies suggest they are multiple (c.f. Banerjee & Seneviratne 2006; Thumin 2012). What is deemed proper and useful for PSM to do? Different constituencies have diverse and contradicting views about that. And how should a discussion about PSM's role or activities take place? Experience to date suggests it isn't easy to make the dialogue work in practice. Even when it works the results aren't always very useful and figuring out what to do with what comes of the effort is challenging (Baker 2011).

Section III of this book considers the definition of publics in operationalising public value through a series of case studies. Each presents an approach to formulating public value by better understanding diverse audience/user needs and values. Takanobu Tanaka and Toshiyuki Sato kick things off with their investigation of NHK's response to the Great Eastern Japan Earthquake, the summary description for the devastating earthquake, tsunami and nuclear disaster in August 2011. They explore NHK's distinctive relationship to Japan's broadcast audiences, the victims and their extended social networks, and its emerging connection with online users.

Since 1961 when NHK was legislated to perform a disaster mitigation role, the organisation has developed guidelines to ensure the provision of rapid, accurate and ethical information in traumatic circumstances. The authors introduce the idea that the NHK perspective can usefully be understood as a new principle for public value in action, which they term "human security". This view is widely pertinent today where nations confront international risks with global stakes, as also highlighted by Moore and Benington (2011) in the conclusion of their edited collection on public value theory and practice.

In the study reported here the authors examine procedural considerations in disaster reporting, especially the need for calm and sensitivity, and to put public guidance before news value. This evaluation illustrates that the Japanese population at large *expected* NHK to provide more responsive online services than other operators, and valued new services that NHK provided to fulfil the expectations – such as Twitter conversations that informed individual or local needs and function for reporting on missing persons. Organisational transparency and recognition of user-led innovation have since indicated the need for further future improvements in communicating post-disaster information.

The re-orientation of values to co-production of knowledge is an enormous shift for broadcasters because their professional identities and characteristic communication modes are based on the transmission model. Even among the majority that have embraced online publishing and interactive platforms, the process of figuring out the best approaches, practises and limits is complicated and often contradictory. Some PSM organisations have developed advanced downward accountability to their publics via editor's blogs, hosted forums and document repositories. But so far, at least, online services and programmes are rarely built *on the basis* of audience feedback, community consultation or social production models. This illustrates that regardless of rapid socio-technological change institutional values are predictably difficult to change.

Davis and West (2008) proposed three approaches to putting public values into action. These approaches are certainly evident in political battles over the transition from PSB to PSM organisations:

1) *Values amplification* (incorporating a wider range of values to better align the organisation with its environment).

2) *Values maintenance* (defending and keeping faith with existing values that are typically inherited or received as legacy values).

3) *Values contraction* (jettisoning some values that were previously maintained, often today associated with focusing on 'core competencies' or the 'core business').

Option three is evident where public service has been forced to retreat from online and new media markets, as in Germany. It is also evident in the policy-driven collapse of PSB in New Zealand. Option two is evident in appeals for public support when governments threaten to withdraw financial support, as in the USA where the political atmosphere has been toxic and recently in Greece. The amplification option, the most important for evolving media markets, is evident during negotiations about introducing or expanding PSM, as in recent years in Taiwan, for example. Thus it should not be surprising that despite increased public expectations for PSM development online, the new principles signalled in scholarship for more than a decade, and developing in various ways in practice, including connectivity (Martin 2002), participation (Enli 2008) and reciprocity (Jackson 2013), are taking time to operationalize and coping with real complications in policy formulation (Gripsrud & Moe 2010).

Key challenges are apparent in the chapter by Jonathan Hutchinson,which documents an ABC experiment in content co-creation. ABC Pool was designed to foster users' social and cultural capital in new media production, and to diversify ABC cultural input. Pool staff provided ABC users with access to archival material, supported creative collaborations between users and staff, offered professional advice on production, and help commissioned audio-visual material for ABC programmes. However the project depended on the mediating work of a community manager who developed production guidelines, communicative and regulatory strategies to facilitate conversations and to arbitrate disputes. It required some effort to represent institutional values and professional standards to contributors as well as user interests to programme-makers and executives. Hutchinson's theoretical analysis of this 'innovation system' concludes that such "cultural intermediaries" are one of the keys to fostering online community governance within an institutional PSM setting.

Co-creation is an ambitious and extended form of co-producing public value, and arguably doesn't always reveal the thoughts and feelings even of majority interests – much less of disadvantaged minorities. Only a small percentage of PSM users may ever be inclined to generate content, or even to comment on programming. Georgie McClean provides an inside look at practices of audience consultation that were instrumental in commissioning two successful documentary series produced by SBS. These projects took a more formalised and traditional approach to programme evaluation of public value via commissioned audience research. The study gauges how well SBS programmes deliver on its charter obligations to nurture pluralistic values, representational diversity and greater understanding across cultural divides on topics of national importance, in this case immigration.

From a conservative perspective, these documentaries can be seen as provocative or even unbalanced in their political focus – particularly in one case when a reality television format was used to explore a contentious topic with the goal of reaching a younger audience. The study is an excellent example of why PSM institutions and institutionalised practices are primary grounds for values contestation – not just because of their normative or ethical approach to constructing debate, but because they are deeply embedded in the historic shaping of particular political, social and cultural environments and bring essential expertise and authority to the process.

In its emphasis on co-production as a form of knowledge exchange, Moore's public value framework aligns with the economic theory of 'convention'. This argues that markets operate on the basis of efficient co-ordination of social and economic interdependencies that are characteristic of diverse interests in complex social systems. In Hartley's view (2011), public sector organisations should be part of an "open" system for developing public value, and need to maintain many and intricate productive relationships with the external environment in which they are embedded. Benington (2011) takes networked approaches a step further, arguing not only their importance for improved service provision, but also in developing governance for public sector institutions.

Networked relations are an adaptive response to increasing social heterogeneity, political complexity and market volatility. Such changes destabilise traditional hierarchies and signal "a shift in the centre of gravity of governance away from the state and towards civil society" (ibid: 36). This shift necessarily requires restructuring in institutional relations of power. Today already, and even more in the future, public services will involve as a constellation of formal and informal partners, operating sometimes co-operatively and at other times competitively, but which seek to respond to changing public values and to create ideas and relationships of lasting public value.

Conclusion

It strikes us as ironic that public media professionals seeking to create new and better forms of public value online, along with closer and more varied public relationships, have met with so much pushback from government and commercial competitors. When seen from a public value perspective – the very perspective that grounds policy preferences for public sector institutions today – PSM is engaged in a logical, principled and appropriate adaptation to a changing media marketplace, to the evidenced interests of diverse publics, and the multiple uncertainties in service delivery that are essential concerns not only for output, but more importantly for outcomes. These institutions are doing what is expected and required in the public value framework, and yet often find themselves in what amounts to a no-win game. It's difficult not to think that a lot of what is going on in the pushback against PSM is based on misunderstanding at best, and a deplorable hypocrisy at worst.

The same point is applicable to the drive to limit PSM's innovation efforts. Public sector risk-taking, where it is well managed at least, has potential for contributing significant and cumulative added public value that benefits everyone. As Stuart Cunningham (2013: 93) argues, PSM can provide important innovation functions within their national context because:

> [They] typically straddle the boundary between the market and the community or civic space. They have complex nation-building roles, delivering key information and news and current affairs unburdened by commercial interests and thus performing a key informal educative function (and, in so doing, maintaining a 'trust' relationship in a 'risk' society), but also providing experimental domains for new technology and creative R&D, while connecting with a broad-based audience.

Cunningham further proposes that PSM can have a sponsoring effect, rather than the chilling effect on innovation that is often claimed, wherever competitors are not already in position and where the PSM provider in is not the dominant market player.

In this collection we recognise that questions about how PSM's public value is constructed and measured may never be answered fully, and never finally. As Hartley observes, there will always be:

> ...different assessments according to context and organizational capacity, according to short-term and longer-term perspectives, according to whether this reinforces particular strengths and weaknesses of the organization – quite apart from the different judgments, values and priorities that varied stakeholders may place on the innovation or improvement (2011: 180).

However, this collection takes up the notion of public value as a useful if politically contentious lens for exploring the current significance and future potential of PSM in a period and context when just about everything that is pertinent to the phenomenon is in flux. The contributions demonstrate that for PSM, at least, the public value framework and notion is most useful in just the way that John Benington suggests – as a heuristic tool "to stimulate debate between competing interests and perspectives, and to generate dialogue about how to improve services, about who gains and who loses, and about relative benefits and costs" (Benington & Moore 2011: 49).

References

ACMA (2013) *Community Broadcasting: State of the sector. Australian Communications and Media Authority.* October 2013. Accessed at: http://www.acma.gov.au/~/media/Community%20 Broadcasting/Publications/CBA_FINAL_web%20pdf.pdf

Ang, I., Hawkins, G. & Dabboussy, L. (2008) *The SBS Story: The Challenge of Cultural Diversity.* Sydney: University of New South Wales Press.

Baker, P. (2011) Expectations, experiences & exceptions: Promises and realities of participation on websites. In Lowe, G.F. & Steemers, J. (eds.) *Regaining the Initiative for Public Service Media,* RIPE@2011. Göteborg: Nordicom, pp.237-252.

Banerjee, I. & Seneviratne, K. (eds) (2006) *Public Service Broadcasting in the Age of Globalization.* Singapore: Asian Media Information and Communication Centre and Nanyang Technological University.

Barreto, M. & Godhino, I. (2013) Portugal's forthcoming privatization plan. Lexology. July 18th 2013. Accessed 1 December: http://www.lexology.com/library/detail.aspx?g=2084e4a8-bae3-439e-b82f-ddaf8c09b5d2

BBC (2004) *Building Public Service Value: Renewing the BBC for a digital world.* London: British Broadcasting Corporation. June 2004.

Beninger, J. (1989) *The Control Revolution: Technological and Economic Origins of the Information Society.* Harvard: Harvard University Press.

Benington, J. & Moore, M.H. [eds] (2011) *Public Value: Theory and Practice.* Basingstoke, UK: Palgrave Macmillan.

Brown, A. & Althaus, C. (1996) Public Service Broadcasting in Australia. *The Journal of Media Economics.* 9 (1) pp. 31-46.

Castells, M. (2004) *The Power of Identity, The Information Age: Economy, Society and Culture, vol. II,* 2nd edition. Oxford: Blackwell Publishers.

Charles, M.B., de Jong, W.M & Ryan, N. (2011) Public values in Western Europe: A temporal perspective. *The American Review of Public Administration, 41*(1): pp. 75-91.

Collins, R. (2007) *Public Value and the BBC: A report prepared for The Work Foundation's public value consortium.* May 1 2007. Accessed August 24 http://www.theworkfoundation.com/downloadpublication/report/174_174_publicvalue_bbc.pdf

Collins, R. (2011) Public Value, the BBC and Humpty Dumpty Words – does Public Value Management Mean What it Says? In Donders, K. and Moe, H. (eds.) *Exporting the Public Value Test: The Regulation of Public Broadcasters' New Media Services Across Europe.* Göteborg: Nordicom. pp. 49-57

Coyle, D. & Woolard, C. (2012) *Public Value in Practice: Restoring the ethos of public service.* BBC Trust. Accessed 20 September http://www.bbc.co.uk/bbctrust/governance/tools_we_use/public_value_practice.html

Crabtree, J. (2004) The revolution that started in a library. *New Statesman,* 27 September. Accessed at http://www.newstatesman.com/node/148947

Craig, G. (2000) Perpetual crisis: The politics of saving the ABC. *Media International Australia,* 94. pp. 105-116.

Craik, J. & Davis, G. (1995) The ABC Goes To Market. In Craik, J. Julie James Bailey, J. and Moran A. (eds.) *Public Voices, Private Lives: Australia's Media Policy.* Sydney: Allen & Unwin, pp. 117-129

Cunningham, S. (2013) *Hidden Innovation: Policy, Industry and the Creative Sector.* St Lucia: University of Queensland Press.

Davis, P. & West, K. (2008) What do public values mean for public action? Putting public values in their plural place. *American Review of Public Administration, 39*(6): pp. 602-618.

DBCDE (2012) *Strengthening Our National Broadcasters.* Department of Broadband, Communications and the Digital Economy. Australian Government. Accessed at http://www.archive.dbcde.gov.au/2012/may/abc_sbs_review/strengthening_our_national_broadcasters

Donders, K. & Moe, H. [eds.] (2011) *Exporting the Public Value Test: The Regulation of Public Broadcasters' New Media Services Across Europe.* Göteborg: Nordicom.

European Commission (2009) Commission Recommendation of 20 August 2009 on media literacy in the digital environment for a more competitive audiovisual and content industry and an inclusive knowledge society. European Commission. OJ L 227, 29.8.2009, p. 9-12.

Enli, G. (2008) Redefining Public Service Broadcasting: Multi-Platform Participation. *Convergence: The International Journal of Research into New Media Technologies.* 14(1) pp. 105-120

McClean, G. (2011) Multicultural Sociability, Imperfect Forums and Online Participation. *International Journal of Communication.* 5, pp. 1649-1668

Forde, S. Meadows, M. & Foxwell, K. (2002) *Culture, Commitment, Community: the Australian Community Radio Sector.* Sydney: Community Broadcasting Association of Australia and the Community Broadcasting Foundation.

Foucault, M. (2000) (2000a) Governmentality. In Michel Foucault: *Power: The Essential Works of Foucault 1954-1984 Volume 3* (ed. James D. Faubion) (French original published 1978) London, Penguin/The New Press, pp. 201-222.

Frazer, M. & O'Reilly, J (eds) (1996) *Save Our ABC: the case for maintaining Australia's public broadcaster.* Sydney: Hylland House and the Friends of the ABC.

Freedman, D. (2008) *The Politics of Media Policy.* Cambridge, UK: Polity Press.

Giddens, A. (1990) *The Consequences of Modernity.* Cambridge: Polity.

Gitlin, T. (1998) Public Spheres or Public Sphericules? In Liebes T. & Curran, J. (eds), *Media, Ritual and Identity.* New York: Routledge, pp. 168-175.

Gripsrud, J. & Moe, H. [eds.] (2010). *The Digital Public Sphere: Challenges for Media Policy.* Göteborg: Nordicom.

Hartley, J. (2011) Public value through innovation and improvement. In Benington, J. & Moore, M.H. (eds.) *Public Value: Theory and Practice.* Basingstoke, UK: Palgrave Macmillan, pp. 171-184.

Horner, L. & Hutton, W. (2011) Public value, deliberative democracy and the role of public managers. In Benington, J. & Moore, M.H. (eds.) *Public Value: Theory and Practice.* Basingstoke, UK: Palgrave Macmillan, pp. 112-126.

Inglis, K. (2006) *Whose ABC? The Australian Broadcasting Corporation 1983-2006.* Melbourne: Black Inc.

Jackson, L. (2013) Participating Publics: Implications for Production Practices at the BBC. In Glowacki, M. & Jackson, L. (eds.) *Public Media Management for the Twenty-First Century: Creativity, Innovation, and Interaction.* Routledge: New York.

Lee, D.J., Oakley, K. & Naylor R. (2011) Giving Them What they Want: The Construction of the Public in 'Public Value'. *International Journal of Cultural Policy*, 17(3): pp. 289-300.

Lilleborge, M.T (2012) Norway: The First Ex Ante Test Completed. IRIS Merlin: *Legal Observations of the European Audiovisual Observatory.* IRIS 2013-1:1/31. Accessed 9 December http://merlin.obs.coe.int/iris/2013/1/article31.en.html

Lowe, G.F. & Jauert, P. [eds.] (2005) *Cultural Dilemmas in Public Service Broadcasting*, RIPE@2005. Göteborg: Nordicom.

Lowe, G.F. & Steemers, J. [eds.] (2011) *Regaining the Initiative for Public Service Media*, RIPE@2011. Göteborg: Nordicom.

Lowe, G.F. (2009) Beyond altruism: Why public participation in public service media matters. In Lowe, G.F. (ed.) *The Public in Public Service Media*, RIPE@2009. Göteborg: Nordicom, pp. 9-36.

Lowen, M. (2013) Greek police clear former broadcaster ERT's offices. *BBC News*, 7 November. Accessed 13 December http://www.bbc.co.uk/news/world-europe-24847278.

Martin, F. (2002) 'Beyond Public Service Broadcasting?: ABC Online & The User/ Citizen' *Southern Review*, 35 (1): 42-62

Moore, M.H. (1995) *Creating Public Value: Strategic Management in* Government. Boston: Harvard University Press.

Mulgan, G. (2011) Chapter 13: Effective supply and demand and the measurement of public and social value. In Benington, J. & Moore, M.H. (eds.) *Public Value: Theory and Practice.* Basingstoke, UK: Palgrave Macmillan, pp. 212-224.

Nevradakis, M. (2013) Chronicling the Greek Government's Shutdown of ERT, *Daily Kos*, Mon Jun 17, 2013. Accessed at http://www.dailykos.com/story/2013/06/17/1216716/-Chronicling-the-Greek-Government-s-Shutdown-of-ERT

Rose, N. (1999) *Powers of Freedom: reframing political thought.* Cambridge: Cambridge University Press.

Roxborough, S. (2013) Public broadcasters pull plug on German 'Hulu'. The *Hollywood Reporter*, 18 September. Accessed 3 December at: http://www.hollywoodreporter.com/news/public-broadcasters-pull-plug-german-630449

Skene, W. (1993) *Fade to Black: a Requiem for the CBC.* Vancouver: Douglas & McIntyre Ltd.

Thumin, N. (2012) *Self-Representation and Digital Culture.* Basingstoke, Hampshire: Palgrave MacMillan.

Touraine, A. (2011) *Beyond Neo-Liberalism.* London: Polity Press.

Tracey, M. (1998) *The Decline and Fall of Public Broadcasting*. New York and London: Oxford University Press.

Van Den Bulck, H. & Moe, H. (2012) To Test or not to Test: Comparing the Development of Ex Ante Public Service Media Assessments in Flanders and Norway. *International Journal of Media & Cultural Politics*, 8(1) pp. 31-49.

Whiteside, N. (2011) Creating public value: The theory of the convention. In Benington, J. & Moore, M.H. (eds.) *Public Value: Theory and Practice*. Basingstoke, UK: Palgrave Macmillan, pp. 74-88.

Woldt, R. (2010) *Three Steps to Wisdom? Public Value Tests for Germany*. Paper presented for the RIPE@2010 conference and available online at: http://ripeat.org/wp-content/uploads/tdomf/2071/Woldt.pdf

I.
Defining & Critiquing 'Public Value'

Chapter 2

Defining Public Value
in the Age of Information Abundance

The Hon. James Spigelman AC QC

The RIPE@2012 conference was opaened by the then newly appointed Chair-
man of the Australian Broadcasting Corporation, Mr James Spigelman, who
delivered his first official address on public service broadcasting.

As in every nation represented at this international conference, the Australian
media landscape is today dominated by the challenges of digital technology,
with radical effects already apparent and the scope of future effects inherently uncertain. For many participants in the media this is a time of fear and
trepidation. It was always thus with revolutions in communication technology.

In the *Phaedrus,* Plato has Socrates recount a legend about the origins of
writing, which the mythical Egyptian inventor Theuth presented to his pharaoh
as an aid to memory. In reply, the king asserted that it would adversely affect
the human capacity for memory. As Socrates put it:

> (Writing) will introduce forgetfulness into the soul of those who learn it: they
> will not practice using their memory because they will put their trust in writ-
> ing... You have not discovered a potion for remembering but for reminding.[1]

The next great technological revolution in communications was the invention
of printing. It was greeted in the same way. Before the upstart entrepreneur
and goldsmith turned printer, Johan Guttenberg, transformed publishing, it
had been conducted for millennia by scribes who, in Europe, were controlled
by the Church. A limited form of mass production was achieved in the large
scriptoria of monasteries. Printing was a major threat to this business.

Filippo di Strata, a Dominican friar from the convent of San Cipriano on
Murano, an island in the Venice lagoon, proclaimed in the late 15th century:
"The world has gone along perfectly well for 6000 years without printing and
has no need to change now". He was particularly critical of the German inter-
lopers who took work from Italian scribes. Fra Filippo called them "ignorant
oafs" who "vulgarised intellectual life". He said that printers, unlike scribes,

did not really understand what they were doing. He was concerned that the editorial expertise and writing skills of the scribes would be lost, as would the educational value of having to write things out in longhand, at a pace that enabled a monk to absorb and contemplate the text.

There was also a serious threat of intellectual freedom – I emphasise *of* not *to* intellectual freedom. Lascivious Roman love poetry, such as the works of Ovid, was widely circulated for the titillation of the young and impressionable. Cheap printed versions of the Bible were now becoming available to individuals without the intermediation of a priest. All this was a threat to the authority of the Church. The impact was, of course, worse because printers could produce enormous quantities of books that anyone could get. Indeed, Fra Filippo complained: "It was hardly possible to walk through the streets of Venice without having armfuls of books thrust at you 'like cats in a bag' for 2 or 3 coppers".[2]

This was an early form of information overload. Now we have what one commentator has called "data asphyxiation". If you do a Google search of information overload in quotes, you get the self-satirical answer of 3,620,000 hits in 0.14 of a second. The radical transformation in data availability is well expressed by Clive James who described the words "to Google" as "the infinitive that could search infinity".[3]

Fra Filippo's complaints about printing have almost precise parallels in some responses to the digital revolution – responses that will share the same fate.

Making sense of information abundance

Accumulating information today is like trying to drink from a fire hose. How can one cope with this flow and stay in control of one's time and intellectual development? We all need help. How we get it is a work in progress. Deceptive shortcuts like Google pretend to give you what you need, but an automatic algorithm has no rational discriminatory basis. How many of us go beyond, say, the 20th or even the 10th page of Google results – through the commercial messages, the repetitive entries and the transparently useless junk – so that we are not subject to a mere popularity contest? Yes, we can refine the search, but the fact that a particular word combination appears in a text does not mean that the text is worth reading.

When you need a quick fix, Google and Wikipedia are a good place to start. However if you want depth of any kind, and if you care about quality, you need intermediation by a real person who has applied a mind, rather than a formula, to screening the information. Furthermore, the process of compilation must be trustworthy. Neither search nor aggregation algorithms can promise that.

In the field of broadcasting, the parallel technical change arises from the virtual disappearance of spectrum scarcity, which has always been the focus of broadcast planning and development. The very concept of broadcasting is under challenge as new modes of delivery enable any viewer or listener to arrange their own program schedules to be accessed whenever they feel like it, and to do so from an ever expanding range of sources, all accessible from rapidly converging hardware of extraordinary, and increasing, power. It is in such a context that public service broadcasters, like the Australian Broadcasting Corporation [ABC], must now find their place.

If anything, the editorial role of a trustworthy intermediary to find, select, organise and analyse the abundance of material has become more important, not less. Of course, one can focus on specialist web sites and media for this purpose. Here lies one of the hidden dangers of the digital revolution. It is now possible to retreat into an electronic village or insulate oneself from any opinion with which one may disagree. The role of public broadcasters in promoting social cohesion and providing a forum for debate for a democratic polity as a whole – not just for those who can penetrate pay walls – remains of critical importance. As the ABC's Managing Director Mark Scott put it in his 2009 Commonwealth Broadcasting Association Lecture: "The ABC ... is a commons, a shared space ... a shared reference point within Australian life, a cultural experience we all have in common, at a time when common cultural experiences are becoming harder to come by."[4] Such a role is best performed by an institution that is accountable, and accountable only, to the people as a whole – in the case of the ABC, to the Australian people represented in the nation's Parliament.

Ensuring diversity in the organising principles of a nation's key institutions is as important for the health of society as biodiversity is for the health of the environment. A monoculture is inherently unstable, as we all experienced after the Global Financial Crisis of 2008, and earlier, with the sudden collapse of the USSR and Eastern Europe's Communist regimes.

A commercial monoculture in the media will either not deliver the broad range of content that public broadcasters have traditionally delivered, or will not deliver such content to the whole community. This is the fundamental justification for the mixed public/private model of the Australian broadcasting environment which has existed from the outset of radio (1920s) and television (1950s), and to which were more recently added community broadcasters (1970s) and subscription or pay TV (1990s).

Maximising and satisficing

The theme of this conference, "Value for Public Money–Money for Public Value", fits with precision a key statutory statement of the ABC's purpose. Our legislation expressly provides, as the first stated duty of the Board: "to ensure that the functions of the Corporation are performed efficiently and with maximum benefit to the people of Australia" (section 8(1)(a)).

The value for money theme has been a dominant consideration in public management debate for several decades. It developed as a result of the perceived inadequacies of the traditional approach to decision making in public sector organisations not fully subject to market pressures. Until comparatively recently, public bureaucratic conduct did not always – perhaps even did not usually – display an acceptable balance between "maximising" public outcomes, or seeking optimal solutions to problems, and merely "satisficing", in the sense of making acceptable or satisfactory decisions.[5]

Such imbalances are not unique to the public sector. Any large organisation is prone to distortion in its decision making in order to serve the institutional interests created by its separate existence and its internal structure. This institutional imperative can often become a form of defensive tribal loyalty, both in the responses of the organisation as a whole towards outsiders and of sub-units within the organisation towards other sub-units and the organisation's central decision-makers. At the risk of seeming exceedingly cynical, it sometimes appears that decision-makers in such contexts assess their personal success by maximising two variables: first, the total amount of resources available to the organisation (or to the relevant sub-unit) and, secondly, the extent of their institutional autonomy and freedom to act.

Efficiency, in the sense of value for money, is thus often something to be satisficed, rather than maximised. Similarly, effectiveness, in the sense of achieving the purposes of the organisation or sub-unit and of particular programs, is also to be merely satisficed. Such considerations lie behind the flourishing, over recent decades, of management theory and practice both in private corporations and in public organisations. This development has brought to the forefront issues of efficiency and effectiveness as matters to be maximised and not merely satisficed. The literature produced in pursuit of these objectives has consumed many forests.

The ABC has reason to be proud of its achievements over the last two-and-a-half decades in these respects, not in the least in demonstrating value for public funding.

Efficiency and effectiveness at the ABC

Between 1987-1988 and 2012-2013, the ABC significantly expanded the services it provides, and did so with fewer staff and less funding. In 1987-1988, its operational funding was A$967 million and it had 6,400 full-time equivalent staff. By 2012-2013, the ABC's inflation adjusted funding had reduced to A$840 million and full-time equivalent staff to 4,600. However, the expansion of the services to the public over the same period was dramatic.

In 1987-1988, the Corporation had one analogue television channel, two national radio services, 38 local radio stations across regional areas and a youth radio service available only in Sydney. By 2012-2013, there was one analogue and four digital television channels, four national radio services, 60 local radio stations and five digital-only radio services, including specialist jazz and country music channels and triple j Unearthed, a user-generated music channel to which Australian record companies now look, almost exclusively, for new talent. On the other hand, part of the reduction in staff numbers is attributable to the loss of a function – the transfer of the State symphony orchestras.

The transformation was not only quantitative, but also qualitative. The ABC has sought to meet audience expectations as they are transformed by rapid changes in broadcasting and communications technologies. It offers one of the nation's largest websites, radio podcasts, the iview television catch-up service and mobile apps, as well as meeting users' expectations of interaction through online forums, blogs and social media.

In large measure these new services were funded by internal efficiencies, as well as reallocation of resources. No additional funding was provided for the delivery costs of online services, the content of digital radio or ABC2 television, nor for the creation of digital television news channel ABC News 24. To give only one example of the efficiencies made, television news studios that only a few years ago required a 14-person crew now require only four.

I repeat, all of these additional services were developed and deployed with fewer staff and less funding. There was significant progress on the efficiency dimension. It is a tribute to effective management in practice, as distinct from management in theory, about which I will have some more to say.

Audiences as citizens and consumers

I turn to the question of "public value" or, as it is expressed in our legislation, "public benefit". Because of the adoption of "public value" as a central consideration by the BBC, these words are very much in vogue in public broadcasting discourse. So far as I am aware they are words without a universally accepted definition and are, accordingly, deployed in different ways in different contexts.[6] I do not mean to suggest that perfectly ordinary English words like this require definition before they can be used in civilised discourse. However, I do note that some of the literature appears to regard the absence of definition as some kind of barrier to proper analysis. While this is doubtless true for quantitative research or accounting for policy implementation, I have no such inhibitions. In many contexts this concept merely replaces similar overlapping terminology such as "public good", "public interest" and "public benefit". These words have been used with good effect over many decades, indeed centuries, without being burdened by definition.

Any assessment of public value must start with an understanding of the objectives of public broadcasting. I do not think that the Reithian trifecta – to inform, educate and entertain – has ever been bettered. The one additional dimension that I would add is operational, concerning the way a public broadcaster should interact with its audiences.

A defining characteristic of public broadcasting should be that it treats its audiences as citizens and not as consumers. To act in this way is an essential component of an ethos of public service, which the ABC, by force of its statutory Charter, is obliged to adopt. Public service goes well beyond satisfying consumer demand. There is, of course, nothing wrong with being a consumer or ensuring that organisations take into account how well the functions they perform meet the requirements of people as consumers. Nevertheless, it is important to recognise that a person's interests as a "consumer" is only one part of that person's status as a citizen. In much public policy discourse, the consumer analogy became a feral metaphor that acquired a disproportionate prominence. That may now be changing.

Consumers have desires or needs. Citizens have rights and duties. This distinction, which is reflected in the public value literature, is significant not only for the content of programs, but also for the way a public broadcaster interacts with its publics. It is sufficient to give only one example of programming for an audience of citizens. In a democratic polity the provision of a forum for public debate and discussion of ideas creates public value irrespective of whether or not it responds to something akin to popular demand.

Whilst the need to satisfy community demand for mainstream programming may be common to both commercial and public broadcasters, there are process and accountability considerations that commercial broadcasters either do not have, or do not share, to the same degree. Public broadcasters, for example, traditionally offer a diverse array of programs even though specialist and minority content may be costly and is unlikely to attract the large audiences sought by commercial media in pursuit of market share. Even the values of efficiency and effectiveness may sometimes need to be balanced against other public values such as accessibility, openness, fairness, impartiality, accountability, legitimacy, participation and honesty.

Of particular significance is the public value of accessibility of information, both in a technical and practical sense. In Australia, broadcasting has developed on the principle of universal, free availability. The intrusion of advertising on free-to-air television does not undermine that principle. However, pay-walls do. The cost of subscription to pay TV is not consistent with the public value of universal accessibility. Such considerations significantly limit the contribution that pay TV can – and to a significant extent does – deliver on another traditional public value principle, program diversity.

There is a broadly based consensus in Australia that there is a core of programming that must be universally available. In our sports-mad nation this is reflected in an "anti-siphoning" list, requiring major sports events to be first offered to free-to-air TV. However, is it not only sport that can deliver the kind of public value or benefit that should be available to all. Facilitating the discussion of ideas is a good example. Creating social cohesion by ensuring that the whole community understands its heritage and knows its own stories, is another.

Universality and technological change

The digital revolution has undermined the business model of much traditional media. Locally these effects have recently been manifest in dramatic job losses at Australia's two largest print media corporations, the largest of which is News Limited, the Australian arm of Rupert Murdoch's News Corporation. Broadcasters in metropolitan and regional areas are also facing an uncertain future with declining advertising revenues – although the impact has not, or not yet, been as dramatic as that for print.

In such a context, it is entirely understandable that there has been an increase in the frequency with which commercial interests express anxiety about competition from public service broadcasters. There is of course nothing new about this. Public broadcasters, by their very existence, have always had an adverse impact on such commercial interests.

In 1933, when the ABC started an independent news service, the chief executive of one of our major commercial media groups was so concerned with the potential competitive impact on his company's print and radio operations he called for a reduction in the ABC's revenue. That person was Sir Keith Murdoch, Rupert's father. Some things change very little over the decades.[7]

The first thing to say about such arguments is that there has never been a time when the ABC was simply a market failure broadcaster, obliged to fill gaps in the commercial offering. Its obligations are, and have always been, defined positively, not negatively. Specifically, under current legislation, the ABC is directed to provide "comprehensive broadcasting services" and to accept a "responsibility... to provide a balance between broadcasting programs of wide appeal and specialized broadcasting programs".

Unquestionably, a public broadcaster must program for minority audiences in a way that at least commercial free-to-air broadcasters would never do. There could not be a better example of this than this week's comprehensive ABC coverage of the Paralympics – with which, it appears, advertisers would prefer to avoid any association, despite the triumph of the human spirit that is continually on display.

However, as the express statutory obligations of the ABC make clear, we are obliged to offer services to the community as a whole. At a fundamental level, the key role of the ABC is to ensure that *all* Australians have access to quality media services, perhaps particularly reliable news and information about international, national, regional and local matters.

The technological changes to which I have referred are only at the beginning of their impact on traditional modes of delivering news, information, entertainment and education. Already it is apparent that digital technology constitutes a profound challenge for media organisations that have built and sustained businesses on pre-convergence assumptions.

New business models are being tried, in the hope that they will allow established media companies to transform themselves. In the face of confident assertions that these models will work, and that the assumptions on which they are based are sound, the truth is that no one knows where this is going. There is no guarantee that any of these models will prove to be sustainable.

In such a context, the provision of a bedrock of quality services from a trustworthy source, accessible to all Australians wherever they live and without charge,[8] with a degree of certainty that is not now available from other traditional sources, is a fundamental aspect of the public benefit – public value – that the ABC delivers. This is particularly so in the case of news and current affairs programming. It is now clear that present pay walls and online advertising for newspapers can no longer sustain the news gathering infrastructure of the past. It is doubtful whether the pay wall for pay TV can be sustained at the levels extant in Australia. The reduction of commercial TV and radio news and current affairs coverage to a tabloid core has been noticeable for some years. These developments are unlikely to be reversed.

There is no public debate in Australia that seriously questions the continuation of the ABC's traditional services. There is however some, limited, negative commentary about the ABC's expansion into online and mobile platform delivery, which perhaps mirrors some international debate over the extension of public broadcasters' remits into internet protocol publishing and distribution. Yet computers, smart phones and tablets are now so ubiquitous that delivery of a program, or cognate material, to such devices is a form of broadcasting, in the natural meaning of the term. These platforms are ubiquitous in their availability and, in that respect, are becoming the same as traditional radio or television sets.

Any suggestion that such delivery platforms should be restricted because they are new is as dubious as an argument would have been – if advanced, but it was not – that radio programs should not be delivered to transistor radios because they did not exist when radio broadcasting commenced. The change from "desktop" radio to mobile radio is of the same character as the change to contemporary mobile devices.

That is not to say that the ABC's determination to remain technologically relevant, interacting with its audiences in the manner that they prefer, does not have adverse commercial consequences on existing or potential service providers. As I have mentioned, the ABC has always had such effects. Whether, in particular circumstances or for particular services, the employment of public funds constitutes competition that could be regarded as "unfair", is a matter on which reasonable minds can differ. However, "broadcasting", in its ordinary and natural meaning, encompasses delivery of programs to all platforms capable of receiving them.

Public value and competition

I am aware that a significant body of writing in the "public value" literature raises similar considerations of "unfair competition". Such issues arise explicitly in the European public value literature for competition law reasons.

Public expenditure on broadcasting falls within the European concept of "state aid" which is capable of distorting the single market of the European Union. In this context, public value has emerged as a comprehensive description of the benefits that arise from public broadcasting which, pursuant to European competition law, need to be balanced against the market impact of the service so provided. A similar balancing exercise has been adopted by the BBC, in a context where the market dominance of that institution has been controversial for reasons additional to those which arise under European competition law to which, of course, the BBC is also subject.

Australians could perhaps obtain some advantage from the public value literature. However, I must say that the approach may not prove particularly helpful when balancing incommensurable standards like "public value" and "market impact". As one United States Supreme Court judge put it in a different context: it is like asking whether this rock is heavier than that piece of string is long.

Nevertheless, judgments balancing incommensurable values of this character frequently have to be made in public policy decision-making. The major trap to avoid in such a process is not to give the quantifiable components a disproportionate weight. Hard figures portray a concreteness which means they can receive salience not available to narrative propositions. Considerations of quality or equity are not entitled to less weight in a balancing exercise merely because measurement is difficult and, often, impossible.

The approach is unlikely to be of much utility in Australia, where these cross-border competition or protectionist issues do not arise. Nevertheless, similar "crowding out" arguments have been put forward on the basis of "fairness" or "proper use" of public money, rather than in the language of competition law. Such concerns were raised in Australia during the recent national Convergence Review of digital media policy. Yet the final review report noted the leading role Australia's public broadcasters have played in developing innovative online and digital content and recommended their broadcast-era charters be updated to explicitly encompass these new media activities.[9] This proposal acknowledges an important form of "public value" that the ABC produces in the changing media environment.

Public value and managerialism

Despite its widespread use, the managerial origins of contemporary public value discourse should give us pause before accepting and applying the concept. It can be traced to a book by Mark Moore of the Harvard Kennedy School of Government published in 1995: *Creating Public Value: Strategic Management in Government.*[10]

Persons responsible for organisation in the public sector used to refer to their vocation as "public administration". Most of the university courses and academic journals were so entitled. Some still are. Over recent decades this sphere of discourse has come to refer to itself as "public management". The change in terminology reflects a development in which "managers" see their role as more active and interventionist, with a claim, of a professional character, to a broader, indeed sometimes to the universal, applicability of their vocation in all spheres of organised activity: private corporations, the not-for-profit sector and the public sector.

When the focus was on "administration", there was validity in the proposition that the skill set required for administration was similar from one sphere to another. The same claim of universality was, however, carried over when "administration" became "management". However, "managers" purport to be able to determine a much wider range of organisational conduct than they did when they were "administrators".

This claim to institutional territory now encompasses the manner in which the objectives of an organisation are determined and how they are to be achieved. This imperial claim is, in significant respects, a conceit. The decision-making training and experience of "managers" is not necessarily well-suited to the attainment of public objectives. It sometimes offers a falsely, technical answer to political, social, cultural and even moral questions, about which people often, indeed usually, disagree. "Management" often proceeds on the basis that there is a right answer to any question. There isn't.

At the core of management practice, including public management, is a broadly applicable set of principles and practices that distil a considerable body of experience. The concern with value for money, to which I have referred, is an example of the utility of good management. However "management" is also a fashion industry and it is necessary to be aware of the transient elements, particularly in view of the imperial overreach of recent decades.

"Public value" is the latest in a long line of cognate attempts to guide budgeting and decision-making in the public sector: in the 1950s there was "performance budgeting"; in the 1960s came "programme budgeting"; later there emerged "Zero-based budgeting". Thereafter, public budgeting and decision-making began to embrace managerial fads from the private sector: including strategic planning, mission statements (even "vision statements"), business plans, benchmarking, "management by objectives", "strategy", "total quality management", "the triple bottom line", the "balanced scorecard", "business process re-engineering" and many others.

As anyone familiar with the burgeoning management sections of book-shops will know, these fads come and go as rapidly as the equally large and burgeoning sections on personal diets. Scarcely a week goes by without some new volume proclaiming the abiding utility for "managers" or, even better, for "leaders", of the insights to be found in an obscure author whose work is available, if at all, only in the Penguin Classic series, or from some other set of insights which can be deduced from either a catchy aphorism or a promised set of numerical principles, usually 10 in number. Much of this literature reminds me of Clive James's description of "a thin argument gaining altitude", which he said was "like the burnt paper wrapping of an amaretto cookie rising on a self generated column of hot air".[11]

Many of these attempts to draw on private sector experience for public sector decision-making were brought together under a general concept of "New Public Management" or, in the terminology favoured by Vice President Al Gore, "Reinventing Government". The "public value" approach was, originally, self-consciously a successor to the "New Public Management". In some of its iterations "public value" has certain distinct advantages over NPM, in particular by re-emphasising the need for public policy to treat citizens *as* citizens and not merely as consumers, and the assertion of the process values involved in public decision-making. In the latter respect the literature draws to some degree on the deliberative democracy literature.

However, no one should proceed on the basis that this fashion cycle is over. Indeed a rival group in the United Kingdom appears to have stolen a march on advocates of "public value ". Earlier this year the UK Parliament passed the *Public Services (Social Value) Act*, which imposes a statutory requirement on public bodies to apply a test of "social value "to services commissioned and procured. This terminology appears to have emerged from the NGO space, but is now a statutory intrusion into "public value "territory.

The origins of "public value" in the 1995 managerial book, bears its time on its face. As the title itself makes clear, this was a period when Harvard Business School and the management consultants had convinced many that the answer was "strategy". No one talks like that anymore.[12] Even, by 1995, this approach was already being supplemented with a newfound focus on people and agency rather than structure, particularly from a book entitled *In Search of Excellence*.[13] "Excellence" also features in the foundational text on public value by Moore. Unfortunately the list of excellent companies proved more transitory than the management fad. Within five years, about half had fallen from grace and within 15 years only five were left.[14] Neither "strategy" nor "excellence" feature in recent public value discussion.

Of more enduring significance for the public value literature is the proposition, repeated on many occasions, that "public value" is the equivalent in the public sector of "shareholder value" for the management of private corporations. In this respect the public value discourse has not caught up with what has happened in management of private sector corporations. "Shareholder value" has also experienced a fall from grace.

What was called "value-based management" or VBM, in the argot of the consultant business, has disappeared from polite discourse amongst management consultants. It was blamed for managers indulging in asset stripping, destruction of communities, short-term orientation, excessive risk-taking, unconscionable remuneration and scandals such as *Enron*. The financial crisis of 2008 finally put it to bed and even Jack Welch, the poster boy CEO of GE, announced that, "shareholder value is the dumbest idea in the world".[15]

The most recent Harvard Business School offering is a new concept of "shared value", which criticises those who: "... (C)ontinue to view value creation narrowly, optimising short term financial performance in a bubble while missing the most important customer needs and ignoring the broader influences that determined their long-term success".[16] This has much in common with both the "public value" and "social value" approaches. Perhaps most strikingly for observers of the media, the journey of managerial philosophy has an uncanny echo in the journey of the Murdoch family's MacTaggart lectures: Rupert in 1989, James in 2009 and Elisabeth in 2012.

Conclusion: against pantometry

If "public value" is understood as an overarching term to cover the kinds of things we have always talked about in terms of public benefit, public interest or public good, it can do no harm and may do much good. If the aura of managerialist rhetoric assists in selling what is in essence a process of judgment and assessment, then it can be useful. That includes utility in the context of deciding whether or not public broadcasting is operating unfairly to other media.

The principal danger is that some will seek to give this value judgment process a fake air of precision by introducing measurement as the only guide to the formulation of judgements. This tendency in public discourse, a tendency which may now be receding. I did my best to resist this tendency in my earlier incarnation as a judge on a number of occasions. I revived a term that has fallen into disuse – pantometry – which means universal measurement, the belief that everything can be counted. In fact, not everything that counts can be counted. The basic thrust of much of the public value literature affirms that proposition.

The BBC now disaggregates the elements of public value: democratic value, cultural and creative value, education value, social and community value. This is useful and can assist decision-making that requires judgment. There is some danger, however, in the attempt to specify aspects of value that are measurable: reach, quality, impact and value for money.[17] Some of these elements cannot be measured, particularly quality. Broadcast programs are not like manufactured goods subject to objective reject rates. The perils of pantometry must be borne in mind lest the elements that are measurable dominate the decision making process. There are contexts where what can be measured matters most. Public broadcasting is not one of them.

In mid-18th-century London a mathematical prodigy called Jedediah Buxton was taken to see David Garrick perform in Shakespeare's *Richard III* at the Drury Lane Theatre. When asked whether he had enjoyed the play, his reply was that it contained 12,445 words. Jedediah would today be diagnosed as autistic. He did seem to miss some significant things: the sarcasm of "Now is the winter of our discontent, made glorious summer by this son of York" and the desperation of "A horse, a horse, my kingdom for a horse." I do not wish to suggest that pantometry is a medical condition, but sometimes I wonder.

I accept of course, that measurement does have an important role to play. My concern is to ensure that it does not receive unwarranted significance. The ABC recognizes that it is vital to know whether it is providing programs that people value. For some time now, independent surveys have consistently affirmed that about nine in ten Australians believe that the ABC provides "valuable services" to the Australian community and about half believe that the services are "very valuable".[18]

That is worth knowing and worth watching.

Notes

1. Plato. *Phaedrus*, 275a, trans. A. Nehemas and P. Woodruff, in John M. Cooper (ed). *Plato: Complete Works*, 1997. Indianapolis: Hackett, pp. 551-552.
2. The quotation and references are from M. Lowry *The World of Aldus Manutius: Business and Scholarship in Renaissance Venice* Blackwell, 1979 pp. 26-35, generally repeated in V J Hippetts "Yesterday Once More: Sceptics, Scribes and the Demise of Law Reviews" (1996) *Akron L Rev* 267 @ 268-271.
3. Clive James "Sir Thomas Brown" *Cultural Amnesia*, Picador, London 2007 p. 79.
4. Mark Scott. "Commonwealth Broadcasting Association Lecture 2009", Speech at Australia House, London, 9 September 2009. <http://about.abc.net.au/speeches/association-lecture-2009/>.
5. Simon, Herbert A. (1957) *Administrative behavior: a study of decision-making processes in administrative organization*. Second edition. New York: Macmillan.
6. For a recent review of the public value literature see Iestyn Williams and Heather Shearer "Appraising Public Value: Past, Present and Future" 2011 *Public Administration, 1.*
7. K.S. Inglis *This is the ABC: The Australian Broadcasting Commission 1932-1983,* Black Inc., Melbourne, 2006 pp. 65-66.
8. The ABC is unusual in that it is one of very few public broadcasters in the world that is funded through direct government appropriation, rather than a licence fee and/or advertisements. While Australians do pay for the Corporation's services, they do so indirectly and invisibly; there is no correlation between the amount they pay in tax and the amount they contribute to the ABC's operations.
9. Australian Government. *Convergence Review: Final Report*. March 2012, pp. 84-86. http://www.dbcde.gov.au/__data/assets/pdf_file/0007/147733/Convergence_Review_Final_Report.pdf.
10. Harvard Uni P, Boston 1995. A professor in the Kennedy School of Government at Harvard, his frame of reference was "public management".
11. Clive James "Walter Benjamin" *Cultural Amnesia* op. cit. p. 52.
12. See e.g. Walter Kiechel III. *The Lords of Strategy: The Secret Intellectual History of the New Corporate World*. Harvard Business School Press, 2010.
13. Thomas J. Peters & Robert H. Waterman. *In Search of Excellence: Lessons from America's Best-Run Companies*. HarperCollins, 1982.
14. Walter Kiechel III. *The Lords of Strategy*, pp.148-149.
15. (Kiechel supra are at page 324).
16. See *Harvard Business Review* January 2011 "Creating Shared Value".
17. *Building Public Value: Renewing the BBC for a Digital World*, London, 2004, p. 87.
18. Newspoll. *ABC Appreciation Survey*, annual reports (2003-2012); summary versions of the reports are available from http://about.abc.net.au/how-the-abc-is-run/reports-and-publications/.

Chapter 3

Comparing 'Public Value' as a Media Policy Term in Europe

Hallvard Moe & Hilde Van den Bulck

'Public value' is the most central concept in discussions of publicly funded media across and beyond Europe. The concept invokes a redefined remit for public service media, incorporates an economic variable, and pushes the enterprise beyond traditional broadcast radio and television services. Understanding what different stakeholders mean by 'public value' in different contexts and what impact the growing use of this concept has on policy is crucial for anyone interested in the future of public service media.

Much has been written about the so-called *ex ante* public value tests for new service of public service media, the procedures and its impact on public service media policy (e.g. Donders & Moe 2011; Levy, 2011; Michaelis 2010; Moe 2010; Van den Bulck & Moe 2012). However, policy is not just procedures and long trajectories, but also incorporates concepts that often become buzzwords, emerging in policy discourse with life spans that depend on the policy environment. These buzzwords push policy thinking and policy making in particular directions. Therefore, tracing the appearance and spread of policy terms across contexts can provide insight into evolving power structures and meaning creation and re-creation. Studying buzzwords and the mechanisms behind them further enables to take a step back and critically assess the wider impact of current policy development. Based on empirical data from policy debates and legal implementations, and taking an international comparative approach, this chapter scrutinises the history and analyses the meaning of 'public value' and its impact on public service media policy in a cross-section of countries. The aim is to understand the historical roots of 'public value' and its trajectory in European media policy-making. Our approach to the study is based on assessing factors that include relations to the overall policy environment or zeitgeist; the relative power of actors introducing the term; its 'translatability' into different languages and country-specific characteristics; and the ways in which it has been turned into actual policy. Beyond that, the chapter aims to study what counts as 'public value' today, and to reveal significant patterns of consistency and variation in different countries and languages.

What does 'public value' mean, and what are the consequences of the different uses of the term? Our work will demonstrate how despite, or maybe because of, the term's relative success, its actual meaning remains undefined and unspecified, the concept continues to be controversial, and is often used mainly in an instrumental manner to legitimate new development in public service media but in ways that are largely already meant by the terms 'public service' or 'public interest'. Recognising that public service media is in essence a normative construct (e.g. Curran 1991), this chapter offers critical, comparative insights into the varied construction and measurement of public value in media policy-making, and the consequences of policy discourse based on this economic logic. The spread and uses of the term 'public value' have yet to be mapped in media research. Thus we will analyse as wide a range of cases as can be distinguished, rather than doing an in-depth study of a few specific instances. Nevertheless, we aim to move beyond a mere listing of examples to an international analysis of the trajectory and meanings of 'public value'.

Accounting for the service to the public: 'Public value' as a buzzword

The role of public service media in society, how they can perform this role in a transparent fashion and be held accountable for the use of public funds – in short how institutions can best fulfil their public service – remains topical around the world. Across Europe, public service media have undergone a process of debating and redefining their remits, a process which continues today and tends toward a more market- and economic-oriented construct. This follows, and is to a significant degree influenced by, the growing power of commercial competitors as key stakeholders in media systems and policies both nationally and at the EU level (Van den Bulck & Donders 2014). However, policy-making is not just about stakeholders struggling to obtain particular policy outcomes. It is also a struggle over the power to define both the problem and the solution, and thus a matter of establishing a characteristic terminology. As such, policy-making is about introducing and creating momentum for certain terms, here considered as catch phrases or buzzwords (e.g. Freedman 2010; Fairclough 2006).

'Buzzword' has a negative connotation. Its historic roots are within the business and technology sectors (Mjøs et al 2010). The seed of a buzzword is typically planted within a specialist field, where the term has a precise meaning. But as the term is appropriated outside its originating context – for instance being adopted in policy-making discourse – the meaning typically changes, becoming less precise and connoting something that is characteristically vague even if also important and current (Mjøs et al 2010: 4). In what follows, we start from the assumption that 'public value' is a buzzword in this sense (also Lee et al 2011). The term has come to play a key role in European public service media discussions over the past decade, appearing in corporate strategy and governing policy documents at both national and European levels, assuming a position of considerable importance in legislation and academic analyses. We trace this development, looking in detail at the uses of the term and the functions it serves for different actors.

The introduction of the 'public value' term is closely related to evolving views on accountability in public service broadcasting. Until the mid-1980s PSB organisations were typically monopolies in Western Europe and thus accountable first and foremost to governments, a condition that was reinforced through the politicisation of these institutions (notable historic references include Scannell & Cardiff 1991; Van den Bulck 2001; Bardoel & Lowe 2007). From the mid-1980s onwards, technological developments (first cable and satellite, then digitisation), economic dynamics (the concentration of media ownership, the pursuit of economies of scale and scope), socio-cultural trends (postmodern structures, individualisation in audience identities as consumers) and political preferences (neo-liberal political philosophy and deregulatory agenda) are all factors that have resulted in the dissolution of public service monopolies in broadcasting (McQuail & Siune 1998; Blumler 1992; Doyle 2006). Reforms through the 1990s varied across Europe but were heavily influenced by the New Public Management [NPM] doctrine. This introduced entrepreneurial management styles and a business-like orientation to public sector management and governance, describing the public as a client (rather than a citizen), celebrating competition as an absolute good, cultivating marketization and encouraging outsourcing, and contractualising relations (Hood, 1991; Pollitt & Bouckaert 2004). Public sector broadcasters have been both the target of such interventions and an active participant in partly exchanging a cultural-educational logic for those of competition, audience maximisation and channel branding (Lawson-Borders 2006; Van Cuilenburg & McQuail 2003).

Since the year 2000, instruments of control and accountability have become increasingly organised within a competition framework between PSM organisations and other media market players – mainly commercial operators. This competition framework has been legitimated by an increasingly manifest belief that the market can provide diverse and high quality services, embodied especially in EU competition law, that government intervention in broadcasting (and media more generally) should decrease because it disturbs markets and creates distortion, and that the role of publicly-funded media organisations must be defined and monitored more transparently, a change evident in vocal calls for greater accountability and the implementation of instrumentation to determine levels of performance (Armstrong & Weeds 2007; Elstein et al. 2004). One consequence is the adoption of the so-called *ex ante* tests as a requirement to introduce new and/or significant expansions to public media services, procedures meant to control (and possibly constrain) PSM institutional behaviour, particularly in the area of online media services (Van den Bulck & Moe 2012; Donders & Moe 2011).

This phase or phenomenon coincides with and was strongly influenced by the introduction of the concept of 'public value' in a reaction against the NPM public management paradigm (Bennington & Moore 2011; Christensen & Lægreid 2007). The 'public values framework' was introduced by Mark H. Moore at the Harvard Business School. Moore (1995: 10) sees public value as a concept that "equates managerial success in the public sector with initiating and reshaping public sector enterprises in ways that increase their value to the public in both the short and the long run". Collins (2011; 2007; also Lee et al 2011) explained how 'public value' was adopted by the British Labour Government in the early 2000s and how the term was subsequently embraced by the BBC as a key policy tool in 2004 in the legitimation strategy and processes that preceded its Charter renewal (Lee et al 2011; Collins, 2007; BBC 2004). From there, the term travelled into the realm of the European Union, consequentially crossing linguistic and political borders. Indeed, the spread of the term across Europe seems closely related to the growing intervention of the European Union, particularly the European Commission (EC) in public service media policy. The Amsterdam Protocol (1997), the cornerstone of EU policy on PSB, recognises it as a crucial institution in maintaining media pluralism, and confirms member states' competence to provide funding for PSB. Yet, the Protocol stipulates that such funding must not "distort trading conditions and competition rules in the European Union" (Bardoel 2009: 1; Donders & Pauwels, 2010).

On this basis, a wave of cases brought against publicly funded broadcasters by commercial broadcasters and press companies have protested the wide scope of activities, the position of PSB *vis à vis* technological developments and new media services, and the so-called 'market distortion' effect of public funding in broadcasting (cf. Bardoel, 2009). These complaints led the EU to gradually introduce more detailed regulations, and the European Commission to replace the 2001 Broadcasting Communication on state aid rules for PSB with the new 2009 Broadcast Communication,[1] stating that: (1) The public service remit must be clearly defined and formally entrusted upon the PSB institution; (2) Financing must be limited to actual costs; (3) Commercial activities must conform to the market (Soltész 2010: 32). These developments coincided with the growing use of the term public value.

This trajectory will be useful to trace and explain. Did the debates after the BBC Charter introduced the term into public service media policy making, actually lead to the adoption of public value as a rhetorical tool by the

EC, across EU member states (and EFTA), by neighbouring states such as Switzerland and possibly beyond? Where was the term introduced and which factors pushed which actors to introduce it in the particular forms that it took? Equally, if the term was not adopted, we want to understand why not. What is more, it appears that over the course of almost twenty years now, the public value concept has changed meaning and been construed to support varying functions for different stakeholders. Collins (2011; see also Lee et al. 2011) argues that the term was not just adopted but *adapted* considerably from its origin as a critique of NPM. While in Moore's (1995) North American conception the term refers, for example, to public management's 'engagement with [...] users, citizens and communities' (Benington 2011: 21) and European NPM scholars focus on longer-term question on 'what adds value to the public sphere' (ibid.), in contemporary European broadcasting, public value has become a vehicle for more top-down management approaches, extensive and increasingly bureaucratic assessment procedures, and a 'ritual of verification' (Bardoel & Brants 2003), most notably in the development of the BBC's public value test (Donders & Moe 2011). We will interrogate these shifting meanings and applications of public value to generate improved understanding of their implications for public service media.

Analytical framework

To understand the trajectory of the concept of 'public value', its adoption (or not) by stakeholders and policy makers at various (institutional, regional, national, EU) levels, and the various adaptations of the actual meaning of the concept in a meaningful way, we need to identify a number of factors that determine these processes.

A first important set of factors is *the relationship of stakeholders and policy makers to the EU*. As analyses of the EC media policy indicate (Donders 2012; Collins 2011; Michaelis 2011) analyses indicate, the EU has been instrumental in spreading regulatory mechanisms that are inspired by, or directly linked to, the idea of public value. While the 2001 and 2009 Broadcasting Communication Acts both stipulate a clear definition of the public service remit, the Commission failed to stipulate what exactly this public service remit should entail, leaving governments and competing stakeholders to attribute different interpretations and functions to it. Crucial in understanding the potential impact, is the EC role in the development of the so-called *ex ante* tests for significant new services that have been set up in response to EC stipulations following the above-mentioned complaints from commercial competitors. Most notable in this regard, was the development by the BBC of such a test and, more importantly, the labelling of this as a 'public value test'. Together with the German *Drei-Stufen-Test*, it set the tone for much discussion about the development of such tests in other countries (cf. Donders & Moe 2011).

The EU and EC influence is not limited to EU member states. For instance, Norway, Switzerland, Lichtenstein and Iceland all fall under the European Free Trade Agreement (EFTA) and this 'preferential position' *vis à vis* the EU puts them under almost equal EC scrutiny as EU members. What is more, there are indications that EU policy's influence exceeds to wider geo-political areas. A first step in understanding the (non) use of the term public value, therefore, is to identify the relationship between a national policy maker and the EC and to then determine whether or not a particular policy process regarding *ex ante* testing was introduced after the emergence of the term in British policy in 2002.

A second factor is the *characteristics of the media market*. Hallin and Mancini (2004) distinguished three dominant models of European media system: the liberal model (characteristic of the UK), the democratic corporatist model (characteristic of Scandinavian countries) and the polarised pluralist model (characteristic of France). Terzis (2009) proposed a fourth, the East-European post-communist model (e.g. Bulgaria). Each model involves *a set of relationships between media and government, characterised in part by varying terms, degrees and approaches to accountability.* Indeed, in many countries, PSM critics maintain that the absence of a clearly defined remit goes hand in hand with inadequate accountability instruments and a lack of transparency (Brants 2003; Bardoel & Brants, 2003).

A third relevant factor is the *overall size of the media market*. PSM is of particular relevance in smaller media markets, as these are inevitably characterised by more limited resources, higher per capita production costs, and more limited export opportunities compared with big market and global language players. As such, these markets incur higher degrees of vulnerability, coupled with a notable dependence on what happens in neighbouring countries (Edelvold Berg 2013; Lowe & Nissen 2011; Puppis 2009). This makes the position of PSM in dual media markets not only crucial to the economic and cultural health of audiovisual production, but also vulnerable to scrutiny from other stakeholders, particularly commercial competitors.

Finally, we need to analyse *the different meanings attributed to the concept of public value*. Theoretically, we can distinguish a number of, often oppositional, understandings of the term. For instance, Moore's (1995) conception of the term focuses on the bottom-up relationship between citizens and the public institution. In contrast, Power (1999) points to public value within the context of the 'ritual of verification' of top-down management and assessment procedures (Power, 1999). From an economic perspective, public value can be position as a positive alternative to a market failure prespective on public service media. It is also useful to establish how the use of the concept in different contexts relates to older key terms, especially those of 'public service' and 'public interest'.

Methodology

In general, comparative analysis yields a better understanding of intricate, country-specific processes that push seemingly similar processes into different directions. We therefore opted for a 'comparative case study' that can account for complexities as well as for specific circumstances and contexts surrounding a thematic subset of issues (Raats & Pauwels 2011: 25). To analyse the use of the concept of public value in policy debates and legal implementation, we identified and collected *relevant policy documents*. For each case (see below) we collected regulatory frameworks, White and Green papers and other policy documents of national governments, performance contracts and other relevant documents of broadcasters and other stakeholders and actors for the selected cases. These documents were identified according to type of document and 'author' (i.e. policy actor). We consider policy documents as texts (see Fisher 2003), which means 'social products that have consequences in themselves' (Karppinen & Moe 2012: 166) and that incorporate a certain narrative about policy issues. We searched for the occurrence of the keyword phrase 'public value' (in English and possible translations in the various case languages) and its situated meaning. Meaning is here understood and operationalized in terms of the Barthesian (Barthes 1957, 1964) sense of denotation (explicit or direct meaning), connotation (association, implicit or secondary meaning) and myth (ideological and/or meta-meaning). This triple analytical system is applied to occurrences of the term in the collected documents used here. If the term did not occur, we looked for the use of alternative, related terms including public service, public interest and the like. This allowed to understand not just the occurrences of the term public value but also to understand the background of its use (or not).

Following Collins' (2007 & 2011; see also Lee et al. 2011) analyses of the early introduction of the concept of public value in the area of media policy in Britain, our *research period* begins in 2002, the year the British government adopted the term, and analyses a ten-year term (up to 2012). Each case is identified on the basis of *a set of indicators* which include the identification of the media model that is extant (either polarized pluralist, democratic corporatist, or liberal), the existence or absence of an *ex ante* test (on paper, legally, or actually performed), the media market size (large or small) and the occurrence of the term public value in relevant policy documentation.

The above research interest and framework guide the selection of cases. First, as the 'pioneer' of Reithian PSB, the UK is included as a background case. Second, EU member states with different media systems are represented. Third, European non-EU members, preferably also with different media models, add to the analysis. Fourth, the inclusion of non-European cases further substantiates the discussion. Keeping in mind the need to limit the total number of cases to facilitate thorough scrutiny, as well as to allow for pragmatic concerns, including those of the researchers' knowledge of different languages and the kinds of literature and sources available, the following 14 cases were selected: UK, Ireland, Flanders, the Netherlands, Germany, Austria, France, Denmark, Finland and Slovenia (as EU members differing along other factors), Norway, Switzerland and Macedonia (as non-EU members with different systems and relations to the EU), and Australia (as a non-European country).

Table 1.   Overview of factors across case countries

	Post-2002 EU complaint	Ex ante test	Type of media system (cf. Hallin & Mancini 2004; Terzis, 2009)	Size media market (cf. Berg 2011)	'Public value' used (native term)
UK	Yes*	Yes	Liberal	Large	Yes
Ireland ·	Yes	Yes	Liberal	Large	Yes (public value)
Netherlands	Yes	Yes	Corporatist	Large	Yes (publieke (meer)waarde)
Flanders	Yes	Yes	Corporatist	Large	Yes (publieke (meer)waarde)
Germany	Yes	Yes	Corporatist	Large	Yes (public value)
Austria	Yes	Yes	Corporatist	Large	Yes (public value)
Denmark	Yes	Yes	Corporatist	Large	Yes (public service-værdi)
Finland	No	Yes	Corporatist	Large	No
France	Yes	No	Polarised Pluralist	Large	No
Slovenia	No	No	Post Communist	Small	No
Norway	Yes	Yes	Corporatist	Large	Yes (allmennverdi)
Switzerland	No	No	Corporatist	Large	No
Macedonia	No	No	Post Communist	Small	No
Australia	N/A	No	(Liberal)	Small	No

Table 1 provides an overview of the cases and factors. We found the keyword phrase in use in seven of these cases, not counting the UK. We now scrutinise the ways in which the term is used in these cases. On that basis, we can discuss the potential explanations for its different spread and different uses.

The Netherlands

While the term 'public value' is not part of Dutch PSM's (NPO[2]) general mission statement, it appears in several of its documents and in three areas: (1) as part of its overall aims and goals, (2) in relationship to the *ex ante* test and, since late 2011, (3) in relation to audiences.

First, with regard to its *overall aims and goals*, in the NPO policy statement 2010-2016 (NPO 2009) the term 'publieke waarde' (the literal translation of public value) gets several mentions. It is described as a key public service broadcasting characteristic "to be found in all genres" of production. It is also used as a 'container term' that refers to all traditional goals of public service broadcasting (formation, enriching, distinctiveness, "binding, enriching, surprising" (ibid: 8), which are subsequently illustrated in specific examples. In the actual text of the policy plan, mention is made of "public basic values", which are seen as referring to quality, trustworthiness, independence, plurality, innovation, variation, and interaction influence (ibid). Further on, in a section about quality assessment, public service broadcasting's public value is described as its "public value for Dutch society in the area of democracy, culture, education and society". Accordingly, it appears that public value here refers to a contemporary interpretation of longstanding public service goals and objectives.

Second, the term is used with regard to the operation of the *ex ante* testing, as such confirming an (indirect) impact of the EU. Here, more often the translation 'publieke meerwaarde' (public added value) is used rather than simply 'publieke waarde' , most probably as a way to emphasize the necessity of PSM activities demonstrating it being of 'more' value than what commercial media offer, i.e. in a contrastive self-definition.

Third, the term is used by NPO in its self-promotion. For instance, in January 2011, it announced that for any Dutch public service broadcasting organisation, to get airtime (a decision renegotiated regularly between the different broadcasting 'pillar' organisations), it must "prove" the "public added value of each and every one of its programmes" (Trouw 2011). To this end, it is decided that public surveys should include a question regarding the "public added value" of a particular programme.

Flanders

In Flanders, the Dutch speaking, Northern part of Belgium, the text of the 2008 media decree that defines public service broadcasting and its main remit, amongst other media regulatory principles (a decree that was revised in 2012), does not mention the term public value – not even in the section dealing with *ex ante* testing that was the outcome of complaints by commercial competitors against Flemish PSM operator, VRT, lodged with the EC. So there is no straightforward relationship between the EC complaint and assessment processes and the introduction of the term 'public value' into policy form(ul)ation. However, the term 'publieke meerwaarde' (public added value) does appear, primarily in documents drafted by several stakeholders in the lead-up to the new management contract between VRT and the Flemish government, which was negotiated in 2011, implemented in 2012 and remains in force (Flemish Government, 2011, see chapter Donders & Van den Bulck).

First, the advice of the Media Council mentions 'public added value', once again as a term that groups all "duties" or "tasks" of public service broadcasting, even though the phrase itself is not specifically defined (Sectorraad Media, 2010). In further discussion of these tasks, the phrase appears only with reference to entertainment and sports programmes, which are explicitly required to demonstrate their public added value. This provision reflects the critical voice of commercial competitors exerting influence in the media council as one which believes that entertainment and sports should be left to the market. The management contract further uses the term when referring to new services for which it is said that the 'publieke meerwaarde' must be defined (Flemish Government, 2011).

Second, the actual management contract mentions the term as one of the six key elements that make up its 'specific role in the Flemish media constellation' (Flemish Government, 2011: 10). As its second main function VRT has "public (added) value and quality". The explanation asserts that "VRT guarantees high quality standards. The VRT realizes a public added value in all it does and strengthens this added value by emphasizing more the public and ethical quality". The latter refers to an ideological, mythical meaning of public service broadcasting

Germany

The German case stands out because no native translation of the term exists either in media policy debate or in the documentation created by ARD or its component regional broadcasters. Instead, the English-language term 'public value' is used to some extent, especially by academics and stakeholders. For example, in their review of the debate leading up to the German *ex ante* test based on an inductive analysis of legal documents regarding PSM and informed by the minutes of parliamentary debates and PSM policy documents, Radoslavov and Thomass (2011) explain that no specific meaning of the term was evident in this debate. Rather, the term is used in different ways, this usage referring implicitly both to methodological, policy, content, production and/or ideological dimensions which address "different understandings of the common welfare connected to broadcasting" (ibid: 87). They find that discussions about 'public value' in Germany refer mainly to the methodological dimension – i.e. the implementation of a measurement mechanism for determining the validity of new public media service plans – whereas normative or content aspects were largely missing from the debate (ibid: 91). Nevertheless, in our evaluation, the term has made no lasting linguistic-terminological impact, either in media debates or in the name of the *ex ante* test (called 'Drei-Stufen-Test' or the Three Step Test).

Austria

Austria differs again from other European cases. As with Germany, Austria uses the term 'public value' in its original English-language form. However, in contrast to the German case, Austria's ORT has embraced the term in a particularly explicit way. Already in 2007, the institution set up a *'Public-Value-Kompetenz-*

zentrum' (Puppis et al 2012; ORT 2011), a research centre that undertakes quantitative content measurements as well as surveys for ORT and publishes a yearly 'public value report' that seeks to explain why Austrians should keep ORT as a public service broadcaster. In these reports, the term is used quite frequently, even being connected with specific genres (e.g. comedy). In a short interview in the 2011 report, an ORT programme host, for instance, used the term in a quite off-hand way, stating "it doesn't get more public value than to initiate a climate protection award" (ORT 2011: 21). In this context, ORT defines public value simply as 'Wert über Gebühr' or 'value over charge' (ibid: 2). In the Austrian case, then, the term has been given the overtly 'hands on' meaning of a striving for excellence and ideational 'worthiness', so has taken on yet another meaning. It is also used strategically and actively by the public service broadcaster to legitimate its operations.

Ireland

The Irish case seems to provide a clear example of the EC's influence on the introduction of the term 'public value' into policy development. A 2007 draft letter from the Irish government (O´Brien 2007), written in response to an EC intervention following a complaint, focuses on the term and lists all the criteria believed to be included in 'public value': The list includes concerns about accessibility, compliance with the remit, media plurality, along with considerations regarding RTÉ's contributions to meeting the democratic, linguistic, educational, and social needs of Irish society, among other things. The final provision, of "such other matters as the Minister adjudges relevant and appropriate", allows for a situated extension of the denoted meanings. This is a far-reaching interpretation. Not only does it refer to other supranational policy documents (Audiovisual Media Services Directive) and policy bodies (including Council of Europe), it also incorporates such key concepts as 'plurality'. Furthermore, the Irish Government opens up the literal definition to any future local additions "the Minister" might see fit. In effect, this achieves two potentially conflicting outcomes – of establishing a formalized regulatory definition and formalizing a policy term that is open-ended in practice – at the same time.

Denmark

Denmark, an EU member state, is another case where the term has had policy influence. However the background of the term, the term itself, and its use, all differ again from the previous cases we have looked at. In 2007, directly inspired by the BBC's public value test, the Danish government set up a *værditest* ('value test') of new DR services (Svendsen 2011: 118). An English translation of the document outlining the test's purpose, describes it as "a value test of new public service broadcasting services" (Kulturministeriet 2007: 1). The test itself entails only half the scope of the British instrument, in that only a public value assessment is required, with no obligation to also include a market impact assessment. In the following years, this regime was subject to some criticism for having no practical consequences, and for dealing with miniscule services, but little attention was given to the term 'value test' (e.g. DDF 2008). In 2010 the government introduced a fully-fledged *ex ante* test, adding a market impact assessment to the "assessment of the service's public service value" (Kulturministeriet 2010: 3, our translation). In Denmark, then, 'public value' led directly to the introduction of the notion of 'value' in public service media regulations, a concept later specified in the English-Danish language construct as *public service værdi*. Along the way, "value" also went from connoting a degree of cultural or democratic worth, to incorporating a more specifically economic meaning, as linked to the *ex ante* test.

Norway

Norway is a non-EU member, but all relevant policy measures are equally relevant to it in the wake of the European Economic Area (EEA) agreement with the EU which ensures the free movement of goods, people, capital and services with EU member states. From 2003 onwards, Norway's PSM was subjected to a policy process equal to those run by the EC, but in this case it was run by the EFTA Surveillance Authority (e.g. Moe 2010). The process led to a redefinition of the public service broadcasting remit, as well as to the establishment of an *ex ante* test (see Lilleborge 2011) but the term 'public value' was not at all central to that policy process. Only after the conclusion of this process, did the term even surface. It was introduced by the public service broadcaster, NRK, in a Norwegian translation (*allmennverdi*) as part of a bid to renew discussions about the PSM remit. Much like in the Austrian case, the term was applied in annual reports and strategy documents. Launched in a 2011 strategy document, *allmennverdi* was described as a term the NRK wanted to "link to all kinds of programmes", according to the then-NRK Director General Hans-Tore Bjerkaas. Asked to define the term *allmennverdi*, he admitted: "I cannot give an exact definition. The term has to find its form in the meeting of program makers and schedulers within each genre, in each medium and on each platform" (Bjerkaas in DN 2011). Since then, the term seems to have lost some of its vogue with the NRK, as it is absent from the 2012 annual report.

Scrutiny of these specific cases where we have found the term 'public value' to exist in public service media policy discussions reveals quite different trajectories, definitions and uses. Much of this discourse suggests a large rhetorical role as well as an important instrumental function for this term. We will now compare these findings with the remaining cases in order to clarify and consider where the term (so far) has not made an impact. The aim is to move closer to an understanding of the factors that might affect the uptake of the term.

Understanding correspondence and differentiation

When speculating about the factors, identified in table 1, that have so far affected the dissemination and uptake of the term 'public value', our first observation has to do with the case study countries' relationships with the EU. All cases discussed so far are either located within EU member states or those bound to EU policy through specific agreements (Norway). All these cases have also been subject to an EU-driven state aid policy process concerning public service broadcasting remits and/or funding issues beginning in 2004. More over, these countries all fit the liberal and corporate categories of Hallin and Mancini's schema, indicating the relevance of the specifics of the media system.

If we look further at all European countries where 'public value' is not in policy use, however, we find a 'mixed bag': the six include European non-EU member states (Switzerland and Macedonia) as well as EU members (France, Finland and Slovenia). Switzerland has a large media market, and a long tradition of public service broadcasting, but has chosen a different path when renewing the regulatory framework, namely setting up a test *ex post*, that is after the actual introduction of the service, rather than *ex ante*, that is before the introduction of a new service (Just et al. 2012; Puppis et al. 2013). Slovenia, on the other hand, has a small media market, with a shorter tradition of public service broadcasting, much like Macedonia. The two latter characteristics – fewer commercial competitors and an evolving public service sector – might help explain why the debate so far has focused on other, perhaps more pressing issues.

In Australia, despite long tradition of public service broadcasting, as well as historically and politically close ties to the UK, the term 'public value' has not (yet) made an impact in actual policy. This is possibly because the ABC, and later SBS, were always part of a mixed market model, and smaller market players in revenue terms than their commercial competitors, who dominate a highly concentrated broadcast and online marketplace (Dwyer and Martin, 2010). Thus the term has not been required to legitimate the PSBs' roles in light of existing or growing market influence. The ABC is unlikely to want to adopt a public value test as of now. Still, the term itself, freed from the regulatory set up of an *ex ante* test, is being discussed. However, the ABC chairman has publicly welcomed a quite wide use of the term, stating in a 2012 speech that "In many contexts this concept merely replaces similar overlapping terminology such as 'public good', 'public interest' and 'public benefit'. These words have been used with good effect over many decades, indeed centuries, without being burdened by definition" (Spigelman 2012, see also Cunningham 2012).

The dissemination of public value in media policy and regulation shows that the media reform impact of the EU is worthy of continued scrutiny. Our analysis of France, Finland and Slovenia further show that EU membership and even the existence of an ex ante test do not 'guarantee' the introduction of the term. This suggests the strength of regional policy dynamics.

The policy development role of the EC and subsequent adoption by countries of an ex ante testing becomes even less self-evident as diffusion factors when looking at various definitions and interpretations of the term. While the Irish case shows quite a straightforward relationship, with the term used in answer to an EC complaint letter, other factors suggest a less straightforward relationship. Importantly, key EU documents such as the 2009 Broadcast Communication do not actually use the term public value, only "Added value in terms of serving the social, democratic and cultural needs of society" (Broadcast Communication 2009). So, has the term in fact travelled through EU (EC) intervention or have member states in their use of the term been inspired by other actors, e.g. the BBC, known to be an important benchmark and example for other public service broadcasters in Europe, or by other PSM actors and stakeholders? This needs to be further explored, for instance by taking a closer look at the specific stakeholders that have pushed for the term (or not). Is the term (and a wider policy agenda behind it) pushed by governments, PSM institutions or other stakeholders? As multi-stakeholderism is on the rise in PSM policy making (cf. Van den Bulck & Donders 2013), the role of stakeholders such as commercial competitors, international media companies and other actors should be put under closer scrutiny.

Other issues worthy of further analysis include the political cultures, the geo-linguistic areas of influence and the history of media policy debate in each case. With regard to political cultures, the level to which the New Public Management policy approach has been adopted and codified in relationship to media by the establishment of media policy advice councils and regulatory bodies as well as the growth in specific accountability measures could have a possible influence. That possibility is suggested by the Flemish case where the Media Council had a role in the adoption of the term. One could hypothesize that NRK's late introduction of *allmennverdi* as a strategic term, with no predefined meaning and no link to the conceptual history, can be understood with reference to geo-linguistic issues. First, scholars have found the Norwegian debate over public service broadcasting to be less concerned with overarching normative policy concepts (e.g. 'democracy') in comparison to similar Scandinavian cases (Larsen 2010). For the NRK, *allmennverdi* seems to have substituted earlier consonant cultural concepts, most recently 'societal mission' (*samfunnsoppdrag*). Norway also has a practice of translating English language policy terms rather than directly adopting them, for example *allmennkringkasting* has been used since the late 1980s for public service broadcasting. In contrast, neighbouring

Denmark has stuck to the English adaptation 'public service-medier' – and now, as shown above, has pursued a similar adaptation of 'public value' into 'public service-værdi'. The absence of the term in the Swiss and French cases further suggest the importance of geo-linguistic factors in media policy development, such as the cultural-intellectual gap between Germanic and Romanic language areas (Treffers-Daller & Willemyns 2002).

Finally, an interesting path to explore is the role of academics and their publications in propagating the term. Both the text of the most recent 2012–16 management contract of Flemish VRT and the answer of the Irish government's Draft Letter to the EC were heavily influenced by academics acting as consultants or providing research reports. This opens up a range of interesting questions, not least those concerning 'reactive effects', that is, the ways in which the results of our research as media policy scholars are affected by our roles as media policy actors (Karppinen & Moe 2012).

When it comes to actual definitions, we have shown how they vary across cases from quite simple and straightforward applications (e.g. in Austria), to either elaborate lists or ambiguous references (e.g. in Ireland and The Netherlands), to no definition at all (e.g. in Norway). In some cases, such as that of Norway, 'public value' (*allmennverdi*) seems to replace the notion of 'public service' in strategic policy documents, if only temporarily. In other cases, these terms appear alongside each other – as if interchangeable. In Germany the concept is not used in actual policy but has nevertheless produced a level of debate, while other countries have introduced the term in quite specific policy procedures (e.g. the Netherlands). For those studying PSM, such findings are not novel of course. Scrutinising both politicians' and media researchers' uses of the traditional concept of 'public service broadcasting' in the 1980s, Trine Syvertsen collected over 30 different criteria, none of which were shared by all definitions and several of which were contradictory (Syvertsen 1990: 191-192; 1992: 17-18). She found, in particular, that public service broadcasting had been used to describe such elements as the emphasis of a particular national system, the role of certain institutions, and a prescribed mix of programmes. This suggest a continued need for terms to describe the role of the broadcasting institution that operate as master signifiers, projecting its ideal nature.

Our findings show some similarities. However, one basic difference lies in the concepts themselves. Despite its different uses, the concept of 'public service broadcasting' has had an influential history in media policy, with some clearly defined core values (for further detail, see Born & Prosser 2001; Moe 2011; Tracey 1998). 'Public value', in contrast, has not only had a shorter history but has also had a less clearly defined role. It emerged out of a period of neoliberalism and neo-classical public management doctrine, moving via UK policy making into BBC strategy documents and further through EC deliberations into different uses in varied languages in a range of countries. Influenced by these different contexts and uses, the meaning has changed, substantially diversified, and has yet remained rather vague (Radoslavov & Thomass 2011: 87-88; Lee et al 2011). In addition, the meaning and context as presented here tend to be so far removed from the original intentions and context from which Moore's (1995) perspective originated that a basic understanding of 'public value' could be even more difficult to achieve than a rudimentary sense of 'public service broadcasting'. This vagueness can only enhance concerns that with the use of the term comes an implicit reference to (and acceptance of) a predominant market-oriented perspective on public service media – that these entities are expected to better 'prove' and/or account for the 'public value' of their activities. Together with the factors already analysed, these additional insights will allow us to evaluate whether the evident dissemination of the term can be attributed to the still increasing homogenization influence of the EU or whether, as the findings so far suggest, it shows a clearer path dependency.

Conclusions

Our analysis has been broad, widely tracing the occurences and various uses of the term 'public value' rather than focusing in-depth on a limited number of cases. The latter is definitely required for an even better understanding of the use and impact of the term public value. However, we believe our study contributes to such an understanding.

As the analysis makes clear, in public service media discussions today, 'public value' serves as a buzzword: it has moved far away from its origins (Moore 1995) in a specific purpose with a stipulated definition relevant to a particular field (public sector management) in a concrete context (the USA). The term has travelled geographically and evolved over time, appearing in different situations, been used by different actors and been given various meanings. In this chapter we have analysed the actual adoption (or not) of public value as a policy term in different countries and looked at factors influencing the introduction and use of the term. Finding no direct link between the concept of public value and the existence of an ex ante test procedure for significant new services, we looked deeper into specific characteristics of different policy contexts, showing the influence of various factors but with the overall result of a widespread use of the term public value.

While 'buzzword' suggest temporary use – soon another buzzword may take over – it would be wrong to underestimate the impact of such buzzwords, as the Dutch case suggests. Indeed, the term is rapidly replacing other key concepts with long and important histories (both as concepts and as subjects for analysis) such as public service and public interest, but without really being positioned vis à vis these terms. New concepts can inspire, inform, and contribute to complex, long-standing and unresolved debates. In this respect, the introduction of the Habermasian notion of 'public sphere' into Anglo-Saxon academia after the translation from German to English of key Habermas' texts offers a good example.

The situation is less encouraging for 'public value' so far, at least. We contend that as long as legislators, policy makers, practitioners and academics forego achieving clarity about its meaning and its relationship to other (older) key terms, there is a real concern that in designing policy processes around that phrase we will end up lost in a vast conceptual wasteland – not actually getting anywhere – and, as a consequence, becoming more or less uncertain about where we are at any given point.

As a buzzword, 'public value' can serve several functions for the actors in PSM reform processes (see Mjøs et al 2010). First, it can simplify something that is unusually complex. When discussing detailed EU competition law requirements and elaborate regulatory mechanisms, it makes sense to use a catchphrase that more or less covers the topic in question. But simplification comes at a price: a loss of depth and complexity of meaning and a loss of clarity, considering that simplification can mystify issues. Moreover, as a buzzword, 'public value' serves to promote a novel idea (Mjøs et al 2010). For some, it is a new regulatory concept meant to discipline public service broadcasters, while others see it as a way to 'defend' and promote what public service institutions do. This relates to a third function, that of legitimating a line of action or a strategy (Mjøs et al 2010). Those public service broadcasters that have embraced the term, use it strategically to gain support in a new political and technological context that is dominated by a belief in the market and a related call for accountability instruments to legitimate public service media's call on public funds. 'Buying into' the buzzword therefore implies buying into a whole paradigm of economic rationality, which, as has been demonstrated here, is in fact a reinterpretation of the 'public value' of these public service institutions.

Notes

1. In early 2010, the EEA issued new guidelines for application of state aid rules to broadcasting which corresponds to the EC Communication (ESA 2010).
2. NPO: Nederlandse Publieke Omroep is the umbrella organisation that governs all public service media organisations in Neetherlands and also determines strategy and programming in cooperation with the different organisations.

Acknowledgements

The authors would like to thank Sally Broughton Micova and Kari Karppinen for valuable help with the data collection.

References

Armstrong, M. & Weeds, H. (2007) 'Public Service Broadcasting in the Digital World', in Seabright, P. & Hagen, J. von (eds) *The Economic Regulation of Broadcasting Markets: Evolving Technology and Challenges for Policy*. Cambridge: Cambridge University Press, pp. 81-149

Bardoel, J. (2009) 'Media Policy Between Europe and the Nation-State: The case of the EU Broadcast Communication 2009', paper presented at the *ECREA Law and Policy Section Conference*, Zurich, November.

Bardoel, J. & Brants, K. (2003) 'From Ritual to Reality: Public Broadcasters and Social Responsibility in the Netherlands', in Lowe, G.F. & Hujanen, T. (ed.) (2003) *Broadcasting & Convergence: New Articulations of the Public Service Remit*. Göteborg: Nordicom, pp. 167-187.

Bardoel, J. & Lowe, G.F. (2007) 'From Public Service Broadcasting to Public Service Media: The Core Challenge', in Lowe, G.F. & Bardoel, J. (eds) *From Public Service Broadcasting to Public Service Media*. Göteborg: Nordicom, pp. 9-26

Barthes, R. (1957/ 1987) *Mythologies*. New York: Hill & Wang.

Barthes, R. (1964/1967) *Elements of Semiology* (trans. Annette Lavers & Colin Smith). London: Jonathan Cape.

BBC (2004) *Building Public Value: Reviewing the BBC for a Digital World*. London: BBC.

Benington, J. (2011) 'From Private Choice To Public Value', in J. Benington & M.H. Moore (eds) *Public Value: Theory and Practice*. Basingstoke: Palgrave Macmillan, pp. 31-51

Berg, C.R. (2011) 'Sizing Up Size on TV Markets. Why David would Lose to Goliath', in G.F. Lowe & C.S. Nissen (eds) *Small Among Giants. Television Broadcasting in Smaller Countries*. Göteborg: Nordicom, pp. 57- 90.

Born, G. & Prosser, T. (2001) "Culture and Consumerism: Citizenship, Public Service Broadcasting and the BBC's Fair Trading Obligations." *The Modern Law Review* 64(5): 657-687.

Blumler, J.G. (ed.) (1992) *Television and the Public Interest: Vulnerable Values in West European Broadcasting*. London: Sage.

Brants, K. (2003) 'Auditing Public Broadcasting Performance: Its Theory and Practice', *Javnost The Public*, 10(5): 5-10

Broadcasting Communication (2009) Communication from the Commission On the Application of State Aid Rules to Public Service Broadcasting (Text with EEA Relevance). Brussels: European Commission, 2009/C 257/01.

Christensen, T. & Lægreid, P. (2007) 'The Whole-Of-Government Approach to Public Sector Reform', *Public administration review* 67(6): 1059-1066.

Collins, R. (2007) 'The BBC and 'Public Value'', *Medien & Communikationswissenschaft*, 55(2): 164-184.

Collins, R. (2011) 'Public Value, the BBC and Humpty Dumpty Words: Does Public Value Management Mean What it Says?' in K. Donderrs & H. Moe (eds) *Exporting the Public Value Test: The Regulation of Public Broadcasters' New Media Services Across Europe*. Göteborg, Nordicom, pp. 49-58.

Cunningham, S. (2012) *Hidden Innovation: Policy, Industry and the Creative Sector*. Brisbane: University of Queensland Press.

Curran, J. (1991) 'Rethinking the Media as a Public Sphere' in P. Dahlgren & C. Sparks (eds) *Communication and Citizenship: Journalism and the Public Sphere in the New Media Age*, London: Routledge, pp. 27-57.

Dagens Næringsliv (DN) (2011) *NRK hopper av markedsjaget*, 19.09, p. 36.

Danske Dagblades Forening (DDF) (2008) *I konkurrence med staten. DR truer dagbladene på nettet*. København: DDF.

Donders, K. (2012) *Public service media and policy in Europe*. Basingstoke: Palgrave Macmillan.

Donders, K. & Moe, H. (eds.) (2011) *Exporting the Public Value Test*. Göteborg: Nordicom.

Donders, K. & C. Pauwels (2010) 'What if Competition Policy Assists the Transfer from Public Service Broadcasting to Public Service Media? An Analysis of EU State Aid Control and its Relevance for Public Broadcasting', J. Gripsrud & H. Moe (eds), *The Digital Public Sphere: Challenges for Media Policy* Göteborg: Nordicom, pp. 25-61.

Doyle, G. (2006) *Media Ownership*. London: Sage.

Dwyer & Martin, F. (2010) 'News Diversity In Online Media Systems: A Preliminary Report on the Concept of Voice', *International Readings in Media and Mass Communications*, Mosco: Lomonosov Mosco State University.

Edelvold Berg, C. (2013) *As a Matter of Size: The Importance of Critical Mass and the Consequences of Scarcity for Television Markets*. Frederiksberg: Copenhagen Business School.

Elstein, D., Cox, D., Donoghue, B., Graham, D. & G. Metzger (2004) *Beyond the Charter: The BBC After 2006*. London: the Broadcasting Policy Group.

ESA (2010) The application of the state aid rules to public service broadcasting [http://www.eftasurv.int/state-aid/legal-framework/state-aid-guidelines/]

Fairclough, N. (2006) *Language and Globalization*. London: Routledge.

Fisher, F. (2003) *Reframing Policy Analysis: Discursive Politics and Deliberative Practices*. Oxford: Oxford University Press.

Flemish Government (2011) Management Contract between VRT and the Flemish government 2012-2016. Brussels: Flemish government.

Freedman, D. (2010) 'Media Policy Silences: The Hidden Face of Communications Decision Making.' *The International Journal of Press/Politics* 15(3): 344-362.

Hallin, D.C. & Mancini, P. (2004) *Comparing Media Systems – Three Models of Media and Politics*. Cambridge: Cambridge University Press.

Hood, C. (1991) 'A Public Management for All Seasons', *Public Administration*, 69(1): 3-19.

Humphreys, P. (1996) *Mass Media and Media Policy in Western Europe*. Manchester/New York: Manchester University Press.

Just, N., Latzer, M. & Saurwein, F. (2012) "Public Service Broadcasting put to the test: Ex post control of online services." *International Journal of Media and Cultural Politics* 8(1): 51-65.

Karppinen, K. & Moe, H. (2012) 'What We Talk About When We Talk About Document Analysis' in Puppis, M. & N. Just (eds) *Trends in Communication Policy Research: New Theories, Methods and Subjects*. Bristol: Intellect Books, pp. 177-194

Kulturministeriet (2007) *Value test of new public service broadcasting services*. Appendix to the 'media agreement'.

Kulturstyrelsen (2010) *Fokus på kvalitet og mangfoldighed: Mediepolitisk aftale for 2011-2014*. http://www.bibliotekogmedier.dk/medieomraadet/tv/medieaftalen-for-2011-2014/

Larsen, H. (2010) 'Legitimation strategies of public service broadcasters: the divergent rhetoric in Norway and Sweden.' *Media, Culture & Society* 32(2): 267-283.

Lawson-Borders, G. (2006) *Media Organisations and Convergence*. London: Lawrence Erlbaum.

Lee, D.J., Oakley, K. & Naylor, R. (2011) 'The Public Gets What the Public Wants'? The Uses and Abuses of 'Public Value' in Contemporary British Cultural Policy', *International Journal of Cultural Policy* 17 (3): 289-300.

Levy, D. A.L. (2011) 'Negotiating Europeanization: State Aid Guidelines, Public Broadcasting and New Services in three major member states.' *OxPo Working Papers 2011-2012*. Oxford: Oxford Sciences Po Research Group.

Lilleborge, M.-T. (2011) 'The Public Service Remit in Norway. what's in and What's out?' in K. Donders & H. Moe (eds) *Exporting the Public Value Test: The Regulation of Public Broadcasters' New Media Services Across Europe*. Göteborg: Nordicom.

Lowe, G.F. & Nissen, C.S. (eds.) (2011) *Small Amongst Giants: Television Broadcasting in Smaller Countries*. Göteborg: Nordicom.

McQuail, D. & Siune, K. (eds.) (1998) Media Policy: Convergence, Concentration and Commerce. London: Sage.

Michaelis, M. (2010) 'Is The Public Interest Under Threat? Public Service Broadcasting Market Failure and New Technologies: The View From the EU', *Interactions: Studies in Communication & Culture*, 1(2), 185-202.

Mjøs, O.J, Moe, H. & Sundet V.S. (2010) 'The Function of Buzzwords: A Comparison of Web 2.0 and Telematics', paper presented at the Norwegian Media Researchers' Conference.

Moe, H. (2010) 'Governing Public Service Broadcasting: 'Public Value Tests' in Different National Contexts.' *Communication, Culture & Critique* 3(2): 207-223.

Moore, M. (1995) *Creating Public Value: Strategic Management in Government*. Cambridge (MA): Harvard.

NPO (2009) *Beleidsplan 2010-2016.* Hilversum: NPO.

O´Brien, K. (2007) *Draft letter to the EC,* Irish Government, 14.12.07

ORT (2011) *Wert über Gebühr – Public Value Bericht 2010/2011.* ORT.

Pollitt, C., & Bouckaert, G. (2004) *Public Management Reform: A Comparative Analysis.* Oxford: Oxford University Press.

Power, M. (1999) *The Audit Society: Rituals of Verification.* Oxford: Open University Press.

Puppis, M. (2009) 'Introduction. Media Regulation in Small States', *International Communication Gazette,* 71(1-2): 7-17.

Puppis, M., Künzler, M. & Steinmaurer, T. (2013) 'Public Service Broadcasting in the Digital Age: Regulation and Organizational Strategies in Ireland, Austria and Switzerland' in M. Löblich & S. Pfaff-Rüdiger (eds) *Communication and Media Policy in the Era of the Internet. Theories and Processes.* Baden Baden: Nomos, pp. 95-106.

Raats, T. & Pauwels, C. (2011) 'In Search of the Holy Grail? Comparative Analysis in Public Broadcasting Research', in Donders, K. & Moe, H. (eds.) pp 17-29 *Exporting the Public Value Test: The Regulation of Public Broadcasters' New Media Services Across Europe.* Göteborg: Nordicom.

Radoslavov, S. & Thomass, B. (2011) 'ZDF's Three-step Test as a Societal Debate about the Future of Public Service Broadcasting' in Donders, K. & Moe, H. (ed.) *Exporting the Public Value Test: The Regulation of Public, Broadcasters' New Media Services Across Europe.* Göteborg: Nordicom, pp. 83-95.

Scannell, P. & Cardiff, D. (1991) *A Social History of British Broadcasting, Volume One 1922-1939: Serving the Nation.* Cambridge: Basil Blackwell.

Sectorraad Media (2010) *Advies SARC Sectorraad Media Beheersovereenkomst tussen de openbare omroep en de Vlaamse Gemeenschap.* Brussel: SARC, December.

Soltész, U. (2010) 'Tighter State Aid Rules for Public TV Channels', *Journal of European Competition Law & Practice,* 1(1): 32-36.

Svendsen, E. Nordahl (2011) *'Two Steps Towards a Public Value Test: Danish Public Service Broadcasting Between Two Lines of Control'* in Donders, K. & Moe, H. (eds) *Exporting the Public Value Test: The Regulation of Public Broadcasters' New Media Services Across Europe.* Göteborg: Nordicom, pp. 117-126

Syvertsen, T. (1990) 'Kringkasting i 1990-åra: Hvem er mest 'public service'?' in Carlsson, U. (ed.) *Medier, Människor, Samhälle – 14 artiklar om nordisk masskommunikationsforskning.* Göteborg: Nordicom, pp. 183-195

Syvertsen, T. (1992) *Public Television in Transition.* Oslo: Norges allmennvitenskapelige forskningsråd.

Syvertsen, T. (1999) 'The Many Uses of the 'Pubilc Service' Concept' *Nordicom Review* 20(1): 5-13.

Terzis, G. (ed.) (2009) *European Media Governance: National and Regional Dimensions.* Bristol: Intellect.

Tracey, M. (1998) *The Decline and Fall of Public Service Broadcasting.* Oxford: Oxford University Press.

Treffers-Daller, J. & Willemyns, R. (eds) (2002) Language Contact at the Romance-Germanic Language Border, *Journal of Multilingual and Multicultural Development* 23:1/2. ClevedonMultilingual Matters.

Trouw (2011) 'Publieke Omroep meet meerwaarde', Trouw, 7 January http://www.trouw.nl/tr/nl/4324/Nieuws/archief/article/detail/1842368/2011/01/07/Publieke-omroep-meet-meerwaarde.dhtml

Van Cuilenburg, J. & McQuail, D. (2003) 'Media Policy Paradigm Shifts: Towards a New Communications Policy Paradigm', *European Journal of Communication* 18(2): 181-197.

Van den Bulck, H. (2001) 'Public Service Television and National Identity as a Project of Modernity: The Example of Flemish television', *Media, Culture and Society,* 29(1) 83–99.

Van den Bulck, H. & Donders, K. (2014) 'Of Discourses, Stakeholders and Advocacy Coalitions in Media Policy: Tracing Negotiations towards the New Management Contract of Flemish Public Broadcaster VRT', *European Journal of Communication.*

Van den Bulck, H. & Moe, H. (2012) 'To Test or Not to Test: Comparing the Development of Ex Ante Public Service Media Assessments in Flanders and Norway', *International Journal of Media and Cultural Politics,* 8 (1).

Chapter 4

The Price of Everything and the Value of Nothing?

Economic Arguments and the Politics of Public Service Media

Peter Goodwin

For the first half-century or so of its existence, public service broadcasting in most places did not have to bother much with justifying itself in terms of the market. This was for two interconnected reasons. First, from radio through to television, from monopoly through to (regulated and licensed) commercial competition, in many countries all broadcasting was officially regarded as a public service. In the UK, at least, which provided the model for many other PSBs, this conception was enshrined in law (Goodwin 1998b: 13). Second, the institutional arrangement of public service broadcasters in the narrower sense – as a public corporation or authority at arm's length from government – was a familiar and widely used organisational form in a wide range of sectors of European economies and across the British Commonwealth.

The public sector corporation was fashionable in the UK when the first PSB, the British Broadcasting Corporation, was established in the 1920s. It became increasingly fashionable with the wave of nationalisations in the UK and in wider Europe after the end of the Second World War (Judt 2005: 361-2). This approach to the organisation of swathes of industry and services was a perfectly normal part of the political and economic landscape of the 'mixed-economy' consensus into the 1970s. Far from being something peculiar to broadcasting the public corporation was also often the main form for rail and public road transport, for mining, for power production and distribution, for other services of a public nature and for various areas of manufacturing.

It should be stressed that this 'normality' of PSB is a matter of historical record in the countries where public service broadcasters existed, rather than of any strict and fundamental logic about broadcasting. In the USA from the beginning there was a quite different way of organising broadcasting as regulated commercial competition, albeit with an expectation that broadcasting ought to serve "the public interest, convenience and necessity"[1]. This difference between American and European broadcasting was part of a more general difference between the politics and economic organisation of America on the one hand and Western

Europe on the other. In the USA the public corporation was a far less common organisational form, there was no post-war wave of nationalisations, and huge areas of the economy (from telecommunications to railway transport), which it seemed to Europeans should quite naturally be in public hands, in the USA seemed more natural to run under private ownership as commercial concerns.

The shift to economic-based argumentation

From roughly the mid-1980s the picture changed in Europe. Particularly in those countries where public service broadcasting had been a monopoly provider, its defenders could no longer ignore the market as it developed into the characteristic context in which these corporations must operate. They would now have to use economic arguments to mount their case for the continued existence of public service broadcasters. In the UK this shift in the pattern of argumentation began dramatically with the Peacock Committee, which was set up in 1985 to look at the financing of the BBC and made its seminal report in 1986. The Committee's general long-term approach to broadcasting was firmly expressed in the language of the market: "British broadcasting should move towards a sophisticated market system based on consumer sovereignty. That is a system which recognises that viewers and listeners are the best ultimate judges of their own interests, which they can best satisfy if they have the option of purchasing the broadcasting services they require from as many sources of supply as possible" (Peacock 1986: 133).

Many of the Committee's recommendations were not taken up. But as the authors of a 1988 academic study entitled *The Economics of Television: The UK Case* put it: "The setting up of the Peacock Committee, the evidence that its inquiry has elicited, and the debate on the future funding of UK broadcasting that it has sparked off, have performed the valuable function of placing the economics of broadcasting firmly at the centre of the policy-making agenda" (Collins, Garnham & Locksley 1988: 1). This emphasis has not gone away. Nor has its influence been confined to Britain. Elsewhere the shift in thinking may have come a bit earlier or later, or more gradually, but it has been equally decisive.

From the 1980s onwards argumentation about PSB has not been able to ignore economics and the market. This new focus in broadcast policy was a part of a far wider shift in political and economic thinking – to put it crudely, the victory of free-market 'neo-liberalism' over the post-war consensus of a mixed economy. Again though, in examining this moment in UK history, which produced the Peacock Report, one needs to distinguish between the politics in play and the particular proposal about broadcasting policy that accompanied it.

The Peacock Committee owed its existence to the Conservative administration of Margaret Thatcher, a pioneer in the free-market revolution in Western

Europe and much of the rest of the world (together with Ronald Reagan in the USA). In its recommendations the Committee did not slavishly follow the bidding of the Thatcher administration, however (as evident most notably in its rejection of advertising on the BBC). But in the overt and general free-market standpoint of its leading members, economist Professor Alan Peacock, and economics-trained financial journalist Samuel Brittan, the Committee was very much at one with the new political spirit of the times. Broadcasting, it should be remembered, was a relatively minor concern of neo-liberal governments, which instituted wide scale privatisations from telecommunications to railways, actions that would have seemed unthinkable a decade before. From being a fashionable and widely adopted organisational form, of which public service broadcasters were merely one instance, the public corporation itself became an endangered species.

Alongside this massive and general shift in the political and economic *zeitgeist* went a logically distinct (and also, I shall suggest, logically flawed) argument about broadcasting. Sometimes dubbed the argument for 'electronic publishing'[2], the proposition went like this: public service and regulation in broadcasting were a direct result of spectrum scarcity, something which had been absent in print publication; with advances in broadcast technology (cable and satellite) there would be a plethora of spectrum available, so broadcasting could become like print publishing – i.e. purely commercial, subject to the market, with minimum regulation and without the need for public service organisations. We return to what is wrong in this argument later, but here it should be noted that a) it is historically inaccurate about broadcasting, b) when first advanced it ran way beyond the currently available technology (as indeed recognised by the Peacock Report, when it envisaged three stages of technological development and take-up, and only the third of which would lead to a 'full broadcasting market' (Peacock 1986: 136) and c) it shows touching faith in the reality of print publishing, which has never actually been an Eden of free competition. So the decisive shift in the 'common sense' arguments about PSB to embrace the economic rationale and market orientation that took place in the 1980s owed far less to the inexorable logic of developments specifically in broadcasting technology, and far more to the general shift in a political 'common sense' that legitimated a free-market orientation across the board.

In response, proponents of PSB as an institution and the public service broadcasters themselves have, not surprisingly, taken up their own economic cudgels in its defence. In the context it was quite natural that the BBC commissioned a number of professional economists to produce studies on the new broadcasting environment during the 1990s. The most important of these was the third published study, entitled *Broadcasting Society and Policy in the Multimedia Age*. This was published in 1997, and authored by Andrew Graham and Gavyn Davis. The significance of this slim volume is suggested by the fact that Davis, then Chief International Economist at Goldman Sachs, was soon after appointed Chairman of the BBC Board of Governors. The arguments advanced in their study would become common currency far beyond the UK and the BBC.

The case that Graham and Davies present is based on more traditional (largely normative) arguments for PSB, like raising cultural quality or provision of information for citizenship, but handled in terms more familiar to economists, including especially discussion about 'positive and negative externalities' and 'merit goods'. The thrust of their argument is that a) there are a number of fundamental cases of market failure in broadcasting, b) these would be increased rather than diminished by digitalisation and the end of spectrum scarcity, and c) public service broadcasters are necessary in order to counter these market failures.

They identify one form of market failure as a function of broadcast economies of scale (due to high first copy costs and low or zero marginal costs of reproduction), leading to concentration in the broadcasting market. A similar drive to concentration, they argue, arises from the economies of scope that derive from the repurposing of the same content across several media (Graham & Davies 1997: 11-13). Then there is the drive towards concentration in delivery systems, epitomised by BSkyB (ibid: 13-15). Market failure, they continue, extends from production into the consumption field because radio and television programmes are experience goods, and the assumption that consumers know in advance their own preferences for these goods is "seriously flawed" (ibid: 20). Broadcasting exists in large part to inform and educate and the process of learning and understanding is an important part of how preferences are formed. These preferences cannot, therefore, be taken as "given in advance" (ibid: 20). Further market failures in broadcasting occur when broadcasting production and consumption interact with "adverse feedback effects"; thus, "putting it bluntly, we will be 'dumbed down' as the Americans say" (ibid: 23).

Why the economic argument is inadequate

Overall, there is nothing in this analysis with which I want to quarrel. There is a chapter in this volume (by Berg, Lowe & Lund) that follows much the same logic. Far from quarrelling with it; around the same time as Graham and Davis were writing I also published an article delving at length into one of their themes – the theoretical implications of the digital revolution for media concentration. In keeping with Graham and Davies' position, I attempted to demonstrate that the digital revolution would reinforce rather than ameliorate the drive towards media concentration (Goodwin 1998a). That too is discussed in the chapter I've alluded to. Like many others who have taught classes on the political economy of communication, I have rehearsed these arguments for cohort after cohort of students.

In my view the arguments about market failure in broadcasting that Graham and Davis deploy, especially alongside their other arguments about broadcasting in relation to citizenship and democracy, provide a useful bridge between the perspectives of orthodox economists and the more radical positions characteristic of the political economy tradition of communication research. They are a valuable corrective to the shrill neo-liberal sniping about public service broadcasting that emerged in the eighties and continue in one form or another to this day. We find that characteristic, for example in James Murdoch's now rather embarrassing but then largely unchallenged assertions in the prestigious annual MacTaggart Lecture to the Edinburgh International Television Festival in 2009, where he argued that the BBC exerted a 'chilling' effect on the commercial media (*Guardian* 28 August 2009). It is an altogether positive thing that economic argumentation is now commonly deployed in defence of public service media.

That said, however, I suggest that such arguments, however valuable and important, are inadequate to the purpose of defending public service broadcasting. Why? In my view this approach is inadequate for three reasons:

1. They have clear and logical implications that would imply public service provision is necessary in fields far beyond broadcasting – a conclusion which most who advance such arguments are unwilling to draw. Indeed most would probably be actively hostile to attempts to draw such implications.

2. Economic arguments for PSB or public service media (PSM) do not in practice engage effectively with the 'economic' arguments that are commonly mounted *against* it. They are about aspects that the other side is not debating.

3. Such arguments are still mainly about broadcasting and do not adequately deal with those major changes in media and media markets commonly labelled 'web 2.0', and their implications for PSM.

Let us briefly examine each of these points in turn.

Everything that Graham and Davies (1997) say about the economic characteristics of broadcasting could be equally said about the economic characteristics of any other media form, including pre-digital and pre-broadcasting forms. Graham and Davies rightly assert that, "broadcasting can have adverse 'external effects' (e.g. amplifying violence in society)". True enough, but the same can be said about films, books, newspapers, magazines and music (and in fact has been claimed on many and various occasions – e.g., 'gangster rap' and first-person shooter video games). They also rightly assert that, "good broadcasting is a 'merit good'. Just as with education or training or checking on their health, if left to themselves to decide, consumers tend to buy less than is in their own best long term interests (ibid: 9). The same can certainly be said about 'good' books, films, newspapers, magazines and music.

The same applies to examples of market failure in broadcasting production and consumption. To take just two examples: 1) "The making and broadcasting of radio and more especially television programmes has exceptionally high fixed costs. At the same time they have very low, in many cases zero, marginal costs. Almost by definition, to 'broadcast' is to say that it costs no more to reach extra people" (ibid: 11). True, but digital films, books, newspapers, magazines and recorded music all have exactly the same characteristic. Of course in the past they had low rather than zero marginal costs – e.g. in the cost of newsprint and newsagents margins – but this will not be the case as media move away from producing physical artefacts. And with these zero marginal costs goes exactly the same tendencies towards concentration that Graham and Davies talk about as being specific to broadcasting.

The same applies to example two, the thesis about market failures in television consumption. If television programmes are 'experience goods' then so too are films, books, newspapers, magazines and music. There, as well, the consumer may not know what the good is worth, or even especially like it until it has already been experienced. Hence the reason for previews, reviews and recommendation engines having such an important role in marketing.

In summary, then, exactly the same economic logic that Graham and Davies apply to argue the case for public service broadcasting can equally be applied to argue for public service media in all forms. And I don't simply mean the extension of public service broadcasters onto other digital platforms (itself a politically fraught process), but rather public service films, public service books, public service newspapers, public service magazines and public service music – in both pre- and post-digital varieties. As I shall explain, I accept that logic but I doubt whether most PSB defenders who deploy economic argumentation would agree. Indeed, conventional policy wisdom in Western Europe, even before its neo-liberal refashioning, would have treated such concepts as anathema – flying in the face of conventional notions of the free-market foundations for freedom of the press and publishing.

This is one and a cardinal reason why the impeccable logic of the economic case for public service broadcasting, as outlined above, fails to deliver the killer punch it deserves. Graham and Davies specifically address the possible weak link when observing that while their arguments provide a strong "prima facie case for intervention" in broadcast markets, they deliver "no guidance on the form that intervention should take. Why, one has to ask, could market failures not be dealt with by regulation, as in the case of health and safety legislation?" (1997: 37). Their answer is that such regulation would have to be qualitative (and thus less susceptible to formulation in precise rules), and would often

have to be positive (which presents greater problems than negative requirements), and that the public service broadcaster is needed to serve as a "centre
of excellence" on various matters, training for instance (ibid: 38-39).

This proposal is altogether less rigorous than the preceding analysis of the
broadcasting market. What other sectors of the economy, free-marketers might
argue, demand an exemplary public 'centre of excellence'? More importantly,
the general drift of public policy in Europe and elsewhere for the past thirty
years has been towards market provision with less regulation and declining
intervention, even in the previous heartlands of public provision like health-
care and education – sectors, interestingly enough, which are often chosen to
illustrate merit or experience goods and positive externalities. A free-marketer
might well query why broadcasting should be any different?

The third weakness of the economic defence that Graham and Davies articulated is, not surprisingly, that things have moved on a decade and a half
after publication. Many subsequent industry developments fit their argument
very well, above all that in the world of broadcasting, digitalisation and the
multiplication of channels have marched side by side with growth in media
concentration, rather than providing a flourishing market in small-scale "electronic publishing". The new players in the wider media field, unanticipated
in 1997, have rapidly developed into semi-monopolistic giants (oligopolies at
least), each dominant on their respective platforms – most obviously Google
and Facebook, and the resurgent Apple.

Writing in the second half of the 1990s, Graham and Davies were rightly
cautious about how the Internet might develop (ibid: 15-16). A decade and a
half on newspaper websites and apps look increasingly like television news
websites and apps. Media convergence has become a reality. In 1997 domestic internet users did not have the capacity to compete with broadcasters by
transmitting video and animation online. Today alongside the internet's commercial giants, we have the mass of do-it-yourself, vernacular online creativity,
file sharing and interaction. These web 2.0 developments (and beyond) are
things that conventional public service broadcasters have to respond to in a
big way, whether by incorporating citizen journalism or producing catch up TV
services, and a lot more besides. Hence, in a narrow sense the transition from
public service broadcasting to public service media is a move that established
PSB organisations are forced to make, and with considerable financial, political
and creative difficulties. They must either expand online or risk irrelevancy.
Hence also the emergence of new forms of public service media in a broader
sense – Wikipedia would be a notable example.

In this situation the need to mount economic arguments for public service
media becomes even more pressing. And yet if these arguments are to give
intellectual muscle to anything more than a rear guard action, they need to
change in at least two ways. First, to be rigorous they need to stop substituting

'broadcasting' for media. If the market economics of media lead inexorably to concentration, 'dumbing down' and so on – and in my view they certainly do – then that needs to be clearly spelt out rather than pretending this merely applies to broadcasting and therefore by implication that the market works just fine as it is for films, newspapers, books, magazines and music.

Secondly, to make these arguments rigorously we have to recognise that they have serious ideological implications. They are part of a far more general critique of free-market neo-liberalism, and a far more general movement for the defence and advance of public service – in media, yes, but not only there. The problems of the free-market are not simply a technical question for the media. Media have special characteristics, it is true, but also much in common with, for example, health and education, where merit goods, externalities, concentration and so on are also commonplace, and where the bloated claims made for free-market provision are equally spurious.

Practical issues for an effective defence

This approach raises a number of practical issues for the forthcoming political struggles over public service media. To begin with, it's clear that such an approach is not going to come naturally to most of those who head existing PSM organisations. Indeed, it is likely to be highly unwelcome because it 'politicises' the issue and damages their carefully cultivated relationships with government and market partners. That suggests the political battles over PSM are likely to be fought far more successfully by what we might term 'the friends of PSM' rather than the PSM organisations themselves. But to wage this fight will mean that the friends must adopt a more critical tone in addressing existing PSB organisations. We doubt that will be welcome either.

In point of fact, there is a lot for even consistent advocates of public service media to criticise in those institutions, including bloated executive salaries, conservative programming policies, corporate arrogance, and lack of inclusiveness – to name but four in a list that is not that short. These friends will also find themselves supporting other PSM initiatives, i.e. non-institutional initiatives, for the good reason that there are a growing number of exciting alternatives. Both of these positions stem naturally from the approach I have outlined. But they contain a danger that we need to be equally clear about. The history of recent debates about broadcasting is full of critical notes about the sector and support for other initiatives that are already used by free-marketeers and opponents of PSM to attack the established PSB organisations.

Independent production and top-slicing the licence fee are two evident examples. A significant part of the original support for independent production in the UK came from left-wing critics of the conservatism of the big vertically integrated broadcasters, the largest of which was of course the BBC. But one of the consequences of the government-enforced growth of independent production that followed has been the hollowing out of the production capacity of the BBC, with the resulting outsourced production mainly benefitting increasingly large commercial 'independents' rather than the small outfits as envisioned, and these large producers aren't more radical than the in-house production they have replaced.

Top-slicing the licence fee and giving that slice over to finance public service provision by media organisations other than the BBC can seem similarly attractive to some friends of public service who are critical of the 'monolithic' BBC and eager to support new initiatives and alternatives. But the consequences of top-slicing are likely to be less public finance available for established PSB organisations as a fixed, even shrinking, supply of funds is divided. Instead supporters of PSM, like supporters of other public services, need to be making the unfashionable argument both for more public money for public service media and for new initiatives in it, rather than robbing the already cash-strapped official PSB organisations in the name of innovation.

Thus, in taking a more rigorous and more radical approach the friends of PSM must remember, at the same time, to be absolutely supportive of the existing PSB organisations. We must not let our (often absolutely justified) criticism of the established providers, or our support for new PSM initiatives, to be turned against the continued existence and continued funding of either these established organisations or the more general need for public service development in media for societies.

Mounting an effective defence of public service media will require both vociferous and radical politics, along with considerable tactical sophistication.

Notes

1. This phrase encapsulated the expectation that broadcasters in the United States have responsibilities for public service in consequence of receiving a licence to broadcast. The principle hinged on spectrum scarcity in the sense that only a comparative few would have that privilege and therefore obligations to society beyond purely commercial reasons are fair and reasonable to expect. The principle was dropped in the deregulatory climate of the 1980s.
2. For an explanation of the context of this use of the term, see Congdon et al 1992 :XV.

References

Collins, R., Garnham, N. & Locksley G. (1988) *The Economics of Television: The UK Case*. London: SAGE.

Congdon, T., Davies, G., Graham, A. & Shew, W.B. (1992) *Paying for Broadcasting: The Handbook*. London: Routledge.

Goodwin, P. (1998a) Concentration: Does the digital revolution change the basic rules of media economics. In Picard, R. (ed.) *Evolving Media Markets: Effects of Economic and Policy Changes*.

Turku, Finland: Business Research and Development Centre, Turku School of Economics and Business Administration, pp.173-189.

Goodwin, P. (1998b) *Television under the Tories: Broadcasting Policy 1979-1997*. London: BFI.

Graham, A. & Davies, G. (1997) *Broadcasting, Society and Policy in the Multimedia Age*. Luton, UK: John Libbey Media.

Judt, T. (2005) *Postwar: A History of Europe Since 1945*. London: Heinemann.

Peacock, A. [Chair] (1986) *Report of the Committee on the Financing of the BBC*. London: HMSO Cmnd 9824

Chapter 5

The Concept of Public Value
& Triumph of Materialist Modernity
'...this strange disease of modern life...'

Michael Tracey

In a 1962 House of Lords debate about the introduction of commercial television into Britain, the by then Lord Reith offered this thought about its value:
"As I said ten years ago, somebody introduced Christianity into this country;
somebody introduced the printing press; others the incalculable beneficence of
medical and scientific discovery and application. Somebody brought smallpox,
the bubonic plague, the Black Death, greyhound racing and football pools.
And commercial television was introduced by means conspiratorial and dis-
reputable..." (quoted in Hansard 1962)

An immediate and somewhat clichéd response to this comment might be
that it is simply Reith being the reactionary contrarian. Certainly the BBC's first
Director General was not enamoured with what he saw in much of popular
culture, but then neither were numerous cultural and critical theorists who have
since bemoaned what they see as a 'tawdry' commercialised media culture. I
would suggest, however, that Reith's earlier writings and musings about the
nature and purpose of public service broadcasting [PSB] actually anticipated
that body of contemporary thought, albeit in his own eccentric way. In effect,
Reith's views and concerns, were very much reflective of a Victorian Age that
spilled over into the 20th century with a characteristic deep concern about the
depredations of industrial modernity and the debasing of culture.

In this sense Reith is at one with such figures as Arnold, Eliot and Leavis.
The relevance of his perspective on the issues addressed in this collection,
which in part questions the idea of performance measures of value, can be
seen in a comment Reith made in 1924 in his seminal book, *Broadcast Over
Britain* (p. 205):

> In almost all other lines of business it is possible to tell pretty accurately
> whether one's efforts are meeting with success or not. There is usually some
> unit of measurement available. It may be tonnage output per week, or com-
> parative weekly costs, or a dozen other equally satisfactory tests, around

which one can build one's comments, complimentary or otherwise, at the weekly staff conference. I should be grateful to anyone who would suggest a really reliable criterion for this business. I cannot find one...

This sentiment is echoed in a comment by a very different thinker on the face of it. Theodore Adorno, in response to a failed effort to work with Paul Lazarsfeld on a quantitative study of American popular culture (note, not high culture, however that might be defined), said: "When I was confronted with the demands to 'measure culture,' I reflected that culture might be precisely that condition that excludes a mentality capable of measuring it" (in: Bailyn & Fleming 1969: 343). If one thing can be said with a level of certainty about the efforts to provide metrics of PSB performance, it is that very little can be said with certainty. It remains a remarkably opaque idea (Collins 2006; Jowell 2006).

No one doubts that aspects of "performance" and "culture" can be measured – viewers viewing, listeners listening, cultural products bought. What Adorno, Reith and others of like mind were arguing was that what lies beyond algorithmic measurement, beyond a metric, is the *experience* of culture. An example. In 2003, a UK poll conducted by the Poetry Book Society, found that Philip Larkin was Britain's best loved poet of the past 50 years and in 2008 The Times declared him Britain's greatest postwar writer. One could readily count the numbers of copies sold of such collections as "The Less Deceived," "The Whitsun Weddings," and "High Windows." It remains difficult, however, to see how one could "measure" the power that they hold over the imagination and the emotion that their reading brings forth. No metric explains the emotive force of what is perhaps his most celebrated poem, "An Arundel Tomb," and its deeply moving final line, "What will survive of us is love." That there is no such measurement, one might claim, is what makes us human.

Pursuing performance measures

There is a fairly widespread sense, and in my view accurate, that PSB is today under siege from a variety of significant forces – ideological, political and technological. The varied forces perceive a need to reinvigorate global capitalism at the expense, if necessary, of more cultural, even democratic, perspectives. It seems that most national and transnational governmental and neo-governmental organisations and corporations overwhelmingly prefer to view public policy through the lens of the economy rather than democratic and cultural practice. That is a very different situation than the context that characterised PSB at its creation. Out of sheer necessity, if not necessarily desire, PSB has to find *some* way of legitimating its existence and establishing contemporary relevance; proponents must make the case that it is worthy of continued public policy support. Commitment to the notion of 'public value' [PV], of demonstrating some metric of worth, was conceived in this context of a perceived existential threat. Of course the issues don't only apply to public broadcasting (or media), as evident in the scholarly foundation of the public value theory and practice notion (see Benington & Moore 2011).

This concept raises a rather awkward question: how does one measure that which in considerable part is not inherently measurable? That is a key question for treatment in this chapter. The pursuit of 'performance measures' for public broadcasting has to be placed within the context of larger national and global shifts in economic practice, and attendant cultural practices. As public service broadcasters grapple with the digital revolution, the general mood favours the dominance of market economics with a co-related sense of the need for accountability whenever and wherever public funds are spent. This general mood is less and less tolerant of traditional modes of thought, which are seen as lofty, elitist, and skewered for being 'out of touch' with populist appetites (see especially Hartley 2002).

The challenge to PSB has already produced an extensive literature that can be read as the searching for a grail that can balance measurements of 'performance' with the maintenance of primarily non-economic values, which have historically informed the practice of PSB (Collins 2006; Coppens & Saeys 2006; Hastings 2004; Born 2003, etc). Much of this work characteristically grapples with the intractability and real conceptual difficulty of being anything other than instrumental. Certainly, for example, one can to an extent 'count' the forms of culture by tallying up how many hours of this or that genre was broadcast, or how much domestic production was purchased from independents. But it is vastly more difficult to measure the intrinsic *qualities* of culture – the worth and actual substance of that.

Some of the most intense and extensive debates by broadcasters, policy makers and scholars over the evolving nature and about the future of PSB and public service media have taken place in Europe. Debate is evident both at the national level of EU members states and in the context of European Commission politics. Historically, Europe has had the world's greatest concentration of national public broadcasters, and the most robust dual system in broadcast media (after 1985). Since 1989 countries in central and eastern Europe have also sought to transform their former state broadcasting institutions into PSB organisations – generally with less success than simultaneous efforts to introduce commercial broadcasting. But on the whole, it still seems fair to say that in Europe there is a well established and comparatively rigorous commitment to the notion that broadcasting should serve the public interest, nurture the public sphere, enable democratic society and feed the culture with merit goods.

I would characterise this as the tradition, but it has lately been under siege and, in my view, mainly as a consequence of the creation of the European

Union and the adoption by member states of neo-liberal economics. These policies favour competition and support development of new digital technologies as a matter both of industry and innovation policy. The EU agenda is not, however, keenly focused on cultural policy. This is in considerable part due to the European Commission's privileging of the dominion of the economic over the cultural and democratic, a proclivity rooted in its origins (the basis on which unionisation has been built – such as it is). This accounts in part, as well, for EC responsiveness to complaints from commercial broadcasters regarding the 'incursion' of PSB in market terrain they deem to be their own – claims of 'market distortion' (Michalis 2009; Donders & Pauwels 2008; Humphreys 2007; Harrison and Wessels 2005).

Karen Donders and Carolyn Pauwels (2010: 1) point out that the European Commission is increasingly involved in encouraging national broadcasters "to introduce an ex-ante test for the evaluation of the public value and market impact of new media services of public broadcasters." They ask whether such tests can "add to the rethinking of broadcasting policies in a public service media oriented way?" The answer so far, at least, seems to be – no, they haven't. Numerous studies have looked at developments in European broadcasting and the implicit, increasingly explicit, clash between public service values, the imperatives of the market, and competition as defined by the European Commission (Tracey 2013; Gil 2010; Iosifidis 2010; Potschka 2010; Jakubowicz 2007; Steemers 2001). The recent book co-edited by Donders and Hallvard Moe (2011) on "exporting the public value test" make the situation abundantly clear, and empirically verified.

There is, then, a clear sense in the research literature that in developing and employing metrics to evaluate PV, public service broadcasters are responding, whether they wish to or not, to the objective reality of an evolving ecology of communication and media, in particular by making the case that their traditional values can and should be part of the fabric of new digital platforms. Perhaps surprising to some, this is not a new problem.

In his lengthy and excellent overview of the BBC's adoption of the concept of Public Value, Richard Collins (2006) noted:

> The BBC is currently caught in a vice. Its claim on the licence fee depends on fulfilling two contradictory obligations. First, it must retain a sufficiently large share of viewers' and listeners' consumption of broadcasting for them to feel that the requirement to pay the licence fee is not unacceptably onerous... Second, the BBC must continue to provide merit goods which, by definition, viewers and listeners are not aware that they want or need...Moreover, because there is no point in providing merit goods unless they are used, the BBC must find ways of squaring the circle and making the good popular and the popular good (ibid: 52).

An earlier version of this dilemma was sketched by Arthur fforde, the vastly underrated Chairman of the BBC from 1957 to 1964. In a letter to Reith, dated 24 November 1958, he wrote:

> My chief feeling is one of inadequacy…as to do what is possible to prevent a further slide in the direction of commercialisation. The dilemma is that (a) if we turn our backs on all blandishments in the way of 'entertainment' or 'background music', and lose the large audiences in those fields, it will be said that we are not giving the public, en masse, what they pay their licence fee to get; (b) if we don't, it will said that there is no distinction between the BBC and the 'Independents', so why have a BBC? (quoted in Stuart 1975: 490).

One of the most laudable, and lengthy, attempts to provide a kind of performance metric was undertaken by Shaun Hargreaves-Heap (2005: 112-157), a British economist who quite literally sought to develop algorithms to measure performance. In a lengthy account he develops a number of "performance indicators" which, taken together, might provide a set of definable characteristics to suggest the "role" of PSB in "a digital age". The proposed indicators are information provision; standards of decency; horizon stretching; innovation; intense preferences; and home country subject matter. However admirable the effort, it is not clear how these are particularly new.

Certainly one could measure, for example the number of hours broadcasting news and current affairs programmes or the level of audience trust in the supplier (see Ofcom 2012 for what is being done in this aspect). But the situation is far more problematic when considering the 'standards of decency' aspect. Debates about decency are as old as broadcasting, highly variable in and between societies across space and time, and always contentious due to the very basic and inherent problem that what some people find indecent and offensive others find artistic and laudable. This was evident, for example, in the intractable struggle between Hugh Greene, the BBC's Director General from 1960 to 1969, and moral campaigner Mary Whitehouse (Tracey & Morrison 1979). Conflict over standards is inevitable because questions of taste are in play and these are inherently a function of personal and cultural preferences in particular and changing contexts. There is not, and never will be, an objective metric for decency / indecency – and certainly not one that can be expected to persist.

Programmes that are "horizon stretching", as Hargreaves-Heap seems to suggest, are not restricted to a particular audience demographic but have broad appeal across age, gender and socioeconomic categories. This would presumably characterise programmes such as, say, *Frozen Planet* or *Downton Abbey*. Other programmes break down along ethnic or class lines. Again there is nothing especially new here. 'Innovation' is certainly vital and can be recognised, but can it be quantified? In this case possibly by, for example, pointing to new platforms on which to communicate. Most public service broadcasters have long provided programming about the home country, and elsewhere but in native languages (often via dubbing or subtitles). Again that could be measured in terms of programming hours or budget expenditure, but what would such measurement really mean? That is largely a matter of presumptions. It is much less clear how one would pin down the relationship between such programming and an audiences' sense of, say, national belonging. Hargreaves Heap is no fool, and having introduced his performance measures he immediately writes, "Each of these indicators is imperfect" (ibid: 135). Indeed.

The changing nature of PSB: the case of the United Kingdom

In articulating its mission to include new digital platforms and by incorporating the idea of PV, it seems widely understood that the BBC very much took the lead in responding to the new media world order (so to say). The wider industry context within which this has happened provides a useful case study for situating the shape-shifting of public service broadcasting on an historical continuum. As 20th century Britain approached the new millennium the deepening role of market forces in the social, economic, cultural and political fabric of the nation, begun under Margaret Thatcher's Conservative government and pursued by Tony Blair's Labour government, gathered ever greater force. It was clear that Conservative governments under Thatcher and then John Major were eager to change the landscape of British broadcasting, and that the bell was tolling for those public service values that Reith had birthed.

One of the most significant measures (significant because they made clear that both Conservative and Labour Parties now thought of communication, including broadcasting, as basically an economic rather than a cultural practice) was keyed to the development of new satellite- and cable-enabled programme services – the Cable and Broadcasting Act 1984. Six years later the Broadcasting Act 1990 implemented parallel proposals in a Conservative government White Paper titled "Broadcasting in the 1990s: Competition, Choice and Quality." Here one strikes the Orwellian trifecta: Britain could have it all – market values and cultural values communicated with range and élan.

This was a questionable proposition, to say the least, but it became law a few days before Margaret Thatcher's forced resignation as Prime Minister. The Broadcasting Act abolished the Independent Broadcasting Authority, which had regulated commercial television since 1973, replacing it with the Independent Television Commission [ITC] whose mandate for regulating the regional commercial television network, ITV, was with a "lighter touch", meaning less regulation. That furnished the basis for the gradual shift of ITV away from any commitment to public service values. The Act also allowed for growth in multi-channel satellite broadcasting, deepening the competitive environment for broadcasting. Crucially it further allowed companies within ITV to take over other ITV companies after 1994, a process that would end with today's concentrated ITV public limited company (plc.), which now owns 11 of the 15 regional franchises.

The 1990 Act was described by Ray Fitzwalter (2008), a former senior ITV executive and author of *The Dream That Died: the Rise and Fall of ITV*, as one of the most shameful pieces of legislation of the last 50 years. Historically, ITV franchises had been awarded on the basis of the quality of the proposals for the kinds of programmes that the franchisee would offer in their region, say the northwest or the southwest. Once awarded the franchisee was granted a monopoly on advertising in their region – surely echoes of Reith's "brute force of monopoly" (Stuart 1975: 470-471) – and, in return, were expected to deliver on their promise to supply quality programming across genres. If they did not deliver, they should expect the real possibility of their franchise being removed.

Under the 1990 Act franchises were to be awarded on the basis of blind, one-time bids that would inevitably, as Fitzwalter pointed out, take large amounts of money from programme budgets. The Act also separated ITV from Channel Four (which had previously been funded from ITV advertising revenue), setting up greater competition for ratings and revenue. As Fitzwalter suggested, the Act fatally weakened the regulator, opening the floodgates to lower standards, and allowed for takeovers in ITV that would reduce competition, promote monopoly and destroy the regional network as two companies. That has happened: Carlton and Granada bought up smaller regional companies within the ITV network. It was difficult to see how public service values would survive in such a world. It was clear that these changes would put pressure on the BBC to compete for audiences as it contemplated its own mortality. In other words, the essential narrative of the place of broadcasting in society was being rewritten.

The 2003 Communications Act, produced by the Blair Government, followed on and played to suit. That Act set up a new body, the Office of Communications (Ofcom), with regulatory authority over large areas of communications in the UK, including broadcasting. The Act also further liberalised UK media ownership rules, allowing for the formation of a single ITV company.

These developments have culminated in an environment for British broadcasting that has become, as intended, more competitive and in which a would-be public service broadcaster, the BBC, has been compelled to compete aggressively with an ITV sector that became, for all intents and purposes, rampantly populist despite its ostensible PSB obligations. There was something else going on, however, and that is the rise to prominence of a generation of politicians and broadcasters who were palpably less committed to the ideas and values of public broadcasting. Theirs was a market-based and -driven world, a world view that prioritises growth in margins, slashing budgets, fiscal efficiency, organisational rationalisation, and the importing of market values and principles into public sector institutions – in this case, particularly, the BBC (Born 2003 & 2005).

The most potent symbol of this shift was the rise to power of John Birt, who became the BBC's Director General in 1993. What is perhaps not understood about Birt is that he was by inclination a mathematician and by training an engineer. He once said: "I enjoy the puzzle, the solving of puzzles in a methodical way… there's always some interesting problem at the centre of which you have to find a way of resolving, and I enjoyed applying concepts to solving problems" (Tracey 1983: 25). Given this disposition it is not difficult to imagine how he saw a BBC in great danger as one more puzzle to solve with the help of management mechanics and organisational theory, and henceforth the rise to prominence of numerous management consultants during his tenure in the 'hallowed' corridors of Broadcasting House. One way of thinking about Birt is to understand that he was a vector for larger forces at play in the Blairite world of building 'UKplc', – conceptualising the United kingdom as a kind of gigantic corporation.

Of course there were efforts to pushback and by the time he retired John Birt was widely loathed – even if there is a case to be made that through his efforts he saved the BBC as an institution, if not as an institution still overly committed to the idea that broadcasting should be imbued with values that have little or nothing to do with econometrics or measurement. Two of the most brutal but insightful critiques of what was happening inside (and to) the BBC are provided by a journalist, in the first instance, and by a playwright in the second, both brilliant. The journalist is Kate Adie, the former Chief News Correspondent for the BBC. In her 2002 autobiography, *The Kindness of Strangers*, she wrote:

> … in the last ten years of the Twentieth century the Corporation not only saw an alteration to its outer skin, reflecting a fast-moving society, but also changed inwardly, losing many of the old certainties based on experience, and replacing them with a theory of management that owed much to business practice and an increasing sense of insecurity. The audience ceased to be respected and came to be seen as a consumer whose desires were to be catered for, and audience figures achieved a daily influence on production decisions (Adie 2002: 5).

As damning as that was, the most famous – because brutal – assault on Birt's BBC was from the playwright Dennis Potter in his 1993 MacTaggart Memorial Lecture at the Edinburgh Television Festival. John Birt, whom he was about to lacerate and humiliate, was sitting in the front row. He titled his lecture *Occupying Powers* and famously described Birt, and the BBC's then Chairman, Marmaduke Hussey, as "a pair of croak-voiced Daleks." He continued:

Our television has been ripped apart and falteringly re-assembled by politicians who believe that value is a monetary term only, and that a cost-accountant is thereby the most suitable adjudicator of what can and cannot be seen on our screens…The public pressures from market-obsessed radicals, and the huckster atmosphere that follows, has by degrees, and in confused self-defence, drawn the BBC so heavily into the dogma-coated discourses of so-called 'market efficiency' that in the end it might lose clear sight of why it, the BBC, is there in the first place. I fear the time is near when we must not save the BBC from itself, but public service broadcasting from the BBC…

Potter was railing against what he saw as a growing managerialism and a consequent cultural and creative impoverishment of PSB within the BBC. His reference to "croak-voiced Daleks" – soulless creatures, devoid of humanity in the fabled sci-fi programme *Dr. Who* – was meant not only to sting, which it surely did, but to describe and define an emergent condition. What one sees first in the Birtist BBC is the breaking through of forces that had been held at bay for seven decades, but no longer – a constituency that had long favoured establishing culture as commodity with a price, materialist values, the pursuit of metrics of performance, and defining audience as consumers rather than citizens. The process has continued apace and unabated with his successors.

In a speech to the Oxford Media Convention in January 2003, Mark Thompson, who would become the BBC's Director General in May 2004, asked whether the old song that had traditionally lauded the virtues of public service broadcasting would be able to "work its magic again?" In answering his own question, he said:

> …to me, the (Communications) Bill (has) crystallised something which has been apparent for some time now: which is that regulators and policy-makers are increasingly finding themselves having to weigh the benefits and disbenefits (sic) of public service provision quite forensically, almost numerically, against the interests – and pressures – of the private sector.

He seems to have been suggesting that an institution imbued with values that are hard if not impossible to pin down in language – let alone in an algorithm – is nevertheless faced with the need to articulate itself numerically. Would it be a stretch to suggest that the logic unfolding suggests that if there is something that cannot be represented numerically – a value, a principle, a moral commitment, a creative idea – then at the very least a question mark will be placed against its continued viability?

What is immediately brought to mind, of which more in a moment, was the central concern of the great 19th and early 20th century social theorists – one thinks of Weber, Simmel, Tonnies, and of course Marx. An essential concern for all of them hinges on the intrusiveness of the calculative nature of capital in human affairs. But the answer to the earlier question is yes, that is indeed the logic that unfolds. Thompson continued:

> The problem with the traditional public service song is that, no matter how much passion and conviction you bring to the performance, it's just too woolly and abstract to be measured against anything else. And if it can't be weighed properly, in the end it won't be valued properly. The dominant language of the new regulators is going to be the language of economics, competition and public policy rather than the historic language of public service broadcasting, which is the language of culture, and high culture at that. If we want to develop public service broadcasting as a cultural force in this environment we have to find arguments and evidence which make sense in this new language.

There were other clues as to what was afoot. Large moments, deep shifts in the culture and the human response to those shifts, can be revealed in moments of clarity that are nearly blinding. In 2007 one of these occurred when the BBC's Deputy Director General, Mark Byford, appeared before a Parliamentary Committee to explain a series of scandals that had seriously damaged the BBC's integrity and created a sense in both public and political minds that something was seriously amiss inside the Corporation. Byford acknowledged, as he put it, that "the brand" had been harmed. The most famous and successful broadcasting institution in history was reduced to nothing more or less than a *brand*, as if one were discussing a tennis shoe or a tin of beans, as if the scandals were akin to a salmonella outbreak in a fast food chain.

What Messrs. Birt, Thompson, Byford and their ilk have chosen to avert their gaze from seeing is the fact that from Reith onwards what public service broadcasting has sought to address were fundamental questions of the Ages: how to provide for the intellectual, cultural, social, even moral needs as well as the desires of a society; how to define excellence in cultural production; what it is to be properly, fully, human in cultural terms; and in all of that – in the project of being human, so to say – in all of that to address how broadcasting can actually be of help in nurturing the collective condition as a mature, evolved, informed, cultivated and ethical society?

Underpinning the ideological shifts articulated by these managers and their acolytes was a keen awareness of what would become the Blairite importation from America of certain 'new' ideas regarding how the economy, if not the culture, might be reordered to meet the 'challenges' of the 21st century as a Third Way. As if the most fundamental challenges today are not enduring, not really all that different from what has been persistently problematic in the human experience, and which media have earlier been expected to help address.

The rise of public value

Thus it came to pass, with an eye cocked to its upcoming Charter renewal, that the BBC anchored itself to the concept of Public Value. In declaring the corporation's commitment to "Building Public Value" (BBC 2004), it intended nonetheless to develop measures to show that it served citizenship and civil society, promoted education and learning, stimulated creativity and cultural excellence and brought the world to the UK, and the UK to the world. In all of that the BBC was reiterating propositions that decades of public broadcasters would recognise and applaud. In similar vein, Collins (2006: 12) quotes the former Chairman of the BBC, Gavin Davies, as saying that "the core case for the BBC should rest not on money and markets but on culture and citizenship", and that "the concept of public value should lie at the heart of the BBC's Charter bid..." To this the only self-respecting question should be, so what exactly is *new* in this proposal, apart from the fact that historic commitments are couched in a curious but more "modern" sounding, terminology?

Collins also quotes Michael Grade, another former BBC Chairman, who applauded, "the idea of building public value, of generating social capital, of serving its audience not just as consumers but as members of a wider society, of contributing to the quality of life in the UK..." (ibid). That Collins was all too aware of the problems of conception and definition is revealed in this comment:

> Organising to create public value requires that public value is defined – or at least that those charged with making it have a sense of what they are aim-ing for and know when they see it. Public value seems the latest term used during the 80 year or more 'snark hunt' for a definition of what the BBC is supposed to be doing. Definition of each of the successive terms used, public service broadcasting, citizen value, public value, has proven fugitive and many...effectively threw their hands up in the air and stated that though they could not 'offer a tight new definition of PSB they were confident they knew it when we saw it (ibid: 31)

Even the Secretary of State, Tessa Jowell, who was then developing the policy for the future of PSB in Britain, concluded that the concept of public value remained unclear (DCMS 2006). She did, however, make a revealing comment: "The idea of Public Value – which I believe in very strongly – will only survive if we are rigorous in its definition and application. Mark Moore, the inventor of the public value concept, said that 'Public value is what the public value.' There is a profound truth behind that simple definition." Indeed there is, because as a comment it is a remarkable echo of a 1981 statement by Mark Fowler, U.S. President Reagan's first Chairman of the FCC, who, in repudiating the language of the 1934 Communications Act that stipulated the station licence holder should broadcast in "the public interest, convenience and necessity," advanced the policy that from thereon "the public interest is that in which the public is interested". That marks the beginning of the process of broadcast and media deregulation, which many commentators believed, correctly, would have such a disastrous consequence for the overall quality and performance of American television – amounting to a "vaster wasteland still", to quote Newton Minnow on the 40th anniversary of his "vast wasteland" speech.

It is here that the rooting of PSB in Reith's original thinking remains crucial. As with other critics, he was setting his face against those aspects of modernity that would inhibit the realisation of its humanistic and non-materialistic sides of life. That is not necessarily how Reith would have articulated it, but it is what he implies. In this sense, if we take the views of Reith and Adorno quoted at the beginning of this essay and place them against those of Birt, Thompson, Byford and associates, one sees a dramatic philosophical, even moral, gulf between a view of the media audience as citizens with the capacity, patience and desire to flourish, and a view which sees the world as consumers ambling through the vastness of an Asda or a Walmart, existentially drained of any larger human purpose and ambition, "I am not, therefore I shop 'til I drop."

Public service broadcasting was never just about educating, informing and entertaining; the PSB mission was about living – its ethos is about pursuing the cultivated life – however old-fashioned that might sound today. The assumption behind the argument for public service broadcasting is straightforward if, admittedly, opaque: that the society in which it is present will be the *better* for it. Immediately one hears the riposte, better how? To which one might reiterate, more informed, democratic, tasteful, educated, pursuing of excellence, enriched in multifarious ways. In short, more *mature*, the life well lived. It is interesting, in this context, that late in his life Reith's mantra – paradoxically alongside "I'm a total failure" – was "life is for living," a phrase given to him by his mistress, Dawn MacKay, when he asked her advice on what he should say in a talk to a boys' school. What this meant, it seems clear, was that the meaning of life is living well, recognising that life isn't always lived well but this doesn't mean that it couldn't be, or shouldn't be – and especially that it is a worthy ambition.

In this vein there is a fascinating letter dated 20th August 1963 to Reith from Oliver Whitley, a key figure in Greene's BBC in the 1960s, a kind and gentle man, very much in favour of the BBC evolving but also very much the keeper of its conscience:

> …What do I think of things nowadays? I think thoughts of dismay but not despair at the corrupt misguided society…Government appears nowadays to imagine that its job is done when it seeks material advance and adopts a neutral stance in morals and ethics. Like Goethe's Faust, it creates by its neutrality between Heaven and Hell, simply a new kind of Hell in the form of a society without meaning for the soul…These things one tries to disseminate

atmospherically rather than didactically at BBC management conferences and on other occasions in the BBC, contending against the Faustian thesis that the BBC's job is to simply inquire, inform, expose without adopting an unequivocal attitude on the side of what humanists and Christians must, if they think hard enough, both recognize as the right if in the long run life is to be worth living (in: Stuart 1975: 509).

There is something unusually potent in that phrase "if…life is to be worth living", and the conjoining of both humanists and Christians to that notion. It suggests that the underlying purpose of public service broadcasting was never only about an instrumental involvement in educating, entertaining and informing, but rather that these are a *means* to a greater end, that properly engaged they provide *for* that very pursuit of living well. They are a resource for its accomplishment. What never occurred to Oliver Whitley was that if one could not provide a performance measure – of whatever kind – for the life lived well, then the ambition, the desire, the pursuit would somehow be deemed to lack authority and legitimacy.

The problem was, and is, how to sustain such commitments in the face of a newly rampant, market driven economy, governed by neo-liberal and post-industrial economics and an attendant apparently necessary assault on the post-1945 collectivist settlement that favoured PSB and other vital public goods, such as public education and public health care. It is in this sense that one might argue that the attempted "metrification" for judging the value of PSB was, in effect, inevitable; that in broad historical terms PSB was an anomaly because its values were manifestly out of step with the mercantilist values of a broader order of modernity. One can get at this through the work of the social theorist Georg Simmel.

In his 1903 essay, *The Metropolis and Mental Life*, Simmel writes that at the heart of the "metropolis" – a simile for modernity – was the money economy that is premised on exchange value. He argued, somewhat presciently, that as capitalism matured – not in an emotional or moral sense, but as an economic formation – and as urban environments metastasised, everything, all modes of living and being, would be reduced to one question: "How much? …Man is reckoned with like a number, like an element which is in itself indifferent." The result is that the modern mind has become ever more calculating: "The calculative exactness of practical life which the money economy has brought about corresponds to the ideal of natural science: to transform the world into an arithmetic problem, to fix every part of the world by mathematical formulas" (Simmel 1950: 411-412). This, he suggests, is no more exemplified than by the precision offered in life from the growing use of pocket-watches: "Punctuality, calculability, exactness are forced upon life by the complexity and extension of metropolitan existence…" (ibid: 413).

If one accepts the notion that within capitalism much or all of life is reduced to a kind of fiscal calculus, then one can readily see the dilemma that public service broadcasting has faced since it originally and explicitly set itself *against* such calculation in the early part of the 20th century. It was about asking not the question of "how much?" but rather "how good?", with the corollary that one may not be able to measure this, but you can recognise it. If one also sees in recent decades a deepening populist crassness, captured for example in the cold, cruel schadenfreude of much of what is called "reality television," the shabby populism of much of the tabloid press and the emblematic obsession with tales of gruesome crime and celebrity, then its not that difficult to see that public service broadcasting has been battered, as was the culture writ large, by forces over which it has had too little or no control. And the most profound evidence of this lies within its own walls, in the kinds of internal policies, such as PV, viewpoints and functionaries that have come to prevail within PSB that rest easily with the mercantilist side of modernity.

We need, therefore, to go back to the basics, to argue that the BBC, and those modelled on it, had their roots firmly in the soil of the humanistic project of Enlightenment, and particularly, because of Reith's influence, the Scottish Enlightenment. This view was marinated in the *lese majeste* of an Arnoldian world view, all of which embodied, in various ways, a sense of culture which, as Lionel Trilling has written, "does not signify what the word commonly does, a vague belletristic gentility; it means many things but nothing less than reason experienced as a kind of grace by each citizen, the conscious effort of each man to come to the realization of his complete humanity" (Trilling 1949: 252). In this sense public service broadcasting is but the latest site of a long-standing feud, at the heart of which is a basic question: what should be the forces by which society and the individual are formed and the principles that shape them? The BBC, viewed in that light, can be seen as one of many historical critiques that sought to wrestle to the ground the materialism of modernity and to propagate non-material, more humanistic values.

It is here that the intellectual and philosophical influences on Reith become crucial in understanding how contemporary policies are such a radical inversion of what might be called Original Intent. In 1929 Reith was asked by the former Prime Minister, Stanley Baldwin – who had been elected Rector of St. Andrew's University in Scotland – if he had any ideas that he might use in his inaugural address. Reith recommended Tyndall's 1874 address to the British Association, urging Baldwin to study the ideas of Dr. Thomas Chalmers "in his view one of the greatest Scotsmen who ever lived..." as well as Proverbs and the Book of Job (McIntyre 1993: 177.) What McIntyre doesn't do – nor indeed has anyone else – is explain what it was about Tyndall's or Chalmer's work and thought that so appealed to Reith. His recommendation of Tyndall's address is on the face of it slightly odd. Tyndall was a secular humanist who loathed the reactionary role he believed religion had played in slowing up progress in society. Perhaps it merely suggests that Reith actually had a rather open mind.

Thomas Chalmers, is perhaps more relevant to the discussion here. He was a Church of Scotland minister and social reformer, born on 17 March 1780 in Anstruther, Fife. His birth occurred towards the end of what historians have termed the Scottish Enlightenment, the core concerns of which were moral theology, history, economics and the vital question of whether the acquisitive ethics of capitalism were, or could ever be, compatible with traditional virtues of sociability, sympathy and justice. Adherents believed it could not. His biographer, Stewart J. Brown, writes in an essay in the *Dictionary of National Biography*, that what Chalmers sought to confront were the material and, vitally, spiritual depravations, in particular a drifting away from religious practice, which he saw as having been wrought by industrial capitalism. It is not difficult to see how this aspect of his thinking and work would have appealed to Reith. Both, as Brown writes of Chalmers, "betrayed an Enlightenment optimism concerning human nature: a belief that ...human character could be improved." And both believed that there was a necessary co-relation between achieving these ends of moral elevation, of perfecting the human condition, and the creation of powerful "establishments" – in Chalmers case defined by the *Kirk* (church), in Reith's case by the BBC.

It was this philosophical rooting that would, over time, shift from the language of religion to that of secular humanism. This led Reith and those who came after to define a form of broadcasting that was **not** bound by the tendrils of capitalist economics. The values of public service broadcasting embodied that other version of modernity; not its materialism, its impulse to produce, sell and acquire "things," and moreover things that could be *measured*. Rather, the side of values that embodied a humanism which sought to elevate the human spirit, that saw in us, individually and collectively, possibility not as consumers, but as citizens; mature, ethically informed, thoughtful, creative, understanding with George Steiner that "the great and final things" cannot, and should not, belong under any law of mercantile exchange (Steiner 2003).

References

Adie, K. (2003) *The Kindness of Strangers: The Autobiography*. London: Headline.
Adorno, T. (1969) Scientific experiences of a European scholar in America. In Bailyn, B. & Fleming, D. (eds.) (1969) *Intellectual Migration*. Boston: Harvard University Press, p.343.
The BBC (2004) *Building Public Value: Renewing the BBC for a Digital Age*. London: BBC.
Benington, J. & Moore, M.H. (2011) *Public Value Theory & Practice*. NY: Palgrave Macmillan.
Born, G. (2003) From Reithian ethic to managerial discourse: Accountability and audit at the BBC. *The Public, 10*(2), pp.63-80.
Born, G. (2005) *Uncertain Vision: Birt, Dyke and the Reinvention of the BBC*. London: Verso
Collins, R. (2006) *The BBC and Public Value*. Working Paper No. 19. Centre for Research on Socio-Cultural Change, Milton Keynes: Open University Press, pp. 1-71.

Coppens, T. & Saeys, F. (2006) Enforcing performance: New approaches to govern public service broadcasting. *Media, Culture and Society, 28*(2), pp. 261-284.

Donders, K,. & Pauwels, C. (2008) Does EU policy challenge the digital future of public service broadcasting? An analysis of the Commission's state aid approach to digitization and the public service remit of public broadcasting organizations. *Convergence: The International Journal of research into New Media Technologies. 14*(3), pp. 295-311.

Donders, K. & Pauwels, C. (2010) The introduction of an ex ante evaluation for new media services: "Europe" asks it or public service broadcasting needs it? http://ripeat.org/archive.

Donders, K., & Moe, H. (2011) (eds.) *Exporting the Public Value Test: The Regulation of Public Broadcasters' New Media Services Across Europe.* Göteborg: Nordicom

Fitzwalter, R. (2008) *The Dream That Died: The Rise and Fall of ITV.* Leicester: Matador.

Hansard, HL Deb. (1962) 240 (cc 223-334). House of Lords debate, UK Parliament. London: HMSO.

Hargreaves-Heap, S. (2005) Television in a digital age: What role for public service broadcasting? *Economic Policy, 20*(41), pp. 112-157.

Harrison, J. & Wessels, B. (2005) A new public service environment? *New Media and Society, 7*(6), pp. 834-853.

Hastings, C. (2004) Discussion of performance measures in public service broadcasting. *Aslib Proceedings, 56*(5), pp. 301-307.

Humphreys, P. (2007) The EU, communications liberalization and the future of public service broadcasting. *European Studies: A Journal of European Culture, History and Politics, Media and Cultural Policy in the European Union*, pp. 91-112(22).

Iosifidis, P. (2010) *Reinventing Public Service Communication: European Broadcasters and Beyond.* Basingstoke, England: Palgrave Macmillan.

Jakubowicz, K. (2007) Public Service Broadcasting: A Pawn on an Ideological Chessboard. *Changing Media, Changing Europe* (4). pp. 115-150.

Jowell, T. (2006) *A Public Service for All: the BBC in the Digital Age.* Department for Culture, Media and Sport. London: HMSO.

McIntyre, I. (1994). *The Expense of Glory: A Life of John Reith.* London: HarperCollins.

Ofcom. (2012) *UK Audience Attitudes to the Broadcast Media.* London: HMSO

Potschka, C. (2012) *Towards a Market in Broadcasting: A Comparative Analysis of British and German Communications Policy.* London: Palgrave Macmillan.

Simmel, G. (1950) *The Sociology of Georg Simmel.* London: Collier-Macmillan

Steemers, J. (2001) In search of a third way: Balancing public purpose and commerce in German and British public service broadcasting. *Canadian Journal of Communication, 26*(1), pp/69 – 87

Steiner, G. (2003) *Lessons of the Masters.* Cambridge: Harvard University Press

Stuart, C. (ed.) (1975) *The Reith Diaries.* London: Collins.

Tracey, M. & Morrison, D. (1979) *Whitehouse.* London: Macmillan

Tracey, M. (1983) *In The Culture of the Eye: Ten Years of Weekend World.* London: Hutchinson

Tracey, M. (2013) *Public Service Broadcasting.* New York: Oxford Bibliographies On-line, Oxford University Press.

Trilling, L. (1949) *Mathew Arnold.* New York: Columbia University Press, pp.252.

Van den Bulk, H. & Moe, H. (2010) *Public Service Media Governance after the Crisis: Comparing Assessment Practices in Flanders and Norway.* RIPE@2010 conference in London, 9-10 September.

II.

Dimensions of Contemporary
Public Service Value

Chapter 6

A Market Failure Perspective on Value Creation in PSM

Christian Edelvold Berg, Gregory Ferrell Lowe & Anker Brink Lund

The legitimacy of public service broadcasting [PSB] rests on normative political arguments about the role of media in society. Claims derived from economic theory legitimate PSB as one method to resolve the problem of market failure in broadcasting. The argument was persuasive in the era of spectrum scarcity, but some find it less convincing in the era of digital abundance. Our chapter investigates whether the market failure argument is still valid for legitimating publicly funded broadcasting, in the first instance, and goes on to consider its pertinence to argumentation about broadband provision via public service media [PSM].

The concept of public service in media is culturally situated and contested. Our perspective is European, broadly speaking. Each EU Member State has the 'competence' to define, organise and confer what PSM is supposed to do (based on the 1997 Amsterdam Protocol). The results certainly vary, but there are common elements in mandates, such as requirements to provide reliable and robust news and information services, take care of cultural needs, and ensure domestic production. In recent years commercial companies have protested PSM for many reasons, especially their involvement in new media and even for their participation in emerging markets that owe much to the institution's pioneering role (Lund & Lowe 2013). Commercial operators argue against a continuing need for public provision in what is construed as an era of plentiful choice, arguing that PSM distorts markets and enjoys unfair competitive advantages due to public funding and ambiguity in remits.

Such argumentation has made significant headway. The 2001 Communication on State Aid from the European Commission [EC], the executive branch of EU governance, stipulates that "commercial broadcasters, of whom a number are subject to public service requirements, also play a role in achieving the objectives of the [Amsterdam] Protocol *to the extent that* they contribute to pluralism, enrich cultural and political debate and widen the choice of programmes" (EC 2001; emphasis added). This perspective was extended to print media in the 2009 update: "Moreover, newspaper publishers and other print media are also important guarantors of an objectively informed public and of democracy. Given that these operators are now competing with broadcasters on the internet, all these commercial media providers are concerned by the potential negative effects that State aid to public service broadcasters could have on the development of new business models (EC 2009). We agree that media operators of all types ought to have mandated public service obligations and that media law should be enforced. In practice, however, the crunch is in the italicised clause because the extent is diminishing everywhere, even in the UK where the broadcasting system overall has been mandated with public service responsibilities (Ofcom 2009; BBC Trust u.d.).

In this chapter we discuss consequent concerns, focusing on market failure as a premise that continues to legitimate the roles and purposes of PSB. We go on to argue that the premise has increasing pertinence in the rapidly commercialising context of broadband media, which speaks to and about PSM. Our perspective is based on distinctive characteristics of media content as complex goods, an element we variously treat in the flow of discussion. We do not claim that PSM is the only method for correcting market failure, or suggest that normative argumentation isn't actually more important for PSM legitimacy. Although many agree that economic value can't fully capture social or cultural value, that claim is arguable and proper methods might be developed over time (see Mulgan 2011).

Further, while market failure continues to legitimate public intervention in media markets, what counts as 'failure' is determined by a society's ambitions for its media system (CtMD 2005), especially in the expectations that media can be effective in promoting beneficial social outcomes and guarding against those that cause harm. This inherently means that normative argumentation is as vital to economic theory as for all other social sciences. Normative claims legitimate assumptions about how markets should work and ought to be organised. Finally, we do not presume that economic theory is capable of pristine objectivity or that human agency is as rational as typically assumed in classical liberal economic theory (see Kahneman 2011 and Lonergan 2009). All that given, normative argumentation is not our concern here although, as we will see, it's not possible to entirely escape this because it is the essential defining element.

We begin with discussion to clarify the notion of 'market failure' and then consider the roles and functions of the public sector in media systems with regard to their instrumentality for correcting market failures in the provision of media goods. We then make a case for its applicability for legitimating PSM.

Why do media markets fail?

A key assumption in classical liberal economic theory is that left to their own dynamics commercial markets will achieve a condition of perfect competition. Under 'free market' conditions, meaning government doesn't intervene (or 'interfere'), all goods and services in demand will be supplied on a competitive basis over time, and thus on balance resources are allocated efficiently (Rosen & Gayer 2010). The thesis of market failure is a critical reaction to key assumptions in this body of theory. Some goods and services have high social value but aren't commercially viable, aren't as profitable as alternative products, or if provided on a purely commercial basis could not be made universally available because the cost threshold for access is a barrier to people lacking sufficient resources.

The concept of market failure hinges on an expectation that all goods are not equally profitable for a commercial enterprise to produce or distribute at an optimal quantity or quality, and therefore what the 'market will bear' is insufficient to meet every legitimate social, cultural and political need (Samuelson 1954 & 1955; Bator 1958; Sutton 1991 & 1998). Market inefficiencies are the result of underproduction of some types of goods, which is especially characteristic of media goods (Berg 2012; Picard 2011a; Reca 2006). Markets are efficient to the degree that they achieve 'equilibrium', a condition in which no individual is better off doing something differently (called 'Pareto efficiency' or 'optimality').

Market efficiency presumes self-correction as a characteristic dynamic (Weimar & Vining 1991). Based on the individual as a consumer, the aggregate of all self-interested, private pursuits cumulatively and systematically lead to improvement in general economic conditions – the rising tide that floats all boats. Any change in market conditions, typically as a consequence of competition, will eventually resolve into a new equilibrium after some period of shakeout in which less efficient players die out and more efficient players take over. Weimer and Vining (1991: 30) offer a succinct summary of the "idealized economics" and conclude "economic reality…never corresponds perfectly with the assumptions of the basic competitive model" (ibid: 41).

When the conditions for perfect competition are not met the result is a failure of the market to provide what is needed. The production and distribution of some types of goods and services are more prone to market failure than others because efficiency is harder for them to achieve. Also at issue is whether efficiency in the economic sense is the priority in aspects that are fundamentally about socio-cultural worth. According to Rosen and Gayer (2010), causes of market failure are keyed to conditions of 1) asymmetric information, 2) externalities, and/or 3) the nature of products as public goods.

Asymmetric information describes situations where the buyer and seller lack equal access to information that has a bearing on the economic transaction. A study of 'lemons' in the used car market (Akerlof 1970) is seminal and provides a good example of what happens when the seller knows more about the product than the buyer, which is typical. The systemic problem posed by Akerlof is that all things being equal, "most cars traded will be the 'lemons' and good cars may not be traded at all…. [So] the 'bad' cars tend to drive out the good" (ibid: 489) and buyers therefore come to assume a lower overall quality than is factually true. Under conditions of symmetric information, market failure is less likely and also less achievable as a deliberate strategy. This legitimates calls for greater 'transparency'. When applied to media goods, the relevant difficulty for audiences is in knowing whether the content is good or bad before it is experienced. One must buy the proverbial 'pig in a poke' and hope for the best. That is why media goods are characterised as experience goods. Moreover, one can't be sure that the content was as good as needed or better than an alternative that was not experienced (hence they are also credence goods).

Externalities are effects that are indirectly related to the transaction, which means the full cost isn't reflected in the price for consumption (Weimar & Vining (1991). Externalities are about broad impact and the consequences can be positive or negative. Positive externalities are beneficial to society. For instance, persistent and consistent media content that emphasises healthy lifestyle choices can have positive externalities if this plays a role in encouraging reductions in obesity that result in lower health care costs. Negative externalities are harmful, such as consumption of extremely violent or pornographic content if this has a role in causing higher incidence of related crime. Thus, externality effects "arise because certain goods are not [subject to] prices – for example the air we breathe or the river through our town – and hence consumers (and producers) either under-consume (or produce) or over-consume (or produce), depending on whether the externality is positive (e.g., education) or negative (e.g., pollution)" (Estrin & Marin 1995: 5).

For media goods the chief difficulty is the impossibility of taking all costs into consideration to ensure the most efficient allocation of resources, a condition that avoids all negatives and accomplishes only positives. A related and thorny difficulty is related to subjectivity because what some people consider a positive others see as a negative, premised in part on normative preferences (i.e. ethics and codes of morality). Thus, economic costs are mainly taken into consideration rather than the less obvious and highly variable social costs.

We suppose it is impossible to empirically demonstrate the total costs for all of the relevant relational categories in media production and consumption: producer-to-producer, producer-to-consumer, consumer-to-consumer and consumer-to-producer (Weimar & Vining 1991: 59). A positive externality in one relationship could be negative in another. For example, a news story about a crime could have positive consumer-to-consumer externality if discourse leads to societal deliberations about the general causes and ways to remedy the source of the problem. But at the same time the externality could be negative if the news media (producer-to-consumer) sensationalise the story in pursuit of economic profits, and in so doing condemn an innocent person before the matter is decided in court. In Denmark the National Board of Industries Injuries Committee on Occupational Diseases recognizes such cases as causing 'mental injuries'.

Public goods are characterised by non-rivalry and non-excludability in consumption, in contrast with private goods that are both rival and excludable. If a person watches a television show or reads a newspaper this does not prevent other people from doing the same. The cost for additional consumption is equal to zero, and thus there is no rivalry. Private goods are different. When one person eats an apple others can't consume the same apple. Thus, a non-rival good can be used without diminishing its value. In fact, multiple uses can make it more valuable due to network effects (the telephone is a typical example). Excludability means that one person retains control over the good, while non-excludability means that one persons' use of it can't limit others from consuming the good even at the same time (Rosen & Gayer 2010; Weimar & Vining 1991).

Although mass media content as traditionally conceived and distributed satisfies both criteria, in the digital era we observe more of what Rosen and Gayer (2010) describe as "impure public goods". Free riding has been a persistent problem for media companies and is possible due to the non-excludable character of public goods. Free-to-air broadcasting has grappled with this for decades. People who don't pay for the content are able to consume and benefit from it nonetheless, riding 'free' as it were. Of course it is not free because other people have paid the freight for them. Digitalisation increases both opportunity and ease in applying encryption technologies, making it possible to erect 'artificial barriers' that create conditions of greater scarcity. This is one reason or rationale for universal access to public media because that presumably maximises public value (i.e. benefit) from the investment. Of course this also creates complications for commercial media online, especially in the news industry, because people are arguably less willing to pay for subscriptions when they can receive quality news and information at no charge beyond whatever the state collects in revenue to fund PSM.

As the authors observed (ibid: 55), consumption of an impure public good is, to variable degrees, made rival or excludable. This issue is important due to the potential consequences of a 'digital divide', increasing fragmentation of audiences and related concerns about the waning of the 'public' as such. An important point to keep in mind is that markets are typically inefficient in the provision of non-rival goods, irrespective of whether those goods are excludable or non-excludable (ibid). Media content remains non-rival in consumption even as subscription creates 'artificial barriers' that enable greater excludability. This suggests that some degree of inefficiency is inevitable in allocation of media content as public goods.

We should define what we mean by 'goods'. Our understanding follows Alfred Marshall who, in *Principles of Economics* (1920 [1890]), posited that something can be characterised as a good when it satisfies a human need or desire and thereby has 'utility'. Utility presumes economic value because the good can be traded and is therefore subject to supply and demand. A media good in this context can be a tangible product such as a published book or DVD, or intangible such as a website or broadcast. A media good can also be a service, as evident in social media, and such services may be characterised as products. Media goods have economic value, but can also have considerable non-economic value and social utility, which are difficult to quantify or even to comprehensively determine (UNESCO 2012).

Discussion about market failure in media content often hinges on a principle first articulated by Richard Musgrave in the 1950s and 1960s. He argued the basis for government intervention in markets of many kinds, including broadcasting, on the basis of anticipated effects that are meritorious or non-meritorious to the wider interests of a society (2000: 126-127):

> The distinction between private and public or social goods arises from the mode in which benefits become available, that is, rival in the one and non-rival in the other case…. But whether met through market or political process, both choices and the normative evaluation of outcomes rests squarely on the premise of individual preference. Consumer preference is taken to apply to both cases. The concept of merit (or for that matter, of demerit) goods questions that premise. It thus cuts across the traditional distinction between private and public goods [and incorporates]…issues which do not readily fit into the conventional framework of micro theory as based on the clearly designed concept of free consumer choice.

Governments decide whether a category of products is meritorious or de-meritorious. The determination in either case may legitimate some degree of market intervention. This is contrary to the principle of 'consumer sovereignty' because governments intervene in efforts to shape or change patterns of consumption. If the market would prefer to deliver some type and amount of goods that the state judges either inadequate or inappropriate to the best interests of society at large, it intervenes (Musgrave 1959 & 1969). One problem is that intervention presumably represents a majority but is often undertaken by an elite that is attempting to inhibit, alter or encourage changes in consumption patterns to best suit their selfish preferences, but are not be in the best interests of all citizens. Musgrave and Musgrave (1980) suggested that the merit goods concept is relevant to policy when there are questions about whether the sum of individual preferences and choices are adequate to satisfy the broader social, cultural and political interests of a collective group as a whole. Thus, one is ultimately dealing with normative issues in a political process and the perception of merit or demerit is often a contentious matter – not for economic reasons, but for socio-political purposes.

Critics of the public goods notion, and related concerns about market failure, base their stance on the potentially damaging effects of state intervention on market performance and development. In their view, the market will provide any service that is actually needed – eventually and as much as people are willing and able to pay for. This view prioritises the individual and in the role of consumer, conceiving the collective as an aggregate of personal choices. Economic value serves as a reasonable proxy for social value.

Although attractive in many respects, this view doesn't provide satisfying answers for what to do about, or how to avoid, situations where the consequences of consumption are potentially harmful for others. This perspective resists and resents interventions that substitute or elevate collective interests above individual choices, accomplished by introducing regulatory measures to either deter or encourage types of consumption. In practice this means prohibiting or penalising certain choices (actually activities, such as drinking alcohol or smoking tobacco) by imposing 'sin taxes' on the one hand, or providing subsidies (in part or in total) to guarantee provision of goods considered meritorious on the other (Musgrave 1969). Musgrave had earlier noted (1959: 85) that, "such interference is not accidental but the very purpose of public policy".

Correction is important because market failure leads to losses for a society overall, potentially including economic loss (Armstrong & Weeds 2005). For example, a poorly educated population is not as productive of wealth as an educated population, even if some proportion is well educated. Of course the losses can be difficult to quantify, perhaps impossible. The difficulty of measurement is precisely the same problem that frustrates public value theory in practice (Mulgan 2011). And it's certainly true that state intervention often produces unintended consequences, doesn't work but carries costs regardless, or is actually counterproductive. That said, market failure remains one essential component of the case for PSB (Davies 2005) because a defining dilemma for many countries is securing a sufficiency of domestic media content due to the constant risk of market failure, which is particularly high for media products because these are 'talent goods' (Picard 2011a). The problem is especially acute in smaller markets (Berg 2011; Picard 2011b).

The funding mode is a determinant factor in this because the source of revenue focuses operational priorities in the interests of organisational sustainability (Lowe & Berg 2013). Where market funding relies strongly on advertising, media can be expected to provide a sufficiency of goods for audiences that are important to advertisers, but to neglect (or resist) goods that are not instrumental in that pursuit. Where funding relies on subscription, media can be expected to provide goods that satisfy segments that are gratified enough to pay the price and (only) those that can afford it, but to neglect people outside those 'target markets'. Where market funding relies on public monies, media can be expected to provide goods that are necessary to satisfy broad public interests (social, cultural and democratic) and, interestingly, to also cater for the needs of minorities and the disadvantaged because that is inherent to the ethos (and typically mandated). In the USA where public media funding is largely donor-driven, however, the characteristic strategy is to "super serve the core" group of contributors (Stavitsky & Avery 2003).

At this point we have a fair idea of what market failure is, but not enough clarity about what causes the problem. For answers we turn to the seminal work of Francis Bator (1958: 351) who defined market failure as "the failure of a more or less idealized system of price-market institutions to sustain 'desirable' activities or to stop 'undesirable' activities. The desirability of an activity is, in turn, evaluated relative to the solution values of some explicit or implied maximum welfare problem". As our book is premised on public value theory (Benington & Moore 2011), "the authorising environment" is where decisions are taken about what is desirable because that is the source of legitimation (Moore 1995). Again we are entangled with the normative dimension and the issue is about deciding a solution to achieve optimal value for the general welfare of a population. Bator proposed five types of market failure, which could also be seen as causes:

1. *Failure of existence* happens when there is no optimal point to balance the cost for production with the cost for consumption, i.e. when the 'correct price' is ambiguous, subjective or unknown. This applies when the total benefits and costs are not immediate or direct, or subject to financial calculation. It is difficult to establish equilibrium because there are no "price-like constants", which are the necessary fulcrum on which to balance. This is characteristic for both public value and public goods, and is a general problem for media content, which has many types of value but all of them aren't equally amenable to financial calculation. Given that media industries typically function on the basis of 'managing against failure' due to high risks caused by market uncertainty (Picard 2011), establishing the optimal point of balance is a characteristic dilemma.

2. *Failure by signal* happens due to inadequate demand relative to the costs for production. Correction requires public investment either by subsidy or tariff. Limited demand provides no 'signal' for the market to respond to, and this creates failure. This is evident in the historic rationale for PSB, which posits that people don't always know or appreciate what they need, but they need to have those things anyway – hence the 'enlighten-

ment mission'. This is also evident in the rationale for PSB as a mandated institution that is required to provide all and everything that has been (politically) determined to have merit for the general welfare of a society.

3. *Failure by incentive* happens when market conditions make it difficult or impossible to realise a profit. Whereas type 2 is premised on problems with demand, type 3 is more linked with supply. This problem can be overcome by state mandates that require services to be provided as 'the cost for doing business', although 'gaming behaviour' is a persistent problem (i.e. clever ways to evade or limit compliance with regulations). In some cases the company generates profits from other activities that subsidise the cost, for example profits from entertainment pay for news production or public subsidy makes good the losses. This later approach is historically characteristic of press subsidies in northern Europe (Picard 2007).

4. *Failure by structure* happens when markets are not competitive enough, obviously characteristic of monopolies but also in co-related behaviours (collusion), and to a lesser but important degree for oligopolies, which is a typical market structure in media industries (Berg 2012; Oliver 2005). Correction requires increasing the number of companies to grow competition, or imposing regulations that mimic the results 'as if' there were more (e.g. requiring lower prices or more variety, etc.). The 1984 EC directive, *Television Without Frontiers*, supposes that deregulation of media industries would create more competition (which it has) and thereby increases media pluralism and diversity (which are less certain). Ironically, deregulation typically encourages oligopoly (Croteau & Hoynes 2006; Horwitz 1991) due to the imperative for economies of scale.

5. *Failure by enforcement (regulation)* happens with two types of resources, 1) natural (water, air, etc.) and 2) public (highway systems, electricity, etc.). Both are 'common properties'. Taking care of these assets carries costs that are often imposed on markets by various means that include taxation, licensing, quotas, and usage fees. This type of market failure is a consequence of the difficulty of profiting from non-excludable goods. The problem with 'free riding' is relevant, as discussed earlier. This type of failure also happens in media industries when there are rules on the books that regulators don't – or can't – enforce.

Media markets are particularly subject to market failure of all types, as the brief examples illustrate. Market failure is especially characteristic of information goods due to five inherent traits: a) non-rivalry in consumption, associated with high first-copy cost for production but low marginal costs for additional copies or numbers of people that consume the good, b) (some degree of) non-excludability, meaning barriers must be artificially created to ensure economic viability, c) the value of the good for the individual is only known after the product or service has been consumed, d) high potential for indirect externalities linked with consumption, and e) mediated information is a perishable product, hence the reason it is 'news'.

From a commercial perspective the essential questions are 1) which products are most viable for the expense of production? And 2) how much of which types of resources are a wise investment? Media industries cope with a higher degree of uncertainty than most others (Doyle 2013; Picard 2011) because consumers are fickle, markets are increasingly fragmented, popularity is mercurial and product lifecycle varies considerably. Thus, many products (movies, books and music recordings) depend on a 'hit model' to realise profits because the majority of productions lose money while the handful that become hits can produce enormous margins.

Even if a particular category of media goods (such as natural history programmes), produce a profit, the margin might not be as large as would be realised if producing in another category. Production carries 'opportunity costs' because more lucrative options must be foregone due to the constant of scarce resources. This dilemma is evident in the reasoning of former ITV Chairman, Michael Grade, when he argued at a 2009 hearing of the UK House of Commons that this commercial public service company should be allowed to cut regional news. Grade said the *X-Factor*, a breadwinner for ITV, attracted 8-12 million viewers and concluded, "that's what the viewers really want. Yes it's nice to have regional news, but it's not viable for us" (Hedges 2009). Broadcasters' pursuit of financial viability in news increasingly favours taking a deliberate editorial 'slant' that reflects and connects with a particular segment's way of thinking (*Economist* 2011), as illustrated by the commercial success of Fox News in comparison with decline for CNN. Fox News might be an important contributor to discourse in the USA, but it is highly partisan by design – for both commercial and ideological reasons (Wemble 2013; Lee 2012).

Non-excludability is a continuing challenge for media goods, not only in broadcasting but also in the broadband environment. The film and recording industries have been thoroughly disrupted by the ease of copying and 'sharing' content, illegally or not. This facility undermines historically successful business models. It has also become a problem for the newspaper industry, which gave away content online for years before recognising this is one cause of financial trouble for the industry in the West. Although consumption of information goods like news, current affairs, cultural, educational and democratic discourse have beneficial effects for both individuals and societies, if provisioned on a purely commercial basis there are considerable difficulties to ensure an adequate supply – as well as the complications of ensuring that audiences actually consume these goods.

As Ronald H. Coase (1966) observed nearly forty years ago, private commercial media must produce profits for shareholders and at as high a margin as possible. "I am quite certain that the broad pattern of programming will be determined by profitability. My view is that we should not bewail the fact that businessmen maximize profits. We should accept and use it. The task which faces us (and the task of good government policy) is to devise institutional arrangements which will lead the businessman, as it were by an invisible hand, to do what is desirable (by making it profitable for him to do so)" (p. 444). The problem with this view today is that it is less reasonable to expect that something unprofitable could be made profitable, or that enforcement can be guaranteed. Both are less likely as competition and operation have become both more complex and more international. Even at the time Coase made his argument, Harold J. Barnett (1966: 470) noted in response: "As Professor Coase points out, it is rather too much to expect profit-seeking broadcasters not to seek profits or, I might add, non-profit broadcasters to suffer unrecoverable deficits". Economic dynamics play a decisive role in explaining the expectations, orientations and behaviours of media firms.

Thus, the issue for commercial media business is the inescapable, implacable requirement to produce profits. When the potential market is limited, as is the case for many types of content including poetry and fine art, religious programming, content for minorities or mainly for educational purposes, the level of provisioning that is provided willingly (at least) by the market will typically be less than considered optimal for society. We understand that what is 'optimal' will vary according to the socio-cultural context. And of course there is ebb and flow in supply as well as demand for varied genres, often in co-relation with events (e.g. the 9-11 attack on the USA fuelled interest in news, current affairs and documentary production about that event and its consequences). But on average and overall, there are limits to what commercial operators in any media market can provide at a satisfactory profit across a range of genres and for a variety of audience segments.

The argument against PSM is mainly that it distorts competition and this hinders profitability for the commercial sector. But there is evidence in the UK, at least, that the BBC's output has encouraged more and better programming overall and has therefore been a driver of quality, variety and competition rather than an obstacle (Oliver 2005). Barnett (1966) suggested that the essential problem in producing content for smaller audiences isn't necessarily that such services are entirely unprofitable but rather that the revenue is too much less than what can be realised from serving mainstream audiences. Similar points were made in the Peacock committee report on the BBC and public financing in 1986, and in a UNESCO handbook on public service broadcasting from 1996. Analyses on broadcasting in smaller nations (Lowe & Nissen, eds. 2011) suggest that entire nations can be construed as 'international minorities' due to small populations that speak unique languages. For example, with a global population of about seven billion, the roughly 5.5 million Finns would qualify as an international minority. '

The commercial market in media, which is increasingly international, will deliver sufficient supply of some types of content for large enough segments, but not enough of all necessary types for enough segments – especially at the domestic level.

The public service sector in electronic media

The market failure thesis became essential to PSB defence after the introduction of commercial broadcasting in Europe (Lilley 2008; Armstrong & Weeds 2005; Davies 2005). But in the digital media environment a plethora of public service goods are provided by museums, galleries, scientific foundations and associations, and by a variety of media organisations. This is why many think, "the objectives of PSB have too often been defined in terms of market failure" (Gardham 2008: 20). There are at least two thorny problems with arguing the case for PSB on this basis. First, the market failure thesis creates a potential trap because sufficiency of any type of public good that is satisfied by the market undermines legitimacy for continuing PSB provision. Another problem is that the market failure thesis says nothing about the appropriate scale of intervention (Whittingdale 2008: 42-43). As Dieter Helm (2005b) observed:

> Whilst anything can be brought within the market failure framework it does not follow that interventions should be based only on this framework. Markets, it can be argued, exist within a social context, with all its politics, freedoms and cultures, rather than the other way around. At stake here is something very fundamental" (p. 4)…[because in] the economic marketplace people are treated unequally – what matters is how much they are both willing and able to spend. In the democratic political market, ability to pay is not a relevant criterion (p. 5).

Although there are problems in basing argumentation on the market failure thesis, even in an era of increasing media abundance the thesis remains valid for at least two reasons. First, the causes of market failure "have not disappeared simply because technology has gone digital, despite assumptions to the contrary" (Davies 2005: 134). Helm (2005a: xi) expected "pervasive", on-going market failures in broadcasting in the digital environment because the fundamentals of broadcasting as a market encourage oligopoly due to economics of scale and scope. The economic dynamics don't change merely because the delivery mechanism is different.

Second, although more abundant due to greater efficiency in spectrum use, and because digital media rely more on wired delivery, digitalisation facilitates easier conversion of media content into excludable goods (i.e. 'club goods') via encryption and subscription. Without PSB many countries would have far less domestic content than at present (Lowe & Nissen 2011). Analyses suggest that although commercial media companies are often mandated with public service obligations, governments are increasingly challenged by complication in enforcing them. The historic "compact" with commercial networks is collapsing as trans-border signals and rules create conditions where regulators can't rely on scarcity of opportunity that is imposed by licensing in order to leverage public service provision as a cost of doing business in media (Oliver 2005: 40).

Opponents of PSM make much of the benefits and exuberance of commercial competition, but this is just as relative as market failure. As Helm (2005b: 11) observed, "Markets have varying degrees of competition and there are many dimensions and kinds of competition. The policy question is whether there is enough competition to negate the need for intervention?" Oliver (2005: 41) noted that many believe "the more competitive the commercial market the greater the investment in programming and the higher the quality of output", but found that the empirical evidence suggests the reverse: "A market with many separately owned commercial channels is likely to see revenue spread thinly, yielding individual channel schedules of relatively cheap and, outside the USA, often imported programming".

This problem is compounded by the fact that competition for advertising incentivises channels to serve the most profitable markets. Oliver furthered observed that "commercial channels' reliance on advertising makes them especially vulnerable to fragmentation" (p. 45). This partly explains the growing emphasis on pay TV that is beginning to endanger the free-to-air ecology of broadcasting systems. That is evident especially in sports, one genre still able to assemble mass audiences. Competition for live sports programming drives up the cost to acquire rights and partly accounts for the growing popularity of strategies that put sports content behind pay-walls both to generate revenue and grow uptake of subscription TV.

Those who assume the digital environment will always encourage an expanding range of entrants, that barriers will remain low and that consolidation is unlikely, are on the wrong side of the evidence (Helm 2005b). Over the past twenty years convergence, consolidation and globalisation together account for persistent problems with market failure in varied domestic markets, although in cyclical patterns with highs and lows over time and across markets. That said, as Helm (ibid: 14) observed: "the fact that markets fail does not, in itself, mandate intervention. All markets fail: the issue is whether the market failures are greater than the costs for intervention". The answer is often yes for broadcasting because failures are cumulative rather than singular:

The first – and generally neglected – point to make about market failure is that it is typically multiple. Whereas most economic analyses take each market failure in turn for reasons of analytical simplicity, the policy problem is set in the context where these failures happen simultaneously, and indeed may reinforce or offset each other... A second point is that market failures rarely point straightforwardly to state provision or single-form solutions. Markets fail relatively, not absolutely, and because the failures are multiple, so the policy instruments tend to be multiple too (Helm 2005b: 6).

In our view the case for PSM as a legitimate intervention to correct market failure is mainly based on ensuring ample provision of meritorious public goods, and this enjoys legitimacy irrespective of the platform for delivery (i.e. it pertains as well to broadband as to broadcast media in the digital environment). The scale and scope of public services provided by PSM is a policy issue, of course, and therefore political and normative in nature. But the need for some form of intervention is as valid today in the light of developing trends in digital media as has been the case historically in analogue broadcasting. PSB organisations are doing precisely what commercial media firms are also doing – developing operational capacity and competence to function on diverse platforms in order to reach and satisfy audiences that are increasingly fragmented and differentiated. But PSM must grapple with unique problems.

First, public service operators have come increasingly into direct competition with formerly adjacent industries (particularly with newspaper publishers). Second, the fragmentation of audiences has produced significant problems for commercial operators to generate what they (or their investors) consider a reasonable margin. Today's direct conflict with the newspaper industry is important because it has taken an increasingly oppositional tone and position in relation to PSM, which is now a core competitor in the online marketplace (see for instance Murdoch 2009). Big profit margins were common for newspapers historically and the come down has been hard and a long time in the making (see Meyer 1995 & 2009). And although significantly smaller today, margins remain comparatively healthy in comparison with other industries (Egmont et al. 2013; Edge 2012). But the point to make is that PSM faces a range and degree of competition that PSB did not. A third unique problem is discussed in the contribution from Peter Goodwin, who suggests that broadcasting per se has been fundamental to the legitimacy of the public service enterprise. We refer the reader his work in chapter 4 to clarify.

Discussion about the transition from PSB to PSM needs to incorporate an understanding that production and distribution of meritorious public goods is platform-neutral and related more to content genres than modes of distribution. Fulfilment of the public service mission in media today requires a range of activities across diverse platforms. The challenge is no different for commercial media firms. Public service organisations have legitimate interests in developing web and mobile presences to ensure delivery of services. Demand for online content is growing and there is no convincing reason the sector should be prevented from using their considerable production capabilities and extensive archives, all paid with public money, to produce services that are valued by their publics. It doesn't make sense in terms either of social or economic value that public institutions would be inhibited or forbidden from creating more value for the monies already invested by publics who have a right to expect access to all they are paying to receive.

The dual system in today's media ecology

As noted, a common theme in the discourse of abundant digital media suggests that dedicated public service institutions are no longer necessary because there is so much content available across an increasing range of platforms. The danger is that although there are significantly more sources and abundant supply of some kinds of content, "civic understanding and well-informed debate" appears to be declining rather than growing (Gardham 2008: 14). Moreover, the supply is uneven with regard to what is on offer. Foster (2008) highlighted the importance of treating media as an ecology whenever the goal is to guarantee higher standards of quality than could otherwise be expected, along with a greater diversity of voices and perspectives than would otherwise be represented, and given the continuing need for universal access to secure a more inclusive availability than is likely to be realised otherwise.

Private commercial media will cater for segments that are attractive either to advertisers or as subscribers insofar as such provision is sufficiently profitable. Netflix is an interesting case in the broadband market because this on-demand service has begun to make original content (with the drama series *House of Cards*). The interesting aspect is not only that the company invested in original content at high professional standards, and offered it first on demand, but also the method of development. By analysing big data gleaned from users of their service they were able to identify the profit potential for such a series (*New York Times* 2013[1] and *Technology Review* 2013[2]). Netflix is of pointed interest for attempting to establish a stronger market position in the broadband environment in direct competition with the broadcast environment.

Similar trends have been evident in satellite television for some years. Discovery Communications, for example, targets several niche markets with content that is 'culture-neutral' (e.g. nature series, travel series, science series). While such programming caters to minority interests, profitability depends on assembling a mass audience *across* domestic markets. Although the non-mass audience argument is compelling from a perspective that emphasises cultural distinctions and domestic needs, creating aggregated mass audiences produces significantly higher profits and is pursued via strategies that deliberately avoid domestication of content. International media market success can be construed as serial failures in domestic markets.

PSM is arguably a vital component of the domestic media ecology in most countries because the institution is mandated to ensure provision of content that mainly caters to domestic populations, and to do so with sensitivity to variation in domestic cultures and social relations under local conditions. PSM must provide content that services both mass and non-mass audiences, which is especially important as societies in the West increasingly feature a multicultural complexion. Without intervention, a commercial market will not provide all or as much in meritorious public goods, in this case having merit because they are from and about domestic issues. The smaller the market is, the bigger the potential for failures.

The same needs and principle are arguably valid in the rapidly developing broadband environment, especially as use grows and the media ecology develops in ways that make broadband a vital element. PSM has many purposes keyed to content provision that serve socio-political, democratic and cultural needs, and thereby correct failures in on-demand as well as on-air markets. One can argue that it's too soon or too early in the broadband game to know how much failure there will be, where and in what exactly, and thus the degree to which PSM will be a corrective. That is fair. But there is a case for being safe now rather than sorry later, especially when recognising that systemic properties create path dependencies that are later very difficult – often impossible – to change. Ward (2006) believes the commercial market can provide public service media to some degree and in limited areas of programming, but that the degree is likely to decrease as competition increases.

Digitalisation is thus likely to aggravate the historic problem, rather than resolve it. To reiterate a key point, the need for public service provision isn't declining in the emerging digital media ecology. PSM in its institutionalised form has advantages that render it more likely to secure adequate provision of meritorious public goods and to correct market failures in broadband as well as broadcast platforms. Those advantages include obligatory mandates, historically trusted brands, the scale of facilities and talent available for handling production, their role in supporting the independent sector, and an ethos that prioritises social responsibility. The role and influence of public financing is certainly a factor, as well.

The dual media system in electronic media has been effective in Europe since the mid-1980s, and in some countries even earlier (e.g. Finland and the UK since the mid-1950s). This remains a viable solution to the problem of how to internalise the costs of potential negative externalities that can arise from *either* public service or private commercial operations if one or the other is the only sector. Coase (1966) observed that responsible government policy doesn't condone continuing a harmful practice, whatever the means for 'covering' the cost (if even possible), but requires *fixing the cause* of the problem in the first place. He also observed that potential ill effects on the market caused by intervention must be balanced against the general gains that are realised as a result, and that profits (broadly construed) don't only benefit a particular private interest but also the wider society. Avoiding the harm may also hinder the benefit (for a concise summary see Baffi 2007).

The problems of market failure in electronic media are more likely to be avoided when and where two sectors are in simultaneous and competitive operation than by either sector alone. PSM will cause some distortion in media markets, but that is the purpose it is supposed to fulfil. The rational for PSB continuation, and for PSM development, makes good sense in the light of its potential to correct market failures in order for a society to reap as many and as great a range of benefits as possible. Any other option will create higher costs without assurance of higher benefit.

There will always be market failures of the varied types categorised by Bator, thus it isn't reasonable to expect commercial companies to produce all the domestic content that is merited across all genres because the potential for profit is so variable and risks are high. That holds especially for the rapidly developing but still immature, and therefore unstable, digital environment. That it is not mature for industrial purposes is evident in the frantic, sometimes seemingly desperate, search for business models to realise sustainable profitability (e.g. Kaye & Quinn 2010; Picard & Dal Zotto 2006). We find reasonable grounds for the continuing need of intervention in media markets, all of which are rapidly becoming electronic and digital. This is especially vital in efforts to secure sufficiency in domestic content production at comparable quality standards for both broadcast and broadband provision. PSM is well positioned to guarantee competition within dual media markets and, together with private commercial operators, a sufficiency in media goods that reduces the potential for market failures.

Conclusion: A proven solution

Cases where media goods are characterised by both non-rivalry and non-excludability are shrinking in the digital environment because excludability can be more easily established. Some aspects and degrees of excludability are certainly acceptable, even appropriate, within limits determined by media policy that decides what is socially desirable and most generally beneficial for a society. Universalism has continuing merit for satisfying the greatest range of social, cultural and democratic needs. Requirements for diversity in production can be mandated and private operators provide a range of meritorious public goods. But the causes of market failure in the provision of media goods remain pertinent and digitalisation doesn't resolve historic problems. Moreover, rules must be enforceable and enforced, an evident problem today.

Characteristic structures and dynamics in media industries indicate we are not dealing with 'business as usual'. The costs and the benefits of intervention, and non-intervention, in media markets must be weighed in the balance of what is best for mutual as well as individual interests, and in the light of a society's overall objectives for its media ecology as a whole. It is difficult to estimate in advance what would be lost in setting aside the PSM component of European media ecologies. Clarity might come too late to correct when path dependencies are already set. We can say, without equivocation, that the dual structure has worked very well in European societies for both the provision of content of all types and for all publics engaged with broadcasting. In our view that provides fair reason to expect that the approach will be as effective for maturing the broadband environment in ways that have the highest probabilities for avoiding the damage of market failures.

We understand that claims about market failure in the provision of media goods are sometimes exaggerated for the self-serving interests of PSM organisations, and that commercial media provide a range of goods that benefit publics and are services. That has been evident in the United States for decades. It is equally clear, however, that commercial priorities and mission parameters are different and this has consequences. There have been declines in the production of less popular genres even by PSB providers that prioritise competitive success over other objectives. This is evident in children's programming in the UK, for example (Steemers & D'Arma 2012). In the USA successive cuts in federal funding encourage greater reliance by public broadcasters on commercial revenue via 'underwriting' and direct sponsorship, fuelling varied concerns (Winship 2007) and indicating worrisome influences on the character of content (see FAIR 2013; Mayer 2013; Hall 2011; Rosen 2010).

The roles and purposes of PSM are similar in key aspects to the historic broadcast mission. PSM can be required to provide meritorious public goods across whatever platforms people access to correct various kinds of market failure in the digital environment. Production requires facilities and depends on talent of many kinds, often highly specialised in media. Higher quality goods typically entail higher costs for talent, in design and for production. There is no convincing reason to think that production of such goods for the broadband interactive environment will remain as inexpensive as in the past, or that competition for users and revenue won't drive up costs for all kinds of talents and goods.

PSM will distort markets, but in light of our discussion it's arguably the case that a 'non-distorted' purely commercial market is more prone to failure of various kinds and in varying degrees. The argument for self-correction is not very convincing. There is a continuing need to balance commercial interests with public interests. We think this finds reasonable application in the broadband environment as it becomes increasingly commercialised. PSM organisations have the experience, expertise and will to develop new media services and to play a decise role in the on-going development of the dual market system in Europe (and beyond, where applicable). Moreover, we don't think it makes sense to suggest that goods paid for with public money should not be distributed via all the preferred and generally used means of distribution.

PSM is not the only way to secure meritorious public goods, nor is it always the best approach for every type of service or in every country. But it is a proven approach in Europe's already highly developed dual system and a method through which a sufficiency of domestic content has been well provisioned in audiovisual media for decades. While argumentation to end PSB and to prohibit PSM has rhetorical power in the self-interested designs of private commercial media, we don't find it convincing when assessing the creation of value that adds to the public sphere.

Note

1. Text available at: http://eur-lex.europa.eu/en/treaties/dat/11997D/htm/11997D.html# 0109010012.

References

Akerlof, G.A. (1970) The market for 'lemons': Quality uncertainty and the market mechanism. *Quarterly Journal of Economics, 84*(3), pp. 488-500.

Armstrong, M. & Weeds, H. (2005) *Public Service Broadcasting in the Digital World.* Accessed 3 October 2013: *http://economics.ouls.ox.ac.uk/15248/1/PSB_Armstrong_Weeds.pdf.*

Baffi, E. (2007) *The Problem of Internalisation of Social Costs and the Ideas of Ronald Coase.* Available online at: *http://mpra.ub.uni-muenchen.de/7277/1/MPRA_paper_7277.pdf.* Accessed 18 April 2013.

Barnett, H.J. (1966) Discussion. *American Economic Review, 56*(1/2), pp. 467-470.

Bator, F.M. (1958) The anatomy of market failure. *Quarterly Journal of Economics, 72*(3), pp. 351-379.

Benington, J. & Moore, M.H. (2011) *Public Value: Theory & Practice.* Basingstoke, UK: Palgrave Macmillan.

Berg, C.E. (2012) *A Matter of Size: The Importance of Critical Mass and the Consequences of Scarcity for Television Markets.* Doctoral dissertation at the Copenhagen Business School: defended February 2013.

Berg, C.E. (2011) Sizing up size on TV markets: Why David would lose to Goliath. In Lowe, G.F. & Nissen, C.S. (eds.) *Television Broadcasting in Smaller Countries.* Göteborg: Nordicom, pp. 57-90.

BBC Trust (u.d.) *BBC Response to Ofcom's Second Public Service Broadcasting Review, Phase 1.* Accessed 15 August 2013 at: http://downloads.bbc.co.uk/aboutthebbc/insidethebbc/how-wework/reports/pdf/bbc_submission.pdf.

Coase, R. (1966) The economics of broadcasting and government policy. *American Economic Review, 56*(1/2), pp. 440-447.

CtMD (2005) *Can the Market Deliver? Funding Public Service Television in the Digital Age.* Eastleigh: John Libbey Publishing.

Croteau, D. & Hoynes, W. (2006) *The Business of Media: Corporate Media and the Public Interest,* 2nd ed. Thousand Oaks, CA: Pine Forge Press.

Davies, G. (2005) The BBC and public value. In *Can the Market Deliver? Funding Public Service Television in the Digital Age.* Eastleigh: John Libbey Publishing, pp. 129-150.

Doyle, G. (2013) *Understanding Media Economics,* 2nd edition. Thousand Oaks, CA: SAGE Publications.

EBU (2007) *Broadcasters and the Internet.* Available online at: *http://www.ebu.ch/CMSimages/en/ Broadcasters%20and%20the%20Internet%20_Full%20report_eng_tcm6-61459.pdf.*

European Commission (2001) *Communication from the Commission on the Application of State Aid Rules to Public Service Broadcasting.* (2001/C 320/4). Available at: *http://eur-lex.europa. eu/LexUriServ/LexUriServ.do?uri=CELEX:52001XC1115(01):EN:NOT.*

European Commission (2009) *Communication from the Commission on the application of State aid rules to public service broadcasting.* Available at: http://ec.europa.eu/competition/state_aid/ legislation/broadcasting_communication_en.pdf

Economist (2011) Back to the coffee shop: Special report on the newspaper industry. 9 July. Available online at: http://www.economist.com/printedition/2011-07-09

Edge, M. (2012) *Not Dead Yet: Newspaper Company Annual Reports Show Chains Still Profitable.* Paper resented at the 2012 conference of AEJMC in Chicago. Available online at: http://www. marcedge.com/Notdeadyet.pdf.

European Union (1997) *Protocol on the system of public broadcasting in the Member States.* Available at: http://eur-lex.europa.eu/en/treaties/dat/11997D/htm/11997D.html#0109010012

FAIR (2013) PBS drone coverage brought to you by drone makers: Lockheed's Nova sponsorship violates underwriting rules. *Fairness & Accuracy in Reporting,* 28 January. Available at: http:// fair.org/take-action/action-alerts/pbs-drone-coverage-brought-to-you-by-drone-makers/.

Foster, R. (2008) Plurality and the broadcasting value chain – relevance and risks? In Gardam, T. and Levy, D.A.L. (eds.) *The Price of Plurality: Choice, Diversity and Broadcasting Institutions in the Digital Age.* Oxford University: Reuters Institute for the Study of Journalism, pp. 25-35.

Gardham, T. (2008) The purpose of plurality. In Gardam, T. & Levy, D.A.L. (eds.) *The Price of Plurality: Choice, Diversity and Broadcasting Institutions in the Digital Age.* Oxford University: Reuters Institute for the Study of Journalism, pp. 11-21.

Hall, H. (2011) NPR's scandal serves as a cautionary tale for fund raisers. *The Chronicle of Philanthropy,* 18 March. Available online at: http://philanthropy.com/article/NPR-s-Scandal-Serves-as/126765/.

Helm, D. (2005a) Executive summary. In *Can the Market Deliver? Funding Public Service Television in the Digital Age.* Eastleigh: John Libbey Publishing, p. xi.

Helm, D. (2005b) Consumers, citizens and members: Public service broadcasting and the BBC. In *Can the Market Deliver? Funding Public Service Television in the Digital Age.* Eastleigh: John Libbey Publishing, pp. 1-21.

Horwitz, R.B. (1991) The Irony of Regulatory Reform: The Deregulation of American Telecommunications. UK: Oxford University Press.

Kahneman, D. (2011) *Thinking, Fast and Slow.* London: Penguin Books.

Kaye, J. & Quinn, S. (2010) *Funding Journalism in the Digital Age: Business Models, Strategies, Issues and Trends.* NY: Peter Lang.

Lee, E. (2012) News Corp profit tops analysts estimates on TV ad gains. *Bloomberg Business Week,* 7 November. Available online at: http://www.businessweek.com/news/2012-11-06/news-corp-dot-boosts-profit-after-making-gains-in-tv-advertising.

Lilley, A. (2008) The fertile fallacy: New opportunities for public service content. In Gardam, T. & Levy, D.A.L. (2008) *The Price of Plurality: Choice, Diversity and Broadcasting Institutions in the Digital Age.* Oxford University: Reuters Institute for the Study of Journalism, pp. 95-100.

Lonergan, E. (2009) *Money: The Art of Living.* Durham: Acumen Publishing Ltd.

Lowe, G.F. & Berg, C.E. (2013) The funding of public service media: A matter of value and values. *International Journal on Media Management, 15*(2), pp. 77-97).

Lowe, G.F. & Nissen, C.S. (eds.) (2011) *Small Among Giants: Television Broadcasting in Smaller Countries*. Göteborg: Nordicom.

Lund, A.B. & Lowe, G.F. (2013) Current challenges to public service broadcasting in the Nordic countries. In Carlsson, U. (ed.) *Public Service Media from a Nordic Horizon: Politics, Markets, Programming and Users*. Göteborg: Nordicom, pp. 51-74.

Marshall, A. (1920 [1890]) *Principles of Economics – An Introductory Volume*, 8th edition. London: Macmillan and Co.

Mayer, J. (2013) A word from our sponsors: Public television's attempts to placate David Koch. *New Yorker*, 27 May. Available online at: http://www.newyorker.com/reporting/2013/05/27/130527fa_fact_mayer.

Meyer, P. (2009) *The Vanishing Newspaper: Saving Journalism in the Information Age*, 2nd edition. Columbia: University of Missouri Press.

Meyer, P. (1995) Learning to love lower profits. *American Journalism Review*, December, pp. 40-45. Available online at: *http://www.unc.edu/~pmeyer/ajrprofits/profits1.html*.

Moore, M.H. (1995) *Creating Public Value: Strategic Management in Government*. Cambridge, MA: Harvard University Press.

Mulgan, G. (2011) Effective supply and demand and the measurement of public and social value. In Benington, J. & Moore, M.H. (eds.) *Public Value Theory and Practice*. Basinstoke: Palgrave macmillan, pp. 212-223.

Murdoch, J. (2009) *The Absence of Trust*. MacTaggart Lecture, 28 August 2009.

Available at: www.abc.net.au/mediawatch/transcripts/0937_mactaggart.pdf

Musgrave, R.A. (2000) *Public Finance in a Democratic Society: Vol. 3, The Foundations of Taxation and* Expenditure. Cheltenham: Edward Elgar, pp. 126-127.

Musgrave, R.A. (1969) *Provision for Public Goods*. In Margolis, J. & Guitton, H. (eds.) *Public Economics*. London: Mac Millan

Musgrave, R.A. (1959) *The Theory of Public Finance*. New York: McGraw Hill Book Company.

Musgrave, R.A. & Musgrave, P.B. (1989) *Public Finance in Theory and Practice*. New York: McGraw-Hill.

Ofcom (2009) *Ofcom's Second Public Service Broadcasting Review: Putting Audiences First*. Accessed 15 August 2013 at: http://stakeholders.ofcom.org.uk/consultations/psb2_phase2/statement/.

Ofcom (undated) Annex 11 *Market Failure in Broadcasting*. Available online at: http://stakeholders.ofcom.org.uk/binaries/consultations/psb2_1/annexes/annex11.pdf.

Oliver, M. (2005) The UK's public service broadcasting ecology. In *Can the Market Deliver? Funding Public Service Television in the Digital Age*. Eastleigh: John Libbey Publishing, pp. 39-59.

Picard, R.G. (2011a) *The Economics and Financing of Media Companies*, 2nd edition. NY: Fordham University Press.

Picard, R.G. (2011b) Broadcasting economies, challenges of scale, and country size. In Lowe, G.F. & Nissen, C.S. (eds.) *Television Broadcasting in Smaller Countries*. Göteborg: Nordicom, pp. 43-56.

Picard, R.G. (2007) Subsidies for newspapers: Can the Nordic model remain viable? In Bohrmann, H., Klaus, E., & Machill, M. (eds.) *Media Industry, Journalism Culture and Communication Policies in Europe*. Köln: Herbert von Halem Verlag, pp. 236-246.

Picard, R.G. & Dal Zotto, C. (2006) *Where NEWS?* The media future research initiative report on existing and potential business models of newspaper publishing companies. Darmstadt: IFRA.

Reca, A.A. (2006) Issues in media product management. In Albarran, A.B., Chan-Olmsted, S.M. & Wirth, M.O. (eds.) *Handbook of Media Management and Economics*. Mahwah, NJ, USA: Lawrence Erlbaum Associates, Publishers, pp. 181-202.

Rosen, J. (2010) NPR news analyst: How Juan Williams got fired. *Press Think*, 24 October. Available online at: http://pressthink.org/2010/10/npr-news-analyst-how-juan-williams-got-fired/.

Rosen, H.S. & Gayer, T. (2010) *Public Finance*, 9th edition. NY: McGraw-Hill

Samuelson, P.A. (1954) The pure theory of public expenditure. *The Review of Economics and Statistics*, 36(4), pp. 387-389.

Samuelson, P.A: (1955) Diagrammatic exposition of a theory of public expenditure. *The Review of Economics and Statistics*, 37(4), pp. 350-356.

Stavitsky, A.G. & Avery, R.K. (2003) U.S. public broadcasting and the business of public service. In Lowe, G.F. & Hujanen, T. (eds.) *Broadcasting & Convergence: New Articulations of the Public Service Remit*, RIPE@2003. Göteborg: Nordicom, pp. 137-146.

Steemers, J. & D'Arma, A. (2012) Evaluating and regulating the role of public broadcasters in the children's media ecology: The case of home-grown entertainment. *International Journal of Media and Cultural Politics*, 8(1), pp. 67-85.

Sutton, J. (1991) *Sunk Costs and Market Structure – Price Competition, Advertising and the Evolution of Concentration*. Cambridge, MA: MIT Press.

Sutton, J. (1998) *Technology and Market Structure – Theory and History*. Cambridge, MA: MIT Press.

UNESCO (2012) *Measuring the Economic Contribution of Cultural Industries: A Review and Assessment of Current Methodological Approaches*. NY: UNESCO Institute for Statistics. Available online: http://www.uis.unesco.org/culture/Documents/FCS-handbook-1-economic-contribution-culture-en-web.pdf

Ward, D. (2006) Can the market provide? Public service media, market failure and public goods. In Nissen, C.S. (ed.) *Making a Difference: Public Service Broadcasting in the European Media Landscape*. Eastleigh: John Libbey Publishing.

Weimer, D.L. & Vining, A.R. (1991) *Policy Analysis – Concepts and Practice*, 2nd edition. NY: Prentice-Hall.

Wemble, E. (2013) Fox news all day: Hard and conservative. *The Washington Post*, 27 March. Available online: http://www.washingtonpost.com/blogs/erik-wemple/wp/2013/03/27/fox-news-all-day-hard-and-conservative/.

Winship, M. (2007) Back to the future of public broadcasting. *Common Dreams*. Available at: http://www.commondreams.org/views07/0130-25.htm.

Chapter 7

What Media Value?

Theorising on Social Values and Testing in Ten Countries

Josef Trappel

Values are good fellows of both media business practice and communication research. While the former has always been interested in the economic value of its business, the latter used news values as an analytical tool to understand why some events become news and others don't. The traditional understanding of value in the context of media production is challenged today. Media business is reshaping its concepts fundamentally in attempts to address the decline of readership for newspapers, stagnation of the television audience, the erosion of advertising revenues for traditional (mass) media and the digitalisation of content distribution on the Internet. Some consider these challenges a crisis (Imhof 2011; Almiron 2010; Schudson 2010) and others as a process of transformation (Winseck & Jin 2011).

In this chapter I argue, first, that orientation towards economic and business value alone is not appropriate for media business in the 21st century; second, that social values increase in importance in ways that are contrary to any purely economic (and shareholder) perspective on value; and third, that public service media are well prepared to adopt social values in their operations. In the second part of the chapter empirical evidence is provided to validate the claims.

Economic and business values

During much of the 20th century, private commercial media firms were highly successful in business terms and that was largely a result of orienting their operations to more highly prioritised economic values. Current processes of comparatively radical change might require different business orientations, however, as the ways by which information, deliberation and entertainment are manufactured and distributed is changing rapidly, and corresponding to changes in the ways that people (as audiences, users, etc) receive, use, and organise media use to satisfy their communication needs and wants.

In theoretical terms, business orientation in the later half of the 20th century was strongly influenced by Michael Porter's compelling and prominent theory for understanding and explaining the production, delivery and service process as a "value chain", and the approach for using that concept in analysis [VCA] (Porter 1998 [1985]: 36ff). Nearly 30 years later its long lasting paradigmatic effects on business operations are still evidently important, and merit discussion. The essential idea is that every step (link) of the production, delivery and service process either contributes to or detracts from the value the product has for a customer.

Porter's value chain model focuses on the individual firm and its ability to create value for customers. In his view, this value is evident in "the amount buyers are willing to pay for what a firm provides them. Value is measured by total revenue, a reflection of the price a firm's product commands and the units it can sell" (Porter 1998 [1985]: 38). The level of generalisation is high because in theory his model should apply to all firms in all segments of a competitive market economy.

Media firms and academic studies in media economics and management have commonly used and applied Porter's model and approach, classifying the links variously but always as a chain that features production/creation (of content), packaging/production, distribution, and delivery/exhibition (e.g. Albarran 2010: 57; Zerdick et al. 2000: 52ff). Lucy Küng (2008) applied the model to various media (TV, newspapers, film) to demonstrate differences in the complexity of links in the chain for each, and similarities between them. Despite differences, these authors adhere to a shared perspective in which value is understood as the "ability to command money or other goods in exchange for the commodity or service in the market" (Picard 1989: 35).

Focussing on the economic value according to the VCA by contemporary media and communication firms does not provide fully satisfactory results for four reasons that are important to consider.

The first reason refers to the fundamental fact that most media firms are simultaneously operating in a dual-product market comprised of 1) the audience market for content and 2) the advertising market for audience attention. These 'products' are different (content vs. attention), the customers are different (business-to-consumers vs. business-to-business), and the pricing models are different (low/no cost vs. competitive pricing). Optimising the strategy in one market affects performance and success in the other market (Albarran 2010: 57f; Picard 2011; Picard 1989: 17f). Applying VCA to distinct but related markets often creates contradictions because optimising the quality of content provision does not always correspond with advertisers' requirements concerning the amount and quality of audiences delivered.

A second weakness of VCA in application to media is keyed to an implicit preference for vertical business integration, corresponding well with the paradigm of the industrial age of mass production and mass consumption of the 20th century. In this respect the extraordinary business success of media firms in the 1970s and 1980s can be explained in part by a strategy of vertical integration that made them highly profitable enterprises in a generally favourable business environment of economic growth. Such high profits come at a cost, however. As much as vertical (and horizontal and diagonal) media integration advanced, resulting in increasing concentration, competition within media markets of all sizes declined. Media monopolies in local markets has long been characteristic of newspapers and broadcasting in Europe, for example, and powerful media oligopolies have been increasingly characteristic in national, supra-national and global media markets (for an overview see Downing 2011 & Sparks, 2007). Such large media conglomerates are less acceptable nowadays, however (McChesney calls media concentration a "poison pill for democracy" 2008: 427), and they are required to justify their market power. Anti-trust legislation sets limits and prevents some of them from further growth in varied national markets.

Third, as mass media are transformed into "mass self-communication" (Castells 2009: 58ff), the vertical integration model no longer fits as well. VCA cannot easily cope with influencing factors from outside the constrained focus on a business setting. In Porter's model civil society is relevant only in the role of consumers for goods and services, and in the case of media industries especially for 'audience as product' whose attention can be sold to advertisers. The VCA approach doesn't really accommodate the "active audience" (Hartley 2012: 8) either in the initial link in the value chain, content production, or most of the rest of the subsequent links (distribution, delivery). They really only appear as the evaluators of the value, and this is constrained to the amount of money they are willing to pay for a media product or service.

Fourth, VCA does not provide fully satisfactory results because in contrast to firms producing mainly material goods, media firms are in the business of providing immaterial goods that are strongly bound to the tastes, preferences and values of consumers, i.e. audiences. Of course some media industries produce tangible goods, such as books and DVDs, but the use value isn't in material aspects of those goods – it is in the enjoyment of the experience of reading or viewing, and therefore largely in the intangible characteristics. Explaining and understanding media business merely in terms of money in exchange for services neglects this additional but important business element. Successful media firms always represent more dimensions and kinds of values than competitive and economic value. They represent distinctive views on current events in politics, economics and cultural life, for example. News and entertainment contribute fundamentally to the definition of values in society, and facilitate a never-ending process of public negotiation, deliberation and "working through" (Ellis 1999). In this respect, values obtain additional importance beyond commanding money. Creating, shaping or neglecting value-definition by media firms is, in fact, a major success factor even in business terms.

Thus, the question arises as to whether optimising efficiency along the lines of Porter's value chain model is sufficient to explain performance or success of contemporary media (and communication) firms. Is it appropriate (and socially acceptable) to reduce cost in content production and acquisition (e.g. by cost cutting, downsizing and content syndication), optimise packaging and distribution by advancing for example digital platforms and streamline delivery to make media firms fit for the challenges of the world of mass-self communication? These questions can only be answered by extending the analytical view beyond economic value.

Introducing and defining social value

In this section I argue that the ongoing process of change requires media firms, both private and public, to reconsider the value creation model. I hypothesise that the more media firms concentrate on the creation of *social value* alongside economic and business value, the better these firms will perform and succeed in the age of mass self-communication. Furthermore, I argue that public service media are intrinsically better positioned to deliver social value than commercial media. Obviously, this is an extensive hypothesis and requires close examination of the term *value* in different connotations.

Values, in general terms, are essential for directing behaviour. In the context of media – and in particular in the context of news – values are prominent features that explain why some news items achieve predominance over others (news values). Robert Picard's essay on *Value Creation and the Future of News Organizations* (2010) elaborates on various values with regard to news production. He distinguishes exchange value from use value, individual value from social value and asks questions of fundamental importance: Value for what? Value for whom? (ibid. 47ff). These are basic questions and useful for a critique of claims made by neoclassical economics that "the value of goods and services are whatever the market will bear" (ibid. 48). This over-simplification corresponds well with the VCA model discussed above. From this perspective the question of "value for whom?" is easy to answer: Value for the firm and its owners, investors and managers. The implicit assumption is that whatever is good for the firm is (eventually) good for consumers.

The term *public value*, first expounded in the US public administration literature on effective government administration and management (Moore 1995; Benington & Moore 2011), prominently entered the media reform policy debate in 2004 when the BBC in the UK based its argument for continued legitimacy and relevance during the renewal of its Royal Charter on redefining its remit around that term (BBC 2004). According to the BBC, public value is created by serving people both as individuals and as citizens, and does so by offering additional benefits over and above individual value by contributing "to the wider well-being of society, through its contribution to the UK's democracy, culture and quality of life" (ibid: 29). The basic argument for charter renewal was that the BBC would extend its public value work on three levels:

1. By building a digital Britain, that is, creating innovative services, technologies and content that encouraged citizens to "use, understand and enjoy" digital information technologies (ibid: 65ff)

2. By supporting active and informed citizenship, for example by offering "everyone a democratic voice and a means of contributing to the national debate"; and

3. By providing programmes that enrich lives and culture (ibid: 60ff). This included producing genre crossing productions, multimedia interactive resources and participatory story-telling projects.

A key proposition was that public value should not only be developed in theory but should be measurable in practice. A complex and ambitious procedure, called the public value test, to assess both the BBC's capacity to meet public value objectives and the market impact of its activities (Collins 2007). In this respect the term 'public value' refers to the BBC's political and cultural objectives, and therefore its social value. The market assessment dimension recognises that this cannot be entirely divorced from its economic performance and, especially, impact on the market.

By successfully applying the public value test the BBC finally managed to renew its charter, demonstrating how well the BBC is embedded in British society. In retrospect, the introduction of public value as a core concept in PSB media policy has been highly successful for the BBC's purposes – with consequences for other member states as the European Commission has encouraged, even requires, variations of the test to be developed by other member states to assess the (market) impact of new media services of public service broadcasters (Donders & Pauwels, 2010; see also the chapter by Hallvard Moe & Hilde Van den Bulck in this volume).

The term public value is therefore closely connected to the BBC's context of charter renewal and this instrumental pursuit (Oakley et al 2011) has subsequently become a defining element of media policy discourse related to public service media and their remits. Apart from this British context, however, the specific meaning of this term has not been clearly defined and the term is used widely and in various contexts (Donders & Moe 2011). Analytically, this depreciates the term.

In contrast to public value as elaborated here, the term *social value* (following Picard 2010: 61) refers to values for society, not for single stakeholders, highlighting collective benefits. This overlaps with the BBC's understanding of public value:

> Social value is created when news organizations inform and explain events of the day, monitor the integrity of public representatives, chastise and laud the behavior and performance of institutions, organizations, and enterprises, and stimulate public discussion and engagement (Picard 2010: 61).

Thus, social value addresses mid- to long-term collective needs and wants, is rooted in the communication requirements of democratic societies and provides "a society with a better understanding of itself and its place in the world, and a shared sense of identity and place" (Flew 2013: 82, with reference to Throsby 2001)

At this crossroad, different schools of thought meet. On the one hand, media economists propose social value as an essential element of good media business governance; on the other hand (political) theories seeking to analyse the development of democracy refer to essential values for democratic societies. These ends can be tied together. Irrespective of what (political) model of democracy is chosen for analysis – pluralist, administrative, civic or direct democracy (see Glasser 2009: 97ff) – one can identify fundamental normative values that need to be protected, proceeded and respected by leading (news) media:

Equality and *liberty (freedom)* are the most frequently mentioned social values when looking into the relevant literature on media and democracy (Glasser 2009). In the media context, equality as a media value refers to the fundamental democratic requirement to offer a voice to all relevant groups in society. Michael Schudson used the terms "social empathy" and "advocate for various viewpoints" (2010: 104) to describe this value. Liberty (freedom) is a value materialised in the independence of the media from all sorts of power in society and enables media to act in a non-partisan or "objective" way (Baker 2006: 115). Curran argues that both of these values, equality and liberty, should not be misinterpreted. Equality does not simply mean that media should enable equal representation of interests but also the expression of conflict. Core media "should enable divergent viewpoints and interests to be aired in reciprocal debate, and alert mainstream society to the concerns and solutions of minority groups" (2007: 40). Freedom needs to be interpreted not only as independence from the state but also from other power-holders in society.

Another key social value is *control*, often referred to as the watchdog function of the media to hold political authorities to account by monitoring their activities (among many others, cf. Voltmer 2006: 4) and reporting on those activities. Contemporary understanding of this value extends beyond the classical understanding: "The watchdog role of the press is perhaps best viewed as mediating the investigative resources of a free society – its whistleblowers, dissenting elite members, civil society watchdogs, independent think tanks, and critical researchers – rather than acting as a substitute for them." (Curran 2007: 35)

Other social values within the media and democracy discourse are *solidarity* (Dahlberg and Siapera 2007: 2) and *participation* (Carpentier 2011). Solidarity is closely related to the broader value of equality but underlines the role of the media and can be regarded as "a central communication value according to the definition of communication as increasing communality and sharing of outlook and experience" (McQuail 1992: 68). Participation in general means greater public involvement in decision-making, although it is understood that more participation "may not necessarily lead to a particular enlightened debate (...)" (Downey 2007: 110).

Social values in the media arena are thus defined as values because they provide collective benefits in democratic societies, enhancing non-partisan and independently informed citizenry, augmenting social empathy and equality among citizens by providing platforms for participatory controversy and discourse, and controlling the powerful in society by holding them to public account. But are these social values behavioural guidelines for media firms? Picard's analysis of social and democratic values created by the news media ends on a pessimistic note:

> Given the poor value produced for society today by many news organizations (...), we may need to seriously consider whether the conditions that led the press to become the fourth estate still exist or whether the diminished role that many news organizations play today will make them irrelevant in the future (Picard 2010: 133).

While acknowledging the criticism, there are good arguments for why leading news organisations (still) deliver social value. Looking at the news output alone cannot explain differences between leading news media. Following Kaarle Nordenstreng (1999: 30), structural conditions need to be taken into account when news output should be explained. He asked: "Is not content just a reflection of structures of production and distribution, ultimately ownership? Is not content after all an ahistorical category?" Similarly, Denis McQuail suggested three levels for analysis of media performance. Quality of media output needs to be complemented by the structural and the organisational levels, thus ownership, control and conduct become part of the analysis (1999: 30).

To conclude this part of our discussion, social values are success factors for media, both public and private, in the age of *active audiences*. Media firms are required to carefully analyse how they address active audiences with their products and services. Delivery of social values seems especially pertinent as key for establishing and maintaining trust in a context that very clearly demands continuous customer relations with media firms in the 21st century. It is up to respective media firms to decide how social values are defined, made available and delivered for and to their specific audiences, which differ considerably between 'low key' entertainment media and 'high brow' informational and educative contents.

The terms public value and social value overlap to some extent. Social value, however, is more inclusive and less connected to the British and European Union debates on public service media. I therefore use social value for the following empirical analysis.

Testing social value in ten countries

The structural perspective taken in this chapter goes beyond content production and is chosen to provide empirical evidence on how leading news media respect and further social value. The research question is whether and to what extend leading news media are prepared to support social values? Are social values any part of the internal organisation of a newsroom? Are they reflected in mission statements and in daily journalistic practices and routines? And are public service media any different from private commercial media?

Empirical evidence is provided by the *Media for Democracy* (MDM) project, scrutinising leading news media in nine European countries and in Australia (Trappel et al. 2011). Within this project, interviews were conducted with journalists and editors-in-chief of leading newspapers, magazines, radio and television broadcasters and online-media as well as representatives of journalism unions, supplemented with document analyses. The analytical framework builds on three dimensions: freedom/information, equality/interest mediation, and control/watchdog function. For each dimension several indicators have been applied to establish the extent to which the leading news media in each country contribute to the function of democracy. Some indicators represent social values as discussed.

Out of the total of 26 indicators used for the MDM project, five are clearly and directly connected to *social values* as discussed in this chapter and these provide empirical evidence about the extent to which social values are evident at leading news media in ten countries: Australia, Austria, Finland, Germany, Lithuania, the Netherlands, Portugal, Sweden, Switzerland and the UK. In the following analysis, each indicator is briefly introduced and described, followed by significant findings from all or selected countries. The sources for all country information can be found in Trappel et al. 2011. Here the sources are cited only once when first mentioned.

Independence of the news media from power holders

This indicator refers to the social value of independence of the newsroom, which is essential for being able to inform citizens, to explain complicated matters and to report on relevant issues in an objective and non-partisan manner. The normative assumption is that newsroom members do not feel obliged to power holders in society but rather are beholden to their internal principles and rules – and ultimately or to their audiences. Furthermore, this indicator establishes ways and means that explain how journalists are shielded from vested interest and how strong – if at all – non-media organisations (such as financial investors, political parties, churches etc) are in having a say inside a media company. Moreover, financial conditions are relevant: It is assumed that more and long-term available financial means enhance independence. Empirical data were derived from interviews, company information, mission statements and the remit of public service media.

The protection of journalistic independence is not as obvious as one might expect. In several countries, vested business interests are present in the leading news media. For example, the two financial investors KKR and Permira own the second largest private broadcasting company in Germany (*ProSiebenSat1*) (Marcinkowsi & Donk 2011), and partly own *SBS Nederland* in the Netherlands (d'Haenens & Kik 2011). The financial group *Raiffeisen* is part owner of some of the largest news media in Austria, *Kurier* and *Profil*) (Grünangerl & Trappel 2011).

The Catholic Church owns media in Portugal (*Rádio Renascença* and a number of small regional newspapers) and Austria (*Styria Group*). Furthermore, in the Netherlands the investment group *Talpa Media/Cyrte* of John de Mol is part owner of the *Telegraaf Media Groep* (TMG) and *RTL Nederland*. The financial investor *Mecom* owns 87% of the shares in *Koninklijke Wegener*. In Germany, the Social Democratic Party owns the publisher *DDVG*, among the top ten publishers in this country. In Portugal, the *Sonae* group, who runs supermarkets and shopping centres, owns the daily newspaper *Público* and the advertising company *Controlinvest*, also is active in the football industry and in the trade of football transmission rights, as well as owning three daily newspapers (Fidalgo 2011). The strongest influence of non-media companies on leading news media is reported in Lithuania: there, most news media are owned by strong business groups with interests outside the media field such as real estate agencies, logistics and construction firms, hotels, health care organisations, heavy industry, and finance. Even at the newsroom level, some conflicts of interest have been reported where journalists are being businessmen in Lithuania (Balcytiené 2011).

At the other end of the spectrum, the survey on Sweden and the UK did not reveal any major threats to editorial independence, especially because the public service broadcasters are carefully shielded from politics. The Royal Charter stipulates that the BBC is independent in all matters concerning the content of its output and the management of its affairs. The degree of independence from government can be considered outstanding (Humphreys 2011). In Sweden there is a large institutional distance between policy and the public broadcaster, who enjoys financing over periods of six years (von Krogh & Nord 2011). In Lithuania, in contrast, the independence of public service broadcasting is compromised by the fact that funding decisions are taken by the government on an annual basis, thus preventing independent long-term planning.

Overall, the social value of independence from power holders in society shows some connections between business and other social forces (Church) and newsrooms. Direct influence at the journalistic level, however, has not been reported. Conditions for impartial and non-partisan journalism are good. Public service media show a mixed record. Depending on the institutional setting, the independence varies. The Swedish and British model excels in this respect. More information on how ownership and editorial newsroom interplay is provided in the following indicator.

Company rules against internal and external influence on newsroom / editorial staff

This indicator addresses the problem of compromised editorial independence by internal and external influence. *Internal* influence might originate in the sales department for advertising, but also in shareholders' interests or in the owner or patron. *External* influence might come from pressure or lobby groups, from government or from (large) companies interested in favourable coverage or portrayal of their products, or simply to polish their public reputations. In all such cases of internal and external influences, the question is about what kinds of measures are taken by media firms to resist attempts to influence editorial decisions. Internal rules are one option, e.g. the strict separation of the advertising sales department from the newsroom. Another aspect concerns economic independence that should exclude any single (advertising) customer from achieving dominance over the revenue stream. The more balanced revenues from different sources of commercially funded media are, the better for editorial independence. If companies rely on just one single source of income (such as non-commercial public service media), independence needs to be assured by legally binding rules and practices of distance between the revenue source and the news media. Empirical evidence has been gathered by interviewing journalists, editors-in-chief and other management staff as well as representatives from journalists' unions.

In most countries the leading news media are well shielded from interventions from their owners. In Portugal, Sweden and the Netherlands, there are editorial by-laws that prohibit any editorial influence by the proprietors. In the

UK, large newspapers are clear of editorial interventions, notably Tony O'Reilly (*The Independent*), the Scott Trust (*Guardian*) and Lord Rothermere (*Daily Mail*) are quoted as examples (Humphreys 2011). In contrast, Rupert Murdoch (*The Times, Sunday Times, Sun, Sky News*) is portrayed as being hands-on both economically and editorially. Interventions by the Murdoch family are also reported from Australia, where a recent court case (2010 *Herald Sun* in Melbourne) indicates interventions by media owners (Josephi 2011).

Several countries report blurred borders between newsrooms and company management where editors-in-chief are at the same time also CEOs of their companies, creating potential or real conflict of interests. In the Austrian sample, three editors-in-chief were also part of the management board, and the same situation was found at Sanoma Corp. in Finland (*Helsingin Sanomat, Iltalehti*), and in the Netherlands. Just one such case was reported from Sweden.

The separation of the newsroom from the advertising sales department is formally and strongly enforced by legal tools in all countries under scrutiny and attempts to influence content by advertising clients are normally vigorously rejected. Full separation is the rule in public service broadcasting where advertising is managed in a separate business entity in Austria, Germany and Sweden; in the Netherlands NOS separates editorial and commercial interests by outsourcing revenue collection to a foundation. Such strict separation applies generally less to online media and smaller news media where advertorials, non-spot advertising, and hidden advertising occur.

The social value of uncompromised editorial independence is respected by leading news media in the MDM sample. Large newspapers do not suffer from interventions from their proprietors, but exceptions to this rule are reported. Commercialism and the weak economy, however, seem to erode the otherwise strict separation of editorial content and advertising, in particular in online-media and in smaller media firms. Public service broadcasters in Sweden, Finland, Germany and the UK are well shielded from any interventions – regardless whether from government or from advertisers.

Citizens' participation

Participation is considered a social value for media companies in so far as they offer citizens the opportunity to voice their own views and to react to news stories they see, read or hear. In addition, media might encourage citizens to participate in the production of news. If citizens become more active agents in the process of public deliberations, more social value is created because public issues are then discussed more controversially, more voices are expressed and finally more voices might be heard. It can be argued that the larger the number of citizens who participate, the greater the chance of having a multitude of opinions. Because of their potentially interactive technological architecture, online media are very well suited to establish citizen-centred participation. The question, therefore is, whether and to what extent leading news media offer opportunities for participation to citizens in ways and to degrees that go beyond classical feedback in the form of letters-to-the-editor? It is assumed that more active participation of citizens creates more social value by intensifying public deliberations. By interviewing editorial staff information is gathered on how open newsrooms are for participation, how well practices of reply by citizens are established and to what extent participation is welcome within the newsroom.

Empirical findings show that the leading news media are reluctant to fully implement interactive features and to offer participation options to the audience. In most cases leading news media only provide feedback opportunities by sending-in letters or emails to the editors. Portuguese, Dutch and Swiss leading news media do not offer much more than this (Meier et al. 2011: 309f).

Some public service broadcasters, however, provide best practice examples. The BBC has pioneered formats for providing audience participation, such as the weekly television programme *Question Time*, which is highly popular. In Australia, the ABC and SBS have high profile programmes *Q & A* and *Insight*, which are built on the basis of audience participation. In Germany, public service operator WDR has *Listeners Days*.

Open newsrooms are not well established in the ten counties. The overwhelming majority of newsrooms are never open to citizens. Some interviewees expressed their doubts about quality issues when citizens become journalists and consider participation more as a supplement to journalism than as a forum for self-expression. In Finland, participation is widely recognised as a value among journalists and editors, but productive and meaningful means of implementation are lacking. One example of an open newsroom is reported at the local level, (*Borgåbladet*), which is well accepted and frequently used by citizens. In Sweden newspapers encourage participation and offer multiple mechanisms. *Svenska Dagbladet* runs an online project to combine traditional reporting and user participation.

These findings reveal that leading news media typically ignore, or at best only tentatively explore, the social value of citizens' participation. The traditional model of agenda setting and gate keeping continues to dominate self-understanding among journalists and editors. Citizens are by and large denied access to newsrooms and public deliberations do not primarily happen on the websites of traditional newspapers. Only a few and only public service broadcasters allow for extensive citizens' participation.

Rules and practices on internal pluralism

Internal pluralism is an important social value. It aims at reflecting the variety of opinions and ideas within a society and their appropriate representation in the newsroom. This social value is well respected when there are defined processes for how to handle divergent views within the newsroom. Hierarchical top-down decisions by the editor-in-chief in journalistic routines do not enhance internal pluralism (although of course at least occasionally necessary for a final decision). Sophisticated internal procedural rules to ensure pluralism can be considered to have increased importance to the extent that external pluralism has fallen prey to media concentration. It is usually the responsibility of news organisations to define rules and procedures internally. One important aspect of pluralism concerns the pool of experts that news media usually consult. Experts are preferred sources of information and are also used for interpreting events and issues, and sometimes appear as guest-authors. Again, interviews with journalists and editors are the source for empirical evidences.

While pluralism is valued in all countries and all newsrooms, rules on how to ensure pluralism generally don't exist. The editors-in-chief interviewed refer to informal mechanisms in meetings and conferences where all journalists have a say, but codified guidelines are rare. The public service broadcaster in Austria, ORF, has rules stipulating how to ensure diversity in the choice of experts. In Finland, two national newspapers (*Helsingin Sanomat* and *Iltalehti*) have a policy of including opinions that diverge from the main editorial line (Karp-pinen et al. 2011: 132). In Switzerland, internal pluralism is highly respected by the news media and they strive for balanced representation. Restrictions, however, result from media economics. Journalists lack time for investigation and suffer from precarious job conditions. Furthermore, changes in the profession diminish expert knowledge by journalists and increase dependency on external experts (Meier et al. 2011: 310).

Although well respected by news media, rules on internal pluralism are not popular in the newsrooms of the ten countries, irrespective of whether the organisation is public or private. This finding does not suggest the social value of pluralism isn't respected and that newsrooms don't strive for the representation of a wide variety of ideas and opinions. Certainly both are characteristic. But this important value would be better respected if there were internal rules to certify who and what opinions are reflected in the news.

Watchdog: mission statement and resources

Most journalists and observers agree that the social value of investigative reporting and watching over current affairs is of outstanding importance. Although there are other institutions (and persons) that watch over public affairs, such as Courts of Auditors or even whistleblowers such as Wikileaks, news media are able to confront broad audiences with results from investigations. In what way are news media prepared to respect this important social value? There are two assumptions: First, watchdog journalism requires skills and a sense of responsibility that needs to be anchored in the mission statements of a news media organisation. Second, investigative reporting requires logistical and moral support by the news organisation by providing sufficient financial resources. Both assumptions are conditions for socially responsible watchdog journalism. Newsrooms are required to provide their staff the necessary support to make watchdog journalism possible. The question, therefore, is whether and to what extent are watchdog journalism and investigative reporting part of the mission statement of news media are sufficiently resourced to enable journalists to work on investigations? Empirical findings come from interviews with journalists, editors and representative of journalists' unions.

European news media's reference to watchdog or investigative journalism in mission statements is weak. In most cases no reference is made, with the exception of Sweden where both public service media and newspapers refer to their roles as watchdogs of power holders. *Svenska Dagbladet* claims critical scrutiny of power holders in society and public *Sveriges Radio* requires its journalists to review and investigate different forms of power. However, even in the Swedish case such statements do not mean much in day-to-day routines. In Finland, contrary to the European trend, watchdog journalism enjoys increasing importance in written editorial principles. Other news media in Europe rate information higher than investigation in their mission. Australia is different in this respect. There, journalistic self-understanding is strongly composed of investigation, which is considered the most important role. Media companies (e.g. *The Age; West Australian*) commit themselves expressly to their role as fourth estate in their editorial policy.

Reluctance to include investigative reporting in the mission statements does not prevent news media from allocating resources to this task, which basically means person power. Respondents in Australia confirm that sufficient resources are made available. Equally, German, Finnish, and Dutch media are well equipped for investigative reporting. Cut backs in staff and financial resources are expressly reported from Lithuania, Portugal, Switzerland, and the UK, however, and there the economic crisis has lead to the downsizing of newsrooms and to less available time for the remaining staff to do investigations.

Special task forces for watchdog journalism exist in public service broadcasters (e.g. YLE in Finland has a specific investigative group; the same in Sweden and Switzerland) but not in small newsrooms. In particular online media do not have sufficient means to do investigations. The only reported exception is the Swedish tabloid paper, *Expressen,* which has a special unit with three reporters for investigative projects.

Overall, the social value of investigative reporting is less prominent than the familiar BBC tripartite mission to "inform, educate and entertain". Special journalistic task forces are the exception, despite the fact that journalistic investigations would set media firms apart from their competitors. The economic crisis is eroding watchdog journalism further and new formats of news provisions online are particularly weak in investigative reporting. Some public service media can still afford to maintain special task forces for this function.

Conclusions

In general, we can say that values are important components of normative theories of media communication, and have historically been understood to have particular significance for mass media. While media economists reference value mainly in monetary and business terms, others have emphasised the specific role value plays for the meanings and practices of contemporary societies. Consideration of social values suggest how essential it is to embed media firms in their host societies. Economic value is measured by revenue. That is comparatively much easier and straightforward than attempts to measures public and social value. While *public value* is easily defined in negative terms as being the opposite of private value (i.e., that which profits a firm and its owner / investor interests mainly), *social value* goes far beyond the economic worth to include many more aspects that are closely related to the role and functions that media play in democratic societies.

The value chain paradigm is popular but inadequate for media applications because it suggests that accumulating and concentrating media business activities vertically and horizontally (or even diagonally) is a priority. Michael Porter's model is useful and has utility, but is cannot cope with *active audience* and doesn't accommodate identities and roles outside of consumer-oriented practice. That is far from the whole story for media, and in many respects (as hopefully demonstrated in this chapter) isn't the most important part of the story. As inadequate as it has been shown to be even for traditional mass media, it is even more deficient for the rising tide of mass self-communication identified by Manuel Castells.

An approach that prioritises social value provides a theoretical perspective that does not exclude economic success, that is to say the worth of media companies and industries, but focuses on values that are of mid- to longer-term importance and is at the same time collectively focused (rather than only individually). At issue is what is most beneficial to a public at large, and not only for markets and or for people purely as consumers.

Empirical analyses of selected indicators of the Media for Democracy Monitor project in 2011 (MDM) reveals that social values are not very well incorporated in leading news media in ten countries. It turns out, however, that public service media still generally pay more attention to social values, and prioritise these to a higher degree. That is undoubtedly due in large part to their public service remits, which obligate them to focus less on profit (if at all, actually most are not-for profit) and more on the public and social benefits they must provide in return for public funding and other support. But it seems fair to suggest that respecting social values strengthens the public legitimacy of any media firm, private or public. The severe crisis affecting newspapers (declining readership), magazines, online-media and television (less willingness to pay), explains widespread calls for re-orientation of media firms. As new forms and platforms of public discourse emerge with development in digital technologies that in parallel and in competition with traditional mass media, the incumbents can be urged to redefine and develop business models according to a "social value chain" analysis.

References

Albarran, A.B. (2010) *The Media Economy*. NY: Routledge.

Almiron, N. (2010) *Journalism in Crisis. Corporate Media and Financialization*. Cresskill: Hampton Press.

Baker, C.E. (2006) Journalist performance, media policy, and democracy. In Marcinkowski, F., Meier, W.A. & Trappel, J. (eds.) *Media and Democracy: Experiences from Europe*. Bern: Haupt, pp. 115-126.

Balcytiené, A. (2011) Lithuania: Mixed professional values in a small and highly blurred media environment. In Trappel, J., Niemienen, H. & Nord, L.W. (eds.) *The Media for Democracy Monitor: A Cross National Study of Leading News Media*. Göteborg: Nordicom, pp. 175-201.

BBC (2004) Building Public Value: Renewing the BBC for a Digital World. London: BBC.

Carpentier, N. (2011) The concept of participation: If they have access and interact, do they really participate? *CM Communication Management Quarterly, 21*, pp. 13-36.

Castells, M. (2009) *Communication Power*. Oxford: Oxford University Press.

Collins, R. (2007) *Public Value and the BBC*. A report prepared for The Work Foundation's public value consortium. London: The Work Foundation.

Curran, J. (2007) Reinterpreting the democratic role of the media. *Brazilian Journalism Research, 3*(1), pp. 31-54.

d'Haenens, L. & Kik, Q. (2011) The Netherlands: Although there is no need for dramatization, vigilance is required'. In Trappel, J., Niemienen, H. & Nord, L.W. (eds.) *The Media for Democracy Monitor: A Cross National Study of Leading News Media*. Göteborg: Nordicom, pp. 203-234.

Dahlberg, L. & Siapera, E. (2007) Introduction: Tracing radical democracy and the Internet. In Dahlberg, L. & Siapera, E. (eds.) *Radical Democracy and the Internet: Interrogating Theory and Practice*. NY: Palgrave MacMillan, pp. 1-16.

Donders, K. & Moe, H. (eds.) (2011) *Exporting the Public Value Test: The Regulation of Public Broadcasters' New Media Services Across Europe*. Göteborg: Nordicom.

Donders, K. & C. Pauwels (2010) The introduction of an ex ante evaluation for new media services: Is 'Europe' asking for it, or does public service broadcasting need it? *International Journal of Media and Cultural Politics, 6*(2), pp. 133-148.

Downey, J. (2007) Participation and/or deliberation? The Internet as a tool for achieving radical democratic aims. In Dahlberg, L. & Siapera, E. (eds.) *Radical Democracy and the Internet: Interrogating Theory and Practice*. NY: Palgrave MacMillan, pp. 108-127.

Downing, J.D. (2011) Media ownership, concentration, and control: The evolution of debate. In Wasko, J., Murdock, G. & Sousa, H. (eds.) *The Handbook of Political Economy of Communications*. Chichester, UK: Blackwell, pp. 140-168.

Ellis, J. (1999) *Seeing Things: Television in the Age of Uncertainty*. London: I.B. Tauris.

Fidalgo, J. (2011) Portugal: A young democracy still in progress. In Trappel, J., Niemienen, H. & Nord, L.W. (eds) *The Media for Democracy Monitor: A Cross National Study of Leading News Media*. Göteborg: Nordicom, pp. 235-264.

Flew, T. (2013) *Global Creative Industries*. Cambridge, Malden: Polity.

Glasser, T.L. (2009) The principles and practice of democracy. In Christians, C.G., Glasser, T.L., McQuail, D., Nordenstreng, K. & White, R.A. (eds.) *Normative Theories of the Media: Journalism in Democratic Societies*. Urbana-Champagne ILL: University of Illinois Press, pp. 91-113.

Grünangerl, M. & Trappel, J. (2011) Austria: Informal rules and strong traditions'. In Trappel, J., Niemienen, H. & Nord, L.W. (eds) *The Media for Democracy Monitor: A Cross National Study of Leading News Media*. Göteborg: Nordicom, pp. 79-112.

Hartley, J. (2012) *Digital Futures for Cultural and Media Studies*. Chichester, UK: Wiley-Blackwell.

Humphreys, P. (2011) UK news media and democracy: Professional autonomy and its limits'. In Trappel, J., Niemienen, H. & Nord, L.W. (eds.) *The Media for Democracy Monitor: A Cross National Study of Leading News Media*. Göteborg: Nordicom, pp. 319-345.

Imhof, K. (2011) *Die Krise der Öffentlichkeit. Kommunikation und Medien als Faktoren des sozialen Wandels*. Frankfurt, New York: Campus.

Josephi, B. (2011) Australia: Committed to investigative journalism. In Trappel, J., Niemienen, H. & Nord, L.W. (eds) *The Media for Democracy Monitor: A Cross National Study of Leading News Media*. Göteborg: Nordicom, pp.51-77.

Karppinen, K., Nieminen, H. & Markkanen, A-L. (2011) Finland: High professional ethos in a small, concentrated media market'. In Trappel, J., Niemienen, H. & Nord, L.W. (eds.) *The Media for Democracy Monitor: A Cross National Study of Leading News Media*. Göteborg: Nordicom, pp. 113-142.

Küng, L. (2008) *Strategic Management in the Media: From Theory to Practice*. Thousand Oaks, CA: SAGE Publications.

Marcinkowski, F. & Donk, A. (2011) Germany: The news media are still able to play a supportive role for democracy. In Trappel, J., Niemienen, H. & Nord, L.W. (eds.) *The Media for Democracy Monitor: A Cross National Study of Leading News Media*. Göteborg: Nordicom, pp. 143-174.

McChesney, R.W. (2008) Rich media, poor democracy: Communication politics in dubious times. In McChesney, R.W. (ed.) *The Political Economy of Media: Enduring Issues, Emerging Dilemmas*. NY: Monthly Review Press, pp. 425-443.

McQuail, D. (1992) *Media Performance: Mass Communication and the Public Interest*. Thousand Oaks, CA: SAGE Publications.

McQuail, D. (1999) On Evaluating media performance in the public interest: Past and future of a research tradition. In Nordenstreng, K. & Griffin, M. (eds.) *International Media Monitoring*. Cresskill, NJ: Hampton Press, pp. 25-38.

Meier, W.A., Gmür, A. & Leonarz, M. (2011) Switzerland: Swiss quality media: A reduced protection forest for democracy. In Trappel, J., Niemienen, H. & Nord, L.W. (eds.) *The Media for Democracy Monitor: A Cross National Study of Leading News Media*. Göteborg: Nordicom, pp. 289-317.

Moore, M.H. (1995) *Creating Public Value. Strategic Management in Government*. Cambridge, MA: Harvard University Press.

Nordenstreng, K. (1999) Toward global content analysis and media criticism. In Nordenstreng, K. & Griffin, M. (eds.) *International Media Monitoring*. Cresskill, NJ: Hampton Press, pp. 3-13.

Oakley, K., Naylor, R. & Lee, D. (2011) The public gets what the public wants? The uses and abuses of 'public value' in contemporary British cultural Policy. *International Journal of Cultural Policy, 17*(3), pp. 289-300.

Picard, R.G. (2011) *The Economics and Financing of Media Companies*, 2nd ed. NY: Fordham Univesity Press.

Picard, R.G. (2010) *Value Creation and the Future of News Organizations: Why and How Journalism Must Change to Remain Relevant in the Twenty-First Century*. Barcelona: Formalpress.

Picard, R.G. (1989) *Media Economics: Concepts and Issues*. London: SAGE.

Porter, M.E. (1998 [1985]) *Competitive Advantage: Creating and Sustaining Superior Performance*. NY: Free Press.

Schudson, M. (2010) News in crisis in the United States: Panic – and beyond. In Nielsen, R.K. & Levy, D.A.L. (eds.) *The Changing Business of Journalism and its Implications for Democracy*. Oxford: Reuters Institute for the Study of Journalism, , pp. 95-106.

Sparks, C. (2007) What's wrong with globalization? *Global Media & Communication* 3(2), pp. 133-155.

Trappel, J., Niemienen, H. & Nord, L.W. (eds.) (2011) *The Media for Democracy Monitor: A Cross National Study of Leading News Media*. Göteborg: Nordicom.

Throsby, D. (2001) *Economics and Culture*. Cambridge: Cambridge University Press.

Voltmer, K. (2006) The mass media and the dynamics of political communication in processes of democratization. In Voltmer, K. (ed.) *Mass Media and Political Communication in New Democracies*. London: Routledge, pp. 1-20.

von Krogh, T. & Nord, L.W. (2011) Sweden: A mixed media model under market pressures. In Trappel, J., Niemienen, H. & Nord, L.W. (eds.) *The Media for Democracy Monitor: A Cross National Study of Leading News Media*. Göteborg: Nordicom, pp. 265-288.

Winseck, D. & Jin, D.Y. (eds.) (2011) *The Political Economies of Media. The Transformation of the Global Media Industries*. New York: Bloomsbury Academic.

Zerdick, A., Picot, A., Schrape, K. (2000) *E-Economics: Strategies for the Digital Marketplace*. Berlin: Springer Scientific.

Chapter 8

The 'Digital Argument'
in Public Service Media Debates

An Analysis of Conflicting Values in Flemish
Management Contract Negotiations for VRT

Karen Donders & Hilde van den Bulck

For many years now, policy makers, industry stakeholders and scholars alike have proposed that media policy in general, and public service media (PSM) policies in particular, must be revised due to the technological changes in production, carriage, and consumption associated with digitisation. This quasi-automatic causality between technological change on the one hand and the perceived necessity of policy change on the other hand is referred to as *the digital argument* in this chapter. The digital argument is evident in discussions on PSM policies more or less everywhere today. It is closely related to the debate on public value, the focus of this book, as the digital argument questions PSM's 'added value' to existing broadcast arrangements, as will become clear.

Debate on the public value and future role of public broadcaster VRT in Flanders, the Dutch-speaking region in Belgium, provides a useful contemporary case for analysis. As Flanders is a small region and media market (6.5 million inhabitants), it cannot be considered representative of wider transformations in Europe – much less beyond. It is nonetheless fruitful, we think, because studying a specific policy debate and looking carefully at the outcomes (here the newly updated regulation of VRT), provides insight into how the digital argument is both used, and abused, in a policy field that is not entirely unique. Lessons can be drawn that will have value for understanding developments in other European countries, like the Netherlands, the United Kingdom, and Ireland, where PSM policies are being similarly revised in alignment with the digital argument.

From the end of 2010 to mid 2011, the Flemish government and public broadcaster VRT negotiated on the latter's funding and contractual obligations for the period 2012-2016. The results of these negotiations are legal provisions specified in a 'management contract' (*Beheersovereenkomst*) – an instrument governments in several European countries adopted mainly in the 1990s to deal with public broadcasters in a more management-oriented style, but intended also to allow sufficient operational freedom for institutional decision-making about development objectives (Bardoel & D'Haenens 2004 & 2008).

The VRT discussions were characterised by considerable complexity. Three political parties were involved, two of which are on the political right and one on the left, comprising a Flemish coalition government with a Socialist minister in charge of media. The inclusion of an increasing number of stakeholders in a previously bilateral process of management contract negotiations added to the complexity. This trend in *multi-stakeholderism* for negotiations (see Donders and Raats 2012; Padovani and Pavan 2011) responds to demands from the European Commission (Donders 2012) and is a legal requirement of the Flemish media decree, which envisions formalised, multi-stakeholder procedures to assess the public value and market impact of PSB. Intrinsically, this gives an additional forum to private media companies to contest public service delivery in whole and in part. It also allows citizens, and groups representing them, to express opinions and declare preferences about public service media, although the latter are not as well represented or as professionalised as the private media lobbies.

This chapter assesses which stakeholder coalitions were formed in order to affect the process of negotiations and the results, whether in favour of PSM or not. Our research method is Advocacy Coalition Framework Analysis, drawing on document analysis, an audience survey (carried out in the beginning of 2010) and interviews with media companies, the cultural sector, civil society, etc (also conducted in the beginning of 2010). We explore the concept of policy advocacy coalitions, proposed by Sabatier and Jenkins-Smith (1993 & 1999), which centres on relationships between actors who share similar values and beliefs. Such actors can form loose or tight coalitions that cut across governmental and non-governmental boundaries, but are united in their beliefs and views regarding the best solution to a particular policy issue. Different coalitions, typically two to four, exert influence on policy deliberations and seek the power to control key instruments in policy-making and implementation (Van den Bulck 2012).

While our empirical focus is on a specific case, the evolution of public service media policies in Flanders, this study has wider relevance in terms of the methods employed, the processes and dynamics we investigate, and 'lessons-learned'. As multi-stakeholderism becomes a feature of media governance in most European countries (Puppis 2008), it is crucial to develop methodological approaches to properly analyse the phenomenon; to conceptualise the 'multi' in multi-stakeholderism; to understand how this works in practice; to identify which stakeholders join forces and form the most powerful coalitions; and to clarify how all of this is related to policy-making and implementation. Does policy become more evidence-based as, for example, the European Commission would like to see (Donders & Pauwels 2010), or is the 'value' stakeholders and coalitions assign to public service media highly subjective and, perhaps, a rather weak basis for further policy development?

Moreover, the Advocacy Coalition Framework Analysis allows us to broaden the scope of public service media policy analysis. We avoid an over-focus on broadcasters and governments and, by including a broader field of stakeholder perspectives and acknowledging power asymmetries, we avoid research bias and gain a more comprehensive and balanced understanding of the issue at hand.

We begin with discussion about the digital argument, focusing on the potential overlap between today's technological optimism and the historic problem with technological determinism. Then we provide an overview of Flemish media policy and VRT, highlighting the negotiation process between stakeholders leading to a new management contract. We next analyse the stakeholder groups with regard to composition and comparative positions, before briefly comparing the case with the broader range of similar processes underway elsewhere in Europe. We conclude with discussion of the implications related to the two broad coalitions identified in this project, economics first versus society first.

Technological determinism and optimism: Two worlds apart?

As typology, one can distinguish two main perspectives on public service media. The first is a contested understanding of the market failure approach, which in this case seeks to limit PSM to areas of digital service provision that are not provided by commercial media companies. We say it is contested because the market failure notion is historically, and still importantly, a vital element of the justification framework for PSB (see chapter 8 by Berg, Lowe & Lund). The second has been generally characterised as a social responsibility approach, which argues that media functions are too important for the health and vitality of democratic societies (at least) to be left solely to market forces to determine what is and is not provided, and for whom (Donders 2012; Van den Bulck 2008; Jakubowicz 2007; Bardoel & Lowe 2007). These are theoretical and normative perspectives, both evident in policy debates about PSM. The approaches are conflicted in key respects and explain a characteristic division (even cleavage) between those advocating for, and against, a bigger role for public broadcasters in the digital environment. Protagonists often invoke arguments about technological evolution to make their case, as we will explain.

Broadcasting policy in Europe since the 1970s has strongly favoured the abolition of monopoly strucures in media, largely opposing the formerly strict governmental control over and ownership of broadcasting. The presumed end of spectrum scarcity (or more correctly the possibility to make more efficient use of increasingly contested spectrum space), the advent of cable and satellite platforms, and then the internet with broadband connections, and widespread demands for a roll-back of the State from every kind of market have all played a role in deregulatory trends (McQuail et al 1992: 10-11; Dyson and Humphreys 1988). The market failure thesis (see chapter 8) has become the standard for defining acceptable areas and degrees of government intervention, and has been used with varying degrees of success in efforts to roll back PSM to PSB (i.e. to restrict development beyond traditional radio and TV services).

The drive to reduce public media funding is premised on the idea that digital media markets can perform far closer to optimum efficiency due to "technological development" (e.g. Peacock 1986: 126) and the presumed superiority of commercially financed private sector operations. In this schema media content with 'positive externalities' (for example historical documentaries, information programmes, indigenous children's programming) could and would be provided by the market, undermining the 'public' value of PSM and providing a diminished basis for government intervention through public broadcasting.

While one can legitimately argue that "the public interest does not disappear because we have broadband cable" (Tracey 1995: 126), and while research has revealed that certain types of socially valuable content remains under-provided (see, for example, Steemers and D'Arma 2012), the market failure argument has gained fresh momentum in debates over PSM development of internet and mobile media. Many scholars, notably those with a background in media economics, have argued that technological evolution will eliminate historic market failures in the provision of media services of every kind. This belief legitimates the rhetorical conclusion that in the digital era PSB should not be encouraged, or even permitted, to evolve into PSM; the institution should be confined to the provision of niche services with demonstrable public value (see Armstrong & Weeds 2007; Appelman et al 2005).

Protagonists of the social responsibility approach counter that the market failure approach looks at PSM from the 'wrong end of the telescope', equating societal value with the sum of individual consumer value (Barnett 2002). UK sociologist Nicholas Garnham (1990: 120) was a ferocious early critic, arguing that the value of PSB is not as a complement or supplement to market provision but in actually being superior to the market "as a means of providing all citizens, whatever wealth or geographical location, equal access to a wide range of high-quality entertainment, information and education, and as a means of ensuring that the aim of the programme producer is the satisfaction of range of audience tastes rather than only those tastes that show the largest profit."

This proposition is still seen as a relevant starting point in crafting media policies for 21st century conditions. Despite a quantitative increase in commercial media services, and the growth of citizen-generated media content, genuine plurality and diversity of voices is not the automatic consequence of an exponential increase of channels or, even necessarily, a related expansion of content choice (Dwyer and Martin 2010). In this respect PSM's deployment of online services can be seen as an essential part of strengthening public broadcasting's reach and capacity to nurture and represent inclusive public dialogue (see especially Moe 2008, and also Bardoel & Lowe 2007 and a report for the Council of Europe by Lowe 2007).

Proponents of the social responsibility approach criticise the market fail-ure approach for technological-determinism. And yet one can also observe a variant of the same essential problem in what we characterise as 'technology optimism' i.e. the belief that PSM can redress historic problems in service provision by relying on new media. Technology is represented here not as a limitation but as an opportunity for public broadcasters to demonstrate public value by becoming more relevant to their audiences. For instance, Humphreys (2008: 6) argues that "it is vital that the public broadcasters engage fully with the new digital media and develop new niche channels, on-demand services and Internet services". Public broadcasters need to connect with citizens as active participants (Martin 2002, Bardoel and Lowe 2007: 17) and open the doors to genuine interaction and co-production (Lowe 2010; Murdock 2004).

An explication of the Flemish media market and PSM policies illustrates how these contrasting policy approaches have shaped the focus of VRT's operations.

Flemish media policy, *PSB and PSM:* Values and pragmatism

In general we can say that the existing Flemish media policy is characterised by widespread consensus on a certain social value of the public broadcaster VRT and is a pragmatic solution to contrasting, to some degree also contradictory, political efforts to please both commercial media and the public broadcaster. It is useful to begin with an overview of PSB in the Flemish part of Belgium, one of three language communities. Flanders is the biggest community with approximately 6.5 million inhabitants; the French speaking community (*Wal-lonia*) counts approximately 4.5 million inhabitants. The German speaking community is the smallest with about 200.000 inhabitants.

Public service radio began at the national level in 1930 and television was incorporated in 1953. Gradually, political competencies over the Flemish and Walloon public broadcast institutions were regionalised. Today, public service broadcasting is completely the responsibility of respective Flemish and Wal-loon regional governments (Van den Bulck 2001). This development reflects market reality as Flemish consumers do not watch Walloon television, do not read Walloon newspapers, and do not visit Walloon websites – and vice versa.

The opening up of the Flemish television market to domestic competition began with the adoption of the 'cable bill' in 1987 and hit public broadcaster VRT hard. Flanders' first commercial television station, VTM (owned by news-paper publishers and holding a monopoly on advertising) was an immediate success. This exposed the weakness of a centralistic, hierarchically organised and strongly politicised PSB institution, which could not stem the dramatic decline in audience ratings (Saeys 2007).

Only in the mid-1990s did a far-reaching restructuring of the public broadcaster, and the legal framework within which it had to work, allow VRT to regain the initiative. A flexible management structure was put in place, independence from government was enhanced, and management contracts – to be renewed every five years – were introduced. Accountability and performance measurement became keywords in Flemish public broadcasting policy.

The transformation was successful as VRT once again became a trendsetter. VRT modernised (some say commercialised) its programme offerings on the two television channels and five radio channels. Audience reach went up, provoking frustration among commercial competitors. Frustrated with the VRT's renewed success and struggling for commercial revenues in what was after all a small and quite competitive media market, encouraged commercial players' to intensify their lobbying efforts at both Flemish and European levels, where a complaint was filed with the European Commission in 2004 against the funding arrangements of the public broadcaster (Donders 2012).

The commercial complaint is familiar to students of PSB: that VRT disturbed market competition, broadcasting mainly popular, entertainment programmes. VRT was thus believed to be neglecting the provision of content characterised by added value for the public. It was also considered unfair that VRT received commerial revenue from advertising in addition to public subsidy. In response, the public broadcaster was compelled to limit commercial revenues and to refrain from television advertising all together (Van den Bulck 2008).

Today, VRT has fairly stable market shares in radio (circa 60%) and television (35-40%), with additional online activities. Its main TV competitors are VMMa (the mother company of VTM and a portfolio of channels) and SBS Belgium (recently acquired by a consortium of Flemish newspaper publisher Corelio, Flemish production company Woestijnvis and Finland's Sanoma Group). Although competition is fierce, VRT and the two main commercial players co-operate on several innovative projects, e.g. in trying to fight the powerful position of distribution company Telenet (a daughter of Liberty Global, delivering television services to over 80 per cent of Flemish population).

Generally speaking, VRT has a fairly solid position in Flanders – as PSB operators tend to enjoy in much of western Europe. Despite fierce criticism and considerable challenges (e.g., with the arrival of commercial television), support has been relatively stable. The composition of commercial challengers, both in identity and argumentation, is more or less the same as elsewhere in Europe and might reflect a general strategy employed by commercial opponents to PSM (see Nord 2012). But there is a general belief in the added public value of public broadcasting to and for society, especially in a small media market such as Flanders where the market on its own cannot be expected to cater for a lot of diversity (for a broader treatment see Lowe & Nissen 2011). With regard to new media services, however, the potential added value to the public is disputed.

A snapshot of Flemish media policies for public service media

The basis of Flemish PSM policy is the management contract, which transposes the fairly generic principles of the Flemish media decree into specific, contractual obligations for VRT. The management contract 2007-2011 focused on the organisation's cultural remit and performance regarding quality, moving towards a more explicit focus on the particular public value of PSM and away from an emphasis in earlier contracts on growing audience reach (to counter VRT's dramatic decline in popularity after the introduction of commercial television). That newer contract also specified a number of ceilings on commercial revenue and continued the prohibition of television advertising. Moreover, online services were not entirely embraced in the remit. Although there were few explicit restrictions (Vlaamse Regering & VRT 2006) and technological innovation was emphasised, VRT was essentially still positioned as a radio and television broadcaster. In the management contract commercial broadcasters and publishers stressed the absence of prohibitions on new services, but we observe that the contract included a corresponding absence of new media obligations. This 'silence' on new media services demonstrates that the Flemish government was undecided about the actual policy changes that digitisation required. Whereas some favoured the commercial media companies' stance, others obviously did not. In that sense, the silence speaks volumes.

The management contract is renewed every five years and the procedure has been affected by European State aid formulas, in which Flanders was involved as a litigant (Donders 2012). Article 20 of the media decree specifies that each management contract renewal must be preceded by a public consultation. The Sectoral Council for Media (*Sectorraad Media*) is in charge of this consultation. The Council's composition reflects the Flemish media sector, with representatives from VRT, commercial broadcasters, newspaper publishers, media distributors, radio broadcasters, etc. Consumer organisations and academia are also represented. In its consultation the Council is required to look at:

- Evolutions / trends in the media market and technology;

- International trends;

- Economic changes in the media market;

- Available offers in the market;

- The expectations and needs of media users; and

- The protection and promotion of Flemish culture and identity.

The consultation was outsourced to some extent as the Sectoral Council commissioned an audience survey (Dhoest et al 2010) and a stakeholder consultation (Donders et al 2010) on the future role of VRT in Flanders, executed by two university research groups. In both studies respondents were consulted on the values PSB/M should represent, what it actually stands for, and possible issues related to market distortion. Subsequently, and based on this input, the Council had to produce an advisory document that was published on its website and taken into account by the Flemish Government in negotiations with VRT.

Before we elaborate on the opinion of the audience and other stakeholders' positions, two additional notes will be useful. First, it remains difficult to see how the advice of the Council is related to the studies that it commissions. There are no spelled-out procedures that clarify how, exactly, scientific expertise must be taken into account by the members of the Council. Theoretically, their advice can deviate entirely from the 'evidence' provided by academia. Second, it is even less clear what significance the advice has in the negotiations that produce the management contract between VRT and the Flemish Government. Again, the media decree is not very detailed in this respect.

Overall, Flemish media law stipulates fairly transparent and rational procedures for the preparation of a new management contract, which should ensure that tasks for VRT are clearly linked to well-defined public service objectives. However, as the next section shows, negotiation on its public value and the choice of tangible and measurable indicators to demonstrate this, is a 'messy' political process in which some stakeholders are more equal than others.

Analysing stakeholder coalitions: Identifying conflicting values

Negotiations on the current management contract commenced in late 2010 and the agreement was signed on 20 July 2011, entering into force on January, 1, 2012. Negotiations intensified towards the end of the process and, where many stakeholders were involved at the beginning, the field narrowed towards the end. Divergent opinions on the future role of VRT were apparent during negotiations, revolving around three familiar aspects: 1) the desirable effects of technological evolution on VRT's scope of activities, 2) the scope of VRT's commercial activities, and 3) symbolic issues related to diversity and representation. On most issues, the three government parties (i.e. socialists, Christian-democrats, and Flemish nationalists) were divided. Diversity and representation was an action point of the left wing party in government. An action point of the Flemish nationalists was keyed to identity and Flemish music on VRT radio. Christian-democrats put much emphasis on the scope of VRT's commercial activities. For the purpose of this chapter, we focus on the role of the 'digital argument' in the policy process leading up to the renewal of the management contract.

Our analysis of stakeholder positions and coalitions is based on advocacy coalition framework analysis (cf. supra). In this light, we consider the management contract a policy decision that results from a process characterised by the formulation of different views and interests, expressed by various stakeholders adhering to particular (possibly shared) logics expressed in different forums (Hutchinson 1999; Blakie & Soussan 2001). Here the essential stakeholders are defined as: citizens, political parties, regulatory institutions, media organisations, civil society, unions, and the advertising industry. Within this constellation a distinction is made between the core 'informants', meaning those stakeholders having the most direct influence on policy making – and peripheral 'inform-ants' where the impact is lower or indirect. For each stakeholder we identified their overall views on PSM , their interpretation of the 'digital argument', the coalition of which they are part, and their impact on policy decisions.

We identified two advocacy coalitions, pictured in Figure 1 below. Each coalition shares a similar view on the desired course of media policy and works in concert towards the achievement of their respective view. The intensity with which they do this determines, in part, the success of their coalition. Specific circumstances and, very importantly, the actual (often, economic) 'weight' of the coalition are other key explanatory factors.

Figure 1.   Advocacy coalitions in the Flemish management contract negotiations

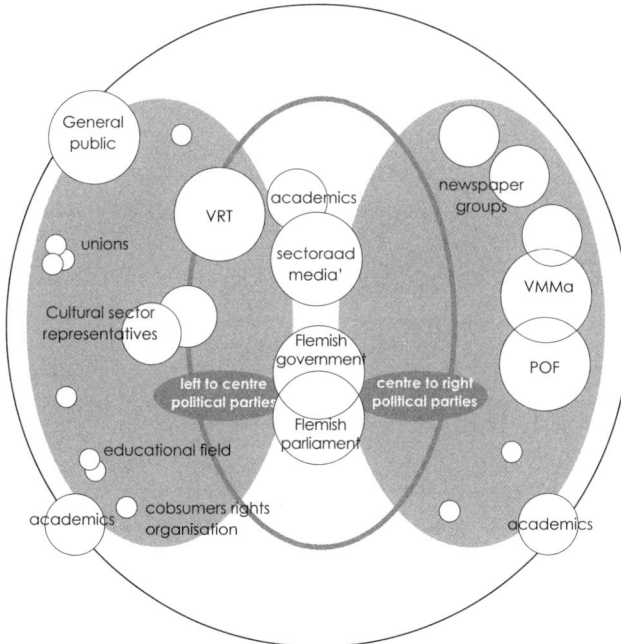

Note: Reconstruction based on Donders et al. 2010; document analysis; newspaper coverage of the management contract negotiations between October 2010 and July 2011; participatory observation with one of the authors be-ing a member of the Sectoral Council for Media and one of them acting as a consultant for the Flemish Cabinet of Media during the negotiations.

Table 1.   **Views of stakeholders on PSM and new management contract**

Stakeholder	View on PSB evolving into PSM	View on the democratic role in society	View on the management contract
VRT	PSM	Social responsibility	Status quo
Media Minister	PSM, no new media means terminal care for PSB	Social responsibility	Status quo
General public	PS(M)	Social responsibility, general satisfaction with VRT	Status quo
POF (private television alliance)	PSB(M), less critical of new media activities then newspapers	Market failure, though with acceptance of broad radio and television activities, asking for more regulation and less commercial revenues	Change, more rules on commercial communication
Newspaper groups	PSB, against online presence	Market failure, no need for VRT doing online news	Change, more rules on commercial communication and new media
VMMa	PSB(M), less critical of new media activities then newspapers	Market failure, though with acceptance of broad radio and television activities, asking for more regulation and less commercial revenues	Change, more rules on commercial communication
Socialist party (of which minister of media is part)	PSM, no new media means terminal care for PSB	Social responsibility, focus on diversity	Status quo
Christian Democrats (government party)	PS(M), new media, but also receptive for vision newspaper groups	Between social responsibility and market failure, focus on efficiency, transparency	Moderate change, focus on transparency and accountability
Fl Nationalists (government party)	PS(M), new media, but not a priority	Between social responsibility and market failure, focus on Flemish language, culture and identity	Moderate change, focus on output requirements regarding Flemish content
Parliament	PSB/M, divided with right wing parties being more critical of PSM and left wing parties in favor	Between social responsibility and market failure	From status quo, over moderate change, to change
Consumer rights group	PSM, but focus on radio and television	Social responsibility, focus on citizens, not politicians	Status quo
Media Council	PSM, though focus on constraints of digital activities	Between social responsibility and market failure (caused by the heterogeneous composition of the Council)	Moderate change, clarification of online remit
Cultural sector	PSM	Social responsibility, focus on culture, education, and participation	Status quo
Educational sector	PSM	Social responsibility, focus on education (but not 'school television')	Status quo
Trade unions	PSM	Social responsibility	Status quo

Markets first: Coalition 1

One of the two identified advocacy coalitions is composed of stakeholders that adhere to the market failure and technology determinist perspective on PSM. Unsurprisingly this coalition is comprised of private broadcasters and newspaper publishers and – although not entirely, or on all issues – right wing political parties.[1] Private broadcasters and newspaper publishers do not oppose the existence of public broadcasting in principle, or VRT as such, but question its scope of activities, its allegedly commercialised behaviour, and a reputed lack of control and transparency mechanisms. In sum, their essential position on the 2007-2011 contract was that, "the current management contract foresees an overly wide definition of the remit … it is not clear what the priorities are" (translated from Dutch; commercial television company VMMa in Donders et al 2010: 34).

Generalising to some extent, this *markets first* coalition, as we describe it, wanted a management contract that contains very specific provisions on what VRT can and cannot do, i.e. a clear definition and restriction of activities to what comprises the added public value of VRT. Specifically with regard to new media activities, such as mobile services and online (sports) news, they asked for a smaller role for VRT. New media services for public broadcasters are considered "accessory activities" (ibid: 34). This would warrant a more hesitant, cautious approach for VRT's role and presence in new media markets. Collecting commercial communication revenues (like bannering, pre-rolls, etc.) for online services is completely rejected (ibid: 89) and the corporate stakeholders in this advocacy coalition pleaded for an extensive *ex ante* test regime for any and every new service that would be "significant".

All corporate stakeholders in this coalition oppose the launch of a third, analogue (but also available as digital) television channel by VRT. At the time of negotiations, VRT had one generalist channel (*één*) and another, more targeted channel that was partly profiled as an information service for adults and partly as a children's channel (*Canvas* for information and *Ketnet* for children). The idea was to split these into separate channels, but maintaining the profile for each respecrtively in their own channels. As would be expected, private television company, VMMa, opposed that plan, arguing that an additional public service channel in an era of abundance was unnecessary, that they had invested considerable capital in children's programming, and that VRT already occupied a dominant position in the market for children's television.

They lost this fight, however, as the new management contract allows VRT to start the third channel. In part this victory for VRT was due to the Minister of Media's, Ms. Ingrid Lieten, desire to increase attention on youngster's needs in public service television, incorporating targeted television services (after 8pm on the children's channel) into a coherent multimedia strategy. However, the third channel for VRT was also very much a 'political' issue. Once the Minister said she was not against a third public television channel, it would have meant political defeat for her not to grant the channel because of political opposition from the other government parties. Again, this illustrates that the third channel not only became a reality because of perceived public value of the additional offer, but was also the result of real political bargaining.

The views of private broadcasters and newspaper publishers were to a large extent shared by the Christian-Democrat and Flemish nationalist political parties in government. However, at the end of negotiations these parties gave in, as is clear from the eventual contract that was agreed. The most plausible reason for this loosening of ties between stakeholders in the 'markets first' coalition is horse trading between the different political parties. Indeed, the VRT management contract was but one of the many issues the Flemish government had to deal with at the same time, and deals between the coalition's partners were made across policy issues. Newspapers reported on the Minister of Media paying a high price (with regards to other government issues) for a management contract that firmly recognises VRT as a public service media provider, that grants it a third television channel, and increases ceilings on commercial communication (Donders & Raats 2012).

As we will demonstrate next, to an important extent this 'markets first' coalition gave in to the *society first* coalition. The market-oriented discourse of the former coalition lost out to a public value argumentation of the latter, setting out as it did from the democratic value of PSM. This view was adhered to by those representing citizen interests (unions, educational field, public institutions in the cultural field, etc).

Society first: Coalition 2

Stakeholders favouring an elaborate public service media project (the public broadcaster, the socialist party, unions, cultural organisations, the educational field, etc.) were supported by the Flemish audience, a representative part of which was consulted in a study by Dhoest and colleagues (Doest et al. 2010). That study showed that over 90 per cent of Flemish citizens support a 'holistic' public service media project, and assign this responsibility firmly to VRT.

Flemings appeared more fond of radio and television services and less enthusiastic about new media activities, however. Only 40 per cent of respondents were of the opinion that VRT should encourage people to use new technologies, with as many being undecided and few being opposed. But this moderate percentage went up significantly when more specific questions on new technologies and new services were formulated. For example, 74 per cent considered online news a key task of VRT. The desire of Flemings to participate or interact was modest, however, with (only) 25 per cent expressing an eagerness to personally contribute to online services (Dhoest et al 2010: 72ff). Unfortunately there is no existing data of which we are aware with which we could compare the results. Overall, however, it is clear that Flemish support for new media activities was quite high when one takes into account that the survey was representative (in terms of sex, age group and socio-economic circumstances). Interestingly, while 74 per cent of respondents said public services should be distinctive in comparison with commercial offers, few accepted a market failure approach. A broad remit that also proivisions entertainment services alongside information and culture, was strongly and quite generally supported. Only 24 per cent of respondents thought a broad remit might cause market distortion; with 45 per cent manifestly disagreeing with that view (Dhoest et al 2010: 81).

Many stakeholders, including the public broadcaster, the socialist party, unions, cultural organisations, and the academic field used the results of the audience survey to support their arguments for VRT as a public service media provider. Largely, they made four points about the public value of VRT.

First, they argued that public service media were related to the wellbeing of democratic societies[2]:

> The citizen has to have access to objective information, which cannot always be guaranteed by private broadcasters whose operating revenues are commercial (Testaankoop, in Donders et al 2010: 32).

> A healthy and independent public broadcaster is crucial for the democratic functioning of society [because] it informs the citizen, provides for a variety of perspectives and opinions and creates a stage for engaging in a democratic debate (Socialist Union, ibid).

Second, VRT should have a comprehensive, multi-platform remit. Excluding VRT from particular platforms would mean as much as a 'death warrant' for the future of public service broadcasting in Flanders (Lieten 2010: 7). The 'society first' coalition favoured the evolution from public service broadcasting to public service media, considered to be a 'natural' evolution. To prohibit that evolution would amount to consigning PSB to 'terminal care'. Adhering instead to a technology neutral approach, VRT should be encouraged to reach all citizens on all relevant platforms. Certainly for children and youngsters this would need to include innovative new media services.

Third, the existence of VRT was seen as an assurance (and insurance) of quality, a key term in discussion on VRT's public value. The public broadcaster was expected to set the bar for all of Flemish radio, television and, increasingly, online quality standards. The cultural heritage centre, FARO, maintained that "without the public broadcaster, informative and cultural offers would diminish" (translated from Dutch by the authors, Donders et al 2010: 32). Although VRT has developed a quality assessment method, it is fair to say that this is a fairly qualitative assertion and not empirically substantiated.

Fourth, and actually more of an economic argument, most stakeholders in this coalition are convinced that a strong public broadcaster benefits all market players. Minister Lieten pushed this argument especially, saying that in new media markets public broadcasters are necessary to co-create consumer demand (Lieten 2010: 8). Again, no empirical evidence exists to substantiate this claim, at least in Belgium (see Lund & Lowe 2013 for more). One might reasonably assume that a player holding a 65 per cent market share in radio and a 40 per cent market share in television in a small media market such as Flanders has considerable market influence.

Thus although this 'society first' coalition emphasised public value arguments, it also interjected the economic value of public broadcaster VRT. This coalition explicitly rejected the market failure and market distortion discourse of the 'markets first' coalition, refusing downsizing scenarios for public service media and discursively supporting the notion that PSM has market strengthening effects (Lieten 2010: 7).

Social responsibility triumphs in Flanders – but loses the battle elsewhere in Europe

The 'society first' coalition had a definite, discernible impact on the management contract 2012-2016. This contract, first and foremost, confirms the status quo. VRT can continue its offer in radio, television and new media services. All radio brands are validated in the remit. This includes MNN, a multiplatform operation that includes an FM radio channel, digital radio, thematic digital radio, and other web-based services. MNN is popular with audiences and was heavily contested by the 'economics first' coalition. VRT's television activities are destined even with expansion with the government's approval for launching a third, analogue channel. Different from the former 2007-2011 contract, VRT's tasks in the online realm are specified in the contract, which now explicitly – albeit without much elaboration, which concerns private media companies – states that the delivery of online services is not merely accepted but is considered a public service obligation, operationalised through several quantitative and qualitative performance indicators.

Core public values appear to be important throughout the contract, in which very specific obligations can be found regarding information, culture and co-operation with the cultural sector, diversity and representation of minorities, and children and youngsters. The role of the public broadcaster in strengthening, rather than weakening, the market is reflected in several provisions. Co-operation with distribution companies, regional broadcasters, private broadcasters and newspaper publishers is encouraged. The quota obligation to invest 25 per cent of the television production budget in independent productions is maintained. At the same time, going against the 'economics first' coalition, the ceilings on commercial communication (including radio advertising, television sponsoring, product placement, and Internet sponsoring) are increased (Vlaamse Regering and VRT 2011; Donders & Van den Bulck 2012), which seems obviously intended to compensate for government funding that will not increase.

This reading could create the impression of a 'winner takes all' scenario for the 'society first' coalition. That would be inaccurate. The 'markets first' coalition saw some of its main concerns reflected in the new management contract. The remit is more clearly defined and operationalised, now with over 100 performance indicators. In addition, the new management contract introduces a stricter regime for any new services that VRT might desire to launch through 2016 and not covered by this management contract. Whereas the addendum to the previous management contract with regard to new media services was pragmatic, listing an exhaustive amount of services that were considered "not new" and leaving virtually no services that could be considered otherwise, the new management contract "finally" prescribes a full-fledged public value test. No full procedure has been developed yet, but categorising services as existing, new and grey zone categories (for the latter category a government assessment of a service's 'newness' is required) changes the approach considerably and makes an actual public value test of a new media service conceivable.

It is interesting to see how the 'society first' coalition was so successful in Flanders, whereas sister coalitions have largely lost the fight in other EU Member States, including the Netherlands and Germany. In the Netherlands, funding of public broadcasting organisations has been cut dramatically and their scope of activities is considerably smaller than the scope enjoyed by VRT today. In Germany, thousands of websites were de-published as a consequence of newspaper publishers' lobbying, and over 40 *ex ante* tests for signifcant new services have been conducted so far (Donders 2012; Donders & Pauwels 2010).

An explanation for this Flemish 'exception' can be argued on the basis of our advocacy coalition framework analysis, explained because ties between stakeholders in the 'society first' coalition were stronger and remained strong until the end of the negotiations on the management contract. Minister of Media Ingrid Lieten could, moreover, rely on a the strong support for VRT's activities and intentions among the Flemish public, evidence in the audience survey.

It is fair to say that the economic clout of the 'economics first' coalition is much bigger than that of the 'society first' coalition. Moreover and related, while stakeholders like cultural organisations, the educational field, and socio-economic actors were surveyed in the stakeholder consultation of the Sectoral Council for Media and expressed high confidence in and assigned a lot of value to public broadcaster VRT, they were certainly not part of the group of 'core' stakeholders (including private broadcasters and newspaper publishers) that discussed issues directly with government parties. Yet, ties in the 'economics first' coalition turned out to be rather loose by the end of the negotiations. The

Christian Democrats and Flemish nationalists in government, traditional allies of the corporate media sector, decided to trade their victory in non-media dossiers for a (small) 'victory' for the Minister in the VRT management contract dossier.

Conclusions: A battle won but the 'war' is far from over

The findings in this article show that despite a head start enjoyed by the 'economics first' coalition, the 'society first' coalition won the most recent battle in deciding the particulars of the 2012-2016 management contract between the Flemish government and public media operator VRT. The findings also show that the 'digital argument' is not what divides stakeholders in debates about public service media, at least in Belgium. Coalitions continue to split on traditional market versus society arguments, however disguised by shiny new digital gift wrapping. Put differently: the 'digital argument' is instrumental only in terms of arguing for more or less government intervention, and in that sense is important, but it is not an explanatory factor in the analysis of stakeholder positions undertaken in this study. In a similar vein, negotiations were highly subjective with different stakeholders arguing either in their own corporate interest, or with an eye on the achievement of normative values like diversity, pluralism, quality, etc.

Although VRT and Flemish citizens cannot complain about the outcome of the 2012-2016 management contract negotiations, it would be overconfident to assume the 'society first' coalition will continue to 'reign' in public service media discourse in the coming years. As private media companies are facing harsh economic times (being confronted with phenomena that are difficult or impossible to 'control', like catch-up television, declining advertising revenues, and Google News) they will be inclined to challenge the public broadcaster again – and repeatedly, we suspect. This means that proponents of public service media will have to build a stronger case for it (Picard 2012) and work continually at strengthening 'society first' coalitions. One can hardly rely on occasional dysfunction by the other coalition to win a war that still has plenty of fight left.

For the coming years it appears that the public value of public service media in Flanders has been reconfirmed. Its public value is accepted in the realms of information, culture and co-operation with the cultural sector, for diversity and representation of minorities, and services for children and youngsters. It has also been accepte that this public value extends to new public media services, not only in radio and TV broadcasting. However, recent debates in Flemish parliament, questioning the 'added' value of online news services of VRT – even and especially with regard to online news – not only echo critical voices in other national contexts but indicate that the proponents of Economics First have not given up and are playing a long game aimed at undermining support for and about the added value of public service media.

Notes

1. For broad European perspectives see Biggam (2011) and Wolswinkel (2011).
2. Quotes translated from Dutch by the authors.

References

Armstrong, M. & Weeds, H. (2007) Public service broadcasting in the digital world. In Seabright, P. & von Hagen, J. (eds.) *The Economic Regulation of Broadcasting Markets: Evolving Technology and Challenges for Policy.* Cambridge, UK: Cambridge University Press, pp. 81-149.

Appelman, M.; van Dijk, M.; Nahuis, R.; Vollaard, B. & Waagmeester, D. (2005) Een economisch vooronderzoek ten behoeve van het rapport van de WRR over de media. In van de Donk, W.B.H.J.; Broeders, D.W.J. & Hoefnagel, F.J.P.M. (eds.). *Trends in het medialandschap: vier verkenningen.* Amsterdam: WRR and Amsterdam University Press, pp. 11-66.

Bardoel, J. & Lowe, G.F. (2007) From public service broadcasting to public service media. The core challenge. In Lowe, G.F. & Bardoel, J. (eds.) *From Public Service Broadcasting To Public Service Media.* Göteborg: Nordicom, pp. 9-28.

Bardoel, J. & D'Haenens, L. (2008) Reinventing public service broadcasting in Europe: prospects, promises and problems. In *Media, Culture and Society* 30(3), pp. 337-355.

Bardoel, J. & D'Haenens, L. (2004) Media responsibilty and accountability: new conceptualizations and practices. In *Communications: the European Journal of Communication Research* 29(1), pp. 5-25.

Barnett, S. (2002) Which end of the telescope? From market failure to cultural value. In Cowling, J. & Tambini, D. (eds.) *From Public Service Broadcasting To Public Service Communications.* London: IPPR, pp. 34-45.

Biggam, R. (2011) Ex ante regulations, the EU and its Member States. Back to Brussels? In Donders, K. & Moe, H. (eds.) *Exporting the Public Value Test: The Regulation of Public Broadcasters' New Media Services Across Europe.* Göteborg: Nordicom, pp. 39-48.

Blakie, P. & Soussan, J.G. (2001) *Understanding Policy Processes.* Leeds: University of Leeds.

Dhoest, A.; Van den Bulck, H. Vandebosch, H. & Dierckx, M. (2010) *De publiek omroepdracht gewikt en gewongen: Publieksbevraging over de toekomstige taak van de VRT.* Antwerpen: Universiteit Antwerpen en Sectorraad Media.

Donders, K. (2012) *Public Service Media and Policy iIn Europe.* Basingstoke: Palgrave Macmillan.

Donders, K. & Raats, T. (2012) Analyzing national practices after European state aid control: are multi-stakeholder negotiations beneficial for public service broadcasting? In *Media Culture and Society* 34(2), pp. 162-180.

Donders, K. & Van den Bulck, H. (2012) *De VRT in de 21ste eeuw: overbodige luxe of maatschappelijke noodzaak?* (edited collection). Antwerpen: UAP.

Donders, K. & C. Pauwels (2010) The introduction of an ex ante evaluation for new media services: 'Europe' asks it or public broadcasters need it? In *International Journal of Media and Cultural Politics* 4(2), pp. 133-148.

Donders, K.; Raats, T.; Moons, A. & Walravens, N. (2010) *De toekomstige plaats en rol van de openbare omroep in Vlaanderen: Stakeholderbevraging.* Brussel: SMIT and Sectorraad Media.

Dwyer, T. & Martin, F. (2010) Updating diversity of voice arguments for online news media. In *Global Media Journal, Australian edition* 4(1) (published online: http://www.commarts.uws.edu.au/gmjau/v4_2010_1/dwyer_martin_RA.html).

Dyson, K. & Humphreys, P. (1988) *Broadcasting and New Media Policies In Western Europe.* London: Routledge.

Garnham, N. (1990) *Capitalism and Communication: Global Culture and the Economics of Information*. London: Sage Publications.

Humphreys, P. (2008) Globalization, Digital Convergence, De-regulatory Competition, Public Service Broadcasting and the 'Cultural Policy Toolkit': The Cases of France and Germany. Paper presented at the ECREA Conference, Barcelona, 28-29 November.

Hutchinson, D. (1999) *Media Policy: An Introduction*. London: Blackwell.

Jakubowicz, K. (2007) Public service broadcasting in the 21st century. What chance for a new beginning? In Lowe, G.F. & Bardoel, J. (eds.) *From Public Service Broadcasting To Public Service Media*. Göteborg: Nordicom, pp. 29-50.

Lieten, I. (2010) *Visienota: de VRT als uitdager en partner in het Vlaamse medialandschap*. Brussel: Vlaamse Regering.

Lowe, G.F. & Nissen, C.S. (2011) *Small Among Giants: Television Broadcasting in Smaller Countries*. Göteborg: Nordicom.

Lowe, G.F. (2010) *The Public in Public Service Media*, RIPE@2009. Göteborg, Nordicom.

Lowe, G.F. (2007) *The Role of Public Service Media for Widening Individual Participation in European Democracy*. Report for the Council of Europe's Group of Specialists on Public Service Media in the Information Society (MC – S – PSM), report H/Inf (2008) 12. Available for download at: http://www.coe.int/t/dghl/standardsetting/media/Doc/H-Inf(2008)012_en.pdf.

Lund, A.B. & Lowe, G.F. (2013) Current challenges to public service broadcasting in the Nordic countries. In Carlsson, U. (ed.) *Public Servcie Media from a Nordic Horizon: Politics, Markets, Programming and Users*. Göteborg: Nordicom, pp. 51-74.

Martin, F. (2002) Beyond public service broadcasting?: ABC online & the user. In *Citizen' Southern Review* 35(1), pp. 42-62.

McQuail, D.; de Mateo, R. & Tapper, H. (1992) A framework for analysis of media change in Europe in the 1990s. In Siune, K. & Truetzschler, W. (eds.) *Dynamics of Media Politics: Broadcast and Electronic Media In Western Europe*. London: Sage Publications, pp. 8-24.

Moe, H. (2008) Discussion forums, games and second life: exploring the value of public broadcasters' marginal online activities. In *Convergence: The International Journal of Research into New Media Technologies* 14(3), pp. 261-276.

Murdock, G. (2004) Building the Digital Commons: Public Broadcasting In The Age Of the Internet. Paper presented at the 2004 Spry Memorial Lecture, Montreal, 22 November.

Nord, L. (2012) Losing the battle, winning the war: Public service media in Scandinavia 2000-2010. In Lowe, G.F. & Steemers, J. (2012) *Regaining the Initiative for Public Service Media*, RIPE@2011. Göteborg: Nordicom, pp. 45-62.

Padovani, C. & E. Pavan (2011) Actors and interactions in global communication governance. In Mansell, R. & M. Raboy (eds.) *The Handbook of Global Media and Communication Policy*. Oxford: Wiley-Blackwell, pp. 543-563.

Peacock, A. (chairman of the committee) (1986) *Report Of the Committee On Financing the BBC*. London: Her Majesty's Stationary Office.

Picard, R. (2012) The changing nature of political case-making for public service broadcasters. In Lowe, G.F. & Steemers, J. (eds.) *Regaining the Initiative for Public Service Broadcasting*. Göteborg: Nordicom, pp. 27-44.

Puppis, M. (2008) National media regulation in the era of free trade: The role of global media governance. In *European Journal of Communication* 23(4), pp. 405-424.

Sabatier, P. & Jenkins-Smith, H. (1993) *Policy Change and Learning: An Advocacy Coalition Approach*. Boulder: Westview.

Sabatier, P. & Jenkins-Smith, H. (1999) The Advocacy Coalition Framework: An assessment. In Sabatier, P. (ed.). *Theories of the Policy Process*. Boulder: Westview, pp. 117-66.

Saeys, F. (2007) Statuut, organisatie en financiering van de openbare televisieomroep in Vlaanderen. In Dhoest, A. & Van den Bulck, H. (eds.) *Publieke televisie in Vlaanderen: Een geschiedenis*. Gent: Academia Press, pp. 23-52.

Steemers, J. & D'Arma, A. (2012) Evaluating and regulating the role of public broadcasters in the children's media ecology: The case of home-grown television content. In *International Journal of Media and Cultural Politics* 8(1), pp. 67-85.

Tracey, M. (1995) The role 2007 of listeners and viewers in the future of broadcasting. In Groombridge, B. & Hay, J. (eds.) *The Price of Choice: Public Service Broadcasting In a Competitive European Market Place.* London: John Libbey Publishing, pp. 124-127.

Van den Bulck, H. (2012) Towards a media policy process analysis Model and its Methodological Implications. In Just, N. & Puppis, M. (eds.) *Trends In Communication Policy Research. New Theories, Methods and Subjects.* Bristol/Chicago: Intellect. pp. 217-232.

Van den Bulck, H. (2008) Can PSB stake its claim in a media world of digital convergence? In *Convergence The International Journal of Research into New Media Technologies* 14(3), pp. 335-349.

Van den Bulck, H. (2001) Public service broadcasting and national identity as a project of Modernity. In *Media, Culture and Society* 23(1), pp. 53-69.

Vlaamse Regering and VRT (2006) *Beheersovereenkomst 2007-2011. Brussel: Vlaamse Regering.*

Vlaamse Regering and VRT (2011) *Beheersovereenkomst 2012-2016.* Brussel: Vlaamse Regering.

Wolswinkel, H. (2011) Publishers' fight for fair competition in the digital era. In Donders, K. & Moe, H. (eds.) *Exporting the Public Value Test: The Regulation of Public Broadcasters' New Media Services Across Europe.* Göteborg: Nordicom, pp. 145-154.

Chapter 9

Multi-stakeholderism
Value for Public Service Media

Minna Aslama Horowitz & Jessica Clark

> The varied problems PSM companies have today are most likely to find last-
> ing solutions through collaboration with people outside the firm, particularly
> those who are most intimate with their services and products. (Lowe 2010, 26)

In the past decade, redefinitions of what 'public' media means have begun to
emerge in a variety of contexts: from debates about the role of conventional
public television broadcasters in the digital 'era of plenty' (Ellis 2000); to the
possible public service functions of commercial media; to analysis of the function of new independent, Internet-based, not-for-profit media producers, and
the influence of user-generated, social media driven phenomena that may
indeed 'serve the public' or 'publics' (see, e.g., Clark & Horowitz 2013; Lowe
2010). Recently, a growing body of scholars has begun to study new media
ecologies from the perspective of *de jure* public service broadcasting [PSB] and
other public service media [PSM], as well as *de facto* public media that are not
institutionally designed and mandated to act in public service, but that do so
(Bajomi-Lazar et al, 2012). Their interest is in how these two broad categories
of media can create a truly vibrant and diverse democratic public sphere. In
addition, various research groups and networks have emerged to discuss public
interest media and 'public service communication' (Collins 2010; Iosifidis 2010).

These initiatives are not isolated scholarly pursuits. Since 2002 the growing RIPE network of PSM professionals and scholars has focused on the need
for reinvention of public service broadcasting strategies in the commercialising media landscape, defined by drastic technological changes. Similarly, the
U.S.-focused *Beyond Broadcast* conferences (2006-09), conceived by Harvard's
Berkman Center for Internet and Society, have aimed at bringing together
'legacy media' representatives with researchers and new media practitioners
in order to foster innovation and collaboration. The authors of this chapter
have been involved as organisers and shapers of these emerging public media
networks as researchers for the *Mapping Digital Media* initiative referenced

below, and as shapers of such participatory public media projects as Localore and the Public Media Corps. The analysis that follows is informed by their practice of the so called 'engaged scholarship' (see, e.g., Aufderheide & Clark 2009; Napoli & Aslama 2011).

When less than a decade ago European countries and EU legislation still struggled with indecisiveness and a multitude of approaches related to PSM digital mandates (e.g., Aslama & Syvertsen 2006), RIPE participants and others had already begun to rethink historic notions and possibilities for reinventing the public media enterprise for conditions in the 21st century. The motivating sentiment was never about competition or exclusivity. These discussions and networking opportunities deliberately pursued collaboration across pertinent borders – geographical, professional and institutional. The implicit quest has been to understand what the public value for all kinds of public media consists of in this new and very challenging media environment.

This chapter proceeds with the quest by suggesting a conceptual and normative approach to the public value of public media, and the role of PSM in the process. The framework suggested here is 'multi-stakeholderism'. The concept of multi-stakeholder collaboration has few precise definitions, but is often used in the context of international decision- and policy-making, as well as other forms of governance intended to counter elitist, centralised formations of power (see discussion, e.g., in Cammaerts 2011). 'Multi-stakeholderism' has an implicit promise of participation (Cammaerts 2011: 134) and, accordingly, the potential for the incorporation of more diverse perspectives and more publicly visible values. It is in the latter sense that multi-stakeholderism is used in this chapter – a concept denoting a participatory framework for diverse actors in and across the arenas where public media is being governed, produced, distributed, and consumed.

In addition to providing theoretical discussion about the forms and remits of PSM, this chapter draws on several empirical studies, most notably the comparative data gathering and analysis project of the Open Society Foundation's, *Mapping Digital Media* (MDM) project (2010-2013).[1] The MDM, as noted in the introduction of each of its country reports, assesses the global opportunities and risks that are created for media by digitalisation, including the growth of new media platforms as sources of news and the convergence of traditional broadcasting with telecommunications. MDM has addressed issues that are broadly relevant to PSM, from spectrum allocation to other legislative approaches, audience structures, and financial aspects of national media markets around the world. Furthermore, the project has produced special reports, and a designated section in each country report, about the role of publicly owned media. The results of comparative mapping of public media institutions over 40 countries is used in this chapter to contextualise the conceptual discussion of multi-stakeholderism and the role of PSM in that framework.

Finally, this chapter illustrates the interconnectedness of three circuits of power (Clegg 1989) that traditionally have not collaborated. These circuits are conceived as macro-level policy-making, institutional meso-level practices of media organisations, and micro-level participation of individuals and civic organisations. This chapter suggests that public value can better be created through diverse actors engaging with one another, across institutional borders, but that public media *de jure* can be a central catalyst in the process. The chapter concurs with Benington and Moore (2011) that the context in which social life is lived today requires a networked approach to governance of the public sector, and provision of services for the public, and thus depends on developing broadly inclusive processes and practices to ensure the best quality of life results for the legitimate collective interests of civil society in every country.

Context: Crossing borders

In many countries, PSM makers and distributors are in the process of transitioning, or have already crossed over, from broadcasting to other media platforms. There is urgent need to continue to reach out to new platforms and productive relationships. Although conventional PSB has been a strongly national project, the urgency of collaboration, inclusiveness and engagement with new partners is relevant to 'mature' PSM organisations in globalising marketplaces. It is equally important in contexts where state media are being transformed into public service media (e.g., former Eastern Europe, some Asian countries and many Latin American countries), or where public interest media (including PSB, community, and local media) face severe commercial competition and/or the need for revitalisation. Non-institutional public actors – from crowd-sourced projects such as *Wikipedia* and *Ushahidi*, to *Massive Online Open Courses* (MOOCs), advocacy and news efforts of local minorities via radio, as well as internet and mobile platforms (MDM India 2013, 62)[2] – embody 'public service functions' in media, such as emergency communications, free educational opportunities, and minority voice representation. In addition to cute cat videos and homemade hip hop clips, *YouTube* and *Soundcloud* offer culture from classic cinema to opera for anyone with access to the Internet.

As the MDM overview of EU countries[3] and the MDM USA report[4] highlight, in liberal democracies internet users have improved access to whistleblowers (most notably through online intermediaries such as *Wikileaks*), experts and alternative news sources, while institutional take-up of the web has made information held by public bodies and institutions more widely and readily available. Digitalisation and widespread domestic internet access, together with lowered software production and distribution costs, have led to innovative methods of information gathering and sharing that include wikis, social networking, and crowdsourcing. They also expand capacities for storing, indexing and securing the raw material of investigative reports. Furthermore, digital media networks, platforms and tools have reduced the costs of dissemination, enabling controversial issues too often ignored or neglected by generalist legacy media to find a home in journalistic blogs and online-only news sites.

But who should be expected to provide these functions that are clearly 'in the public interest'? In recent years, numerous initiatives outside the orbit of institutional PSM are addressing concerns at the heart of those organisations' remits. Non-institutional actors promote diversity of access, ownership, content, and participation. Such endeavours include 'media reform' and 'media justice' projects and organisations, large and small. Some well-known initiatives include the activist/advocacy umbrella organisation *Free Press* (U.S.)[5], not-for-profit journalism projects from *OhMyNews*[6] to *ProPublica*[7], and global community/ alternative media collectives such as *OurMedia*[8] and *Global Voices*[9].

This is not to imply less need for or relevance of institutional provision of public services in media. Nations and national-regional institutions continue to support PSM *de jure*. Although the purpose of PSM in national media landscapes differs greatly between countries (e.g., Iosifidis 2012)[10], as do conceptual questions about PSB / PSM as well as perceptions regarding what is appropriate to the remit, the significance of these institutions in creating public value continues to matter. To understand the scope of the discussion on public media *de jure* around the world, a total of 42 Mapping Digital Media country reports[11] were reviewed for this chapter. The MDM project, one of the most extensive comparative empirical studies of media systems and markets ever undertaken, is a descriptive, partly quantitative but largely qualitative account of the current state and the impact of digitalisation of communications in many countries. MDM's emphasis is on assessing the nature and impact of media-related problems. For our purposes here the most important aspect is to assess the extent to which public media *de jure* is understood to be in crisis, or at least in trouble, in different countries and to grow a deeper understanding of the role of public media *de facto* in those countries.

A basic survey of *Mapping Digital Media* (MDM) country reports makes it quite clear that the assessment of the status and future of PSM is generally agreed to be a core challenge in about half of the researched nations. Figure 1 depicts the full suite of digital media challenges most often identified in MDM reports. The report template[12] includes specific questions about the provision and status of public media, so it is no surprise that PSM is mentioned as a challenge in 20 out of 42 reports. At the same time, the figure highlights other problems in which public media *de facto* has a stake: policy debates about media concentration, the provision of quality journalism, press freedom, the visibility of minority voices, and so forth. All of that and more is closely linked to the ideal and practices of conventional PSM.

Figure 1.   Media-Related challenges in MDM countries

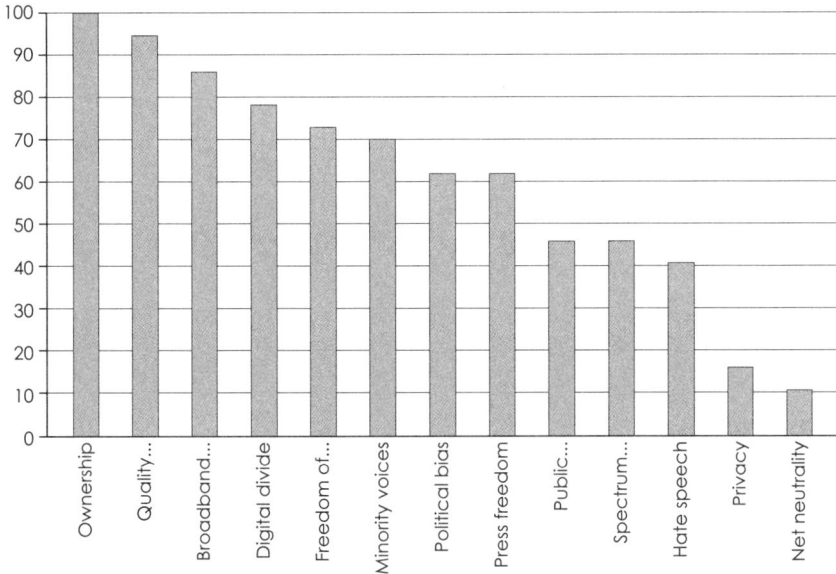

Note: % of the reports, N=42

The public media organisations of the 42 countries that were assessed are not directly comparable. Media systems and policies differ, as do the cultures of different countries. Yet, there are some general observations that emerge from the MDM mapping effort and one of the key findings is that PSM still matters to many citizens. This is perhaps unexpected good news. Only three years ago Richard Collins (2010: 53-54) reiterated the fear of many scholars since the 1990s that traditional PSB institutions would "dumb down" their output by following similar strategies to their commercial competitors, hence corroding their distinctiveness and legitimacy. MDM study results don't confirm that as the characteristic reality.[13] MDM reports suggest that especially in countries with a long public service tradition, PSM content remains respected and trusted. This positive image of PSM institutions, in terms of providing depth, trustworthiness, and diversity of content, is also present in a European-wide survey of over 800 'media experts' from 34 countries (Popescu 2011: 53-59).

Many MDM reports highlight that institutional PSM should play a role in ensuring the public value of communication domestically, and in many cases does that. For example, while internet activism as well as diverse forms of *de facto* public media are growing, they seldom last very long unless they are attached to an established institution. As one MDM report notes, "these campaigns needed to attract the attention of mainstream media, in essence becoming news, before they could generate wider public support beyond the internet-savvy, but fragmented, activist groups" (MDM Hungary 2012: 8).[14] The challenges of providing public service functions and characteristics, such as universal access to reliable, relevant, educative content that recognises diversity and minority voices, are exponential in contexts from Kazakhstan to Kenya – where PSB or any other forms of public media barely exist, exist only nominally, or are perceived as state-controlled media.

Several MDM reports underscore a need for public service organisations to secure a social contract, an agreement of trust and social responsibility between *de jure* PSM and its audiences, as well as between the new, often online entrants – be they services, platforms, application providers, or even event organisers and individual content-makers. When fragmentation is coupled with approximate infinite supply, PSM can take the role of a hub. These reports suggest that there is both need for and opportunity to rethink the public value of public service in media. The MDM Croatia report (2012: 34-35)[15] suggests that the greatest opportunity for the national public broadcaster lies in developing new media content and interactive services in order to grow audiences (op cit., 35). To take a second example, the MDM Colombia Report (2012: 6)[16] observes that "[There is] a moment of opportunity to review and rethink the duties and obligations of public television in light of the educational and cultural value of public media." Collins (2010: 54) seems to have been right in his expectation that "internet based content provides potentially greater opportunities … to extend, pluralise and deepen provision of public service content beyond what public service broadcasters provide". All of that, as this chapter argues, requires a systematic multi-stakeholder, approach.

Model: A multi-stakeholder approach to collaboration

Multi-stakeholder collaboration as a governance model has increased in popularity (Ansell & Gash 2008). This kind of collaboration is necessitated by problems that are complex, involve interdependent actors, and require cooperation with non-state actors (Markopoulos et al. 2012; Benington & Moore 2011). Given the magnitude of media landscape shifts that create new challenges for guaranteeing the public value of public service media, how should we should conceptualise, support, regulate and pay for this ever-broadening field of PSM? How could new public value be created via PSM-public media and other relationships?

Multi-stakeholder modelling provides an analytical framework for understanding not only competing theories about the value of public media, but a template for collaborative analysis and action. The very idea of collaboration is at the core of multi-stakeholderism. Collaboration is here understood in a broad sense, not only in terms of public service media governance but also with regard to how PSM is produced, distributed, and consumed. In addition, most theorising around the concept points to either an instrumental or a process-based rationale for collaboration (Markopoulos et al. 2012): The former stresses improved outcomes due to participants sharing diverse expertise; the latter posits that the process of collaboration is desirable to enhance commitment and ownership of the issues in question. Given that relationships between PSM and other parties can be formal or 'fragile' (see Raats et al. in this volume), not only instrumental but also process-based motivations for multi-stakeholderism are important. The focus is on creating collaborative relationships that foster ownership of the public value that PSM can create.

Multi-stakeholder modelling has been used, for instance, in tracing techno-logical diffusion in media industries by mapping developments in organisa-tional, industrial and environmental levels (Shin et al. 2006). And, as Van den Bulck (2012: 219) notes, media policy analyses tend to be stakeholder analyses becasue "a policy decision is implicitly or explicitly considered as the result of a process characterised by the formulation of different views and interests expressed by actors or stakeholders..." For example, internet governance is often explicitly discussed in the framework of multi-stakeholder interests (e.g., ITU 2013; de La Chapelle 2007).

The field of media management has also embraced the concept of multi-stakeholderism over the last decade. McQuail (2000) discussed the many 'pres-sures' that a media organisation faces from actors, ranging from competitors, news agencies, owners, and unions, to those with legal and political control; from diverse lobby groups to distributors and audiences. McQuail's idea was not to model collaboration and participation between these actors as we intend in this chaper, but rather to depict how three stakeholder groups within a media organisation (management, content producers, and technical experts) react to outside pressures. His model highlights the interest groups that have a stake in a media organisation's decisions. Stakeholder analysis has also been applied to media ethics (Stern 2008), the operation of news organisations (Adams-Bloom & Cleary 2009) and, recently, to PSM management (Kraus & Karmasin 2013). As Donders & Van den Bulk show in this volume, multi-stakeholderism can be detected in the specific national case of Belgium and its public service media organisation, VRT.

The model proposed here seeks to conceptualise the idea of multi-stakehold-er collaboration for a diverse public media landscape. Following Clegg (1989), the model entails three 'circuits of power' evident in participation in public media issues: 1) The circuit of structural issues (macro), 2) the institutional circuit of public service organisations (meso), and 3) the micro-level circuit of individuals participating in civil society. The model we apply was originally developed by Aslama & Napoli (2010) in work undertaken to reconceptualise audiences in media policymaking and to envision a strategic model for PSM

(Aslama 2010). Fuentes-Bautista (2011) has since used it to map different forms and modalities of participation in networked media environments.

The structural, or macro-level arena entails the forums of policy-making and PSM regulation, as well as other governance questions that stipulate how PSM can function. The meso-level circuit of institutions involves the operations of public media organisation, i.e. production and distribution of content and services. The micro-level circuit is associated with varied roles that individuals have in civil society, whether framed as audiences, individual content creators, members of networks or other collaborative constructs engaged in media-making. It is crucial to understand that these power circuits are interrelated in the model; that the practice is dialogic:

1. Structural policy questions set the stage for public media to exist and flourish;

2. Conventional PSM and public media organisations may draw inspiration from community media practices;

3. Media activism and advocacy may influence policy-making and increase public awareness of issues pertinent to public media.

More broadly, based on Clegg's (op cit.) idea of (organisational) power circuits, the model also emphasises the power and potential of different levels to act 'in the public interest'. Traditionally, these separate circuits operate within their own contexts, rules and practices. Yet, the normative implication here is that they overlap in terms of their attempts to create public value, and hence should actively collaborate.

Circuits of collaboration

If public service media *de jure* is indeed still in demand and valued (as the MDM reports apparently validate), the multi-stakeholder model can point out the arenas in which PSM can either become more active, and where they could enable more participatory possibilities for other stakeholders. The idea of circuits of stakeholders working in collaboration offers several outlooks on how different constituencies contribute to different forms of public media – both *de jure* and *de facto*. For example, it may help in analysing entire media systems and their collaborative traditions; that is, how different actors together govern, produce, distribute – and facilitate consumption of – media. In addition, it may illustrate how different individual experiments and efforts engage different circuits of stakeholders as a key characteristic explaining success, or failure.

Our discussion and examples of stakeholder collaboration are focused on the Western context where there are strong institutional public service institutions and long traditions, and also highlight several examples from the U.S. where the multi-stakeholder collaborations with *de jure* and *de facto* realms of public media have been systematically fostered by specific projects. This is not to downplay other contexts that might include a vibrant *de facto* public media, but rather to face challenges in terms of *institutional* public service – the essential focus for our work here.

The examples highlight explicit recognition of, and systematic efforts in, multi-stakeholder collaboration. Today these are more typical to pluralist media ecosystems where public media ideas and ideals are part of the traditional view of the media's role in a society. At the same time, new forms of what could be called public media seem to 'just happen' in the sphere of Web 2.0, emerging from not-for-profit, open access, participatory media forms on varied platforms. These media projects and platforms arise from a wide variety of felt needs and philosophies, ranging from an impulse to express previously excluded viewpoints and minority perspectives, to a valuation of 'open source' culture and production as a viable alternative to top-down editorial methods, to commitment to a free speech ethos. Collaboration is also being experimented with in the meso-level circuit by conventional media institutions, and being mapped and documented by collaborative research efforts. Although relatively few macro-level circuits of policy-making directly foster collaboration for public media, policy issues and regulatory moves can still be discussed within the framework as inspirations or implicit practices that support such goals.

Micro-level: Social media-driven collaboration

Social media is rapidly changing public media ecosystems, especially in terms of journalism, that most trusted-quality product of Western public media organisations. Most Mapping Digital Media (MDM) research reports discussed in this chapter indicate, for example, that Twitter is now a common route to finding news stories and has an important role in defining ('trending') public debates.[17] Albeit not always the most important or trusted news source for media consumers, social media platforms and peer recommendations are more markedly important in the U.S. where the institutional PSM presence has always been much weaker than in Europe.[18] Network scholars such as Benkler (2012) and Shirky (2011),[19] suggest that popular participatory social media sites may, beyond acting as news hubs, serve as more effective tools for informing and capturing public debates than broadcast or print outlets.

Shirky (op cit.) calls this phenomenon 'cognitive surplus': the innate desire for sharing and participation that inspires fast and innovative solutions for communication. As he indicates, not every blog or Tweet has public value, but many forms of participation, from fundraising to crisis mapping, are intended to create just that – to inform, help and engage people for the good of the public and as a public good. Arguably, this kind of public value is potentially fragile. As many MDM reports (2010-2013) indicate, alternative media production, digital activism, and citizen journalism tend to wane without institutional anchoring. Collaborative, partly crowd-sourced efforts in content creation like *localore.net*[20] in the U.S., funded by the Corporation for Public Broadcasting and private foundations, are examples of the possibilities for local and networked communities to co-create original content and thereby strengthen the local community's participation – things that clearly have public value.

Meso-level: Conventional media organisations

Conventional, institutional public service media in the West have in the digital era been engaging people in processes and projects for production of content and commentary (see e.g. Aslama & Syvertsen 2006). One often cited example is the BBC's citizen journalism efforts such as *Have Your Say*.[21] However, public service media in countries with a long tradition of PSB are facing growing pressures from the perceived unfair advantage and over-extension of their remits (Schlosberg 2013).[22] Public broadcasters in many Western European countries, such as YLE in Finland, have faced opposition not only from commercial broadcasters but also from the newspaper industry (which today includes broadcasting operations, as is the case with Sanoma Group) in developing new participatory online and mobile services.[23]

In the U.S., audiences of non-profit public networks (PBS in TV and NPR in radio) have always participated in funding those institutions by making donations (to become 'members'). The continuing importance of localism in American electronic media (not only geographical but also issue, interest and community-driven), is in response to challenges created by chain format radio and economic pressures on the local press in many localities. This has fuelled support especially for public radio, which has also had more freedom to experiment with participatory, co-operative and collaborative approaches to programming as it lacks the commercial pressures of consolidation (Stavitsky & Huntsberger 2010). Some recent innovative U.S. examples include collaborative *Local Journalism Centers*,[24] which pool resources and reporting among regional clusters of public broadcasters, *National Public Radio's Argo* project[25] which supported a clutch of bloggers at local radio stations, each assigned to a particular beat; and the *Public Media Corps*[26] a DC-based media literacy project which the *Center for Social Media* helped to incubate and document.[27]

As the MDM report on the USA highlights (2011)[28], public, educational and government (PEG) access channels of cable TV can be seen as ideological forerunners of *YouTube*. Today, PEG and community stations are working to reposition themselves as hubs for digital literacy and journalism training, and points of broadband access for those who can't otherwise afford it. Community media has also played a critical role in media access and diversity in Canada, Australia, New Zealand and the Pacific, influencing both the form and content of mainstream media (Forde, Foxwell & Meadows 2009; Meadows et al 2008; Robie 2009).

Macro-level: Policy-driven collaboration

Historically, multi-stakeholder participation has been grassroots-driven. Activist and advocacy groups especially in the U.S., but also elsewhere, have worked relentlessly at the grassroots level to influence the macro-level on decisions taken about media ownership, content and access, sometimes with significant impact (e.g., McChesney 2007).

Recent attempts to cultivate multi-stakeholder dialogue, debate and governance have been initiated, or embraced afterwards, by formal governance bodies, evident for example with regard to internet governance and digital rights (e.g., the *Internet Governance Forum*, and the current EU stakeholder dialogue on copyrights[29]). Public service media have received less attention from decision-makers focus on multi-stakeholder dialogue. In its 2009 report on the future of PSM governance, the Council of Europe did suggest exploring the de facto networks for governance models; they suggested that multi-stakeholder participation for PSM could model itself after *Facebook*'s user panels, pursue transparency and support direct voting (CoE 2009: 32-33).[30] Yet little concrete action has emerged in response. A sign of support for a generally more robust public media ecology and broader participation is more evident in the way the European Union has addressed community media. As stated in a resolution of the European Parliament in 2008: "[C]ommunity media fulfil[s] a broad yet largely unacknowledged role in the media landscape, particularly as a source of local content, and encourage[s] innovation, creativity and diversity of content".[31] This is echoed by the findings of the Europe-wide MDM overview (2012: 1)[32]: "EU-level funding initiatives should support new models of investigative journalism, as well as local and minority media".

Currently there are questions about future broadband access and spectrum allocation that significantly raise the policy stakes, given the participatory requirements of digital citizenship and political possibilities of online production, consumption and distribution. Decision-makers are beginning to consult civic groups and invite citizens to comment on digital media policies and implementation. A prime example is the new EU instrument called the European Citizens' Initiative (ECI) for online campaigning EU-wide. One of the first initiatives is a campaign for media pluralism.[33]

Discussion: Collaboration and shared values

Creativity is fuelled by diversity and PSM companies need to reorient from their PSB heritage to invite, encourage, and actively facilitate the participation of the public in order to guarantee the richest, most embedded context of diversity Lowe (2010: 26).

Diverse organizations, *de jure* and *de facto*, as well as public media activists and regulators, share many goals and values: including a desire to foster diversity of media ownership in commercially driven or mixed markets, to secure diversity of voices, and to provide universal access to content. While the definitions and forms of public media may be continuously evolving in the digital era, the core purposes have not changed with developments in online and mobile platforms. However the task of forging alliances is certainly complex, and increasingly so, and the model we present is only a starting point in the work necessary to identify opportunities for new, hybrid public media relationships that build on the public value of PSB in the PSM environment.

The model of stakeholder arenas depicted in this chapter is not unproblematic. More work is needed to clarify how circuits function: Who is included and who is excluded? How is the credibility of different actors established, and also the boundaries of both editorial and financial power? Defining particular public media stakeholders can be a daunting task akin to mission impossible when potential audiences of a digital platform can span the globe (Adams-Bloom & Cleary 2009: 3). As noted earlier, the concept of multi-stakeholderism has been created in opposition to insular concentrations of power and those are inherently difficult to penetrate, break or reconfigure.

For example, the structural level or media policy-making is still very much the business of the chosen few who are supposed to act as representatives of diverse national and/or international interests, but in practice are often tied to corporate or party-political interests. This is precisely the reoccurring critique of the *Internet Governance Forum*. The non-governmental parties may perhaps voice their concerns, but are they given true participatory power? (Maciel & de Souza 2011). Similarly, media reform campaigns tend to be reactionary emergency calls from a civil society in response to types of crises (funding, legitimacy, etc) rather than co-ordinated collaborative efforts to solve problems and decide upon future actions.

Regardless of how these questions are resolved in various national settings, news consumption, civic engagement and education habits will undoubtedly continue to evolve. For those who straddle the meso-level worlds of traditional public service broadcasting and multifaceted new forms of public service media, it seems clear that embracing new kinds of interdependent practice including citizen production and participation can only make public media more interesting, engaging, diverse, creative and relevant. Admittedly, this has so far proved much more difficult to implement in mature digital markets. At the same time, many MDM reports (2010-2013) highlight that in many media ecosystems with state media, or PSM 'in-transition', public media *de facto* functions as the counter-force to what is often perceived (and often is) limited, controlled media content. For emerging public media organisations that want to establish themselves, it may be hard to engage independent, networked initiatives in participation.

In terms of grassroots collaboration, the challenge is for small, vulnerable actors to be able to maintain diversity and vibrancy while gaining wider visibility and achieving sustainability and longevity. Viral trends come and go. As noted in the beginning, institutional PSM is still a brand in Western Europe (as well as in Australia, Japan, and newer contexts like Thailand, where it challenges state media). And as several MDM reports (2010-2013) show, most successful, sustainable digital participatory practices and activities benefit from an institutional backing and affiliation.

Multi-stakeholderism and its practices in application to public service media and an emphasis on developing public value clearly need further scrutiny and much more empirical analyses. Given the challenges of the current media landscape and the role of PSM in diverse contexts, it is clear that more systematic, empirically informed and nuanced scholarly work is needed to understand complexities, identify problems and connections, and develop alternatives and options. We concur with Hilde Van den Bulck (2012: 229) who posited, when discussing the importance of multi-stakeholderism as a concept for media policy research, that:

> The development of media policies seems to be becoming more complicated through shifts from traditional state policy-making to governance and even multi-governance and through an exponential growth in potential stakeholders. Disentangling and analyzing this intricate web is becoming ever more important yet also more complex.

This does not mean that media researchers should vet on these questions as the ultimate experts. Multi-stakeholderism applies here, as well. Especially for communications and media research, questions about social justice require repositioning the conventional, 'objective' Ivory Tower approach in the academy and beginning to establish principles of engaged scholarship for academically rigorous, yet applicable and compassionate work. Universities, too, have been elitist institutions in many instances, at least in the sense that the information they produce often is not very accessible for very many. This is one important reason explaining the scepticism among other stakeholders regarding the relevance of scholarly work. The communications field – relatively new, still relatively undefined, and also rather typically at the lower end of the pecking order in the academic firmament – has long faced difficulties in justifying its existence and value. We contend that the field is gaining fresh momentum, however, precisely because a growing reliance on multidisciplinary approaches. Better suited for multi-stakeholder collaboration by experience and structures, communications and media scholars can help other stakeholders create more value for PSM (Napoli & Aslama 2011).

Despite the challenges and need for more examples, the multi-stakeholder model is useful for discussion and development in perspectives about where public media *de jure* stands and ought to stand in today's media ecosystem. The model doesn't imply that the role of PSM has diminished. It highlights collaborative possibilities while explicitly recognising the different kinds of value created by media and through their interaction with diversity at many levels and in diverse aspects (see Hasebrink 2012: 63). Each circuit in the multi-stakeholder model – micro, meso, and macro – can be assessed in terms of the value of media content and services to and for many and diverse individuals, and more than that for a social collective. Do media policies support variety, pluralism and diversity in what is produced by public media, and that members of 'the audience' can co-create a diverse range of content? Is social value safeguarded, and how, to identify, even police, misinformation, harmful content and trampling on the human rights of a public? And finally, how is public value in the promotion of democracy and support for cultural diversity and vitality both envisioned and realised? That has clearly been a traditional cornerstone of PSB *de jure* and is arguably crucial for PSM *de jure*, as well.

Based on the MDM findings discussed in this chapter, it seems that in many countries this is specifically the position that PSM is still expected to take, to reclaim or to achieve in the first place. But in a media ecosystem where stakeholders continue to multiply, this task is loftier and more complex than before. Arguably, the idea of multi-stakeholderism suggests that optimal public value would be created when a PSM organisation engages with and thereby mobilises different and diverse stakeholders, doing so not only in content production or networked protests, but rather more deeply in the creation and implementation of a set of values that benefit the public as such.

Notes

1. See: mappingdigitalmedia.org (retrieved 12 October 2013).
2. www.opensocietyfoundations.org/reports/mapping-digital-media-india (Retrieved 20 May 2013).
3 http://www.opensocietyfoundations.org/sites/default/files/Mapping_Digital_Media_EU_20121217_0.pdf (Retrieved 20 May 2013).
4. http://www.opensocietyfoundations.org/reports/mapping-digital-media-united-states (Retrieved 20 May 2013).
5. http://www.freepress.net/ (Retrieved 20 May 2013).

6. http://international.ohmynews.com/ (Retrieved 20 May 2013).
7. http://www.propublica.org/ (Retrieved 20 May 2013).
8. http://www.ourmedia.org/ (Retrieved 20 May 2013).
9. http://globalvoicesonline.org/ (Retrieved 20 May 2013).
10. http://www.opensocietyfoundations.org/sites/default/files/mapping-digital-media-digital-television-public-interest-and-european-regulation-20120312.pdf (Retrieved 20 May 2013).
11. Albania, Argentina, Bosnia, Bulgaria, Chile, China, Colombia, Croatia, Estonia, France, Germany, Hungary, India, Italy, Japan, Kazakhstan, Kenya, Latvia, Lebanon, Lithuania, Macedonia, Malaysia, Mexico, Moldova, Morocco, Netherlands, Nigeria, Pakistan, Peru, Poland, Romania, Russia, Serbia, Slovakia, Slovenia, South Africa, Spain, Sweden, Thailand, Turkey, United Kingdom, and United States. Several other country reports were in the process of being published in the late summer and autumn of 2013; see, mappingdigitalmedia.org (retrieved 20 May 2013).
12. See: http://www.opensocietyfoundations.org/publications/mapping-digital-media-research-template (retrieved 29 September 2013).
13. Some studies show that in terms of programming strategies, in today's digital era of channel plentitude, there exists more of a division of labour between commercial and non-commercial channels, rather than competition by "more of the same" (see summary discussion, e.g., in Aslama 2008).
14. www.opensocietyfoundations.org/reports/mapping-digital-media-hungary (Retrieved 20 May 2013).
15. www.opensocietyfoundations.org/reports/mapping-digital-media-croatia (Retrieved 12 October 2013).
16. www.opensocietyfoundations.org/reports/mapping-digital-media-colombia (Retrieved 20 May 2013).
17. See, mppingdigitalmedia.org (Retrieved 4 September 2013).
18. See, e.g., The Pew research report http://stateofthemedia.org/2012/mobile-devices-and-news-consumption-some-good-signs-for-journalism/what-facebook-and-twitter-mean-for-news/ (Retrieved 20 May 2013). http://www.scribd.com/doc/99630943/Germany-Mapping-Digital-Media
19. See also the analysis by Yochai Benkler at The Guardian: Blueprint for Democratic Participation, presentation from the Guardian Activate Summit 2012. http://fora.tv/2012/05/03/The_Guardian_Blueprint_for_Democratic_Participation. (Retrieved 20 May 2013).
20. http://localore.net (Retrieved 12 October 2013).
21. http://www.bbc.co.uk/news/have_your_say/ (Retrieved 29 September 2013).
22. Unpublished presentation at the IAMCR Conference in Dublin 25-29 June, 2013: Mapping Digital Media in Europe: The sustainability of public interest news
23. See, e.g., http://www.hs.fi/english/article/Decision+on+funding+for+Finnish+Broadcasting+Company+to+be+made+next+week/1135248662900 (Retrieved 12 October 2013).
24. http://www.centerforsocialmedia.org/future-public-media/public-media-showcase/cpb-funded-local-journalism-centers-grow-fits-and-starts (Retrieved 20 May 2013).
25. http://www.npr.org/blogs/inside/2010/09/09/129755091/-argo-npr-s-blog-network-sets-sail (Retrieved 20 May 2013).
26. http://publicmediacorps.org/ (Retrieved 20 May 2013).
27. http://www.cmdn.tv/ (Retrieved 20 May 2013).
28. http://www.opensocietyfoundations.org/reports/mapping-digital-media-united-states (Retrieved 20 May 2013).
29. http://ec.europa.eu/licences-for-europe-dialogue/en (Retrieved 20 May 2013).
30. Public Service Media Governance: Looking into the Future. Media and Information Society Division. Directorate General of Human Rights and Legal Affairs. www.coe.int/t/dghl/standardsetting/media/doc/PSMgovernance_en.pdf (Retrieved 12 October 2013).
31. European Parliament resolution of 25 September 2008 on Community Media in Europe (2008/2011(INI)), (2010/C 8 E/14) http://eurlex.europa.eu/JOHtml.do?uri=OJ:C:2010:008E:SOM:EN:HTML (Retrieved 20 May 2013).
32 http://www.opensocietyfoundations.org/sites/default/files/Mapping_Digital_Media_EU_20121217_0.pdf (Retrieved 20 May 2013).

33. See: http://ec.europa.eu/citizens-initiative/public/welcome. Other initiatives include the Finn-ish otakantaa.fi website set up by the Ministry of Justice, and its call in 2006 to comment on the future of public broadcasting; the recent Levenson Inquiry in the U.K., see http://www.levesoninquiry.org.uk/ (Retrieved 4 October 2013).

References

Adams-Bloom, T. & Cleary, J. (2009) Staking a claim for social responsibility: An argument for the dual responsibility model. *The International Journal on Media Management, 11*(1), pp. 1-8.

Ansell, C. & Gash, A. (2008) Collaborative governance in theory and practice. *Journal of Public Administration Research and Theory, 18*(4), pp. 543-571.

Aslama, M. (2010) Rethinking audiences: Diversity, participation and strategic considerations for public media in the Web 2.0 era. In Lowe, G.F. (ed.) *The Public in Public Service Media*, RIPE@2009. Göteborg: Nordicom, pp. 87-100.

Aslama M. & Syvertsen T. (2006) Policies of reduction or renewal? European public service broadcasting in the new media era. In Carlsson, U. (ed.) *Radio, TV & Internet in the Nordic Countries: Meeting the Challenges of New Media Technology.* Göteborg: Nordicom, pp. 29-41.

Aufderheide, P. & Clark, J. (2009) *Public Media 2.0: Dynamic, Engaged Publics.* Washington, DC: Center for Social Media, School of Communication at the American University.

Bajomi-Lazar, P., Stetka, V. & Sukosd, M. (2012) Public service television in European Union coun-tries: Old issues, new challenges in the 'East' and the 'West'. In Just, N. & Puppis, M. (eds.), *Trends in Communication Policy Research: New Theories, Methods and Subjects.* Bristol: IntellectBooks, pp. 355-380.

Benington, J. & Moore, M.H. (2011) *Public Value Theory and Practice.* Basingstoke, UK: Palgrave Macmillan, pp. 1-30, 256-274.

Cammaerts, B. (2011) Power dynamics in multi-stakeholder policy processes and intra–civil society networking. In Mansell, R. & Raboy, M. (eds.) *The Handbook of Global Media and Commu-nication Policy,* Oxford: Wiley-Blackwell, pp. 131-147.

Clark, J. & Horowitz, M.A. (2013) Remixing public media's remit: Networking stakeholders across borders. In Glowacki, M. & Jackson, L. (eds.) *Creativity, Innovation and Interaction: Public Media Management Fit for the 21st Century.* London & New York: Routledge.

Clegg, S. (1989) *Frameworks of Power.* London: SAGE Publications.

Collins, R. (2010) From public service broadcasting to public service communication. In Lowe, G.F. (ed.) *The Public in Public Service Media*, RIPE@2009. Göteborg: Nordicom, pp. 53-69.

De La Chapelle, B. (2007) Towards Multi-Stakeholder Governance –
The Internet Governance Forum as Laboratory. In Kleinwächter, W. (ed.) *The Power of Ideas: In-ternet Governance in a Global Multi-Stakeholder Environment* pp. 265-271. Berlin: Marketing für Deutschland.

Ellis, J. (2000) *Seeing Things: Television in the Age of Uncertainty.* London: I.B. Tauris.

Forde, S. Foxwell, K. & Meadows, M. (2009) *Developing Dialogues: Indigenous and Ethnic Com-munity Media Broadcasting in Australia.* London: Intellect.

Hasebrink, U. (2012) The role of audience within media governance: The neglected dimension of media literacy. *Media Studies, 3*(6), pp. 58-73.

Hindman, M. (2009) *The Myth of Digital Democracy.* Princeton, NJ: Princeton University Press.

Iosifidis, P. (2010) *Reinventing Public Service Communication: European Broadcasters and Beyond.* Basingstoke: Palgrave Macmillan.

ITU (2013) *Supporting Multi-stakeholderism in Internet Governance.* WTPF Backgrounder Series. Geneva: International Telecommunication Union.

Kraus, D. & Karmasin, M. (2012) Multistakeholderism in media management. In Glowacki, M. & Jackson, L. (eds.) *Creativity, Innovation and Interaction: Public Media Management Fit for the 21st Century.* London & New York: Routledge.

Lowe, G.F. (2010) Beyond altruism: Why public participation in public service media matters. In Lowe, G.F. (ed.) *The Public in Public Service Media*, RIPE@2009. Göteborg: Nordicom, pp. 9-35.

Maciel, M. & de Souza C.A.P. (2011) *Multi-stakeholder Participation on Internet Governance: An Analysis from a Developing Country, Civil Society Perspective.* Association for Progressive Communications, September 2011.

Mapping Digital Media reports (2010-2013) http://www.opensocietyfoundations.org/projects/mapping-digital-media

Markopoulos, M., Broekhoven, G. & Fisher, B. (2012) *Collaboration and Multi-stakeholder Dialogue: A review of Literature.* Gland, Switzerland: International Union for Conservation of Nature and Natural Resources.

McChesney, R.W. (2007) *Communication Revolution: Critical Junctures and the Future of Media.* New York: The New Press.

McChesney R. & Nichols, J. (2010) *The Death and Life of American Journalism: The Media Revolution that Will Begin the World Again.* New York: Nation Books.

McQuail, D. (2000) *McQuail's Mass Communication Theory.* London: SAGE Publications.

Meadows, M., Forde, S., Ewart, J. & Foxwell, K. (2008) A Catalyst for Change? Australian Community Broadcasting Audiences Fight Back. In Gordon, J. (ed.) *Notions of Community: An Edited Collection of Community Media Debates.* Oxford: Peter Lang Publications.

Napoli, P. & Aslama, M. (eds.) (2011) *Communications Research in Action. Scholar-Practitioner Collaborations for a Democratic Public Sphere.* New York: Fordham University Press.

Popescu, M. (2011) *European Media Systems Survey 2010: Results and Documentation.* Colchester: Department of Government, University of Essex.

Robie, D. (2009) Diversity reportage in Aotearoa: Demographics and the rise of the ethnic media. *Pacific Journalism Review, 15*(1), pp. 67-91

Shin, D.H., Wong-Yong, K. & Dong-Hoon, L. (2006) A web of stakeholders and strategies in the development of digital multimedia broadcasting (DMB): Why and how has DMB been developed in Korea? *The International Journal on Media Management, 8*(2), pp. 70-83.

Stavitsky, A. & Huntsberger, M. (2010) "With the Support form Listeners Like You": Lessons from U.S. public radio. In Lowe, G.F. (ed.) *The Public in Public Service Media*, RIPE@2009. Göteborg: Nordicom, pp. 257-271).

Stern, R.J. (2008) Stakeholder theory and media management: Ethical framework for news company executives. *Journal of Mass Media Ethics, 23*(1), pp. 51-65.

Van Cuilenburg, J. (1999) On competition, access and diversity in media, old and new. *Television & New Media, 1*(2), pp. 183-207.

Van der Wurff, R. (2011) Do audiences receive diverse ideas from news media? Exposure to a variety of news media and personal characteristics as determinants of diversity as received. *European Journal of Communication, 26*(4), pp. 328-342.

Van den Bulck, H. (2012) Towards a media policy process analysis model and its methodological implications. In Just, N. & Puppis, M. (eds.) *Trends in Communication Policy Research: New Theories, Methods and Subjects.* Bristol: IntellectBooks, pp. 217-231).

III.
Public Service Value in Practice

Chapter 10

Disaster Coverage and Public Value from Below

Analysing the NHK's Reporting of the Great East Japan Disaster

Takanobu Tanaka & Toshiyuki Sato

As the sole public broadcaster of Japan, where earthquakes, volcanic eruptions, typhoons, and other natural disasters are all too common, Nippon Hoso Kyokai [NHK] is expected to play a twofold role in emergency situations. In its usual capacity as an independent, authoritative source of information, NHK reports on the damage caused and the state of the disaster-affected area. But NHK is also a key part of the national infrastructure for large-scale disaster prevention and, when disasters happen, a central actor in Japan's crisis management strategy. So while Japanese broadcast law guarantees NHK's editorial independence, the Disaster Countermeasures Basic Act (National Land Agency 1997) stipulates NHK as one of the designated public organisations which, in order to protect people's lives and property, has a duty to report disaster-prevention information accurately and promptly. While other public service broadcasters strategically contribute to disaster management strategies (see for example ABC 2011) the dual legislative role assigned to NHK is unique. This provides an interesting lens through which to investigate the effectiveness of its public service media [PSM] operations and its diverse contributions to the public value of PSM.

In this chapter we explore NHK's response to the March 2011 disaster in the Tohoku region, the Great East Japan earthquake, and the tsunami and nuclear accidents that followed in consequence. We seek to establish the important and potentially unique public value of PSM in the context of such extreme conditions. In the initial natural disasters we discuss here, 15,800 people lost their lives across an area stretching from Hokkaido Prefecture in north Japan to Kanagawa Prefecture where Tokyo is situated, with the devastation concentrated on the Pacific side of the northeast Tohoku region, in which the coastal town of Fukushima is located. Ninety per cent of the deaths were caused by the tsunami. One year after the event 3,000 people were still missing and 344,000 were living as evacuees, nearly a third of them as a result of the Fukushima Daiichi nuclear reactor explosions (Sato 2012). The scale, speed and complexity of the disaster created an unprecedented reporting challenge for NHK.

This case study and content analysis is keyed to understanding some of the most significant lessons learned about NHK's roles during the early days of the aftermath, and its changing relationship with the Japanese public since that time. We begin by examining the history, scope, forms and utility of NHK's considerable investments in disaster reporting technology and expertise. We then analyse the comparatively different roles played by NHK and commercial television in coverage of the events for the first three days following the 3/11 earthquake. Discussion will emphasise how these roles reflect different operational and strategic values in the two approaches and types of mediation. Finally we consider the limitations of NHK's televisual disaster response and examine ways in which the use of online publishing systems may enable more flexible, audience driven, and bottom up approaches to meeting public expectations in future crisis events. Based on our analysis, we pose a new approach to understanding the public value of PSM in an international policy context, that of safeguarding human security in an age of global, catastrophic risk.

NHK and its disaster remit

Tokyo Broadcasting Station, NHK's predecessor, was established in 1925, only two years after the Great Kanto earthquake that devastated most of the Tokyo metropolitan area and killed around 105,000 people. Wrong information about evacuation places and harmful nationalistic and racist rumours against Chinese and Korean residents in Tokyo spread after the quake. These triggered violence and caused much public confusion, which highlighted the need for a broadcasting service to disseminate accurate and prompt disaster information (Nakamori 2008).

Public service broadcasting [PSB] has historically served a number of defined public purposes: democratic, cultural and creative, educational, social and community (BBC, 2004). For NHK disaster reporting has been, and will remain, at the heart of its core mission for Japanese society. Natural disasters that have claimed thousands of lives have been almost annual events over the organisation's history. In the process of re-building the country after World War II and during post-war rapid economic growth, the Japanese government recognised the need to develop an integrated disaster management system as a critical factor for mitigating damage.

This system was codified in 1961 after the Ise-bay typhoon killed more than 5,000 people. The government established the Disaster Countermeasures Basic Act in which NHK was designated as the public institution responsible for the urgent dissemination of emergency information.

NHK's operation as an arm of the State during crisis is not inconsistent with its historical role as an independent public service broadcaster. The organisation was created as an institution that is expected to co-operate with the government during times of crisis and disaster, and has from the start been dedicated to supporting social progress and the considerable efforts required to achieve Japan's modernisation. The State does not control or interfere with content in the terms of the broadcasting law, but has an important role on the basis of legislative authority. Thus the dominant attitude of NHK to audiences in the past has been more or less 'paternalistic', claiming to know what is culturally best for people, similar to the European experience (NHK Broadcasting Culture Research Institute 2002; Krauss 2006). NHK's social responsibility mandate and paternalistic orientation can be seen in its corporate plan, which states that NHK's core mission is "to build a prosperous and secure society, and promote the development of culture of the new era" (NHK 2012, 1) and in its pillars of action that clearly indicate the importance of this institution for disaster reporting in mind. NHK must "provide safety for the public" and "promote the development of the Japanese nation, regions and communities" (Ibid. 1).

Certainly the Japanese public expects NHK to prepare for disaster reporting even though it is costly to maintain the fleet of 14 helicopters that are needed to guarantee live broadcasting coverage whenever disaster strikes anywhere in Japan, as well as 460 remote-controlled cameras located all around the country, and of course the costs required to train NHK reporters and technical staff to be able to cope with emergency situations. Cameras situated at airports are intended to capture airplane accidents. Robot cameras located at volcanoes monitor eruptions and others situated at industrial complexes or nuclear power plants can monitor for fires and other kinds of accidents 24/7 the whole year through. Although this system and all related equipment is especially intended for use during emergencies, making use of them on a daily basis allows NHK to recoup some of its high initial investments. Live images from robot cameras can be used in a variety of programme contexts, for example as backdrops for weather news (Sato 2012).

Yet advanced disaster surveillance and reporting tools and systems can only be effectively mobilised if NHK staff are well trained in emergency procedures. Thus, every employee, whether reporter, programme director or engineer, receives mandatory training in disaster procedures and must be familiar with detailed guides to operational protocols in the case of an event. In most of the regional NHK stations spread across Japan, overnight-shift news and engineering staff conduct routine exercises every day at midnight, as specified in NHK's internal disaster operations manual. In case of an earthquake, responsible news desks must quickly decide where to send the camera crews, how to ensure the circuit of remote-controlled cameras is operational and dependable, and whether to use a helicopter in addition to other basic actions spelled out in the manual.

The fundamentals of disaster-prevention reports include delivering exact, timely information from the Japan Metrological Agency [JMA], urging the audience to remain calm and providing any necessary instructions for what people ought to do. In order not to sensationalize, reporters are trained, for example, not to use strong adjectives in describing disaster events (Harlan 2012). Yoshihiko Shimizu, head of NHK's news department on 3/11, said it was his staff's job to help people navigate the worst moments of the crisis, and to be sensitive about coverage of the human impact:

> We knew people watching or listening might have friends and relatives in the disaster areas, so we were careful not to cause panic that might lead to further injury or damage. Our broadcast guidelines demand that we protect the privacy of individuals when reporting, so we also had to be careful not to cause more distress for survivors (quoted in Fry 2012)

Clearly, disaster-mitigation reporting is an important factor in gaining the trust of Japanese viewers and listeners. As table 1 indicates, NHK and five main commercial broadcasters collectively enjoy more than 90 per cent of the TV viewership in Japan. But when there is an earthquake or a typhoon, or when a volcanic eruption happens, people typically turn to NHK and viewer ratings spike. On 11 March 2011 before the Great East Japan earthquake the rating for NHK General Television was 3 per cent in the greater Tokyo area because households usually have their television receivers turned off in the mid-afternoon period. But as soon as the earthquake hit the eastern part of the country the ratings quickly rose to 15 per cent, then upwards to nearly 22 per cent.

Table 1.   Share of viewership in Japan

	NHK General	Nippon TV	Fuji TV	TBS	TV Asahi	TV Tokyo	Others
2005	14.6%	18.2%	19.4%	16.1%	16.2%	7.7%	5.4%
2010	14.8%	18.2%	18.6%	14.5%	16.2%	6.4%	8.9%

Source: Nakamura, et.al. 2013.

The earthquake had a magnitude of 9.0 and occurred at 14:46. An "Earthquake Early Warning" message was immediately broadcast on all eight TV and radio channels operated by NHK. As shown in table 1, NHK broadcast the early warning less than one minute after the initial earthquake occurrence. In less than two minutes NHK interrupted regular programming and thereafter devoted 100 per cent of its capacity to disaster reporting. Within 63 minutes after the initial impact an NHK helicopter was on the scene providing live coverage. Broadcasting of information about the tsunami and earthquake, and its aftermath, continued around-the-clock for the first week on the main terrestrial TV and radio channels, and via satellite TV.

Table 2. **Time line of NHK coverage during the first hour of broadcasting during the Great East Japan earthquake**

14:46	Earthquake occurred off the coast of the Tohoku region of Japan
14:46:50	NHK broadcast an Earthquake Early Warning System notice on all 8 channels
14:48:18	NHK switched off all regular programming to focus on disaster-related news
14:49	Major Tsunami Warning was issued and NHK focused on calling for evacuation
15:03	Live footage of fire in Tokyo was aired on NHK and commercial stations
15:14	NHK camera captured the massive tsunami's arrival along the Tohoku region coast.
15:49	NHK helicopter started sending live footage of the tsunami in residential areas

On 11 March 11 2011 NHK was obviously well prepared, experienced and equipped to handle the emergency. It must be emphasised that Japan's commercial television networks also have considerable expertise in, and experience with, disaster coverage, and this was also demonstrated during the disaster. Most of the commercial networks skipped commercial messages for a couple of days and broadcast related news 24 hours a day, non-stop.

The authors conducted minute-by-minute content analysis of television broadcasts by NHK and commercial broadcasters to see if there were significant differences as well as similarities in their respective efforts at disaster coverage. As NHK television broadcast the same content both on TV and radio in the initial stages of the disaster, we analysed the broadcast vision and sound separately, noting only the sound was available in radio programming. The latter coverage is particularly relevant as more people, especially in the area where the disaster struck and where power was lost, resorted to radio broadcasts to get disaster information.

McQuail's media performance and public responsibility frameworks (McQuail 2003) were used to guide our analysis because they focus on the social responsibilities of media, and his approach "equates quality with characteristics of media content and media structure in relation to norms and values, under the rubric of the public interests" (as summarised by Ala-Fossi 2005: 38-40). Social responsibility is a core aspect of public value. Especially in times of disasters, both NHK and commercial broadcasters ought to serve public purposes and be socially responsible. We argue differences in disaster coverage between NHK and commercial broadcasters can indicate the characteristic public value of NHK.

With that background in mind, we introduce the results of content analysis, carried out with the support of NHK's independent culture and services research group, the Broadcasting Culture Research Institute [BCRI]. This research compares reporting of Japan's 3/11 disasters by NHK and the major commercial networks. Our analysis was aimed at answering three main questions:

1) Are there any conspicuous differences and similarities in disaster reporting between NHK, which operates primarily in pursuit of public interest, and the commercial television networks, which are basically run on market drive?

2) What do these differences suggest about the relative public value of these services?

3) Are there any signs that the social responsibility model of NHK's disaster reporting, and its top-down, paternalistic approach, has altered? If so, how and which direction is the change heading?

Methodology

BCRI researchers analysed the disaster broadcasting on NHK General TV, NHK's main television channel, and two of the five key commercial networks based in Tokyo: Nippon Television and Fuji Television. Analysis was confined to the first 72 hours after the earthquake, as this was regarded as the critical period for survivors, and thus for NHK to disseminate disaster information to save lives. Nippon Television is Japan's first commercial television station, established in 1953. But Fuji Television had the second highest average rating, following NHK, for these first three days after the earthquake. Monitoring took place from 14:46 on March 11 to 14:59 on March 14.

Since NHK and the commercial networks continued their disaster coverage non-stop, we had to devise an appropriate way to conduct content analysis and decided to rely on random sampling. We analysed television footage vision and sound at the 22nd second of every minute, a moment randomly chosen as the point for examination. In analysing the sound, we listened to the content before and after that 22nd second in order to understand what was being broadcast at that point. Our assumption is that if we add up all the minute-by-minute data, the result represents a good general picture of the entirety of coverage during the research period.

Comparing coverage from NHK
and two commercial broadcasters

During the first 24 hours of the disaster the three broadcasters initially reported on the earthquake and then on the tsunami that followed. This coverage was prominent in images and sounds. Information on the tsunami gradually decreased as that event subsided. During the 24-48 hour period, events at the damaged Fukushima-Daiichi nuclear power plant assumed highest relevance and received heavy coverage. All through the 72 hours of our monitoring, the broadcasters used more than ten percent of their airtime to report information on sufferers and relief activities.

The detailed results of this analysis are reported in papers authored by Tanaka and Hara (2011 & 2012a/b). Here the authors focus attention primarily on findings that demonstrate specific tendencies in, and the stances toward, disaster reporting when comparing NHK and the commercial television networks.

A port in Tohoku versus a fire in Tokyo

In this section three main findings will be introduced; two differences and one similarity. One of the most striking differences was observed in the first hour after the disaster, in the focus of coverage, which gives one example of NHK's public value.

NHK used 70 per cent of its airtime for news about the tsunami, 10 per cent in coverage of the earthquake, and 11 per cent related to a building fire in Tokyo. Nippon Television used 27 per cent of its airtime for the tsunami, 26 per cent for the earthquake and 14 per cent for the fire in Tokyo. Fuji Television devoted 28 per cent to the tsunami, 29 per cent for the earthquake and 19 per cent for the Tokyo fire. When we examined the geographic coverage by areas, 64 per cent of NHK reporting was about the Tohoku region, which was close to the epicenter of the earthquake and was hit severely by the tsunami, and 20 per cent was about Tokyo. In contrast, Nippon Television devoted 42 per cent of its coverage about Tohoku and 41 per cent about Tokyo and Fuji Television devoted only 26 per cent to the Tohoku region and focused 35 per cent on Tokyo

Particularly in the first 30 minutes after the quake, there was a clear contrast between the geographical coverage of NHK and the commercial networks. During this period of time, the tsunami had yet to arrive and NHK was not sure if a significant tsunami was actually approaching. Despite this uncertainty, NHK broadcast live footage of ports in the Tohoku region to observe the changing sea level, and called for immediate evacuation of the coastal region. NHK put its utmost focus on the potential tsunami, whereas the commercial networks spent as much airtime reporting about the earthquake, with lots of video footage of the heavy shaking, as the tsunami warning.

There was another significant difference. About 15 minutes after the quake NHK helicopters and remote-controlled cameras caught a building on fire in Tokyo. NHK reported the fire rather briefly, and as soon as it was confirmed that there were no casualties, turned back to Tohoku. The Tokyo-based commercial networks, in contrast, chose to report more on the fire. Only after NHK broadcast live helicopter footage, showing the massive tsunami devastating farmland and residential areas in the disaster zone did the focus of the commercial broadcasters return to the tsunami.

These differences reflect NHK's prioritisation of disaster prevention, saving lives and protecting property, over damage reporting. It also evidences its responsibility to primarily serve people in the affected Tohoku coastal region. Even though the commercial networks have a national audience, they focused far more news coverage on Tokyo. Naturally they don't have the same national reporting infrastructure that NHK has at its disposal. However there seems to be another interpretation. A senior journalist of Nippon TV confessed that "with a TV man's usual instinct, there were times when I automatically responded to and broadcast the live footage of violent shakings of the earthquake and the fire in Tokyo...knowing the tsunami warning was the top priority" (Tanifuji 2013: 120). In the immediate aftermath of the disaster, as neither NHK nor commercial broadcasters had sufficient time to deliberately think over about what to report, their corporate cultures had an affect on their editorial decisions. Yet NHK had obligations over and above routine news reporting. This responsibility is part of its public value.

Coverage of "rescue operations"

Another difference between commercial and public service operators is evident in the kinds of information delivered during the first 72 hours after the initial disaster. Figure 1 shows how the three networks reported on disaster sufferers and rescue operations, with thematic peaks during the monitored period marked with circles.

At around 10:00 on March 12, NHK news coverage of rescue operations sharply increased as it reported live on the helicopter rescue of people stranded on the roof of an affected building. Soon after NHK shifted its focus to reporting on evacuation centres and evacuees. This was especially apparent throughout the day of March 13, when there were repeated live reports from evacuation centres, providing detailed information about conditions and highlighting the kinds of supplies the evacuees most needed. NHK was able to set up live broadcasting operations from disaster-stricken areas by dispatching remote broadcast vans with professional production capacity.

Nippon Television increased its rescue coverage on the afternoon of March 12, and again on the afternoon of March 13, reporting helicopter rescues of people stranded on building rooftops. Its coverage of evacuation centres increased on the evening of March 13, when it aired a pre-packaged news feature in which a reporter accompanied some evacuees going shopping, to find out what supplies they needed most.

Fuji Television spent the most airtime of all broadcasters on rescue operations during the 72 hours. Most of its reports were live coverage of helicopter rescue operations. On the morning of March 12 it broadcast live relays of rescues in several locations. In addition to commentary from reporters onboard the

Figure 1.   Ratio of Evacuation centers and rescue operations in news coverage during the Great East Japan Earthquake

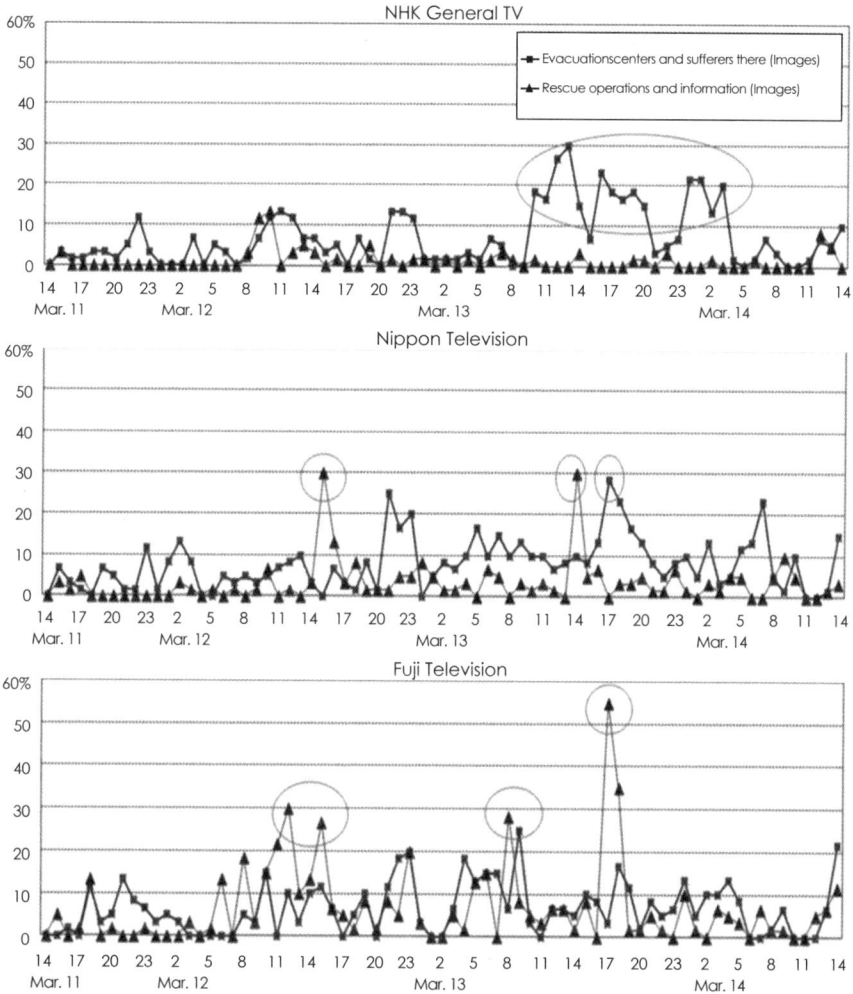

helicopters, newscasters and commentators in the news studio described the ongoing rescue operations, explaining, for example, the difficulty of rescuing people while the aircraft are hovering. Even on the third day, in the evening of March 13, Fuji Television devoted more than half its monitored airtime to rescues.

There are many factors that may have contributed to the thematic differences between the networks, including different interpretations of news values, differing organisational cultures and professional practices, and variable access to sources. However we found that NHK treated the voices of survivors in evacuation camps as having more value for the audience than rescue operations, especially on the third day when its satellite broadcasting trucks reached the evacuation centres, enabling live on-location reporting. Its more intense coverage of evacuee stories, compared to Fuji and Nippon services, is also consonant with its responsibility to help survivors in the disaster struck areas. NHK had helicopters and was capable of reporting the rescue operations, However, in accordance with NHK's public value, it chose to report on the plight of evacuation camps and how people outside could help, prioritizing the public interest.

Coverage of the nuclear accident at Fukushima

One of the reasons the earthquake on 11 March 2011 had such a huge international impact was related to the consequent meltdown of the Fukushima Daiichi nuclear power plant. The plant was built to withstand a tsunami of six meters in height. When the tsunami of more than 10-metres hit the plant, all of the fuel tanks for the emergency diesel generators were swept away and emergency power cells quickly submerged under water. All power supplies were cut and the nuclear reactor went out of control. Assessment of the damage and threat worsened over time and now, according to the International Nuclear Event Scale of IAEA, the Fukushima Daiichi nuclear accident is rated at level seven, the same as the Chernobyl accident (although the amount of radiation leaked remains one tenth of that at Chernobyl). Following the hydrogen explosion at the plant, there were widespread public concerns about whether Tokyo Electric Power Company, or TEPCO (the organisation responsible for the plant), and the Japanese government were dealing properly with the situation, given that their descriptions of the accident changed frequently. The government lost people's trust, as many began to wonder whether it was telling the truth.

Despite the more numerous differences in coverage shown in our analysis, there is one similarity between the networks that stands out. That is in reporting about this nuclear accident. Figure 2 shows changes in the volume of nuclear accident news reports over time, with all three networks showing similar timing in the increase and reduction of news coverage.

The peaks in the line graphs signal when problems were reported. The first peak comes when a hydrogen explosion occurred at Unit 1 of the Fukushima Daiichi nuclear power station. The second peak came when the networks acquired information on the possible hydrogen explosion at Unit 3. The third peak came when a hydrogen explosion actually occurred at 11:01 on March 14.

The fact that the volume of nuclear accident news reports increased at the same time on all three networks can partly be explained by their shared reliance on official information sources, especially news conferences given by the government, TEPCO, and similarly responsible institutions. Why, then, did news reports on this issue decrease as sharply and at a relatively similar time later?

Figure 2. **Ratio of reports on nuclear accidents**

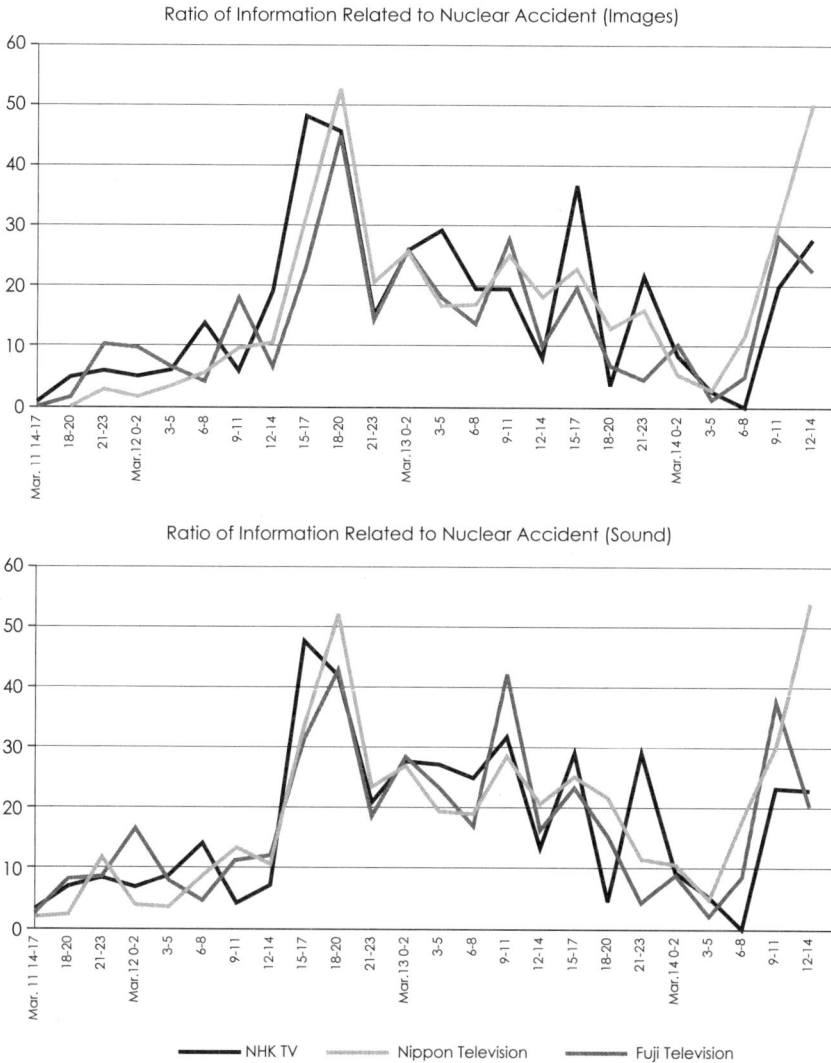

Ratio of Information Related to Nuclear Accident (Images)

Ratio of Information Related to Nuclear Accident (Sound)

———— NHK TV ———— Nippon Television ———— Fuji Television

Again we suggest this can partly be explained by source availability, but also by "source capture" – a phenomenon of noted importance when privileged access to political information results in reduced critical examination of that material (Bruns 2008)

The volumes of news reports on the explosion at Unit 1 on March 12 at 15: 36 remained high until 21:59. The volumes dropped at 22:00 at the three networks. We infer that this has something to do with Chief Cabinet Secretary Edano's statement in a news conference at 20:41. He acknowledged, for the first time, that there had been a hydrogen explosion. However he went on to say that the explosion had caused no damage to Unit 1's containment vessel, in which the nuclear reactor sits. From shortly before noon into the afternoon of March 13, the volume of news reports on the nuclear accident decreased because the government had said there was no reason to fear a hydrogen explosion. After the hydrogen explosion occurred at Unit 3 on the morning of March 14, Nippon Television intensified its reporting of this accident as it had exclusive footage of the moment of the explosion. Fuji Television sharply reduced news reports on the explosion at around noon. NHK reduced them gradually. In its news programme at noon on March 14th, NHK reported Mr. Edano's statement that after the hydrogen explosion, "the integrity of the containment vessel is maintained, and that the possibility is low that a large volume of radioactive materials has been scattered in the air".

One possible explanation for the sequential reduction in news reports on these nuclear accidents is that the news media as a whole accepted information given by the government, playing down the risk of explosion without critically analysing the claims. Even if they had had doubts about government claims and sought out the opinions of independent experts, there was no way to verify their information while government was hiding crucial details. This source capture phenomenon arguably delayed the media's awareness of how serious the accident actually was.

The lack of critical scrutiny is important because this incident was of global concern and NHK's informational role was not limited to the national interest. NHK World broadcast Mr. Edano's press conferences with simultaneous translations in the hourly headline news, *Newsline* and other extended news programmes. The Fukushima accident also had a significant impact on discussions about nuclear power safety around the world. Germany and Switzerland began moving away from nuclear energy in response, partly at least, and the majority of Italian people voted "No" in their referendum on nuclear energy on June 13th, 2011 (Sato 2012).

Limited lifeline information on TV

Table 2 shows how much the three broadcasters reported on information about emergency service lifelines during the first 72 hours. Here, the term "lifeline information" refers to information about electricity cuts or 'blackouts', problems or lack of same with water and gas supplies, telephone and other communications services, the situation for hospitals and medical services, etc.

There are very small ratios of airtime given to lifeline information during the study period compared to other types of programming, but NHK aired relatively more of this information than the other two broadcasters. Transport information, such as trains and bus service, traffic blockage and highway situations, received the most coverage. NHK devoted 7.6 per cent of its airtime in

Table 3. **Ratio of kinds of lifeline information reported**

	NHK TV		Nippon TV		Fuji TV	
	Images	Sounds	Images	Sounds	Images	Sounds
Areas under power blackouts and information on blackouts	0.9%	1.8%	0.5%	1.8%	0.1%	0.9%
Transport information	5.4	7.6	2.3	4.0	2.2	3.8
Information on water and gas supplies	0.3	1.1	0.2	0.7	0.0	0.5
Information on telephone and other communications services	0.4	1.0	0.1	0.4	0.1	0.3
Information on hospitals and medical services	0.5	0.8	0.3	0.2	0.1	0.2

Note: 100%=Entire 72 hours

sounds to this information, whereas for Nippon Television and Fuji Television the amount was about 4 per cent.

Public discontent with NHK and the use of social media

The Great East Japan disaster was a complex, fast moving catastrophe that hit many people across a wide geographic area, affecting them in multiple and different ways. It is safe to say that the scale of this disaster would have presented most broadcasters with problems in delivering effective media coverage, and especially beyond the scope of the general television networks based in Tokyo. Our content analysis shows that overall reporting of the Fukushima Daiichi accidents by the three selected broadcasters was of a similar volume, intensity and timing, and we believe this was at least partly because the news media were largely dependent on government information and had limited alternative sources. NHK knew that the public needed and wanted more information and their reporters commented repeatedly that the government and TEPCO should provide residents and media with more essential information, signifying the frustration that all the news organisations were feeling. NHK nonetheless received public criticism of its nuclear reporting, largely based on audience perceptions that it was a part of a government ploy to play down, even to hide, the actual danger of the accidents.

There were different reactions to the NHK's coverage of nuclear accidents on social media. NHK news has three accounts on twitter: 1) '@nhk_news', 2) '@nhk_kabun' (short for kagakubunka-bu, meaning science and culture news department), and 3) '@nhk_seikatsu' (short for seikatsujyoho, meaning lifeline information). Among these, '@nhk_kabun' handled disseminating information about the nuclear accidents. At first NHK tweeted the short versions of TV news about what was going on and tips for residents in Fukushima, such as in order "to avoid radiation exposure, change clothes and wash your hands and face when coming home from outside". But responses mushroomed, such as "'no immediate danger means there will be in the future?" and "I need detailed explanation of the current radiation level of the Fukushima power plant". NHK reporters tweeted answers, and those question and answer sessions received lots of positive reactions from the followers. Before the 3/11 disaster, the number of followers of NHK accounts was rather small, less than 5,000 for each tweeting account because NHK used Twitter mainly for programme promotion, not for news reporting. At the end of April the number of followers of the three accounts had jumped to nearly 500 thousand. @nhk kabun, which started to disseminate information about the nuclear accidents, had 1.6 million page views a month, up from about 50 thousand a month previously. NHK science reporters were mainly caught up with TV and radio reporting and could not spend enough time and energy on this task for the Twitter audience, but our inquiries suggest they felt the importance and necessity of using social media will increase in the future disasters.

According to a survey NHK conducted in the Tohoku region, the information that people needed but could not get from NHK TV was about food, water or gasoline supplies and electricity or transportation recovery. NHK made a point of periodically reporting the lifeline information it had in an organised way, following news reports related to the disaster. However in the face of such a broad-scale, ongoing catastrophe we argue that TV alone cannot meet individuals' diversified and personalised information needs. We found audiences today expect the internet to play an important part by enabling them to search for, request and discuss the specific kinds of information they need. NHK was slow to realise this demand for online services and it was only 3 weeks after the disaster that it set up a search function on its website. Our research suggests that NHK must improve its system of providing lifeline information, developing a cross-media strategy for broadcast, Internet and mobile phones to meet the needs and wants of the public.

NHK's duty is to disseminate disaster information, which in the past has mainly come from above. Although the public valued this service, as responses to the nuclear accidents clearly showed the public now expects more interaction with and through NHK. Public opinion will play an important part in developing NHK's disaster reporting capacity.

Human security: Public value from below

The discussion just concluded demonstrates that the move from PSB to PSM, and new digital publishing platforms, has not been smooth for NHK. But these problems are not only organisational and operational; they are also structural.

According to the Broadcasting Law, NHK is allowed to put its content online only *after* it is broadcast on TV and radio. To do live streaming requires permission from the Minister for Internal Affairs and Communications. However soon after the occurrence of the earthquake, one high school student began to offer live streaming of the NHK's TV coverage on the U-stream, which is a breach of copyright law. U-stream called NHK to ask whether they should shut it down and NHK decided to let them continue without getting permission. NHK also co-operated with Google to use their Person Finder function for setting up a search system to locate missing persons' names. In these instances NHK's use of all media platforms to provide crisis information caused no complaint or criticism. In the pursuit of saving lives, which is the ultimate public value, everything else becomes secondary. But the essential legal and policy problems remain to be resolved, of course.

Here the authors suggest the concept of 'human security' as a type of public value that is of the highest importance, and should be recognised as an essential duty of PSM everywhere. This is not the same thing as national security. The concept of 'human security' first appeared in the United Nations Development Programme, UNDP 1994 Human Development Report, which provides a people-centred perspective. It is based neither on the interests of any national government nor on market 'fundamentalism'. Traditionally PSB's functions were based mainly on political and cultural nation building, and the predominant attitude to audiences was paternalistic – at least until the era of deregulation in the 1980s (Jauert & Lowe 2005). Today PSM needs to take into consideration the wider context of human security, which sometimes goes beyond national borders, and certainly also will involve more than traditional broadcast services.

For example now that the radiation levels in Tokyo and in most Japanese regions, excepting the restricted area in Fukushima, have returned to normal, it is the role of NHK's overseas broadcasting to report scientific and objective information on radiation safety to its audiences abroad. Since the March 2011 nuclear accidents there has been a domestic ban on consumption of agricultural products from, in and around Fukushima prefecture and fish caught near the coast and in some lakes. In turn, however, exports of agricultural products from elsewhere in Japan have dropped due to health concerns that aren't actually valid. Products such as high-quality rice, fruits and powdered milk for babies were becoming popular especially in Asian and Middle Eastern markets prior to the disaster because of their safety and quality, and were well accepted despite their relatively higher prices compared with local goods. The perceived impact of radiation contamination is an important long-term informational and educational issue for NHK's international services, not only for its domestic services, and in this case, at least, has economic and trade implications as well.

It is widely anticipated that global warming will cause more abnormal weather in many parts of the world; more frequent incidence of torrential rains, stronger typhoons and hurricanes, and the collapse of lakes that hold water from melting glaciers in high mountains, as well as shrinking ice shelves in the polar regions. Today, the role of public service broadcasters in times of disaster is becoming more important than ever, for both domestic use and international use. NHK's accumulated knowledge of reporting in disaster-prone Japan is being used in other countries to prepare for many different types of emergencies. Since the Indian Ocean earthquake and tsunami in 2004, NHK has consulted with Asian public broadcasters on disaster reporting strategies, and hosted international conferences to improve the effectiveness and standards of emergency coverage.

In the past, the public values provided by PSB were conceived from above, via legislative remit and within the framework of national interest. That still remains largely the case. However in this era of global interdependencies, we argue there is a greater need to pursue public value 'from below', i.e. that responds to the self-defined needs of people on the ground rather than primarily being defined by the state Historically the state's role in pursuing human security for its citizens focused on keeping them safe from armed conflict and poverty. A newer critical, non-statist perspective suggests the pursuit of human security should be extended to social and environmental threats, and should promote the involvement of more actors including individuals, cultural groups and non-government organisations in defining relevant goals and activities (Naidoo 2001). In this view human security is in everybody's interest, including the collective needs of the public, because it focuses on securing and protecting individual's "freedom from want" and "freedom from fear" (Futamura, Hobson, Turner 2011). The authors argue, though it might be difficult to generalize, that 'human security' is an important element of public value in a risk society and one key area where PSM can produce valued and valuable outcomes.

At the risk of sounding overly self-congratulatory, we hazard to claim that NHK's role in disaster reporting following the Great East Japan Earthquake has been vital to the nation and with potential importance far more broadly. Its multi-layered, multi-dimensional and in-depth media coverage has been highly acclaimed.

A Nomura Institute survey (Nomura 2011) conducted immediately after the earthquake found that 81 per cent of respondents thought NHK was the most reliable source of information, while commercial television was at 57 per cent, followed by web portal sites at 43 per cent and newspapers at 36 per cent. The later is especially interesting and, we think, has much to do with the live nature of coverage for electronic media. The first ever live aerial image of the huge tidal wave rolling in was shot by an NHK helicopter and relayed overseas, where more than 2,000 television stations aired it. In the United States, at the

Public Television Programmers' Association of the PBS General Assembly held in May 2011, and at the American Public Television's programme distribution meeting held in November 2011, NHK received special awards and a standing ovation. In this sense NHK's decision to expand into overseas broadcasting three years ago has finally paid off through the reception of international recognition for its coverage capacity.

Conclusion: PSM and new public value

The research documented and analysed regarding NHK's coverage of the Great East Japan Disaster in March, 2011 has examined some crucial challenges for public service media in a time when its relevance is threatened by the forces of commercialisation and growing complications and instability related to digitalisation. The public value of a public service media organisation is clearly tested in emergency situations, especially disasters. The research reported in this chapter has found clear distinctions between the roles of NHK and two commercial television networks during the 3/11 crisis in Japan. The commercial broadcasters tended to report incidents characterised by high-impact images, such as a building fire or helicopter rescues, whereas NHK focused more on safety and public service information, such as tsunami warnings and information about evacuation sites, food and water supply, and medical facilities. Of course there were problems with NHK, and the commercial networks did provide needed services for the public as well, but on balance there are clear differences in what was prioritised and how coverage was handled – differences that suggest, at least, the higher public value of this publically funded and oriented institution.

In this study we have demonstrated how the historic paternalism of PSB, which historically also shaped Japan's national political identity and cultural frames of reference, has given way due to the need to satisfy the information needs of a more diversified and international society, as well as the more active consumption and production practices of digital media users. During this disaster we saw greater public use of social media to gather and exchange information. The importance of this highlights the need for NHK to move more quickly and comprehensively in digital media platforms, which had been slow prior to 3/11. Online services for the public clearly became more of a priority, evident in special web reporting pages that have been developed, specialist microblogging channels, improved search facilities, streamed emergency news allowed, and collaboration with Google on missing persons services.

NHK is required by its audiences to serve their information needs in an astonishing variety and depth, demonstrating that the traditional 'public value from above' approach that was characteristic of PSB broadcasting isn't sufficient for managing disaster media and communication today. The organisation must be of value to a much greater extent for a more participative, digitally networked public. Disaster reporting remains a vital social responsibility and a valued role for PSM, but we would argue that the very meaning of being public is changing, and therefore NHK's future depends on addressing its "public value from below". This requires remedying a range of inter-related problems, some operational and others organisational – and some, as earlier noted, also structural. At base, public value is in large part perceptual – it is keyed to what people see as having value. In our view, the highest public value lies in taking care of a society's need for human security.

The Great East Japan Disaster, like the massive floods in Thailand in 2011 or the impact of Hurricane Katrina in the USA in 2005, and in numerous other natural disasters this century – and which seem to be growing in number and intensity as global weather patterns change – all illustrate the far-reaching consequences of events that affect everyone, the collective as well as individuals. All of this has evident implications for the security of individuals and communities, and lies beyond the still acknowledged importance of the security of the nation. The Asian region in particular faces frequent catastrophes and, given the prospect of more extreme natural weather events, disaster reporting is arguably a core need for development as one of the key strengths of public service media everywhere. It is, moreover, an aspect of increasing relevance to cross-border emergencies and dependencies.

References

Ala-Fossi, M. (2005) "Culture and Quality in Broadcast Media. Market Dynamics and Organizational Dependencies"; in Lowe, G.F. & Jauert, P. (eds.) *Cultural Dilemmas in Public Service Broadcasting*. Göteborg: Nordicom, 37-55

BBC (2004) Building public value; Renewing the BBC for a digital world at: http://downloads.bbc.co.uk/aboutthebbc/policies/pdf/bpv.pdf

Bruns, A. (2009) Reporting the 2007 Australian Federal Election, In Citizen Journalism: global perspectives, Stuart Allan & Einar Thorsen (eds.) New York: Peter Lang.

Fry, A. (2012) NHK's rapid response. C21 media and NHK. Accessed at: https://www.nhk.or.jp/japan311/c21-01-nhks.html

Futamura, M., Hobson, C. & Turner, N. (2011) Natural disaster and human security. *United Nations University*. Accessed at: http://unu.edu/publications/articles/natural-disasters-and-human-security.html

Harlan, C. (2011) The Calm behind the Headlines. *The Washington Post*. March 26, 2011.

Jauert, P. & Lowe, G.F. (2005) Public Service Broadcasting for Social and Cultural Citizenship Renewing the Enlightenment Mission; in Lowe, G.F. & Jauert, P. (eds.) *Cultural Dilemmas in Public Service Broadcasting*. Göteborg: Nordicom: 13-33

Krauss, E. (2000) Broadcasting Politics in Japan. Cornel University. New York

McQuail, D.(2003) Media Accountability and Freedom of Publication. *Oxford University Press*, New York

Naidoo, S. (2001) A Theoretical Conceptualization of Human Security. Proceedings of the UNESCO-ISS Expert Meeting, Pretoria, South Africa Moufida Goucha and Jakkie Cilliers (eds.) Accessed at: http://www.issafrica.org/Pubs/Books/Unesco/Naidoo.html

Nakamori, H. (2008) Saigaijyohoron no Keifu~Joho Panic to Saigaijohokenkyu no Tenkai [History of Disaster Information Studies ~Information Panic and Evolution of Disaster Information Studies] in Tanaka., A. & Yoshii, H. (eds.) (2008) *Saigaijyohoron Nyumon* [Introduction to Disaster Information Studies] Tokyo: Kobundo.

Nakamura, Y., Aramaki, H., Higashiyama, I. & Ida, M. (2013) Perceptions of Public Broadcasting: Findings of an International Comparative Survey at: http://www.nhk.or.jp/bunken/english/reports/pdf/report_13050101-2.pdf

NHK 2012 For a Prosperous, Secure and Stable Future – NHK Corporate Plan for 2012-2014 at: http://www.nhk.or.jp/pr/english/publication/pdf/plan2012-2014.pdf

NHK Broadcasting Culture Research Institute (2002) Broadcasting in Japan: The Twentieth Century Journey from Radio to Multimedia. NHK.Tokyo

National Land Agency (1997) Disaster Countermeasures Basic Act (trans. Asian Disaster Reduction Center). Accessed April 20th 2013 at: http://www.adrc.asia/documents/law/DisasterCountermeasuresBasicAct.pdf

Sato, T. (2011) The Great East Japan Earthquake: Japanese TV Coverage and Foreign Reception. 20th JAMCO Online International Symposium, March 2012. Accesses at: http://www.jamco.or.jp/en/symposium/20/3/

Tanaka, T. & Hara, Y. (2011) Higashinihon-Daishinsai Hassei kara 24 jikanTerebi ga Tsutaeta Jyoho no Suii [The Great East Japan Earthquake: Transition of Information Transmitted within 24 Hours after the Quake ~Analyzing TV coverage of the Disaster] in NHK Broadcasting Culture Research Institute, *Hoho Kenkyu to Chousa*. 2011.12: 2-11

Tanaka, T. & Hara, Y. (2012a) Higashinihon-Daishinsai Hassei kara 72 jikan Terebi ga Tsutaeta Jyoho no Suii ~Zaikyo 3 kyoku no Hodo Naiyo Bunseki kara~ in NHK Broadcasting Culture Research Institute, *Hoho Kenkyu to Chousa*. 2012.3: 2-21

Tanaka, T. & Hara, Y. (2012b) The Great East Japan Earthquake: Transition of Information Transmitted within the 72 Hours after the Quake~ Analyzing TV coverage of the Disaster by Three Tokyo-based Stations~ http://www.nhk.or.jp/bunken/english/reports/pdf/report_12030101-3.pdf

Tanifuji, K. (2013) Higashinihon-Daishinsai no Kyokun; Kiikyoku no Shinsai Hodo wo Furikaette ~anohini dekitakoto, dekinakattakoto, korekarashitaikoto [Lessons from the Great East Japan Earthquake; Looking back on our Disaster Broadcast as a Commercial Network ~ what we were able and unable to do and what we want to do in the future.] in Niwa, Y. & Fujita, M. (eds.) *Media ga Furueta~ terebi/rajio to higashinihon-daishinsai* [The Media Quaked; Television and Radio after the Great East Japan Earthquake], University of Tokyo Press,118-125

UNDP (1994) Human Development Report 1994 at: http://hdr.undp.org/en/reports/global/hdr1994/

Chapter 11

Media Literacy Promotion as a Form of Public Value?

Comparing the Media Literacy Promotion Strategies of the BBC, ZDF and RAI

Stoyan Radoslavov

Given the increasing relevance of the public value concept for the institutional legitimation of public service broadcasters [PSBs] in Europe, it has become necessary to study the value to the public of concrete public service functions. This chapter focuses on analysing one such function: PSBs' promotion of media literacy. Following Patricia Aufderheide (1993: 3) media literacy is understood as "the ability to access, analyze, evaluate and create messages in a variety of forms". Promotion is understood as the efforts of public service broadcasters to raise the level of media literacy among their publics, which I argue is a case of creating public value. In order to analyse media literacy promotion from a public value perspective I structure the chapter along three public value dimensions, that have so far shaped the public value debate in Europe: instrumental, substantial and process value (Radoslavov & Thomass, 2011).

In a first step I consider the instrumental dimension, which has up to now dominated PSB's strategic relation to media literacy, and its policy discussion of its achievements in this field. This dimension is best characterised by what I define as a 'best practice approach', which I analyse from an economic perspective, situating media literacy related programmes as merit goods, premised on the work of Richard Musgrave (1957). The chapter then works to grasp the substantial dimension of media literacy with a particular focus on academic and political readings. After that I compare and analyse case studies of media literacy promotion strategies in three PSB organisations in Europe: the BBC (UK), ZDF (Germany) and RAI (Italy). These case studies are built on expert interviews and incorporate both the substantial and process public value dimensions of media literacy promotion by addressing its definition (what), authorisation (why), operationalisation and evaluation (how) within the three institutions.

The instrumental dimension of media literacy promotion

In the beginning of 2012 the European Broadcasting Union [EBU] issued its first viewpoint on media literacy. The paper demonstrates the strategic position of PSB in Europe regarding the promotion of media literacy and highlights its value for society. Here media literacy is defined as "the ability to access the media, to understand and critically evaluate its content and communicate over a range of platforms" (EBU 2012: 1). The viewpoint distinguishes three purposes, central to the promotion of media literacy: 1) bridging the digital divide, 2) empowering citizens to democracy, and 3) creating a trusted space. Importantly it explains how these purposes are realised by showcasing best practices by 15 broadcasters or PSB alliances that demonstrate how those organisations create public value by means of media literacy promotion. Examples are provided, as illustrated in Table 1 below.

Table 1.

Encouraging online engagement
First Click, BBC, UK

First Click helps people who would not ordinary use a computer to access a step-by-step beginner's guide to computers and the internet. The guide demystifies the internet and builds online confidence.

www.bbc.co.uk/connect/campaigns/first_click.shtml

Platform for expression
Logo! Wahlcity, ZDF, Germany

This interactive game encourages young people to form their own political parties and take part in virtual elections. In this way, they become familiar with the German political system and engage in policy-maling initiatives. After the launch, the project attracted 2.9 million visitors in its first month.

www.tivi.de/fernsehen/logo/start/index.html'

Fostering a media-savvy public
Amnesia, Rai, radio 2, Italy

This daily drama unfolds from the point of view of a radio presenter suffering amnesia, who depends on public input to 'recall general culture and history'. Presented as a 'true story', this multimedia project is fed by live telephone calls from listeners, highlighting the importance to critically follow and interpret media content.

www.radio.rai.it/radio2/amnesia/

Source: EBU Viewpoint on Media Literacy, 2012.

The featured best practices are heterogeneous: interactive platforms, television series, browser games and public campaigns all seem to promote media literacy aspects in their specific and not strictly educational ways. Adopting this broad conception of media literacy promotion allows for greater political leeway when defining the public service mission – media literacy promotion is elegantly used as a legitimating argument for a much broader range of public service programmes[1], and not only for programmes typically described or understood as 'educational'.

When PSBs address the subject of media literacy in policy debates they usually name and praise a broad spectrum of projects and programme examples (Labourdette 2010; ZDF 2010; Mohr 2003), which serve to prove public value. They formulate abstract, normative purposes and then showcase concrete best practices, that demonstrate how those purposes are fulfilled – a discourse strategy I define as a 'best practice approach' and which, I argue, is central to the instrumental dimension of public value.

From a media economics perspective those best practices can be regarded as examples of 'merit goods' because PSBs presume that increasing the media literacy of publics has merit for society at large, beyond the particular benefits enjoyed by an individual (see Musgrave 1957: 34-36 for a fuller discussion of merit goods). The merit goods label is usually applied to specific kinds of media forms and genres, especially news and education programmes, whose production and consumption is considered socially desirable (Kiefer 2005; Collins 1998: 369; Brown 1997), have benefits not just for individuals but society as a whole. Thus where the market is not able to deliver an adequate supply of such programming, at a price that individuals will support, regulators should intervene to ensure its sufficiency through public sector provision.

The insufficient supply of media merit goods has gradually become one of the three characteristic market failure arguments used to legitimate public intervention in broadcasting markets when assessed from an economic perspective (Solberg 2007: 294; BBC 2004: 44-45; Brown1996: 7-9, and see the chapter by Berg et al in this volume). This perspective highlights PSB's merit for the society on the basis of socio-economic rationale that validates, for those in agreement, public intervention in broadcasting markets. The *EBU Viewpoint*, for example, ascribes First Click, (BBC, U.K) as having the merit of bridging the digital divide, Amnesia (RAI, Italy) and Wahlcity (ZDF, Germany) as possessing the merit of advancing active citizenship (EBU 2012: 2-4). Viewed from this perspective media literacy best practice activities can be understood to have instrumental value for the debate that is necessary to legitimate PSB. The best-practice approach can be therefore ascribed to the instrumental dimension of the public value debate. As Radoslavov and Thomass argue, this dimension implies a rather pragmatic understanding of public value, which subordinates the concept to a broader legitimation strategy, based among others on highlighting the provision of merit goods (2011: 175).

This understanding of merit goods has played a role in recent policy and academic interpretations of public value. The BBC, which introduced Mark Moore's (1995) concept to the field of PSB policy in 2004, argued that public value results from the sum of the individual value, economic value and citizen value that its programmes create. Citizen value is defined as an "uplift over and above individual value, that is the additional value that people recognise extends beyond their personal gain, perhaps even from services they don't themselves use" (BBC 2004: 45). Thus, citizen value is based on PSMs' social contribution, and the production of meritorious, collective benefits that go beyond the preferences of consumers (which are largely about seeking individual value), and of market players (largely about securing economic value)[2]. Although the BBC relies on different indicative measures (willingness to pay analysis, expert panels, evidence based impact tracking) to grasp citizen value, in the end the broadcaster concedes that it remains a complex concept dependent on subjective judgement (BBC 2004: 84). This definitional drawback has been central to disputes about merit goods from the concept's formulation and leads inevitably to its most controversial manifestation: paternalism. "Since merit goods imply a more or less intrusive interference with individuals' (revealed) preferences, they have always been accompanied by the suspicion of representing the first step on the slippery slope of paternalism" (D'Amico 2009: 3). The idea of experts deciding which content or services should be delivered to the public, and what is inherently in their best interests – even if contrary to personal preference – has always been the Achilles heel of the concept of merit goods, and of the classical conception of PSB. Even if one accepts the principle that PSBs know better than individual consumers about which content has merit, one still must ask: how might they arrive at those judgements, and ascribe citizen value to their choices? In Moore's view the tendency to idiosyncrasy is common to public managers (1995: 39).

Thus, if public value claims are susceptible to idiosyncratic paternalism, how can we grasp the public value of media literacy promotion by public service broadcasters? How do we make sure that the merits of the EBU's best practices approach are proven rather than simply asserted? Handling that requires that we go beyond the instrumental dimension and look more closely at the substantial dimensions of concepts like media literacy and public value.

The substantial dimension of media literacy promotion

In defining 'public value' Moore highlights roles he considers significant: public sector managers and public service institutions create substantial value for the public in the activities they perform, such as reducing pollution, improving health, preventing crime, and so forth. Policies and institutions should be required, he argues, to produce not only outputs, but outcomes that have inherent and obviously substantial value for society. Can we then ascribe such value to media literacy and its public sector promotion?

Aufderheide's (1993) skills-based definition of media literacy still has a conceptual impact, 20 years on, in both academic and political circles. Of course this is only one definition amongst many[3], but its long lasting career can be attributed to its 'openness' (Livingstone 2004: 4), which renders it flexible enough to accommodate differing, often even controversial, readings.

To date media literacy research has been primarily of a theoretical nature with empirical studies being the exception rather than the rule (Jarren & Wassmer 2009: 47; Livingstone 2004: 3; Baacke 1996: 119). Media literacy remains a variable and normative concept, which imbues the public adoption of new communication technologies, products and processes with normative and often socio-political imperatives. PSBs guided provision of mobile apps is for example often associated with granting universal access and bridging the digital divide (EBU 2012: 2).

The media literacy debate at the EU level is another example of what one might characterise as 'normative overload' for the concept. Since 2006 both the EU Parliament and Commission have been very active in efforts to frame media literacy as an object of EU policy. The EC's Communication from 2007 defines media literacy as "the ability to access the media, to understand and to critically evaluate different aspects of the media and media contents, and to create communications in a variety of contexts" (EC 2007). This definition is in line with Aufderheide's broad understanding and is regarded as the basis for all further actions and initiatives by EU, including the assessment of media literacy levels (Ding 2008: 5). Three years later the EC's Digital Agenda adopts a different reading, however, that focuses on the importance of cultivating digital skills and competencies in a knowledge economy (EC 2010). There the instrumental character of digital literacies becomes central at the expense of the EC's focus on critical media knowledge. It has to be acknowledged though, that there have been efforts on EU-Level to fill the 'empirical vacuum' surrounding the concept of media literacy.

In 2007 the Audiovisual Media Services Directive (AVMSD) introduced a reporting obligation for the Commission on media literacy levels in all Member States (§26). By collecting and analysing media literacy data in different Member States, the European Association for Viewers' Interests [EAVI] "Study on Assessment Criteria for Media Literacy Levels" from 2009 extracted a basic set of indicators on an individual and environmental scale (the latter includes the contribution of public service media) that allows for a both qualitative and quantitative assessment of media literacy levels in the countries and enables comparisons between the Member States (EAVI 2009).

As a result of its inherent normativity, media literacy turns out to be susceptible to divergent political readings. Its substantial dimension can therefore not be assessed without considering the normative purposes media literacy is expected to fulfil. In that regard, the promotion of media literacy can take on different shapes and serve different political ends, as broadly captured by Livingstone et al (2005: 3) in three categories:

1) Democracy, participation and active citizenship

2) Knowledge economy, competitiveness and choice

3) Lifelong learning, cultural expression and personal fulfilment

These normative categories can be weighted differently, depending on the relevant media and political system. It can be argued that the substantial dimension of media literacy depends mostly on the socio-political context in which it is embedded.

The substantial dimension of the public value debate

As earlier chapters have discussed more fully the public value debate that has been shaping PSM policy in Europe since 2004 is about the institution's purpose, first, and also its value in performance. These are also clearly subject to largely normative readings of public value (e.g. Radoslavov & Thomass 2011; Karmasin 2009; Hasebrink 2007), which makes the quest for a common substantial dimension of the public value debate in Europe difficult.

The consensual foundations for a common reading of public value by Europe's public broadcasters were established in the Amsterdam Protocol in 1997, which postulates that: "the system of public broadcasting in the Member States is directly related to the democratic, social and cultural needs of each society". The phrase 'each society' is important because it demonstrates differentiation in the wider 'common market'. Since 1997 broadcasters and legislators in the Member States have been wrestling with the implications, however, as they are under pressure to constantly (re-)define PSM remits and must do so in balance with (and against) the principles of internal market competition. The ex-ante assessment approach described in chapter 3 is the characteristic example of a generalisable policy result.

In 2006 the BBC constructed this fundamental orientation on the claim that, "for us, public value is the sum of the civic, social and cultural benefits the BBC delivers when it meets its public purposes" (Thompson 2006). That formulation was adopted for largely instrumental purposes, however, in the context of BBC Charter renewal (Lee et al 2011). In Germany the approach was adopted in 2009 and the benchmarks for approving a PSM service were directly referred to as the democratic, social and cultural values it would provide (Hasebrink 2009: 10).

Certainly the ways those values are weighed and interpreted within the Member States differ (Donders & Moe 2011) and this can be ascribed to the diverging cultural, political, historical and economic foundations within countries that have shaped their national media regulation and constituted different public value constructs on often distinctive bases. Building upon Hallin and Mancini's (2004) three media system models, Karmasin (2009: 95) identifies three ideal conceptions of public value's substantial dimension, which vary according to the weight they ascribe to different values of public broadcasting: public value as a public good, public value as a cultural good and public value as a democratic good.

The interpretation of 'public value as a public good' highlights the societal relevance of programming and its non-rivalrous and non-excludable aspects, from an economic perspective. The conception is implemented to compensate for market failure in liberal economy systems e.g. in the United Kingdom and Germany. The interpretation of 'public value as a cultural good' connects the merit character of broadcasting to the promotion of cultural and national identity, and thus operates as a counterweight to economic realities impacting the media. This is especially true in France and Italy, but as well in small states including Denmark, Norway and Sweden (Moe 2009: 190). The interpretation of 'public value as a democratic good' is orientated towards the ideal political tasks of the media. In this understanding PSM safeguards plurality of opinions and supports an active public sphere. According to Hallin and Mancini this can mostly be seen with the democratic-corporatist model characteristic of Germany, Austria or the Netherlands.

Looking at both media literacy and public value it seems that neither concept has any inherent or universal substantial public value dimension. The realisation of both depends on normative and often politicised readings that evolve around the idea of PSM purpose. Therefore, when comparing media literacy readings among the broadcasters, it is important to keep in mind that each represents a particular prescriptive context and political process.

The process dimension of media literacy promotion

As indicated earlier three of the essential normative purposes the EBU (2012) associates with improvements in media literacy include creating a trusted space, bridging the digital divide, and empowering citizens to democracy. These aims sound ambitious, which is fine of course, but as Livingstone (2011: 31) has observed, "At the same time, the field of media literacy is characterised by a very considerable gap between aims and implementation, for the means are generally insufficient for the ends". So in order to analyse media literacy promotion from a public value perspective it is necessary to focus on both the aims and the implementation – a process that has been often referred to as media education (Bachmair 2010; Süss et al. 2010; Buckingham 2005).

Media education history has been shaped by two paradigms, protection and promotion, that hinge on variance in defining the way 'the public' is approached (Celot 2008). The protectionist stance, which prevailed in debate before the 1980s, is based on the concept of a passive recipient who needs to be protected from harmful media content. Preventive measures and restrictive sanctions against media providers dominated this paradigm.

The gradual deregulation of media industries in Europe brought also a paradigmatic shift within the process of media education. Within the spirit of self- and co-regulation, media providers were no longer subjects of restrictive regulation (protection of minors, for example) but rather partners in the process of media education. Their goal was no longer to protect the public but to raise public awareness through information campaigns and to encourage users to autonomously access, analyse and evaluate media contents. Protection was gradually replaced by the objective of promotion. In line with the theme in this chapter, media literacy promotion refers to the active participation of PSM in the process of media education.

In Moore's understanding public value strategies have to go beyond the substantial public value dimension, that includes normative definitions and purposes, and to also focus on organisational implementation (Moore 1995: 74). This is about process value[4], which addresses the why and how of media literacy promotion and which involves a complex and interdependent process of authorisation, operationalisation and evaluation[5]. In order to incorporate the process dimension into the case study analysis it will be necessary to go beyond the 'what' of the substantial dimension and include the 'why' and 'how' of the process dimension that media literacy promotion implies. The following case studies are structured along four aspects relevant to this purpose: definition, authorisation, operationalisation and evaluation.

Case studies: BBC, ZDF and RAI

The three PSM case studies originate from countries that represent Karamasin's different public value readings as discussed earlier. The BBC (UK) is therefore expected to put more weight on creating public value as a public good, ZDF (Germany) on public value as a democratic good, and RAI (Italy) on public value as a cultural good. This does not mean, that any of the institutions would neglect the other two readings. The case studies feature large public service institutions from big media markets that have sufficient financial and institutional resources to develop an own strategy of media literacy promotion.

As institutions do not always speak for themselves in documentary terms, the case studies are based on expert interviews with those PSM-practitioners entrusted with the co-ordination of media literacy promotion within their institutions. Martin Wilson, Head of Media Literacy (BBC),Dr. Gunnar Krone, Trustee for the Protection of Minors (ZDF), Markus Nikel, Consultant *RaiEducational* (RAI) and Maria Bollini, Head of Children Programming *RaiTreBambini* (RAI) were interviewed between 12th September and 12th November 2010[6].

This method allowed exploration of the way practitioners read and reason the process of media literacy promotion, with the aim of studying the internal logics of the institutions they represent (Feeling & Gottwald 2008: 8). In accordance with the theoretical reflections so far, the interviews focus on the strategic questions of media literacy promotion: what (substantial dimension), why and how (process dimension).

BBC, United Kingdom

Definition: In defining media literacy, the BBC refers to Ofcom, the British regulator's definition. As entrusted by the Communications Act (2003), Ofcom is responsible for the active U.K. promotion of media literacy and defines it as "the ability to access, understand and create content in a variety of contexts" (Ofcom 2004: 2) The BBC's online media literacy platform was named 'Connect' and places the emphasis on access and digital skills[7]. The BBC envisions the media literate individual as a 'confident user' of new media – it is therefore the BBC's task to accompany people on their learning journeys from *'media rejecters' to 'confident users'* of digital media (Wilson 2010).

Authorisation: The BBC's activities in the promotion of media literacy are largely legitimated by the sixth public purpose in its public value strategy, "helping to deliver to the public the benefits of emerging communications technologies and services" (BBC Trust 2010a: 4). Within that context, the BBC interprets its primary task as improving access to and handling of new digital technologies. This demands achieving one essential objective: universal access for all UK license-fee payers not only to the BBC's digital content, but to public services in general. According to Wilson this approach stems from the implications of the UK government's broadband initiative *Digital Britain* (DCMS 2009): "Because we are going through huge policy changes here, and people are going to have to relate to, talk to government websites in order to get benefits and upload information, with other words there is a level of media literacy now that everybody needs" (Wilson 2010). The UK Government's White Paper on the BBC Charter Review argues that: "the BBC continues to play a leading role in the development of a media literate population in the UK, helping people to understand and access new communications technologies and underpinning personal creativity in the digital age" (DCMS, 2006: 14). The BBC's reach and trustworthiness become powerful aspects of this policy instrument within the framework of a national digital strategy.

Operationalisation: In October 2009, the BBC's Director General, Mark Thompson, established a separate media literacy unit with a core team of six members. Its tasks comprise the co-ordination of media literacy initiatives by working closely with all relevant departments, evaluating available resources, selecting and branding existing output by "making it look like a coherent offering" (Wilson 2010). As the media literacy unit disposes of its own budget, it is also able to commission media literacy programmes within the BBC, out-source campaigns and conduct relevant research. The media literacy unit is also responsible for packaging media literacy content on platforms and linking those assets to each other.

One of the most crucial tasks for the media literacy unit is to raise the BBC's staff awareness of the importance of promoting media literacy, which goes beyond the institutional boundaries of the media literacy unit and is perceived as a task for the whole corporation.*BBC Learning* is primarily responsible for delivering basic educational content, *BBC Academy* offers more advanced voca-tional training, *BBC Marketing* is commissioned with the development of trailers and campaigns, and *BBC Audiences* with long term evaluation of the output.

Evaluation: One of the main purposes for establishing the media literacy unit within the BBC in 2009 has been to deliver tangible results for the promotion of media literacy. The unit relies mostly on quantitative criteria like audience reach, level of satisfaction surveys, quantity of feedback and long term tracking research. It also implements qualitative criteria by inquiring into the extent to which the BBC has helped people to better understand the digital environ-ment and emerging technologies. However, research and assessment are not directly conducted by the unit but rather commissioned from *BBC Audiences* or external research companies, which then develop their own criteria and vari-ables. The *BBC Trust* also actively commissions research in the field of media literacy in its responsibilities for oversight and evaluation of BBC fulfilment of the six public purposes[8].

ZDF, Germany

Definition: ZDF has not undertaken independent theoretical work on the sub-ject so far and employs existing definitions from studies in media pedagogy and quotes Baacke's well established definition of *Medienkompetenz*, which divides media literacy into four basic components: use, knowledge, critical understanding and creativity (Baacke 1997: 123). This definition is considered dynamic enough to encompass the socio-technical changes induced by media convergence: "Until now we have not had enough reasons to consider the Ger-man definition inappropriate. Instead, we have always followed the traditional line" (Krone 2010).

The institutional reading of media literacy embeds the concept into a rather legalistic dichotomy, which differentiates between restrictive and preventive protection of minors in the media (*restriktiver und präventiver Jugendmedi-enschutz*). Promoting media literacy becomes a sub-domain of the preventive protection of minors in the media and serves as a proactive instrument in that special field, which has some implications for the way media literacy is read.

Keywords like 'danger', 'risk' and 'harm' shape media literacy discourse on an institutional scale[9]. The ideal type of a media literate individual is a media user who is capable of recognising and also evading problematic aspects of media communication, like violence, cybermobbing, information overflow, etc. (Krone 2010). ZDF is therefore expected to provide a secure space where users (children, but also parents) can acquire the necessary competencies (ibid).

Authorisation: ZDF's primary involvement in the promotion of media literacy derives from the German Constitution, which underlines the fundamental rights of minors and the necessity for their protection (GG §1, §5 (2) and §6). The position of the media literacy expert is a result of the Interstate Treaty on the Protection of Minors (*Jugendmedienschutzstaatsvertrag*), which obliges television channels with national coverage and more than 50 employees to appoint a trustee for the protection of minors (JMStV: §7 (1)). This explains why the media literacy promotion within the institution adopts a more protectionist stance. ZDF's role here derives mostly from a general responsibility to safeguard minors' fundamental rights and is addressed as "an important element of the social responsibility of public service broadcasting" (Krone 2010).

Operationalisation: ZDF's *Jugendschutzbeauftragte* monitors ZDF's programme output with the purpose of preventing the transmission of potentially harmful content for vulnerable groups, especially children and adolescents. With media literacy being understood as part of the preventive protection of minors, it falls also within the competence of that particular position. So, apart from managing complaints and feedback from the audience, the trustee also works on raising critical media awareness for media consumption. Thus, initiating, co-ordinating and presenting media literacy campaigns and programmes belongs to that second part of his functions.

Other editorial entities, children programming and the department for new media also contribute to the promotion of media literacy – their initiatives are spread throughout genres and platforms. Similar to the BBC, ZDF's *Jugendschutzbeauftragte's* function is to package the delivered output, mostly by submitting media literacy promotion reports to the Director General, the Television Council and to the general public.

The introduction of the ex-ante-assessment (*Dreistufentest*) in Germany has also boosted the impetus-setting function of the Television Council (*Fernsehrat*). Whereas the promotion of media literacy has become an oft mentioned criterion in the process of ex ante assessment of online services, the council has gradually acquired the competence to formulate suggestions that often address the promotion of media literacy as a normative objective of programme making[10].

Evaluation: Although ZDF's research department is very active in gathering data on media consumption of children and adolescents, the concrete impact of ZDF's media literacy programmes and campaigns remains unknown. Developing and institutionalising media literacy research at the broadcaster's level is regarded as unfeasible because such research would go beyond the limits of the public service remit (Krone 2010). When assessing concrete media literacy programmes their makers mostly refer to typical broadcasting data, like audience reach, audience feedback and expert critique. The content analysis of audience feedback remains the most common qualitative research tool the broadcaster implies to explore the impact of its media literacy promotion.

RAI, Italy

Definition: The Italian public service broadcaster doesn't have its own unique definition of media literacy. In fact, the phrase is not common in the relevant policy discourse and there is no Italian translation for 'media literacy'. Instead, both experts interviewed in this study referred to the term 'media education' and its definition was coined by a civil society organisation, MED – the Italian Association for Media Education. They define media education as "an educative and didactic activity which should develop the critical information and comprehension of young people regarding the nature and types of media, the techniques media practitioners use in order to construct messages and produce meaning, the genres and the special languages"[11]. In the view of RAI practitioners the media literate individual is a young media user who is able to critically understand (mostly audiovisual) media communication, differentiate among media languages, and produce his or her own messages.

Authorisation: Although media literacy promotion might be indirectly regarded as part of RAI's educational remit, there is no statutory obligation or requirement. According to the educational remit the public broadcaster is *inter alia* accountable for raising critical understanding of contents among its audiences (Nikel 2010). This vague purpose might legitimate media literacy projects and initiatives, but it does not actively require them.

The rather loose authorisation framework gives more leeway for personal normative readings of RAI's s role in promoting media literacy. On the one hand, Nikel ascribes the promotion of media literacy to the purpose of increasing the public's ability to acquire critical distance from a very commercialised media landscape. Although television is a constant topic in Italian societal discourse, he wishes for more transparency regarding commercial affiliations of Italian television, as well as more critical understanding among citizens of the basics of commercial communication, such as sponsoring, product placement, public relations (Nikel 2010). On the other hand, raising television awareness among children is the main normative objective in Bollini's practical interpretation of media literacy. She perceives it as "the competence to understand what happens behind the screen, how do contents go on air, who works there, how contents are produced"(Bollini 2010). Although they differ in their conception of target groups and normative purposes, both readings find their legitimation in the deficits of Italian television society where fiction and reality are difficult to separate.

Operationalisation: RAI does not have a separate body dealing with media literacy promotion. Media literacy output is primarily delivered by *RaiTre Bambini* and *RaiEducational*, the former a generalist channel's offer for children and the later a thematic channel with marginal audience shares. Whereas *RaiTreBambini* addresses children in an *'edutainment'* mode and promotes media literacy among others, *RaiEducational* is explicitly dedicated to educational and learning purposes. The division of media literacy promotion leads to a lack of a coherent strategy for media education on an institutional level.

Evaluation: Because RAI depends on advertising for more than half of its total revenues, it is not surprising that audience share functions as the main success criterion for programmes overall, including those that promote media literacy (Bollini 2010). On the institutional level there are no specific media literacy criteria. Both educational and children's programming rely on complementary qualitative reception studies to assess the success of particular programmes with an educational profile. Whereas *RaiTreBambini* has developed long term co-operation with the University of Torino for conducting those studies, *RaiEducational* relies on partnership with the Italian Ministry of Education, which co-funds several educational programmes and therefore evaluates their impact among particular target groups (students and teachers mostly). The experts interviewed have to legitimate those complementary studies with the specific nature of educational broadcasting: "Because of their public value and their learning-effects, educational programs need more attention than mainstream broadcasting (Nikel 2010). In an institution that defines itself as a mainstream broadcaster, however, such initiatives of complementary evaluation do not seem to be the established institutional practice.

Summary analysis of the three cases

Definitions: None of the three institutions has adopted a common media literacy definition (say from the EU or the EBU) or developed their own. They use existing, nationally conceived definitions conceived by regulatory bodies (BBC), scholars (ZDF) or civil society organisations (RAI). These place the emphasis of media literacy on different aspects. Whereas the BBC stresses the positive external effects of digital media, ZDF focuses on preventing the negative ones. In contrast, the Italian broadcaster focuses on television and the ability of the user to critically decipher the language of television.

The broadcasters' readings of media literacy promotion depend strongly on pre-existing institutional and political frameworks and therefore diverge in their substantial dimension. The readings of media literacy take different directions and have diverse normative purposes in the three case studies. To some extent the normative readings of media literacy correspond to the public value models, however, as discussed above.

In the case of the BBC, universal access to digital media is perceived as a public good. As the market has difficulties in closing that gap alone, public service media's intervention is legitimated mainly as a compensation for market failure. ZDF's normative approach towards media literacy can be roughly categorised within the reading of public value as a democratic good because there media literacy (*Medienkompetenz*)is perceived as a prerequisite for enjoying the benefits of a democratic public sphere.

In the case of RAI there is little relation between the broadcaster's reading of media literacy and the value of this for the Italian public. RAI's approach towards media literacy in a strongly 'televised' society has a stronger relation to public value as a democratic good than to public value as a cultural good. One possible reason for this discrepancy could lie in the high level of personalised media literacy promotion within the institution. In contrast to the detailed normative backbones that the BBC and ZDF refer to, when translating media literacy into practice, RAI's media literacy practitioners refer to less formal and binding definitions and purposes.

Authorisation: Compared to the other broadcasters, media literacy promotion seems to be of highest relevance for the BBC as it is directly derived from the institution's sixth public purpose. However, the promotion of media literacy is not conceived as a distinct public value strategy but rather as an instrumental asset within a broader governmental policy framework (i.e. *Digital Britain*). ZDF, on the other hand, derives authority from the existing legal provisions on national level as it must contribute to the preventive protection of the rights of minors. Due to the nature of this authorisation process, the institution adopts a more protectionist stance towards the promotion of media literacy. Both BBC and ZDF reflect and advocate their involvement within the context of 'normative backbones'– in each case a national policy, either as a programme in the U.K or with constitutional foundations in Germany. The Italian broadcaster on the other hand derives that task only indirectly from its educational remit, which results in the more traditional understanding of media literacy promotion as media education. Media literacy promotion is primarily authorised by the personal initiatives of its employees.

Operationalisation: The promotion of media literacy in all three broadcasters is decentralised and spread across different units within the institutions. Programme departments, marketing, and research all approach the subject from different perspectives. The media literacy experts interviewed for this study praise this decentralised approach as advocating the heterogeneity of media literacy output and normative readings. In contrast to their Italian colleagues, those responsible for media literacy at the BBC and ZDF are not directly involved in programme making and have a more strategic position. They do affect media literacy output by actively interacting with programme makers and by (re-)packaging and presenting their output.

Evaluation: In all case studies, research departments, external consultancy companies, university institutes apply their own methodologies and respectively their own criteria of evaluation for media literacy. Although all three broadcasters commission qualitative reception studies, audience share and reach remain the key criteria everywhere that decide the success of a particular media literacy programme. All experts interviewed would like to have both quantitative and qualitative assessment criteria tailored for the impact evaluation of media literacy promotion, however.

Conclusions

The chapter explored media literacy promotion by public service broadcasters along the instrumental, substantial and process dimensions of public value. It was argued that the instrumental dimension applied so far by PSBs (in the form of the best-practice approach) does not suffice to prove public value because idiosyncrasy is characteristic in the provision of merit goods, particularly in diverging national media markets and political systems.

The theoretical reflections in the first part have also indicated that media literacy promotion does not have an inherent universal substantial dimension. The variable and normative nature of the concept makes it susceptible to political purposes and readings. As the case studies show, the broadcasters' normative readings of media literacy do not rely on common EU or academic definitions but instead build on the specifics of national media and political systems (*i.e. Digital Britain*) – an insight that once again underlines the significant weight of national culture within the framework of European public service media policy.

The case studies also demonstrate the essential role of the process dimension in shaping media literacy promotion. As the ZDF case shows, the authorisation procedure exerts a massive impact on the way media literacy promotion is understood, in this particular case as protection. The (lack of) institutional implementation in RAI leads to an almost partisan approach towards the promotion of media literacy – the insufficient evaluation procedures subordinates media literacy promotion to traditional assessment criteria of mainstream broadcasting like the audience share.

In conclusion, I would argue that the promotion of media literacy is one way of creating public value, as it goes beyond the interests of individual consumers and benefits society as a whole. Public service broadcasters in Europe have so far been very active in promoting media literacy – in order to qualify these efforts as public value, it is however necessary to actively manage first the process and then the substantial dimensions of media literacy promotion. If the institutions figure out how to take such advice on board, they could tap an additional and arguably also more coherent source of institutional legitimacy.

Notes

1. The final decision on the ZDF's three-step-test mentions the merit of media literacy promotion fifteen times and ascribes it to different genres and platforms (heute.de, tivi.de, etc.)
2. Although public value is not discussed as merit goods per se in Moore's early work, the concept is an evident theme in his more recent edited volume with John Benington (2011: 31). Here public value is redefined 'not just in terms of 'What does the public most value?' but also in terms of 'What adds value to the public sphere?'.
3. In a research period of three years, Gapski (2001) distinguished 104 definitions of media literacy. The study was limited to German scientific literature only.
4. "Creating public value" addresses the process dimension of public value with different terminology. Throughout the book Moore speaks of 'operational value' (300), process virtues (163), 'form and function' (263) and administrative expertise (cited from Banfield 1960: 20-23). Such terms are deliberately distinguished from substantial value. For a clearer understanding the chapter sticks to the term 'process dimension', as applied by Radoslavov & Thomas (2011).
5. The three levels of the process dimension have been elaborated in detail in The Work Foundation (Horner et.al 2006: 27).
6. For the sake of brevity the interviewees will be cited with surname only, e.g. (Wilson, 2010).
7. At the time of writing the BBC's media literacy platform was moved BBC Learning: http://www.bbc.co.uk/learning/overview/about/digitalliteracy.shtml
8. For more details see the Purpose Remit Tracking Study (BBC Trust, 2010a) and the Media Literacy Report (BBC Trust, 2010b).
9. http://www.zdf.de/Kinder-und-Jugendschutz-im-ZDF-26449984.html
10. The 12th Interstate Broadcasting Treaty (2010) explicitly ascribes the promotion of media literacy to public service online services (*Telemedien*) with the purpose of providing orientation and inclusion of all population groups into the information society (RÄStV §11 (3)).
11. http://www.mediaeducationmed.it/associazione-med/cosa-e-la-media-education.html

References

Aufderheide, P. (1993) *Media Literacy: A Report on the National Leadership Conference on Media Literacy*. Aspen, CO: Aspen Institute.

Baacke, D. (1996) Medienkompetenz – Begrifflichkeit und Sozialer Wandel. In: Rein (Ed.) *Medienkompetenz als Schlüsselbegriff*. Bad Heilbrunn: Klinckhardt, pp. 112-124.

Bachmair, B. (2010)(ed.) *Medienbildung in neuen Kulturräumen*. Wiesbaden: VSVerlag.

Benington, J.& Moore, M.H. (eds.) (2011) *Public Value Theory& Practice*. Basingstoke: Palgrave-macmillan.

Bollini, M. (2010) Expert interview conducted on 24.11.2010

Brown, A. (1997) Economics, public service broadcasting, and social values. *Journal of Media Economics*, 9(1), pp. 3-15.

BBC (2004) *Building Public Value: Renewing the BBC for a digital world*. London. *http://downloads.bbc.co.uk/aboutthebbc/policies/pdf/bpv.pdf*

BBC Trust (2010a) *Purpose remit tracking study 2009-2010: Quantitative audience research assessing the BBC's delivery of its public purposes – UK Findings*. London. *http://www.bbc.co.uk/bbctrust/ assets/files/ pdf/review_report_research/ara2009_10/purpose_remits_uk.pdf*

BBC Trust (2010b) *Media Literacy: A report into Research Conducted on Behalf of the BBC Trust.* Leamington Spa: The Knowledge Agency.

Buckingham, D. (2005) *The Media Literacy of Children and Young People: A Review of the Research Literature.* London: Ofcom.

Celot, P. (2008) *Media Literacy in Europa: Leggere, scrivere e parteciparenell'eramediatica.* Roma:Eurilink.

Collins, R. (1998) Public service and the media economy: European trends in the late 1990s. *International Communication Gazette,60(5),*pp. 363-378.

D'Amico, D. (2009) *Merit Goods, Paternalism and Responsibility.* Rome: Società Italiana di Economia Pubblica.

Department for Culture, Media and Sports (2006) *A Public Service for All: The BBC in the Digital Age. http://www.official-documents.gov.uk/document/ cm67/6763/6763.pdf*

Department for Culture, Media and Sports (2009) *Digital Britain Final Report.http://webarchive. nationalarchives.gov.uk/+/http://www.culture.gov.uk/images/publications/digitalbritain-finalreport-jun09.pdf*

Ding, S. (2011) The European Commission's Approach to Media Literacy. In Livingstone, S. (ed.) *Media Literacy: Ambitions, Policy and Measures,* pp. 5-8.

EAVI (2009) *Study on Assessment Criteria for Media Literacy Levels.* A comprehensive view of the concept of media literacy and an understanding of how media literacy levels in Europe should be assessed. Brussels: EAVI.

EBU (2012) Empowering Citizenship through Media Literacy: The Role of Public Service Media. *http://www3.ebu.ch/files/live/sites/ebu/files/Knowledge/ Publication%20Library/EBU-Viewpoint-Media-Lit_EN.pdf*

European Commission (2010) *A Digital Agenda for Europe http://ec.europa.eu/digital-agenda/en/ our-goals/pillar-vi-enhancing-digital-literacy-skills-and-inclusion*

European Commission (2007) *A European approach to media literacy in the digital environment http://ec.europa.eu/culture/media/media-content/media-literacy/c_2007_833_en_1.pdf*

European Union (1997) Protocol on the system of public broadcasting in the Member States *http:// eur-lex.europa.eu/LexUriServ/LexUriServ.do? uri=CELEX:11997D/PRO/09:EN:HTML*

Freiling, T. & Gottwald, M. (2008) *Qualitative Methoden Auswertung von Interviews. http://www. fbb.de/fileadmin/Materialien/Ringvorlesung/ 080704__qualitative_Methoden_fbb.pdf*

Gapski, H. (2001) *Medienkompetenz. Eine Bestandsaufnahme und Vorüberlegungen zu einem systemtheoretischen Rahmenkonzept.* Wiesbaden: Westdeutscher Verlag.

Hasebrink, U. (2007) „Public Value": Leitbegriff oder Nebelkerze in der Diskussion um den öffentlich-rechtlichen Rundfunk? In: *Zeitschrift für Rundfunk und Geschichte* (1-2), pp. 38-42.

Hasebrink, U. (2009) *Publizistischer Wert und Qualitäten der Telemedien des ZDF:* Begriffserklärung und Einordnung. Ergebnisse einer Expertise für die ZDF Medienforschung.

Horner, L., Lekhi, R. & Blaug, R. (2006): *Deliberative democracy and the Role of Public Managers.* Final report of the Work Foundation's public value consortium. http://theworkfoundation. com/assets/docs/ publications/107_Deliberative%20democracy%20and%20the%20role%20 of%20public%20managers.pdf

Jarren, O. & Wassmer, C. (2009) Medienkompetenz Begriffsanalyse und Modell. Ein Diskussionsbeitrag zum Stand der Medienkompetenzforschung. In: *Medien + Erziehung* 53 (3), pp. 46-51.

Karmasin, M. (2009) Public Value: Konturen und Konsequenzen eines Legitimationsbegriffs. In: Brandner-Radinger, Ilser (ed.) *Was kommt. Was bleibt. 150 Jahre Presseclub Concordia.* Wien: Facultas, pp. 91-99.

Kiefer, M. (2005) *Medienökonomik,* (2 ed.) München: Oldenbourg.

Krone, G. (2010) Expert interview conducted on 11.11.2010.

Labourdette, N. (2010): *Media Literacy &Public Service Media.* Presentation at the Media& Learning Conference. Brussels: 25-26.11.2010

Lee, D.J., Oakley, K. & Naylor, R. (2011) 'The public gets what the public wants': The uses and abuses of 'public value' in contemporary British cultural policy. *International Journal of Cultural Policy, 17*(3), pp. 289-300.

Livingstone, S. (2004) *Media literacy and the challenge of new informationand communication technologies.* LSE Research Online: *http://eprints.lse.ac.uk/1017*

Livingstone, S., Van Couvering, E. & Thumin, N. (2005): *Converging Traditions of Research on Media and Information Literacies: Disciplinary, Critical and Methodological Issues*. LSE Research Online: *http://eprints.lse.ac.uk/23564/*

Moe, H. (2009) Status und Perspektiven öffentlich-rechtlicher Onlinemedien. Erfahrungen aus Großbrittanien, Norwegen und Deutschland. In: *Media Perspektiven*. 4/2009, pp. 189-200.

Mohr, I., Breunig, C, Feierabend, S., Nolting, C. & Oehmichen, E. (2003) (ed.) *Medienkompetenz bei ARD und ZDF. Angebote des öffentlich-rechtlichen Rundfunks*. München: Kopaed.

Moore, M.H. (1995): *Creating Public Value. Strategic Management in Government*. Cambridge, MA: Harvard University Press.

Musgrave, R. (1957) A Multiple Theory of Budget Determination. *Finanzarchiv*, New Series, 25 (1), pp. 33-43.

Nikel, M. (2010) Expert interview conducted on 10.11.2010

Ofcom (2004) *Ofcom's Strategy and Priorities for the Promotion of Media Literacy. http://stakeholders.Ofcom.org.uk/binaries/consultations/ strategymedialit/summary/strat_prior_statement.pdf*

Radoslavov, S. & Thomass, B. (2011) Public Value. In: Karmasin, M. et. al.: *Public Value Theorie und Praxis im internationalen Vergleich*. Wiesbaden: VS Verlag, pp. 173-189.

Solberg, H.A. (2007) Sports Broadcasting: Is it a Job for Public Service Broadcasters? A Welfare Economic Perspective. In: *Journal of Media Economics 20* (4), pp. 289-309.

Süss, D., Lampert, C. & Wijnen, C.W. (2010) *Medienpädagogik*. Wiesbaden: VS Verlag für Sozialwissenschaften.

Thompson, M. (2006) *Delivering Public Value*. Speech Online: *http://www.bbc.co.uk/print/pressoffice/speeches/stories/thompson_smith.shtml*

Wilson, M. (2010) Expert interview conducted on 10.09.2010.

ZDF (2010) *Jugendmedienschutz in der Gemeinwohlbildung*. Mainz: ZDF.

Chapter 12

Extending the Public Service Remit through *ABC Pool*

Jonathon Hutchinson

Due in large part to public service broadcasting's decade-long exploration of media convergence, audience participation and multiplatform content delivery, as well as new services created for the online, non-linear environment, it is fair to say that innovation is not a new characteristic of public service media [PSM]. The remit for public service broadcasting [PSB] in most places was not exclusively about broadcasting as such, but typically prioritised initiating and facilitating activities to support a broad cultural infrastructure and to secure national identities in pluralising societies (Wilson, Hutchinson & Shea 2010). The recent focus on developing new content delivery platforms and services (see especially Debrett 2010; Brevini, 2013) signifies a semantic shift from the era of PSB to the emergence of public service media organisations (Flew 2011; Lowe & Bardoel 2007).

On numerous occasions the convergent PSM organisation has been the target of criticism from media industry moguls and conservative policy makers, accused of overstepping its role in a post-scarcity media market, keyed to an argument that PSM is 'crowding-out' the private sector. During his 2009 MacTaggart Lecture, as a distinctive example, James Murdoch questioned the role of regulation within a media rich environment, suggesting that "a heavily regulated environment with a large public sector crowds out the opportunity for profit, hinders the creation of new jobs, and dampens innovation in our sector" (Murdoch 2009). Murdoch's direct attack on the regulatory framework of media industries suggests that governments which interfere with the marketplace through regulation are inhibiting growth and development, bringing into serious question the remit of public service media (beyond traditional broadcasting, at least).

Murdoch's complaint highlights a common critique of the innovative work undertaken by PSM, often performed under the regulatory auspices of institutional governance. If subsidised by government to undertake experimental modes of content production and delivery through information communication technologies, PSM organisations very well can enjoy a significant economic advantage over their commercial competitors. However, a line of enquiry has emerged from the creative industries field that moves discussion beyond the crowding out argument to analyse the marketplace role of PSM. Potts et al. (2008) suggest the crowding out argument is over- simplistic because PSM should be viewed as an instrument that engages in and stimulates innovative practices: making provision for new activity within an abundant media marketplace (see also Cunningham 2013). Others have suggested that PSB long had a pioneering role in new media and technology developments, and has been vital to the project of constructing what only afterwards became a market (Lund & Lowe 2013).

Positioning PSM as an experimenter and developer in, and for, the creation of new investment opportunities in a contemporary marketplace shifts thinking about these institutions from terms that privilege revenue issues and treat them pejoratively as 'innovation sponges'. In this view one sees them as organisations that are responsible for testing the dynamics of online media environments that are prone to rapid change – which is to say, high instability and considerable risk. PSM in this view has the opportunity (and obligation) to become a market organiser for developing social and cultural capital amongst the societies they are mandated to serve, and that is accomplished mainly by explicitly including experimentation as a valid aspect of their public service remits.

In this chapter, I propose a new apparatus to extend the public service remit and develop the value of PSM for its publics. The apparatus is the emergent importance of the mediator role in the production ecology, making the case for what I will call *cultural intermediation*. In brief, this means PSM is a means for developing social and cultural capital, harnessed through co-creative activities, which builds up the creation of new media markets. I define and develop the significance of cultural intermediation in three sections that culminate in that explicate the term.

The first section builds on Cunningham's (2013) 'distinctive innovation' no-tion, which "moves the sector [forward] from Reithian justifications of normative market shaping to a more nimble, facilitative role of performing experimental R&D for the system – a very recognisable role for the public sector from an innovation perspective" (Cunningham 2013: 95). Here I will demonstrate distinc-tive innovation with three examples of audience participation: a) participatory media at Channel 4iP (Jackson 2008), b) DR Youth at the Danish Broadcasting Corporation [DR] (Bechmann 2011), and c) Capture Wales (Kidd 2008). These examples highlight the significance of PSMs for building social and cultural capital through experimental projects in new media products and services, and thereby demonstrate the role of cultural intermediation.

In the second section the focus is on one particular case study at the Austral-ian Broadcasting Corporation [ABC], called ABC Pool (www.abc.net.au/pool). I discuss the context and uniqueness of the ABC, which operates in a dual broadcast licensing system. Established in the 1930s, this system protects the revenues of commercial stakeholders while enabling two government-funded broadcasters, the ABC and the Special Broadcasting Service [SBS]. Both operate at a distance from vested interests. ABC Pool emerged from Radio National[1] as an experimental project to lower the barrier of participation for Australian artists. This platform incorporates the diversity of the ABC audience into the production process of 'cultural artefacts', defined here as creative media products that provide information about the contemporary Australian socio-cultural landscape. By highlighting the social and cultural benefits of the *New Beginnings* co-creative project, ABC Pool (and the earlier illustrations from elsewhere), I exemplify how PSM organisations are incorporating audience participation as an important aspect of their mandated activities.

The final section establishes the concept of cultural intermediation within PSM. Cultural intermediation is defined as "the combination of ... human and non-human actors [to] negotiate cultural artefact production" (Hutchinson 2012). The notion is useful for understanding how cultural and social capital production can be managed within media systems. In this instance, social capital refers to strong personal relationships between the broadcaster and its audience (BBC 2006), while cultural capital refers to externalities or benefits beyond economic value, for example education as a social asset that has general public value (Woolsey & Biggart 2008). PSM engages the audience's production of social capital through multiple production roles from online moderators through to content producers and community managers, while designing and developing the online tools and platforms that enable users to participate in such activities.

The chapter examines multiple cultural intermediaries who explore the diversity of a PSM audience and engage in co-creative practice on the production of cultural artefacts. It highlights the emergence of the intermediary in internet research within the context of public service media. Furthermore, this chapter indicates how some PSM organisations have incorporated online activity into their charters, while others have not.

I want to highlight the connection between cultural intermediation and the value of public service media. Historically, PSM has facilitated projects that increase the social and cultural capital of audiences. But of course there are examples of projects that have not achieved that goal, irrespective of best intentions. This is precisely the role of the cultural intermediary: to manage and ensure the facilitation of the PSM's social and cultural capital building capacities are realised, which requires taking and managing the risk in a highly uncertain and clearly experimental context. Cultural intermediation is the process that ensures the increase in public service media value from not only the perspective of the institution but also in conjunction *with* the audience.

The data presented in this chapter is from a two-year ethnographic research project where I was embedded at the ABC as the community manager of ABC Pool. I was a paid employee for the second half of the research, which provided increased access to participants and processes essential for developing the cultural intermediary framework. Ethical issues associated with my researching role are addressed in Hutchinson (2012). I will discuss the benefits of having a dual role (community manager + ethnographer) because that was instrumental to the development of the cultural intermediation framework.

PSM innovation in practice

Distinctive innovation is a specific form that, as Cunningham (2013) suggests, is particularly suitable for PSM. It is useful for moving the innovation argument beyond claims of crowding out and market failure, and it provides a point of departure for examining how experimental activities affect the production of cultural capital. The incorporation of audience participation in the co-creative production of cultural artefacts is a core activity for a PSM organisation that is exercising distinctive innovation in efforts to develop social and cultural capital. Benefits include an open exchange of cultural and media expertise, access to historical and cultural artefacts, and the inclusion of new media production methodologies. However, such participation displays all the characteristics of a fragmented audience whose focus is on self-service with a desire for highly personalised media experiences (McClean 2008). The challenge for the PSM operator is how to manage the application of funds for experimental research and development in new media services that incorporate the audience as an exercise in promoting distinctive innovation.

Public service media has been in a crisis of legitimacy for some years now (see for example Jacubowicz 2007; Lowe & Hujanen 2003). The core Reithian values that have inscribed PSB include "the application of core principles of universality of availability and appeal, provision for minorities, education of the public, distance from vested interests, quality programming standards, programme maker independence, and fostering of national culture and the public sphere" (Cunningham 2013: 62). Yet achieving all that is quite complicated in a media landscape that features a fragmented audience pursuing niche topics, often described as a "personalised media-use environment" (McClean 2008: 5). Further, PSM is under market pressure to produce content that not only satisfies the core principles of its historic ethos but also adds a degree of populism needed to attract larger audiences (ibid). If PSM is engaging in activities predominantly serviced by commercial media organisations, there is a type of ironic 'non-market failure' characteristic that raises concerns around its role that can specifically challenge its provision for minorities and the inclusiveness of marginalised voices (de Bens 2007).

As chapter 3 notes the premise for the creation of ex ante evaluation tools, famously the UK's 'Public Value Test' and Germany's 'Drei-Stufen-Test' (three-step test), is about holding these organisations accountable for the distribution of services that are funded with public money. The point is to assess the public value of the content and services provided by the public service sector in media by establishing what counts as public service and is also fair for the commercial sector. In this context, public value and the relevance of PSM raise a key question: "Why should taxpayer money... subsidise services used by few, often described as 'elite', audiences?" (McClean 2008: 5).

Adding to the crisis of legitimacy, recent disruptive Web 2.0 technologies challenge the historic production and governance models of PSB. In the spirit of "here comes everybody" (Shirky 2008), PSM is faced with navigating a rapidly changing media landscape in which audiences no longer only consume content but also actively participate in the making and sharing of content. The role of PSM in this situation is to not only produce content, but also to engage in co-creative practices *with* audiences as 'partners' (see Lowe 2010). Burgess and Banks (2010: 298) define co-creation as:

A "descriptive term that highlights the ways that users or consumers, within the constraints and affordances of platforms provided by others, collectively contribute to the social, cultural and economic value of the media products and experiences associated with those platforms; and likewise, it indicates the ways in which platform providers (however imperfectly) integrate user-participation into their own models of production".

Within the co-creation model, PSM may incorporate users into the production process, not only through content production per se but also by utilising user generated techniques and platforms that are traditionally administered by the expert staff of the organisation.

PSM thereby challenges historic and core values of PSB, which featured a generalist and Enlightenment mission, by accommodating the increased engagement levels of niche users that are participating in the production of popular cultural artefacts. The shifting media environment and enabling technologies facilitate user engagement (not simply audience attendance) in new and innovative ways that present opportunities for PSM to strengthen its relationship with audiences.

Concurrently, the shifting media environment's governance system suggests we should look carefully at the historic polity of PSB and couple the core values that have grounded and still legitimate this approach to mediation with emerging, developing methods. This could be less 'revolutionary' than one might surmise. As Moe (2010: 208) noted, "Practices do not swiftly change in the digital era. Rather than replacing established policy tools and regulatory actors, novel mechanisms modify and extend existing arrangements". But extending PSM's remit while also decentralising media governance is unlikely to be a simple process. It inherently requires the co-ordination of multiple stakeholders by specific intermediaries that are skilled both in PSM production and in community cultural development, defined here as the ability to empower individuals through a pedagogy of creative practice.

The inclusion of users engaging with Web 2.0 is not unique to PSM, but also common in other activities of participatory cultures with interest in broadening economic engagement (Benkler 2006), political engagement (Castells 2002), cultural production (Jenkins 2006), and journalism (Bruns 2008). One way to highlight the tensions of participatory cultures within PSM is to explore its key characteristic – the (apparent) absence of gatekeepers. Bruns (2008) argues that in the case of Wikipedia, the 'anyone can edit' slogan has a direct relationship to the granularity of the editorial process because users are experts on a few topics and can contribute their expertise in those areas. By engaging in the 'collective intelligence' (Levy 1994) of all the contributors, the depth and quality of information generated is both unique and potentially very rich. As an approach, a participatory media culture is difficult to facilitate in PSM due to the specific public service requirements mandated for these particular types of institution. That is, it is difficult to align the 'collective intelligence' and contributions of the audience with the specific requirements of PSM, given the crisis of legitimisation argument noted earlier.

The value of participation for public service media, then, is inherently located within the distinctive innovation role of the PSM organisation, as the cases that are discussed next illustrate. Historically, measuring that value has been troublesome when compared against the allocation of public funding to support PSM within a competitive media marketplace, the context in which ex ante public value testing mechanisms are elaborated. I argue that audience participation is crucial for adding to the value of PSM, although difficult to manage by those who facilitate the co-creation of cultural artefacts.

Three cases of PSM participatory cultures under development

The first example of audience participation by a PSM organisation revolves around that as a strategic aspect of public service development as demonstrated by the now defunct Channel 4iP, the digital investment arm of Britain's Channel 4. With 4iP, this commercially financed public service company explored "how users might become involved in the production process" (Jackson 2008: 1). Further, "Channel 4iP encourages both the public and creative media firms to pitch ideas in an open commissioning process" (ibid). The channel did this by providing users a range of "disruptive media tools" while suggesting a number of conditions to successfully pitch an idea, including the principle that ideas "must be suitable for digital networks, foreground participation and collaboration, and the service must be financially self-sustaining" (ibid: 9).

One of the most successful ideas commissioned from this project was the AudioBoo service, an audio production tool that enables users to record, edit and publish their own audio online. AudioBoo proudly boasts, "We want to give everyone a way to say what they want – to the whole world" (AudioBoo 2013). In this regard, Channel 4iP was distinctly innovative by providing a free production tool that enabled users to share their story with the rest of the world, an outcome similar to the BBC *Capture Wales* project described later. Jackson notes the benefit of user testing which incorporates users in the production process, suggesting "the involvement of the public in the development of public services assists producers to ensure content and services are appropriate and of high value" (ibid: 11).

DR, the Danish Broadcasting Corporation, has been experimenting with the web since the early 1990s to encourage dialogue (Brügger 2011). This second case offers multiple examples. Bechmann (2011: 194) examined the role of DR Youth, the "young people's department" as a testing ground for audience participation, which she defines as a way of "creating dialogue and/ or engagement with the public" (ibid: 195). The *Blokken* project, another DR effort, invited users to engage web 2.0 technologies to submit mobile phone videos to a low budget television programme and online channel. Their slogan was "You supply, we present", which elegantly summarises the intentions. Bechmann's research suggests that user-created content was of poor quality and few in numbers, and that DR decided to cease curating the content to broadcast on its channels essentially for this reason.

Here we see a clear example of distinctive innovation where the value of PSM is in the experimentation of new production methodologies that, success-ful or not, are shared with the market system as a whole. We will come back to this important point after presentation of the cases. DR shifted the focus of the project to Spam, a project no longer concerned with user-created content but rather with the sharing of content in a peer-to-peer approach. DR's Spam project indicates that emphasis in the dialogical and community aspects are of significant value for PSM, and not only content creation as such. In this regard the value of the PSM organisation's efforts through audience participa-tion are extending beyond experimentation and production methodologies to also include the strengthening of community networks. That is, the value of interpersonal communication between audience members that would otherwise not have occurred can be aligned with increased social capital.

The BBC has experimented with user created content, evident in their flag-ship digital storytelling project called *Capture Wales*, underway during the early 2000s. "Capture Wales… puts the tools of production in the hands of the public, and in doing so perhaps represents a step toward the 'conversation' which is touted by many as framing the future look, focus, and values of journalism" (Meadows & Kidd 2009: 93). Through a series of workshops around Wales, participants were invited to engage digital storytelling techniques that involved combining digital still photography with a narration and a soundtrack to tell their unique, individualised stories.

In 2002, then Director General of the BBC, Greg Dyke, viewed the pilot at Cardiff University and gave the team the go-ahead which meant that "for the first time in the history of broadcasting, a mainstream player was putting the tools of production and editing into the hands of the audience" (ibid: 100). The media and its associated information and communication technologies produced, and the reflections from the participants confirmed, a broader cultural representation of the diversity of the region (ibid).

The PSM value of representing ' the voiceless' resonates with the BBC's latest user created effort called *The Listening Project* (http://www.bbc.co.uk/radio4/features/the-listening-project), which also provides production tools and asks "people up and down the country to share an intimate conversation with a close friend or relative, to help to build a unique picture of our lives today" (BBC 2013). For the BBC, these user-generated content projects facilitate an increased representation of its public while building social capital amongst its participants. The participants have said, for example, "it has brought me closer to my community" and "allowed me to be proud of myself and who I am" (Meadows & Kidd 2009:111).

To return now to the earlier comment, while some of the case studies of audience participation with PSM have been successful others have been failures. Within the public service media arena, either outcome is indicative of the experimental characteristic of PSB. As a not-for-profit organisation, the experimental ethos of PSM is crucial and these institutions can be expected to tolerate more risk than their commercial counterparts. When experimentation is a failure, however, it is fair to say that there are valuable lessons learned for future development, and that failure in this context is not catastrophic. The real problems emerge, however, when the experimentation becomes a success, and therefore is an innovation. Pressure grows from the commercial sector to limit and even marginalise their continuation by PSM organisations due to the potential profitability that early success signals for developing markets. Thus, the public value of PSM to experiment in developing not only media services but also media relations with the public fuels institutional success but also courts potentially harsh criticism that can backlash.

By engaging audiences in new ways, and to new degrees, PSM aligns with what Hesmondhalgh (2007) characterises as a "pattern of change/continuity" (as theory) to incorporate user-generated content (change) with traditional media practices (continuity). Hesmondhalgh's theory outlining the production model suggests PSM thereby blurs boundaries between producer and consumer. Bruns (2008: 2) defines this phenomenon as "produsage", suggesting that "the role of 'consumer' and even that of 'end user' have long disappeared, and the distinctions between producers and users of content have faded into comparative insignificance". Holly Goodier at the BBC completed long-term research into the activity rates of the UK online population which debunk the ratio of participation that has been commonly regarded as a rule: "The model which has guided many people's thinking in this area, the 1/9/90 rule, is outmoded. The number of people participating online is significantly higher than 10%. Participation is now the rule rather than the exception: 77% of the UK online population is now active in some way" (Goodier 2012). By providing new platforms and tools, the audience participation rate for PSM has increased, compounding the effects of produsage.

How, then, does increased participation via new platforms indicate increased levels of public value? Building on the successes of the Capture Wales project, the BBC began exploring this question and in 2006 produced a document of signal importance, *Building Public Value: Renewing the BBC for a digital world*. One of the foundational arguments suggests that the public broadcaster is crucial for building social capital through programmes that make the public "spruce up [their] houses and improve [their] neighbourhood" (p.6), or more significantly "In a national emergency, the right broadcast information might save [their] life" (ibid). This suggests the value of PSM is distributed across a spectrum of influences and consequences that scale from pedestrian through to matters of life or death.

Social capital is typically defined as "the networks of strong personal relationships, developed over time, that provide the basis for trust, co-operation, and collective action" (Cummings, Heeks & Huysman 2006: 574). *Building Public Value* addresses the historic core values of the public broadcaster to "inform, educate and entertain", and updates that within the existing media environment. The findings suggest it is not enough for PSM to inform, educate and entertain; the objective of building social capital means that improvement to both individual and shared quality of life is a core value today: "Public value is a measure of the BBC's contribution to the quality of life in the UK" (ibid: p.8). McClean (2008) adds content quality as a PSM core value and not just an alternative to lowbrow popular broadcasting, suggesting that quality in PSM provision improves "the vision of a desired public culture, greater participation in public life and genuine cultural pluralism" (McClean 2008: 6). Cultural pluralism is achieved through the inclusion of multiple voices, particularly those that are marginalised, reflected in Enli's (2008) suggestion for the core values of PSM should evolve to "educate, entertain and participate".

Strengthening Relationships
through ABC Pool's *New Beginnings*

The previous section has outlined how PSM is approaching distinctive innovation by developing social and cultural capital through audience participation. This section highlights what this means for developing our understanding of public value through innovative publication and publishing methodologies, in conjunction with increased social and cultural capital. In this section we examine the *New Beginnings* [NB] case, a co-creative project facilitated by the ABC Pool project. Building on innovative producing and publishing methodologies, this project demonstrates the social and cultural benefits of incorporating audiences in the production of cultural artefacts. This underscores how the construction of social and cultural capital is not simply through participation, although that is fundamental, but moreover in the efforts of a cultural intermediary during a co-creative process who enables the realisation of public value. This section provides a practical context for elaborating the 'cultural intermediary' concept, which follows in the third section.

The ABC has moved beyond the 1990s and early 2000s period of 'online' publishing to incorporate Web 2.0 technologies with the goal of fostering new relationships with audiences (Walker 2009) by engaging in production activities with participatory cultures (Jenkins 2006). This shift presents both opportunities and challenges to traditional mass media production, characteristic of broadcasting and related to historic editorial policies and governance models. The shift raises questions about the public value of PSM as a proponent and facilitator of experimental and innovative production activities.

The incorporation of information communication technologies to enable participatory cultures challenges the core values of 'public service' in broadcasting because this is not mainly about transmission. The quality of user-created content often differs from a general expectation that the ABC, as a PSB source, will always and only offer accurate, valid and high quality content. These are associated with the core values of its Charter (ABC 1983) and governed by the organisation's Editorial Policies (ABC 2008). As stated in the Charter, the ABC's content must feature production values that "inform, educate and entertain" (ibid). These core values are problematic when attempting to incorporate the inconsistencies that characterise participatory cultures. Here the ABC faces an integrity problem because the daily practice must simultaneously maintain high production quality, engage broad audiences, and deliver true and accurate information – while also minimising editorial control in a collaborative production process.

The governmental Department of Broadband, Communication and Digital Economy[2] (2008) suggested that the role of PSM in the digital era should 1) enhance the deployment of new media platforms and 2) develop digital technologies that engage the audience in new ways. This view, prefigured by Martin (2002), has been developed in the scholarly work provided by Debrett (2010). In remarks at the 2012 Strategic Forum the Managing Director of the ABC, Mark Scott, pondered a question of crucial importance: "What is the place of the ABC in a media rich environment that has global input?" (Scott 2012). He suggested that the ABC think more carefully about its audience and not only about content delivery platforms.

Both the regulatory framework for the ABC and the organisation's internal strategy require the corporation to increasingly engage the cultural diversity of its audiences via new media platforms. This has been understood as a means for cultivating an increased public value of the ABC and the SBS. The Australian Labor Party during this period delivered a media reform package for "Modernising the ABC and SBS charters to reflect their online and digital activities" (DBCDE 2013), indicative of Australian legislation amending the ABC Act (1983) to align online activities with traditional broadcasting regulation.[3]

Given the recent regulatory amendments, there is an expectation that increased public value may be achieved through cultural pluralism that is encouraged by participation of the ABC audience in order to improve performance or accomplishment in quality, information, education and entertainment. A significant ABC project that is experimenting with collaborative creativity is called *ABC Pool*. This platform facilitates efforts to incorporate creative online communities in, with and for the ABC. *ABC Pool* 'members'[4] can contribute and interact with media (audio, photos, text, videos), engage in conversations with other users, contribute media to themed projects, and have access to the expertise of ABC staff. The ABC furnishes resources that include the platform, professional expertise, a secure online environment and access to ABC archival material, operating under Creative Commons licensing.

One regular activity of ABC Pool is facilitating the broadcast of Pool contributions on RN[5] programmes, where users contribute creative work that is curated and aligned with the production values of each particular RN programme. The case study for this chapter is the recent ABC Pool collaborative project with one of these programmes, the RN 360documentaries programme that broadcasts 53-minute feature length documentaries, called *New Beginnings*. Mike Williams, 360documentaries and NB producer, designed the "call to action":

> ABC Pool wants to hear your New Beginnings story! Starting something new can be exciting, refreshing and stimulating but also very daunting and scary. Whether it's a new job, new family member, new home, or maybe even a new love interest, we're often faced with the challenge of having to start afresh in a new situation. This project is about expressing your stories, your experiences and your emotions when you've gone through a new beginning (Williams 2012).

New Beginnings is exemplary of the co-creative process outlined by Burgess and Banks (2010) because it adds cultural and social value to the production of ABC content while accommodating the needs of the project's contributors. Williams designed a project with broad appeal for *ABC Pool* members and RN audiences that is sufficiently focused to motivate people to contribute as participants in this 53-minute radio feature. By inviting the audience to become 'co-creators' of the feature Williams was able to embed the personal stories of Australians. The project received 87 contributions consisting primarily of audio with some text and video productions. There was also a small but dedicated group of 44 project members who were contributing work and engaging in conversations around those contributions. These conversations included technical discussion on how the contributions were made, the clarification of facts relating to stories, or general encouragement from both Williams and other participants. NB was broadcast on *360documentaries* on Sunday the 8th April, with notable public support:

> What marvellous listening...true story telling. A most enjoyable hour that I will want to hear again and again. Thanks to all ... tremendous contributions & production (Linde, 360documentaries website, 9 April 2012).

Unlike other radio features constructed through a series of decision making points by the producer (Lindgren 2011) – for example researching the subject matter, sourcing experts or creatives to assist in the story-telling, recording the talent, designing the sound, mastering the outcome, broadcasting the finished product – this project sought to include the audience in the process. The NB call-out initialised personal story contributions, where Williams conducted a curatorial selection to reveal the narrative. With the narrative partially realised, a co-creative process refined the contributions, as most did not satisfy technical or stylistic standards required for Radio National. He invited a selection of contributors into the ABC studios around Australia and directed them while they recorded their stories, working to retain the personal aesthetic of each.

During the recording process, NB displayed pedagogical aspects in its design by empowering its contributors and transferring knowledge between the participants. By aligning it with the core principals of a "community of practice" (Lave & Wenger 1991), users became radio feature makers and were empowered as such. A community of practice is defined as a "set of relations amongst persons, activity, and world, over time and in relation with other tangential and overlapping communities..." (ibid: 98). It is also a system of recognised peripheral skills, used and exchanged for additional skills and knowledge.

The participants engaged in the production of cultural goods by contributing their ideas and media, in turn entering into a skills exchange arrangement. The production process outlined here provides a practical example. A member would contribute a story or short audio piece to the project, the producer would engage the new ideas and ensure production methods, and the member was invited to the ABC studio to record the contribution. During the recording session, the participants develop relationships with each other. These ABC Pool members gain knowledge of professional work in making a radio feature while contributing their own skills to the session. The ABC staff members that are involved in the sessions experience the benefits of incorporating user-generated content [UGC] in the production process. Podkalicka and Wilson (2012) outline a similar example in a collaborative pedagogical process of filmmaking in Melbourne that is based on the *Youthworx*[6] project. They note:

> While this process necessarily involves the mastery of new knowledge and skills, it is through the broader capacity for participation, acceptance and acknowledgement by adept practitioners within the community of practice that the meaning of this learning is configured and validated, therefore acting as a motivating force (ibid: 8).

Similarly, the skill and knowledge exchange demonstrated by NB frames the project as both a pedagogical process and collaborative cultural production exercise. Through the interviewing process with the RN professionals, it became apparent that the media production skills of the contributors were varied, however these people were acknowledged as competent radio producers and responded to the role. Simultaneously, the skills exchanged amongst the participants were noticeable. Users were gaining technical knowledge on how to professionally record broadcast standard material while learning the craft of radio feature making from the ABC staff. *New Beginnings* was also an exercise in developing users' skills in creative practices more broadly than just radio production:

> Of all my writing achievements, I have to say hearing my words float out on Radio National, in *City Nights* and *New Beginnings*, is by FAR what I'm proudest of. Thank you so much for allowing me to be part of this; it's really something to put on my resume, and make me feel better whenever I get a rejection from a publisher. I got one this morning and you know, I barely even blinked, for once. After the smile put on my face with the broadcast, I don't think it's going to be wiped off that easily! (Name withheld by request, producer email correspondence 10 April 2012).

Skills were exchanged with Williams who learned from the personal stories of the contributors, built social capital with the audience members, and fostered open participation within the production process:

> Through the New Beginnings process I have a better understanding about the Pool community, what to expect from UGC – the diversity in UGC, the importance of a production model with set times, how much time a UGC project takes, what worked and what didn't work in terms of a production

model, how to keep co-creation as flat as possible – how can users be involved in decisions, the importance of talking to users – the power of interpreting the story, and how a flat production model can help iron out some potential issues (interview 16 May 2012).

The success of NB required the input of one person mediating the interests of all those involved in the process. This role is to be the 'glue' that bonds these social capital exercises and enables them to occur within the institutional setting. We now explore how the role achieves this, how the persona responsible operates within institutional online communities engaging in collaborative production.

The role of cultural intermediation in PSM

The intermediary role takes on many forms within the ABC. These include: ABC Open producers (abc.net.au/open) who engage regional audiences and develop their digital literacy through participatory projects; Social Media Producers who develop online communication strategies and procedural practices for content makers engaging their audiences; and Online Moderators who monitor contributions on platforms including, but not limited to, Twitter feeds, Facebook pages, online forums, and ABC web pages.

One specific form of skilled intermediary work within co-creative practices at the ABC is demonstrated through the project management of collaborative productions. The NB project is exemplary of this, where the intermediary interfaces between multiple stakeholders engaging in co-creative practices. This role combines traditional methods with new experimental modes of production and online community governance, and may assist in developing new regulatory frameworks for public service media. In practice, the cultural intermediary is responsible for facilitating the distinctive innovation of PSM modelled in this chapter in the forms of innovative production and publishing methodologies and increased social and cultural capital, also defined here as the essential long-term public value in public service media.

In an online community, defined as a group of online users sharing in a combination of social capital, social support, and common culture (Bonniface, Green & Swanson 2006), the intermediary role is often referred to as the 'community manager'. Jono Bacon suggests the role of the community manager is to encourage the online community's participants while engaging and fostering relationships with its members (Bacon 2009). The community manager has also been described as an advocate or representative of the online community to the institution that resources it (Banks 2007). Both definitions indicate that the community manager is situated between multiple stakeholders, where a comprehensive understanding of those participants' interests is required for communication between them. By understanding the participants' interests, the community manager uses management techniques to negotiate consensus when complicated situations arise (Collins 2007). This may include using diplomatic negotiating skills to resolve a disagreement between participants on how an activity should be performed.

Figure 1 demonstrates the position of the community manager in relation to the stakeholders for *ABC Pool*, performing the core activity of Project Design (designing themed projects that encouraging member participation for a creative outcome, in practice a broadcast outcome).

Figure 1.   The Community Manager within *ABC Pool*

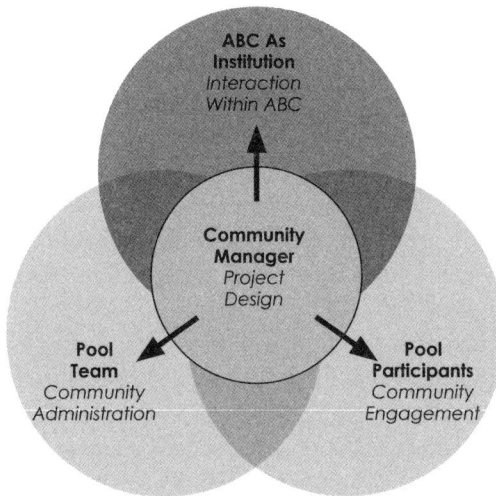

The community manager's role is indicative of how that person interacts with multiple stakeholders. For example, if the community manager is interacting with the Pool participants, he or she represents the interests of the ABC as institution, along with the interests of the Pool team. Likewise, if he or she negotiates with the Pool team, the role highlights the interests of the ABC as institution and the Pool participants in that discussion. Whichever stakeholder the community manager is interacting with, he or she takes the interests and concerns of the other two stakeholders into consideration and must represent them in the interactions. Figure 1 also indicates the types of activities the community manager engages in with the stakeholders: "Community Engagement" is typical of the interaction with the Pool participants, "Community Administration" relates to the day-to-day activities with the Pool team, and "Interaction with the ABC" is any other related interaction with ABC staff not directly related with ABC Pool, for example Legal staff or archival researchers.

For *New Beginnings*, Mike Williams embodied the community manager role, partially in the capacity that Banks (2007) outlined and even more so as described by Bacon (2009). That is why the central circle is realistically positioned at the bottom of the right side to indicate more activity within the community engagement area. Although engaging with the users at a very in-depth level, the community manager was primarily concerned with the production of cultural artefacts from the institutional perspective of the ABC – that is to produce a 53-minute feature to be broadcast on RN *360documentaries*. In this capacity, Williams's role is the cultural intermediary who manages "the division between high art/pop culture and the divide between personal taste and professional judgement (or leisure and work)" (Negus 2002: 503). The creative contributions to NB are a mixture of user-generated content (pop culture) and professionally produced audio (high art), where the intermediary constantly curates the work from both a professional judgement and personal taste perspective.

The *New Beginnings* cultural intermediary was required to utilise, and develop, collaborative creative skills needed to produce and curate the elements of the radio feature. The role also required negotiation skills to engage in communicative activities between contributors and the ABC staff. Power and authority issues often arise between audiences engaging in the produsage of cultural artefacts and the institutions that support these online communities, rationalising the cultural intermediary role.

Within this context, and referring to Figure 1, the central circle of the community manager shifts towards the upper right side of the diagram to indicate a greater emphasis on their negotiating skills, or 'Interacting with the ABC'. By understanding the interests of the project's stakeholders (the ABC, RN *360documentaries* production staff, RN audience members, *ABC Pool* and its members), the cultural intermediary was required to negotiate a consensus to maintain a clear project scope. A grounded example of the cultural intermediary multi-facing was Williams explaining to contributors how to improve their work to achieve an ABC standard, while communicating time and budget constraints with the *360documentaries* management team. The result was a *360documentaries* programme the contributors were proud of that also complied with the high editorial standards of the ABC.

Figure 2 highlights how intermediary roles operate within the ABC more broadly. As outlined earlier, the intermediary role operates in many other capacities from ABC Open Producers to Online Moderators, labelled here as the cultural intermediary. In this capacity, the cultural intermediary is responsible for the specific project being managed, for example ABC Open or the ABC News24 Facebook page. The three stakeholders concerned with any of these activities includes Professional Media Production: ABC staff engaging in the production of media (e.g. Directors, Producers, Engineers); Australian User-Generated Content: contributions to the ABC by audience members (e.g. comments, photographs, stories, talkback); and Site Operation: ABC platforms engaging in UGC activities (e.g. ABC Open, The Drum, QandA). The core activities remain the same, supporting the interchangeable potential of the model developed through *ABC Pool* and *New Beginnings* to the audience participation activities within PSM more broadly.

Figure 2.   The Cultural Intermediary Within The ABC

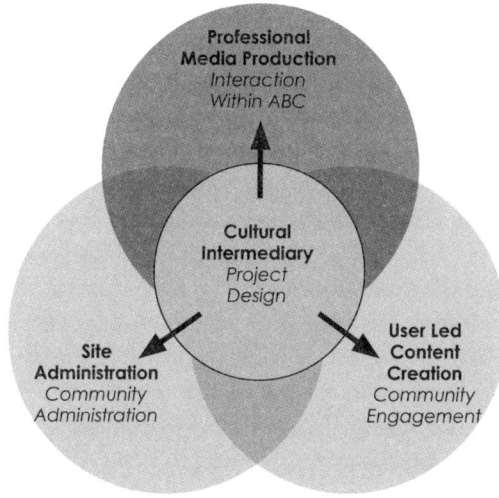

The cultural intermediary role is about securing and deploying distinctive innovation within the ABC as a PSM organisation to enable the development of social and cultural capital, in line with the institution's remit. Cultural intermediation translates and interfaces between the stakeholders, while operating within the fundamental principles of PSM to "inform, educate, entertain" (ABC 1983). It does this uniquely during the co-creative production of cultural artefacts. The cultural intermediary engaging produsage and the pattern of change/continuity philosophies, may champion the notion of 'quality' as the BBC suggest as a core value of PSB (2006). By broadening the engagement levels within the ABC's public service functions, the value of quality increases through improved social capital while the pedagogical experience increases the participant's cultural capital. Audience participation addresses the value of PSM, although still difficult to measure, within the creation and development of cultural intermediary roles that bridge the distance between production and consumption (Negus 2002). Cultural intermediation therefore is the framework that enables and promotes the value of public service media that has been highlighted within the *New Beginnings* case study by understanding and operationalising the social and cultural expectations of the audience and aligning those with the existing PSB remit.

Conclusion

This chapter has highlighted challenges that PSM faces in the current media landscape caused by shifting trends in the ways that people use media and interact as audience-contributors. This raises important questions about new dimensions of contemporary public value for PSM, especially emphasising the relevance of experimentation and risk-taking to realise innovative projects funded and managed by PSM organisations. Here the emphasis is squarely on the contemporary M rather than the historic B in PSB. We have the beginnings of an outline of significant benefits that can only be achieved by engaging in participatory culture-building activities with audiences as contributors. By focussing on *New Beginnings* through a community of practice lens, a significant improvement in audience relations and community cultural development has been demonstrated, increasing the value of activities that build social and cultural capital. *New Beginnings* also highlights the particular skills of the role of contemporary cultural intermediaries to facilitate participatory culture activities where in contributors are engaged with the production of cultural artefacts – captured and curated as creative media products that provide information about the contemporary Australian social landscape.

To that end, further research is required to understand PSM as a market organiser and not an organisation that merely 'crowds out' the commercial sector. As demonstrated through Cunningham's distinctive innovation lens, coupled with cultural intermediation, the value of PSM is in its seedbed approach to develop new forms of media, where the focus of these media is to support the development of social and cultural capital amongst the societies the PSM organisation is mandated to serve. Participation managed through cultural intermediation suggests PSM is effective as a means for developing social and cultural capital. Additional research will provide essential data to support this framework.

This chapter has shown the importance of the cultural intermediaries at the ABC, who operate under various monikers within different departments, engaging the diversity of the PSM audience. I have highlighted one institutional online community governance model trialled in the ABC Pool project, which has provided valuable results already in the work of defining and understanding the role of cultural intermediaries in the negotiation process of production of cultural artefacts. In doing so, the chapter provides a framework for cultural intermediation, understood as the facilitation required to embed online communities within organisations.

Acknowledgements

Mike Williams, Sherre DeLys, John Jacobs, Andrew Davies, Gretchen Miller, Claudia Tarranto, Sheila Pham, Ellie Rennie, Anne Galloway, Fiona Martin, Gregory F. Lowe, Axel Bruns, John Banks, Oksana Zelenko, Jean Burgess.

Notes

1. Radio National is one of the national networks of the ABC's Radio Division. "Radio National's vision and purpose is to nurture the intellectual and cultural life of this country, and to be a vital element of the contemporary Australian conversation" (ABC 2013).

2. The Department of Broadband, Communication and Digital Economy (DBCDE) released the discussion paper during 2008 entitled "ABC and SBS: Toward a digital future", which supports and promotes many of the ideas and strategies addressed so far in this chapter.

3. At the time of writing, Senator Stephen Conroy, the Minister for the Department of Broadband, Communication and Digital Economy had announced the government's official response to the Convergence Review and the Finkelstein Review. There is no clear indication of when the reformation will take place.

4. ABC Pool membership is open to all but certain functionality, for example uploading content to the ABC platform, is reserved for members only.

5. RN stands for Radio National, a national ABC radio network whose "vision and purpose is to nurture the intellectual and cultural life of this country, and to be a vital element of the contemporary Australian conversation" (ABC 2013).

6. Youthworx is media production space that is part practice led research and part community cultural development project. Youthworx "use media arts to engage young people in a process of enrichment and skills development that seeks to build connections to support and community" (Youthworx 2013).

References

ABC (1983) *The ABC Act*. Viewed 14 October 2010 at <http://www.comlaw.gov.au/Details/C2013C00136/Html/Text#_Toc353360751>.

ABC (2009). *ABC Documents – Editorial Policies*. Viewed 10 September 2009 at <http://www.abc.net.au/corp/pubs/edpols.htm>.

Bacon, J. (2009) *The Art of Community*. Sebastopol, CA: O'Reilly Media.

Banks, J. (2007) 'Opening the production pipeline: Unruly creators. In Castell, S.D. & Jenson, C. (eds.) *Words in Play: International Perspectives on Digital Games Research*. NY: Peter Lang Publishing Inc., pp. 143-152.

Bardoel, J. & Lowe, G.F. (2007) From public service broadcasting to public service media: The core challenge. In Lowe, G.F. and Bardoel, J. (eds.) *From Public Service Broadcasting to Public Service Media*, RIPE@2007. Göteborg: Nordicom, pp.9-28.

BBC 2006, *Building Public Value: Renewing the BBC for a Digital World*. Viewed 15 August 2012 at <http://downloads.bbc.co.uk/aboutthebbc/policies/pdf/bpv.pdf>.

Bechmann, A. (2011) User participation at the Danish Broadcasting Corporation 1998-2010. In Burns, M. & Brügger, N. (eds.) *Histories of Public Service Broadcasters on the Web*. NY: Peter Lang Publishing Inc.

Benkler, Y. (2006) *The Wealth of Networks*, 1st edition. New Haven, CT: Yale University Press.

Bonniface, L., Green, L. & Swanson, M. (2006) Communication on a health-related website offering therapeutic support – Phase 1 of the HeartNET website. *Australian Journal of Communication*, 33(2), pp. 89-107.

Brevini, B. (2013) *Public Service Broadcasting Online: A Comparative European Policy Study of PSB 2.0*. Basingstoke: Palgrave Macmillan.

Brügger, N. (2011) The idea of Public Service in the early history of DR Online. In M. Burns & N. Brügger (eds.), *Histories of Public Service Broadcasters on the Web*. New York: Peter Lang.

Bruns, A. (2008) *Blogs, Wikipedia, Second Life and Beyond: From Production to Produsage*. New York: Peter Lang.

Burgess, J. & Banks, J. (2010) User-created Content and Online Social Networks. In S. Cunningham & G. Turner (eds.) *The Media and Communications in Australia* (3 ed., pp. 295-306). Crows Nest: Allen and Unwin.

Castells, M. (2002) *The Rise of the Network Society*. 2nd ed. Oxford: Blackwell Publishers Ltd.

Collins, H, & Sanders, G. (2007) They Give you the Keys and Say 'Drive It!' Managers, referred expertise, and other expertise. *Studies in History and Philosophy of Science, 38,* 621-641.

Cummings, S, Heeks, R, & Huysman, M. (2006) Knowledge and Learning in Online Communities in Development: A Social Capital Perspective. *Development in Practice, 16*(6), 570-586.

Cunningham, S. (2013) *Hidden Innovation: Policy, Industry and the Creative Sector*. Brisbane: University of Queensland Press.

DBCDE. (2008) *ABC and SBS: Towards a digital future*. Canberra.

Bens, Els de. (2007). Media Between Culture and Commerce: An Introduction. In E. d. Bens (ed.), *Media Between Culture and Commerce* (Vol. 4). Bristol: Intellect.

Debrett, M. (2010) *Reinventing Public Service Television for the Digital Future*. Bristol: Intellect.

Enli, G.S. (2008) Redefining Public Service Broadcasting. *Convergence: The International Journal of Research into New Media Technologies, 14*(1), 105-120.

Goodier, H. (2012) BBC Online Briefing Spring 2012: The Participation Choice. Viewed on 7 July 2012 at <http://www.bbc.co.uk/blogs/bbcinternet/2012/05/bbc_online_briefing_spring_201_1.html>.

Hesmondhalgh, D. (2007) *The Cultural Industries* (2nd ed.). London: Sage.

Hibberd, M. (2002) *E-Participation and Democracy in the UK*. Paper presented at the RIPE Conference: Broadcasting and Convergence: Articulating a new remit, Tampere, Helsinki.

Hutchinson, J. (2012) The Ethnographer as Community Manager: Language Translation and User Negotiation Through Tacit Norms. *Media International Australia, 145,* 112-122.

Jackson, L. (2008) *Facilitating participatory media at the BBC*. Paper presented at the RIPE Conference: Public Service Media in the 21st Century: Participation, Partnership and Media Development, Johannes Gutenberg-University Mainz and the Institute of Media Design at the Mainz University of Applied Science.

Jackson, L. (2010) *Harnessing collaborative innovation for the evolution of public service media*. Paper presented at the RIPE Conference: Public Service Media After the Recession, Communication and Media Research Institute (CAMRI) at the University of Westminster.

Jakubowicz, K. (2007) *Rude Awakening: Social and Media Change in Central and Eastern Europe*: Hampton Press.

Jakubowicz, K. (2007) Public Service Broadcasting: A Pawn on an Ideological Chessboard. In E. d. Bens (ed.) *Media Between Culture and Commerce*. Chicago: Intellect.

Jakubowicz, K. (2008) *Participation and partnership: A Copernican revolution to re-engineer public service media for the 21st century*. Paper presented at the RIPE Conference: Public Service Media in the 21st Century: Participation, Partnership and Media Development., Johannes Gutenberg-University of Mainz and the Institute of Media Design at the Mainz University of Applied Sciences, Germany.

Jenkins, H. (2006) *Convergence Culture   Where Old and New Media Collide* (1st ed.) New York University Press.

Kidd, J. (2006) *Digital Storytelling at the BBC: the reality of innovative audience participation*. Paper presented at the RIPE Conference: Public Service Broadcasting in a Multimedia Environment: Programmes and Platforms, University of Amsterdam, Amsterdam.

Kjus, Y. (2006) *A public service format? Audience participation as a discursive element in recent BBC program production*. Paper presented at the RIPE Conference: Public Service Broadcasting in a Multimedia Environment: Programmes and Platforms, University of Amsterdam, Amsterdam.

Lave, J. and Wenger, E. (1991). *Situated Learning Legitimate Peripheral Participation* (1st ed.). Cambridge: Cambridge University Press.

Lévy, P. (1994) *Collective Intelligence: Mankind's Emerging World in Cyberspace*. New York: Plenum Trade.

Lindgren, M. (2011) *Journalism as Research: Developing radio documentary theory from practice*. Murdoch University, Perth.

Lowe, G.F. (ed.) (2010) *The Public in Public Service Media*, RIPE@2009. Göteborg: Nordicom.

Lowe, G.F. & Hujanen, T. (eds.) (2003) *Broadcasting and Convergence: New Articulations of the Public Service Remit*, RIPE@2003. Göteborg: Nordicom.

Lund, A.G. & Lowe, G.F. (2013) Current challenges to public service broadcasting in the Nordic countries. In Carlsson, U. (ed.) *Public Service Media from a Nordic Horizon: Politics, Markets, Programming and Users.* Göteborg: Nordicom, pp.51-74.

McChesney, R. (2008) *The Political Economy of Media: enduring issues, emerging dilemmas*: Monthly Review Press.

McClean, G. (2008) *Maintaining Relevance: Cultural Diversity and the Case for Public Service Broadcasting.* Paper presented at the Creating Value Between Commerce and Commons, Brisbane. Viewed on 17 June 2012 at <http://cci.edu.au/publications/maintaining-relevance>.

Martin, F. (2002) 'Beyond Public Service Broadcasting?: ABC Online & The User/ Citizen' *Southern Review*, 35 (1): 42-62

Meadows, D. & Kidd, J. (2009) "Capture Wales": The BBC Digital Storytelling Project. In J. Hartley & K. McWilliams (eds.), *Story Circle Digital Storytelling Around the World* (pp. 91). Oxford: Blackwell Publishing.

Moe, H. (2010) Governing Public Service Broadcasting: "Public Value Tests" in Different National Contexts. *Communication, Culture & Critique, 3* (2010), 207-223.

Negus, K. (2002) The work of cultural intermediaries and the enduring distance between production and consumption. *Cultural Studies, 16*(4), 501-515.

Podkalicka, A., & Wilson, C.K. (2012) Media 'communities of practice' and youth participation: connecting the social and the creative. *Manuscript submitted for publication.*

Scott, M. (2012) *ABC Strategic Forum 2012*, Eugene Goosens Hall, ABC Headquarters, Sydney.

Shirky, C. (2008) *Here Comes Everybody: The Power of Organising without Organisations.* New York: Allen Lane.

Steemers, J. (2012) *Evaluating the contribution of public service broadcasters to children's media: The case of home-grown content.* Paper presented at the RIPE Conference: Value for Public Money – Money for Public Value, University of Sydney, Australia.

Walker, T. (2009) New Audience Partnerships for the ABC. *Telecommunications Journal of Australia, 59* (3), 43-48.

Williams, M. (2012) New Beginnings. Viewed 16 May 2012 at <http://pool.abc.net.au/projects/new-beginnings>.

Wilson, C.-K., Hutchinson, J. & Shea, P. (2010). Public Service Broadcasting, Creative Industries and Innovation Infrastructure: The Case of ABC's Pool. *Australian Journal of Communication, 37*(3), 15-32.

Chapter 13

Public Value and Audience Engagement with SBS Documentary Content
Go Back To Where You Came From
& Immigration Nation

Georgie McClean

While cultural diversity, immigration and refugee settlement are increasingly ubiquitous characteristics of contemporary societies, they are far from universally supported or understood. Seyla Benhahbib described the increasing gap between 'members and non-members' of nation states emerging from migrations of "aliens and strangers, immigrants and newcomers, refugees and asylum seekers" (Benhabib 2004). Population movements and migrations create significant governance challenges in host nations, and debates that are often fiery about international obligations, local politics and humanitarian responsibilities in a complex area of public policy.

Public service media [PSM] charter obligations characteristically include directions to foster a diversity of views, a pluralistic approach to representing publics and, more generally, 'fair and balanced' coverage of public discourse.

We know that media and their audiences can create symbolic as well as material communities (Silverstone, 1999: 98). In many mature democracies the nature of these communities owes much to public service broadcasting, which has traditionally been aligned with nation-building projects (Hall, 1993; Morley 2000; Scannell 1989). Australian multicultural broadcaster SBS, the Special Broadcasting Service, began as an information service for ethnic communities, but was rapidly established as the country's second PSB and a catalyst for the creation of new ideas about foreignness, cultural difference and cosmopolitanism (Ang et al. 2008). Since then SBS has enshrined official recognition of cultural and linguistic diversity as vital elements of the national broadcasting project. As Ien Ang et al noted in 'The SBS Story' (2008: 3-4):

> SBS *begins* from the idea of difference and diversity as normal. Its organising principle is not to marginalise difference or treat it as an add-on or an afterthought; it assumes what Australians have in common *is* diversity and that the role of public media is to create spaces where the connections and differences between particular groups and perspectives can be understood and negotiated.

Increasingly SBS provides a site for the exploration of challenges and achieve-ments in grappling with contemporary social and cultural diversity. In its 2010 Corporate Plan, SBS set itself the objective of being "the catalyst for the nation's conversations about multiculturalism and social inclusion" (SBS 2010: 9). This involved, among other strategies, commissioning programming that would spark debate about diversity issues, including racism and public ambivalence toward immigration and refugees. This formulation of its role represents the broadcaster's latest interpretation of its Charter remit, which requires it to pro-vide radio and television services that reflect multicultural Australia.

To assess how the organisation was meeting its objectives, in 2011, as SBS Manager of Policy, Research and Community Engagement, I studied audience responses to program content. I was seeking feedback for SBS to steer the development of future productions, influence the way the organisation and its programmes communicate with audiences, and make the case for future funding.

In this chapter I want to analyse the findings of one particular study, that probed the reactions of audiences from a wide range of cultural backgrounds, age groups and geographic locations to two important SBS-commissioned documentaries – *Immigration Nation* and *Go Back To Where You Came From*. Both programmes investigate issues related to Australia's previous racially exclusionary immigration policies and current attitudes to asylum seekers in Australia, the latter using a 'constructed' or reality television format. They represent a unique intervention into Australia's prevailing immigration dis-courses and are powerful examples of SBS's contemporary interpretation of its mission.

This chapter analyses the public value of that programming in encouraging recognition of, affective engagement with, and public debate about, conten-tious national issues. It provides an overview of the role and evolving objec-tives of SBS. It then describes the approach to this audience study, discusses its theoretical context, and reflects on participant responses to the content and the kinds of conversations generated. This analysis contributes to a framework for thinking about the value of PSM as a resource to be used by audiences in engaging with complex, shared problems, in creating common points of reference with which to begin a conversation, and for offering opportunities to better understand differing viewpoints.

SBS and the multicultural nation

Australia's Special Broadcasting Service was created nearly forty years ago. It offers an interesting case study of the key challenges for a multicultural society in developing cultural policy that addresses recognition, representation and social participation. I argue that in each of these areas, culturally inclusive public service media provides an important resource for navigating the complexities of contemporary societies.

This is not a project without challenges. Australia is one of the world's most culturally diverse nations (Jupp 2002). According to the latest census, 24 per cent of the national population was born outside Australia and 46 per cent have at least one parent born outside Australia. Australia adopted multicultural policies in the 1970s. The 'ethnopolitics' of this era emphasised "discrete ethnic communities whose integration into Australian society was to be facilitated by policy" (Nolan & Radywyl 2004), with targeted heath, education and employment strategies to assist different groups to contribute to Australian society.

While the interpretation and implementation of these policies have changed much and have been politically compromised over time, the concept of multiculturalism continues to be supported at both a state and federal level today. This is in contrast to other contemporary liberal democracies, where such policies have been criticised for having 'failed'. (Nasser and Modood 2012). Many Australians are ambivalent about multicultural policy, but most recognise that cultural diversity is a reality in today's Australia (Ipsos, 'Immigration Nation' report 2011). However as Will Kymlicka (1995) points out: "the term 'multicultural' covers many different forms of cultural pluralism, each of which raises its own challenges... Generalisations about the goals or consequences of multiculturalism can therefore be very misleading".

As in many other countries populated by immigration, Australian political policies now typically emphasise strict border control. A highly politicised debate focuses on the 'problems' posed by relatively small numbers of asylum seekers arriving in Australia, possibly drawing from popular discomfort with a growing population. Moral panics and mainstream media hysteria about asylum seekers tend to draw on a level of paranoia about the invasion, and subsequent dilution of, vulnerable 'white Australian culture' that has long been part of Australian public discourse about diversity – though holding less uncontested prominence since the emergence of the multicultural project in the1970s (Hage 2002). An important part of SBS's current and ongoing public value is its capacity to intervene in these debates, and to interrogate and contest the assumptions they are built on.

SBS operates under a multicultural and multilingual public charter requiring it to inform, educate and entertain all Australians through multilingual and multicultural radio and television services that reflect Australia's multicultural society. SBS started as experimental multilingual radio services in 1975, later extended to television in 1980 and then online in 1991. SBS was unique in the Australian broadcasting landscape and brought a national audience international news, multilingualism and content from cultural sources outside the usual Australian, UK and US media fare.

SBS has always received a far smaller Government appropriation than the larger national broadcaster, the Australian Broadcasting Corporation (ABC), and has faced multiple challenges in servicing diverse communities and audience expectations. Never without controversy, its 2000s move to more popular programming has been the source of significant debate for the last ten years (see Enker 2004). As Ang et al (2008: viii) note in *The SBS Story*, the organisation "has been attacked as either too ethnic, or not ethnic enough, too elitist or too populist; its audiences have been dismissed as too small to justify public funding, but when bigger audiences have been sought it has been accused of being too commercial." Thus its investment in commissioning the documentaries considered here is of some public interest.

While its audience share is often small relative to commercial broadcasters, hovering around or below five per cent, SBS does have a significant reach. Its digital television services reach 96.8 per cent of Australians, and its programmes are viewed by around one-third of all Australians in any given week. Audiences can access 24-hour in-language radio stations, community television and satellite services. SBS TV broadcasts programming in 100 different languages and SBS Radio provides 74 specialist language programmes, alongside some English language content with a national, regional or global focus. As such SBS offers a unique case study of attempts to engage effectively with the diversity of Australia's population as part of a public service remit.

Inclusive media spaces and shared terms of reference enable forms of exchange between different groups in society, who may otherwise experience alienation from one another. SBS's current objectives bring to mind the theory of cosmopolitan philosopher Kwame Anthony Appiah (2007), who suggests that through conversation people can get used to one another, a crucial precondition for social harmony. That is an explicit aim of SBS, and clearly has value for a public that is so characteristically multicultural. While resourced by a hybrid commercial and public funding model, SBS's Charter and programming are intended to promote the public interest through policy objectives of social harmony, better mutual understanding and civic participation. These social policy orientations speak to the value of PSM in contemporary, culturally diverse liberal democracies.

The research project

The two documentaries discussed in this chapter are *Immigration Nation: The Secret History of Us,* charting the history of Australian immigration policy, and *Go Back to Where You Came From* described as a 'reverse immersive journey' for six 'ordinary' Australians with strong views about the issue of asylum seeker policy – both commissioned as part of SBS's contemporary interpretation of its Charter remit, and broadcast in 2011.

Immigration Nation is a three part documentary series produced by Melbourne-based production company Renegade Films. The narrative focused on the White Australia Policy, one of the first legislated acts of Australian Federation until its eventual abolition in the 1970s. It explored how this policy gave way to changes that eventually shaped Australia's contemporary cultural diversity. The documentary thesis argues that the working-man's utopia and its supposed egalitarianism were predicated on racial exclusion. The production draws on archival footage and CGI animated images, as well as interviews with historians and migrant descendants or government representatives with direct experience of the policies.

Go Back to Where You Came From (series one) is a three-part factual series produced by Sydney-based Cordell Jigsaw Productions and intended to explore the range of Australian opinion about refugees. The six main protagonists included several who strongly believed that asylum seekers deserve no public sympathy and should not be allowed into Australia. The format introduced these participants, and others with more liberal views, to several asylum seekers residing in Australia. It then set the participants to trace back the journeys made by those refugees from their countries of origin in Iraq and Democratic Republic of Congo via immigration detention, a journey by sea and through refugee camps in countries of transition – exploring through the course of the series the challenges faced by those fleeing their homelands and meeting many people who continue in precarious and dangerous situations.

At the time the documentaries were in development, I was speaking at an Ethnic Communities' Council conference in Victoria. I described the programmes and linked them to SBS's intentions in sparking public debate. A young Sudanese community representative stood up and questioned why SBS would use the title *'Go Back to Where You Came From'* as he felt it was a harmful term of abuse his community heard in the street daily. He saw SBS as a broadcaster that aimed to overcome these views, not promote them. I tried to explain the notion of provocation, the technique of challenging such views by exposing them.

But that exchange left lingering questions with me about the nature of our public debates and how, as a public broadcaster, SBS imagined its audiences. Were we setting out to shock or challenge comfortable middle class Australians? What impact might this have on the way people related to the issues these programmes explore? How would this kind of programming be interpreted by marginalised audiences and Australians who already felt a precarious sense of belonging in and our country? The pursuit of answers led to the research project that I will now discuss.

Given the public service intention of the documentaries, SBS colleagues agreed that it would be useful to evaluate them using in-depth audience feedback techniques, beyond the usual ratings, media coverage and the self-selecting audience responses received via social media. The research model we developed incorporated interviews with programme producers and SBS commissioning editors, as well as focus groups made up of a range of audience groups. It follows on from a similar study of audience responses to SBS drama series, *East West 101* and *The Circuit*, also conducted with research firm Entertainment Insights (McClean 2011).

In this study Entertainment Insights conducted the industry engagement component, talking with the documentary producers about points of difference in their programmes and their perceptions of their audiences. The interviews explored whether the SBS Charter inspires different kinds of storytelling and content making to other broadcasters, and whether the collaboration with SBS would have any impact on their future filmmaking or television production practice.

The audience study was comprised of fourteen focus groups, each with 6 to 8 participants. These were used to gain insight into viewer experiences of these programs, to add depth to the anecdotal responses SBS received via other feedback channels and to expand the understanding of audience engagement that that is afforded by ratings information. The focus groups each started with discussion of television viewing practices and questions about whether the participants tended to talk about what they watched on television and, if so, with whom. Conversations were then directed towards programme responses, eventually moving to representations of cultural diversity on television and what kinds of programs do, or could, best reflect Australian cultural diversity.

Entertainment Insights facilitated these groups and I sat in as an observer for the bulk of them. The groups were divided into SBS 'core viewers' (mixed gender, over 40 years old) and younger culturally diverse viewers, plus groups recruited specifically to reflect on the subject matter of the series. These included audiences who had arrived in Australia as part of the post-war migration boom discussing *Immigration Nation*, and recently arrived refugee groups discussing *Go Back to Where You Came From (hereafter Go Back)*. The focus groups were held in Australia's two largest cities, Sydney and Melbourne, the small city of Newcastle, and Shepparton, a country town in Victoria.

One limitation of this study was that the focus groups were based on a constructed viewing experience. A week or so prior to each group, the participants were posted a DVD of two episodes of one of the two series (selected according to the study sample) and asked to watch them and record their initial thoughts in a pre-task work booklet ('viewing diary') before attending the group. A percentage of each group had seen some or all of the content on television when it screened. Significant proportions of participants chose to watch (or re-watch) the DVD with family and friends, although others viewed it alone. Thus this model did not provide 'natural' or detailed ethnographic insights, but rather it relied on reported attitudes and behaviours.

Further as an employee of SBS, I also had a very strong personal and professional investment in the value of multicultural media overall and approached the study with this bias. I attempted to counter this by engaging with dissenting views amongst participant responses and questioning my own approach throughout the process.

The study findings were discussed in depth by the researchers and the commissioning team. The long version of the report was delivered to SBS, and we assisted in refining this into top-line findings which are published on the SBS website (Entertainment Insights 2012). This shortened version is referenced occasionally in this analysis as the Entertainment Insights report.

The value of media service as public resource

This research draws on understandings of media use as part of everyday life, a source of identity formation and resource that fuels and shapes social interaction. Factual programmes in particular can provide common points of reference for conversations about important issues in a multicultural society (Bird 2011), conversations that are increasingly happening online (Dahlgren 2005; Green & Jenkins 2011; Janssen & Kies 2005). Of our two documentaries, *Go Back* caused a storm on Twitter and other social media sites, trending as the top subject on Twitter on the first night of screening, an example of 'spreadable' media (Green & Jenkins 2011).

Analysis of the comments made by audience participants in this study was conducted with the understanding that responses to television content emerge from the context of individual experiences and subjectivities (Liebes & Katz, 1993: 20). The study includes the perspective of ex-asylum seekers, recently arrived migrants, long-term migrants (products of post-war migration), second-generation Australians and Anglo-Australians. Their experiences and identities inevitably add complex layers of meaning to their interpretation of the series' content – as the series provide points of reference for self-identification and the approaches taken by the filmmakers in grappling with complex content around human experiences.

The subject areas of both series' – immigration and asylum seeking – are considered to be 'difficult' topics that tend to polarise opinion in Australia. Yet drawing on discussions in the focus groups, our analysis suggests that the programmes provided common resources around which audiences could develop identifications or reactions that were interwoven with their responses to important social issues and historically informed understandings of Australian society. John Mepham (1990: 60) has called such resources 'usable stories', stories which can assist us to "make imaginatively informed choices and responses to other people" and to "articulate our feelings and aspirations". These documentaries are also examples of media as "…resources for talk, for recognition, identification, and incorporation as we measure, or do not measure, our images and our lives against those we see on the screen" (Silverstone, 1999: 18).

Roger Silverstone describes how narratives interact with "everyday discourses" of gossip, rumours and casual interactions interdependently to "frame and measure experience" (Silverstone, 1999: 11). The documentary viewing experience and subsequent talk become key parts of an individual's (and a community's) wider experiences of important political issues. Marie Gillespie's work on "TV talk" helps one to understand how media texts are understood through interaction and interpretation. Her work explored how media meanings are negotiated and contested via interactions with others, and how they assist in the generation of new identities (Gillespie, 1995). With this in mind, I will now analyse how audiences articulated their responses to our SBS documentary programmes and consider their utility as catalysts for conversations about multicultural society.

Audience engagement with Go Back To Where You Came From

SBS publicity described *Go Back* as a "reverse immersive journey" for "six ordinary Australians" with a range of views on the issue of asylum seekers, a key issue in Australian political debate that had been making headlines. The six protagonists observed the reverse journeys of two separate groups of refugees they met in Australia – one family from Burundi and one group of young men from Iraq. In interviews conducted for this study, the producers described the format as a "constructed documentary". This format takes so-called 'ordinary people' – albeit people carefully cast in the programme – on a constructed experience focused on a theme and allowing for unscripted responses. The Director, Ivan O'Mahoney, described the format in the following terms:

> The form should be driven by the story and the best way of telling it …You have got to be thinking about the message and what you want to achieve and how you make your programme to draw an audience in and make entertaining television…I think we have a duty to engage as wide an audience as we can because we are being paid by these people [tax payers].

Reality television formats are by now very familiar to Australian audiences, although they have rarely explored such pointedly political issues. The constructed documentary approach is atypical for SBS, and initially confounded some audiences:

> At first, having the contestants, a reality TV show was a bit – I thought this was a bit different, but just the content itself is very much SBS. Certainly entertained viewers learn something, and they did that, about a particular

topic or particular point of interest at the moment, and it did that. It definitely felt like an SBS show. (Male, under 35 years, Anglo background, Sydney).

The producers and commissioners of *Go Back* sought to use constructed documentary to explore issues usually only addressed in the framework of news and current affairs programming. The use of a different, more popular format deliberately targeted a wider audience for the content – including younger viewers. This reportedly had an impact:

It was something you were entertained by in the beginning, so it got you kind of hooked in, and you stayed in. I know some of the guys at work...and they were the ones telling me about it! And these are eighteen-year old guys! If it's not Family Guy and it's not comedy-related, it's not really for them! (Female, under 35 years, Italian/Greek background, Melbourne).

Not all audiences found the constructed documentary format appealing. For some it was considered "just another reality show", or "too set up", particularly when dealing with challenging humanitarian issues.

I tend to think it was the plight and the refugees that, kind of – none of the characters I liked, basically. Every one of them I just didn't...there was just something about them all. Personality traits, whatever. I just couldn't warm to any of them, so I found the show a bit irritating because of that. I liked where they went and what they did and stuff like that, but again, yeah, too set-up...– choosing these individuals seemed too set-up. (Male, over 35 years, Anglo background, Melbourne).

I just flicked through it at the point where that young girl was saying that she didn't like certain – I think Africans, I think she said, and I was just freaked. I thought it was just another reality show, so I turned it off. (Male, over 35 years, Anglo/Albanian background, Shepparton).

This level of discomfort seemed to revolve around both the attitudes of the protagonists of the show, and the format used to explore them. It may be that the discomfort lay in being asked to identify with 'ordinary Australians' who were expressing racist views, or that the juxtaposition of such comments in a form usually considered entertainment was too confronting with reference to such a live and polarising political issue.

Australian attitudes to refugees

While *Go Back* was often described as being 'about refugees', the central exploration focused on the attitudes of the Australian protagonists, and whether their attitudes changed when exposed to new information and situations. The six protagonists, their careful casting and the diversity and extremities of views they represented, eliciting a kind of 'love them or hate them' response, were key to audience engagement with the programme. Participants in this study, and those commenting about the programme on social media, tended to view and critique protagonists' comments and behaviours in relation to their own social or ethical values. Many participants expressed shock and anger about the protagonists' views, and the intensity of this response appeared to drive the need to watch in order to see what would happen and who would be transformed by the experience or 'journey'.

> I think it was a train wreck you could see coming, and just wanted to stick around and watch it in terms of these personalities who are clearly racist – you knew they were going for a bit of a slap-down – and whether they would change. That kept the compelling nature going, where you just wanted to see: is this person going to change? Is this person going to stay exactly the same? (Female, over 35 years, Anglo background, Melbourne).

The refugees in our groups found the representation of the protagonists' views on the issue more enlightening. The Iraqi men living in Shepparton who had been recently released from detention centres were shocked by the views expressed by the programme's participants. Their response speaks to issues of language and media access for these groups, factors that restrict participation in public discourse around issues directly affecting them.

> We got surprised that some people in Australia don't like refugees. They dislike them. Yes. We got surprised…so, there are some people, really, in Australia, who don't like refugees? (*Male, Iraqi refugee through an Interpreter, Shepparton*).

The participants in our discussion groups who had arrived as refugees some time ago were more familiar with views represented in *Go Back*, but they also identified the programme as a resource for better understanding.

> …because of this programme, we refugees, we understand the perception of Australians, what is in Australians' minds about refugees. Through this programme we understand what Australians talk about, what they feel about refugees, so this one is the best mirror to understand what is in Australians' minds. (*Male, African refugee, Newcastle*).

One participant of African refugee background felt that the programme had changed perceptions of him in his local community, attributing its broadcast to an increasing comfort on the part of his neighbours with talking to him and including him in local activities.

Human stories

In his interview for this study, programme producer Michael Cordell said that a key aim of the programme was "to demonstrate that behind all these issues are human stories that are often forgotten" (Entertainment Insights 2012, 6). The affect produced by individual, personal stories amongst audiences, combined with the popularity of the series, created opportunities for identification and empathetic engagement that were lacking in much of the news discourse around refugees in Australia. One study participant described it this way:

> It's making the story a story, not just the facts. Because facts in themselves are fine, but for a long period of time, if you're just seeing facts, you don't feel connected to it. So I guess ... this is a really important part as to why we're interested, because if you feel something, you want to know more about it. (*Female, under 35 years, Anglo background, Sydney*).

While the six protagonists were central to engaging audiences with the programme experience, the stories of the featured refugees had the most emotional impact on viewers. The Entertainment Insights report described it in the following way "As the protagonists walked in the shoes of the refugees so did the Australian audience – seeing what the participants saw, feeling what they felt. Viewers were bought into contact with the refugees through the presence of our Australian representatives".

The majority of study participants expressed strong identification with the refugees whose stories were represented in *Go Back*. For many, it was the first time they'd found a connection with the personal story of a person who was seeking asylum.

> I found the actual refugee stories very compelling and heartbreaking. I didn't feel that much empathy with the characters, as in the people going through the experience, as much as I did with the actual, real refugees. (*Female, over 35 years, Anglo background, Melbourne*).

Almost all of the participants who were not from refugee backgrounds themselves described the programme as an eye-opener on refugee issues about which they had limited awareness in the past:

> I suppose what struck me, really, was the conditions of how people live in these countries. What was shown there, it was really, really shocking. (*Male, over 35 year, Lithuanian background, Parramatta*).

Some of the respondents with refugee backgrounds saw the programme as an important validation that would educate their own children on the refugee experience, doing so in a way they appeared to feel they could not.

> I must say, what I found out from this programme: first of all, it reminds us who we are, and it reminds us where we come from, so that our kids – be-

cause I have kids who have not been in the refugee camp as children, so they'll never understand where we came from [because] some of them grew up in Australia – this programme is helping them understand where they come from. (*Male, African refugee, Newcastle*).

Of course the forms of identification would be vastly different for those who never had the type of experience depicted in the programme, and also between and within refugee groups. Media experiences are attributed with meaning that is interwoven with social and political identities in a range of ways (see (Liebes & Katz, 1993: 20). Many of the participants in this study felt that the levels of engagement they had experienced around the plight of refugees through viewing this programme would, or at least 'should', shift the attitudes of other viewers of the programme.

I felt like it was, you know, trying to expose that side of it, that experience of it. Not necessarily to make people go, "OK, we're going to change how we work," for people to understand it, but maybe that understanding or empathy is a basis. Maybe that's the first step in trying to change...so it's sort of like exposing the situation. (*Female, under 35 years, Anglo background, Sydney*).

Several participants in each of our groups expressed the hope that the transformation of opinions and attitudes to refugees amongst the programme's protagonists would have an impact on the broader Australian community and similarly change minds.

I think the whole point is, mainstream Australians are quite racist, a lot of them. And it's only through experiencing what our fellow human beings are going through in other countries that we've had our military involved in: for example, Afghanistan. To me, seeing that program has given me a little bit of hope that some of these people with their narrow views can be changed by seeing people face to face. (*Female, over 35 years, Anglo background, Melbourne*).

The impact of these mediated 'face-to-face' interactions, offering broadcast audience opportunities to identify, critique, express horror, recommend, share and comment, speaks to the intentions of SBS as a "catalyst for national conversations" about diversity. While there was some ambivalence about the programme format, it did appear to cut through more traditional frames and contexts for debating these issues or connect with audience behaviours around 'liking', sharing and discussing content in a way that providing new points of access on a challenging issue. Two quotes capture this line of thought:

I think it gives everyone a really good insight, it educates people, and it gets people talking...they're important issues that should be discussed, I believe. It's good media... (*Female, under 35 years, Egyptian background, Melbourne*)

And everyone has such an opinion. Like, so many people are so – like, a lot of people on the show, which is what the show was about – people have such staunch opinions and they have almost zero idea of the facts, you know? …But yeah, as you said, like, something bad is happening to someone somewhere, but when a story is in your face like that...maybe I might realign my views, or think twice before saying, 'All asylum seekers should be turned away'. (Male, under 35 years, Anglo background, Sydney).

Many participants described talking about the programme and seeking out others' views and positions on the issue after watching. As the Entertainment Insights report (2011, 8) asserts:

Go Back to Where You Came From was a major topic of discussion in the workplaces, on the radio, in Facebook, Twitter and on TV talk shows during the week it went to air. Groups reported conversations with work colleagues, family and friends. Predominantly, our focus group participants believed their opinions on the issues had shifted with new insights they had gained from the program.

Immigration Nation audience engagement

Immigration Nation was a narrative-driven historical documentary built around primary source archival material and interviews with those who experienced elements of Australia's 'White Australia Policy' first hand, their descendents and academics. For some study participants, the approach seemed to strike the right balance.

That's what I liked, actually, because you have the academic; you have the personal, anecdotal commentary; but then you have some of that real feed, you know, of the propaganda documentaries and things like that. So it was kind of this whole...you're getting the whole-picture, I suppose, view of it all. (*Female, under 35 years, European background, Melbourne*).

For many participants in the study, this element of Australian history, or at least this particular take on it, was both novel and informative. Many expressed shock that they had no prior awareness of the realities of their country's proscriptive immigration policy.

I just felt really embarrassed that I didn't know about it. I hadn't learnt about it. Like, I'd heard the 'White Australia Policy,' the term, in the past, and never thought to actually go and find out about what it really meant and what it was about...It's like, why am I born and raised in this country, never lived anywhere else and never wanted to live anywhere else, and why don't I know about this? (*Female, over 35 years, Italian background, Melbourne*)

I had just always thought of Australia as a multicultural nation until I watched that first episode…Yeah, it blew me away…I was shocked, and 'What the hell is this?' (*Male, under 35 years, European background, Melbourne*).

As in *Go Back*, the personal stories and direct experiences that were an outcome of the Policy had the most emotional impact for viewers in this study. High levels of audience engagement, including high levels of recalled detail, were evident in the individual stories of families and individuals who had been impacted by the Policy.

[That] Immigration Nation episode where they were showing the family where the husband was here, and then his family, with the kids. And they were showing photos of the kids with their mum. That was horrible, you know, that they're dividing the family and those bonds, and the children don't have their father because of the immigration…It was just horrible. But when you see the photos, it does connect you to a face and somebody. It just is more powerful. (*Female, under 35 years, European background, Melbourne*).

Participants from migrant backgrounds, particularly in the older groups, expressed strong levels of identification with the migrant experiences portrayed in this series. One older Italian woman wept when she described the immigration screening processes she and other migrants were subjected to before entering Australia, as represented in the series. In group discussions, there was a high level of 'switching' between describing the programme and relating personal experiences, and many recounted the same occurring when they discussed the programmes with others in their families and friendship circles. For some, this was a painful experience, particularly in recalling prevailing racist sentiments when they arrived in Australia:

Honey, nowadays it's [racism] really diluted. You should have been here in the Seventies, when they tell you 'Piss off, Asians,' and they write across the wall, 'Asians out.' And they tell you to piss off, and all these things. And you know, I was a child at school. I used to go into fights with people that were calling me names and stuff… (*Female, over 35 years, Vietnamese refugee, Parramatta*).

Some younger audiences expressed ambivalence or discomfort over the way the programme highlighted the negative experiences of the past. Several in each of the younger groups expressed renewed anger about the policies that had been, perhaps, poorly understood or latently tolerated. A young Italian woman in Shepparton was particularly affected, and described the Policy as insulting, and by extension felt distanced from the programme that was exposing them to this, although she noted in her viewing diary:

It gave me an understanding of why we experienced the discrimination and racism we received. (*Female, over 35 years, Italian background, Shepparton*).

Anglo-Australians were shocked to learn that the diversity they now took for granted in Australian society had been so hard-won. Some described feeling discomfited after watching the programme, although still claiming high levels of engagement:

It makes me want to learn more. And what I feel we have done to immigrant families makes me so angry, confused and uncomfortable – sad that we really were a racist country and I really don't like that because I have always thought we were the lucky country (lucky if you were white). (*Female, under 35 years, Anglo background, Shepparton, Viewing Diary*).

I felt very uncomfortable and sad watching this and realising that the 'great' country that I was born in and raised in was founded on a very racist and cruel law. I also felt emotional that I didn't know about the White Australia Policy before. (*Female, over 35 years, Italian background, Melbourne, Viewing Diary*).

Some drew parallels with current policy and spontaneously started talking about other issues related to immigration, in particular refugee and asylum seeker policy. There were references to past and contemporary policies in their remarks:

We are actually still doing that. We are separating children in detention now, which I find funny that people seem to detach themselves from that. Do you know what I mean? We can watch that [Immigration Nation] and go, '"Oh, that's really terrible'. 'Oh, hang on a minute'. (*Female, over 35 years, Greek background, Melbourne*)

And for some, the series reportedly generated a new appreciation of multiculturalism.

Seeing as that I have quite a few ethnic friends, seeing what their parents and grandparents had to put up with made me quite sad. But I also gained respect for them because of the love they can still have for their adopted nation considering all we have done. (*Male, under 35 years, Anglo background, Shepparton, Viewing Diary*).

I believe the message reaffirms to me the importance of multiculturalism in Australia. Although racism and discrimination is sometimes apparent, it gives me hope that a positive message is supported in media and greater society for equality. (*Male, under 35 years, Asian background, Sydney, Viewing Diary*).

"Usable stories" and common points of reference

The analysis of audience responses in this study suggests that in these documentaries SBS has provided cultural resources around which audiences could develop understanding, empathies, identifications or reactions that assisted them to negotiate their responses to important social issues. These resources were important to cultivating debate around 'difficult subjects' in a complex multicultural society, providing "usable stories" and common points of reference (Mepham, (1990: 60).

The range of groups included in the study generated a range of unique subject positions in relation to the content. When shown *Go Back*, for example, one group of recent refugees, who had arrived by sea, asked their facilitator – through a translator – "do Australians really feel this way about us?" In the *Immigration Nation* groups, some of the older Italian-Australians who had come through immigration assessment processes and the physical appraisal depicted in the series, became emotional when describing the documentary images and sequences, recounting how dehumanising they had found those experiences. Others expressed more ambivalent responses, such as the Afghani female asylum seeker who triggered a long discussion about the illegitimacy of boat arrivals.

Both programmes featured in this study sought to challenge pre-conceived ideas and to provoke debate. Across the participant groups, a large number of individuals appeared to have responded to the content in this way. They described high levels of affective engagement and some significant discomfort in response to the issues portrayed. Some participants, mainly those from non-English speaking backgrounds, expressed a different kind of frustration, an anger or ambivalence about the issues covered in the programme. This was particularly true of younger culturally and linguistically diverse Australians, particularly those of second-and third- generation responding to *Immigration Nation*'s re-engagement with Australia's racist past. For older migrants to Australia, the series provided an important, if painful, validation.

Although the series did not fully reflect our refugee participants own experiences they hoped it would go some way to bridging the lack of understanding about asylum seekers in Australia. None were more hopeful than refugees about the impact of *Go Back*: some thought it would be likely to transform the debate in Australia and others felt it had already started to have an impact in their local communities. While this may be optimistic, it is revealing of the perceived power of documentaries to provide emotional connection and, through this connection, to communicate ideas, start discussions or even to change minds.

The programmes could not be claimed to have fundamentally changed the political landscape in Australia or radically shifted majority public opinion. They did, however add new layers to audience perceptions of, and responses to, immigration policy, race and intolerance. Focus group conversations and debates revealed a high level of engagement with those issues as audiences navigated their reactions to the content. As both documentaries now have an extended life as educational resources complemented by outreach materials, interactive online components and additional factsheets and information, this impact is ongoing. Go Back series one was the highest rating programme for SBS in 2011 and a second series won a popular television award in 2012 and an international Emmy award in 2013.

It is difficult to assess how much insights from these focus groups contributed to the design of other factual programs, as the creative development process draws on such a range of influences. However, the study certainly helped support this approach to factual content as catalyst for conversation – within the organisation, and with external stakeholders including government. The research findings were quoted extensively in public statements by senior management, annual reports, submissions to government (including funding submissions) and corporate documents. The broad notion of audience that informed this study has since been used in SBS outreach and community engagement activities.

Importantly the findings suggest that as our public lives are increasingly lived in and through media, PSM can create opportunities for better understanding between its constituents. Perhaps one of its most important and valuable contributions is as catalyst, and platform, for national conversations about difficult social issues. When the resources informing these conversations are developed in the public interest, rather than purely ratings and subscription- or advertiser-driven commercial interests, there is some optimism for more inclusive and informed public debates.

References

Benhabib, S. (2004) *The Rights of Others*. New York: Cambridge University Press.

Bird, S.E. (2011) Seeking the Audience for News: Response, News Talk and Everyday Practices. In V. Nightingale (ed.) *The Handbook of Media Audiences*. Oxford: Wiley-Blackwell.

Dahlgren, P. (2005) The Internet, Public Spheres, and Political Communication: Dispersion and Deliberation. *Political Communication, 22*, 147-162.

Gillespie, M. (1995) *Television Ethnicity and Cultural Change*. London: Routledge.

Green, J., & Jenkins, H. (2011) Spreadable Media: How Audiences Create Value and Meaning in a Networked Economy. In V. Nightingale (ed.) *The Handbook of Media Audiences*. Oxford: Wiley-Blackwell.

Hall, S. (1993) Which Public? Whose Service? In W. Stevenson (ed.) *All our Futures*. London: BFI.

Janssen, D., & Kies, R. (2005) Online Forums and Deliberative Democracy. *Acta Politica, 40*, 317-335.

Jupp, J. (2002) *From White Australia to Woomera: The Story of Australian Immigration*. New York: Cambridge University Press.

Kymlicka, W. (1995) *Multicultural Citizenship*. Oxford: Oxford University Press.

Liebes, T., & Katz, E. (1993) *The Export of Meaning: Cross- Cultural Readings of Dallas* (2nd ed.) Cambridge: Polity Press.

Mepham, J. (1990) 'The Ethics of Quality in Television. In G. Mulgan (ed.) *The Question of Quality* (pp. 56-72). London: BFI.

Morley, D. (2000) *Home Territories: Media, Mobility and Identity*. New York: Routledge.

Nolan, D., & Radywyl, N. (2004) Pluralising Identity, mainstreaming identities: SBS as a Technology of Citizenship. *Southern Review, 37*(2), 40-61.

Scannell, P. (1989) Public Service Broadcasting and Modern Life. *Media, Culture and Society, 11*(2), 138.

Silverstone, R. (1999) *Why Study the Media?* London: Sage Publications.

Reports

SBS Corporate Plan 2010-2013.

http://media.sbs.com.au/home/upload_media/site_20_rand_1685307411_sbs_corporate_plan7.pdf, last accessed 4/07/2013

The Ipsos McKay Report (2011). *SBS Immigration Nation: Thought Leadership Research Final Report*.http://media.sbs.com.au/home/upload_media/site_20_rand_2115667245_sbs_immigration_nation_final_report_16_dec.pdf last accessed 28/03/2013

Entertainment Insights (2012). *Audience Engagement with SBS Documentary Content*. http://media.sbs.com.au/home/upload_media/site_20_rand_936875053_audience_engagement_with_sbs_documentary_content_sbs_2011.pdf last accessed 28/03/2013

Chapter 14

Finding the Value in Public Value Partnerships

Lessons from Partnerships Strategies and Practices in the United Kingdom, Netherlands and Flanders

Tim Raats, Karen Donders & Caroline Pauwels

This chapter addresses the value of partnership projects and the constituting elements that contribute to their success. In repositioning themselves as public service media [PSM] organisations, broadcasters have increasingly incorporated the pursuit of partnerships in policies and strategies. Engaged in collaborations and joint ventures with cultural and educational institutions, such as museums, universities and film development bodies, they seek to expand the reach of their remits and increase the quality of their outputs and services. Partnerships have also provided a means to increase return-on-investment by expanding the distribution, and enhancing efficiency by sharing costs.

As such, the idea of partnerships has been explicitly linked to the achievement of public value (Moore 1995; Benington & Moore 2011). The BBC has heavily emphasised the importance of partnerships in strategy documents, gradually developing a 'partnership agenda' (BBC Trust 2008). Other PSM operators have also incorporated partnerships as a key factor for enhancing their public service remits (Aslama & Clark 2012; Raats 2012; Lowe 2010). A focus on public value partnerships [PVP] is considered key in deploying a full-portfolio strategy while also staying true to the traditional rationale and core values of the ethos that legitimates PSB (Lowe 2010; Leurdijk 2005).

Partnership is popular among policymakers, encouraged through media regulation and formalised in management contracts, pushing the partnership agenda as essential to overarching ecosystem and for a multi-stakeholder approach (Donders & Raats 2012). In partnerships, PSM has found a strategic mechanism to legitimate operations and safeguard the organisation (Raats 2014).

Despite the relevance from a policy perspective, this strategy entails a twofold risk. First, policymakers can advance partnership requirements to address short-term needs in media markets with the result that collaboration is pushed to compensate for cutbacks (see the Dutch case in Raats 2012).[1] Secondly, there is a risk that the continuous emphasis on partnerships in policy statements might present collaboration as an absolute and the only solution for addressing PSM challenges. When not evaluated against its practice, this can dilute the actual value of partnership – at worst ending up as an empty box.

In this chapter, we approach public value with an emphasis on two questions: how do partnerships contribute to value, and what are the underlying factors contributing to the value of projects? The chapter has four parts. The first contextualises the academic focus on partnerships and introduces the 'digital commons' as an overarching perspective for PSM in a networked environment. It describes the turn to a partnership agenda and discusses the characteristics of public value partnerships. Drawing on the conceptualisation of public value management (Moore 1995; Stoker 2006; Benington & Moore 2011), we tie partnership to the public value concept and analyse the motives and constituting factors for partnership. Next, PSM literature and organisational theory are combined to develop criteria for assessing PVPs and their outcomes. These dimensions create a framework for analysing three flagship projects: *A History of the World in 100 Objects* (BBC), *De Canvascollectie* (VRT) and *Cinema.nl* (VPRO). The cases are useful for discussing wider partnership commitments within PSM. The last part evaluates the cases from a comparative perspective to enhance the framework for application in other domains.

Evidence is derived from analysis of policy documents (strategy documents, press statements, vision notes, reports, management contracts) and interviews with twenty-two experts who are PSM representatives and other stakeholders involved partnership projects with PSM organisations. The interviews were conducted between February 2010 and June 2012.

Partnerships as a pre-requisite for PSM

In analysing the shift to PSM, scholars increasingly study the organisational role from a network perspective (Himmelstein & Aslama 2003; Collins 2010; Brown & Goodwin 2010; Aslama-Horowitz & Clark in this volume). PSM is described as a pivotal node in an increasingly networked system of media and societal relations. The 'digital commons' notion, first advanced by Graham Murdock (2005: 227), envisages this as "a linked space defined by its shared refusal of commercial enclosure and its commitment to free and universal access, reciprocity, and collaborate activity" … [with PSB] as "the principal node in an emerging network of public and civic initiatives". This notion depends on a fundamental revision in our understanding of audience, resting on the premise of significant participation. The notion also depends on success in building partnerships with other public institutions: schools, museums, archives and arts centres, and civil society organisations. These twin aspects of the digital commons are emphasised in other academic literature on partnership and PSM (e.g. Mjos 2012; Lowe 2010; Aslama 2010; Jackson 2010; Jakubowicz 2008).

The motives for partnership are explicitly linked with the delivery of public value in corporate strategies and promotion, if mainly as something implicit in academic literature (until recently). As noted earlier, the BBC promotes partnership as a means to guarantee fulfilment of its public service remit (BBC 2004 & 2008). Claims about collaborating with public institutions throughout the UK mirror the digital commons notion. As former BBC Director General Mark Thompson (2011) exclaimed, "We're also working more closely than ever before with the UK's cultural institutions, many hundreds of them. We know how important we can be in connecting them, their current work and their rich archives with the public, because we know that we share the same public space". This provides a good example of public service corporations promoting the 'partnership agenda' as a key component of an overarching strategy: "For the BBC, partnership is no longer a theory. It is a proven model – indeed it is now the default model for the BBC when any new large-scale issue or opportunity presents itself" (BBC 2008: 10). In practice, however, the implementation of partnership happens on a selective, incremental and pragmatic basis (Raats 2012).

The collaboration we refer to as 'public value partnership' underscores ventures with other players that serve the core domains of PSM and provides a new service or type of content. As both the partnership agenda and the attachment to public value originated at the BBC (Collins 2007), it is our primary example to discuss the partnership agenda. In the years since, the BBC's focus on public value partnerships has increasingly been adopted by other PSM operators, including the Flemish VRT (VRT & Flemish Government 2011) and the Dutch NPO (2010).

In the BBC's current Editorial Guidelines (2013a) the term is explicitly used to herald collaboration that "seeks to offer the greatest public value by working in partnership with others" in order to "inspire and motivate audiences far more powerfully", said to be advanced by working with others, and to "deliver added value for audiences and our partners" (section 16.4.22). PVP in practice mostly entails joint editorial initiatives for cross-media projects. The scope of these projects, as well as the structure, varies from co-operation between broadcasters and museums to develop a television programme together with an off-air exhibition, to the joint creation of a web platform that integrates archival content from art institutions.

Public value and the partnership agenda

The value that PVP is supposed to create corresponds with the 'public value' framework as conceptualised by Mark H. Moore (1995). It's clear Moore's theory was instrumental to the BBC's 2004 proposal for *Building Public Value*

(Collins 2007). For Moore, public value is evident in whatever is valued by a public as citizens, and not only as individuals or in the guise of consumers (see also O'Flynn 2007). In this light, partnerships can be considered a managerial means for enhancing the delivery of what the public values, and whatever also adds value to the public sphere (Benington & Moore 2011). Some observations are worth noting.

Firstly, public value is more than showcasing distinctiveness and performance; that which adds value to the public sphere effectively contributes to it. The aims must be clear, as well as the proposed outcomes (not simply outputs). The work necessary to build and maintain legitimacy is essential for securing support and resources, what Moore called the "authorizing environment" (1995: 164). Thus, an emphasis on partnership is of central importance to the process of enhancing public value.

Secondly, public value management should be "able to show that the results obtained are worth the cost of private consumption and unrestrained liberty forgone in producing the desirable results. Only then can we be sure that some public value has been created" (ibid: 29). That clearly entails efforts to measure public value outcomes. No easy task, but crucial nonetheless.

Thirdly, scholars in the field of organisation studies have considered public value as the core principle for governance in a networked environment (see especially Stoker 2006 and Benington's work in the co-edited 2011 volume with Moore). Public value management requires securing support from a broad (though variable) set of stakeholders, in the case of PSM among those that recognise the importance of a shared public space along the lines of a digital commons. Public value depends not only on what government and public sector institutions do and provide, but also on voluntary initiatives and private sector contributions (Benington & Moore 2011). Thus, adding public value depends on a broad ecosystem and its realisation requires taking a multi-stakeholder approach, as discussed in recent policy discussions where PSM is conceived as a motor and standard to increase the value and position of other players in the ecosystem (Lund & Lowe 2013; Donders & Raats 2012; Kraus & Karmasin 2012). Most notably, it can be found in studies commissioned or conducted by Ofcom (2009) that present partnership as a means (but not the sole solution) for maintaining the amount of regional programming, children's programming, and the overall percentage of content that is domestically produced in the UK.

Fourthly, Moore (1995) highlights the operational capabilities of organisations as being vital to creating public value. This refers to all the assets, financial, personnel, skills and technology, and an optimal allocation of resource capacity. A transition towards the network configuration is not, despite the similar nature and apparent shared goals of public institutions, seamless and clearcut. Because the digital commons lacks a structural, practical component, the perspective oddly overlooks power asymmetries that have been highlighted by others (Kettle 1993; Clegg 1989). While PSM partnerships have rarely been investigated in-depth, contributions hint at a series of thresholds, situated on the level of broadcasting organisations themselves as well as the surrounding contexts (e.g. Severson 2006; Leurdijk 2005; Alm & Lowe 2003; Hoynes 2003).

Interestingly, the three constituting elements in Moore's strategic triangle (authorising environment, public value outcomes, and operational capabilities) correspond with the underlying motives of PSM to engage in partnerships. The pursuit is framed as an initiative for gaining efficiency and productivity (operational capabilities), to enhance public service provision through synergies (public value outcomes), and to secure the support of various stakeholders to consolidate PSM legitimacy (authorising environment).

A framework for analysing public value partnerships

In analysing the value in PVP we can differentiate between the direct value of partnership projects, the outcomes in terms of audience reach and appreciation, getting more people involved in the PSB remit, increased quality through synergies, etc., and their indirect value, especially involvement with the cultural sector that enhances appreciation of the public service remit. But this poses difficulties for measurement regarding the value of public partnerships, at least as much as in measuring public value per se. Furthermore, one needs to also differentiate between the value of partnerships and the value of partnership projects. Often broadcasters measure the success of projects on the success of the collaboration, rather than the outcome of the project (interview with VRT representative; NPO representative). Obviously these are intertwined, but partnership success as such is not a suitable proxy for the degree to which public value has been created or added. Conversely, public value does not necessarily stem from a seamless partnership. Just because things go well together doesn't mean they have gone right. Grasp public value requires analysis of the underlying factors that contribute to the success of a PVP's outcomes. We therefore draw on PSM literature and insights regarding public-private partnership (PPP) because that has a much deeper history than PVP.

PSM scholars addressing organisational and strategic challenges that are characteristic of co-operation often point to the benefits of decentralising, but equally stress the importance of maintaining core capacity and expertise to safeguard competitive advantage and preserve a distinctive corporate identity (Norbäck 2010; Alm & Lowe 2003). Hoynes (2003) described how an increased commitment to engage in public-private ventures at PBS in the United States resulted in the commercialisation of core competences and eventually eroded a distinctive identity. Alm and Lowe (2003: 230a.f.) referred to both knowledge and capacity dependency as factors meriting consideration in strategies related to decentralisation and co-operation. Thus, distinctiveness in this regard hinges on two components: 1) managing the core competencies and capacity in partnerships, and 2) safeguarding the distinctive character and values of PSM.

Others point to the legislative burden that develops in co-operation strategies. Leurdijk (2007) for example shows through case studies that legislative frameworks are often contradictory, hermetic and insufficiently adapted to the hybrid broadcasting climate that is characteristc of partnerships and co-operation strategies. Media management perspectives discuss the importance of connectedness in media clusters, in both formal and casual aspects (Mjos 2011). Karlsson and Picard (2011: 289) distinguish between density, which refers to the amount of linkages, and intensity, which refers to the amound of activity. They underscore the importance of interdependence because how partners are connected is more important than the domains in which they are connected. From the perspective, we can assume that the closer to the strategic and distinctive core of the remit, the more complex and difficult the partnerships will be.

Perspectives on the dynamics of public-private partnerships (Bovaird 2004; Rosenau 2000) agree the notion is vague and discuss the immense breadth of relevant domains. Brinkerhoff and Brinkerhoff (2010) consider PPPs according to the degree of co-operation, pinned to two concepts that constitute its structure and define outcomes: 1) the degree of 'mutuality' as the ways in which partners have agreed on shared investment, shared outcome, shared objectives and horizontal decision-making; and 2) 'organizational identity' as the ways in which the core defining features of partners are preserved when engaging in partnership. Analysis of project networks (Sydow & Staber 2002) emphasise the importance of flexibility, horizontal structure and informal ties in partnership projects. This also shows the importance of control and co-ordination, as well as reconciling flexibility with existent traditional and often rigid organisational structures. Indeed, partnership projects pose challenges to PSB strategy in the need to reconcile a new and rather high degree of 'openness' with "paradigmatic ways of thinking and acting", and for the PSM organisation in the legacy context of corporations that are "typically big, old and powerful" (Lowe 2009: 15) with deep heritage. Perhaps too often most effort goes into crafting the strategy and not enough into guaranteeing alignment of the organisational structure that bottle partnership initiatives (Raats 2012).

Our framework summarises these findings to create dimensions which contribute to, even determine, both the value and outcomes of public value partnerships:

- *Interdependence* = the modalities of partnership commitments (formal or informal agreement, project-based or long-term, standardised or specified agreements

- *Legislative boundaries* = rules enabling or restricting PVP

- *Mutuality* = the ways in which partners' interest are aligned and whether partners have agreed upon shared motives, objectives, and efforts

- *Distinctiveness* = the ways in which PSM safeguards identity and core strategic functions

- *Organisational structure* = how size and structure of the organisation affect commitments.

The factors will be used to analyse the outcomes of three partnership initiatives in practice. The three cases were selected to fit four criteria. First, they are cross-media projects keyed to partnership between a significant PSM organisation and relevant stakeholders and can be considered as PVPs within the scope of the public remit. This does not mean that all partners are public, as the *Cinema.nl* case shows. Second, they have been considered as flagship projects for successful partnership strategies, showcased by PSM professionals as examples of good practice in this area. Third, they also demonstrate thresholds that are clearly associated with the criteria in our analytical framework, and are therefore symptomatic of the limits of the partnership agenda. Finally, they feature sufficient contextual differences (i.e. Flanders' small market, the BBC's size and financial strength; the Dutch pillarised broadcasting system), which is important for the general relevance of the framework.

PSM partnerships in practice

We begin with our case from the BBC, A History of the World in 100 Objects [HOTW], then examine '*De Canvascollectie*' (The Canvas Collection) at VRT in Flanders, and conclude with our case from VPRO in the Netherlands, Cinema.nl.

A History of the World in 100 Objects

HOTW was a large-scale BBC project based on a PVP arrangement with the British Museum [BM] and various UK cultural institutions. It provides an example of the BBC's co-operation with external stakeholders and a commitment to arts and culture in their programmes and services (BBC 2013c). The partnership providing the basis for *AHOTW*, was unprecedented in scale and outcome. The project consisted of a 100-episode series programmes, broadcast on BBC's speech network, Radio 4 in 2010 (BBC Press Office 2009).[2] Apart from the radio series, a website provided additional background, a website served as a means to interact with the public and other cultural institutions, as users could upload and share details of their artefacts.

The partnership that was central to the project was based on joint investment of capacity and resources, and joint editorial responsibilites. An extensive agreement provided the basis for the collaboration (interview with BM, February 2012). The BBC produced and distributed the radio broadcasts and was responsible for the website (launched as a sub-site on the Radio 4 website); BM staff provided the research and edited their input into draft versions of the scripts. BM director Neil McGregor served as the host of the series and BM organised an exhibition at the museum uner the *HOTW* label.

While the BBC and BM formed the core of the initiative, museums, schools and individuals throughout the country provided objects and descriptions. On a regional level, the museums held events linked to the project and worked together with 44 local BBC radio stations (*The Guardian* 2010). Various agreements existed for the different types of *interdepedence* (interview with BBC strategist, February 2012).

The project was conceived by both major parties and based on shared interest and objectives: making cultural artefacts accessible to the wider audience and telling history through grand narratives. Ideas for the project were developed as early as 2003. In 2008 a workable structure of the project was agreed upon and co-operation in working groups started (interview with BM, February 2012). Partner institutions agreed that the public character and accessibility would be core to the project. Hence, the series was made available for free on iTunes and no commercial exploitation and revenue sharing was pursued.

HOTW reached 4 million people through Radio 4. It was downloaded more than 26 million times worldwide. The BM saw an uptake in visitors of 200,000 people. The website counted around 150,000 daily visitors at the end of the project. Website visitors uploaded more than 3240 cultural items (Goring 2011). Despite the agreed non-commercial set-up, partners agreed on a book publication and that has already been picked up in the *New York Times* bestseller list and in the UK it was the most popular historical non-fiction work of all time (interview with BM, February 2012). In the British press, the project was valued for its high quality content and accessbility, and the bottom-up approach (e.g. Hensher 2010; Kennedy 2010).

The originality and simplicity of the concept were two important factors in *HOTW's* success. A third factor was the 360° commissioning and cross-media delivery of the project. The website allowed ongoing information access during and after the broadcasts, markedly extending the lifecycle of the series online and providing the necessary continuity in the project, allowing bottom-up initiatives to gradually develop and flourish. Local partners were added in process and the project picked up by various other BBC players after its launch. Distribution via podcasting increased audiences after the radio broadcasts. Underpinning these aspects of production, the main factor in the project's success was in the set-up of the partnership itself.

Firstly, project success depends on *mutuality*. Both institutions set out to provide shared input and equal capacity. Both agreed on the type of resources they could make available, without any financial trade-offs being required. Equal sharing of effort was also made more easily because of the significant size of the partner organisations and their mutual investment in cultural development.

Second, *interdepedence* and *distinctiveness* were formalised. The extensive negotiations resulted in a contract that clearly outlined the involvement and commitment of all partners. The BBC's editorial independence and control on the final broadcast were safeguarded at all times and the possible restrains that might later hamper collaboration were addressed up front in contract negotiations.

Lastly as regards the *organisational* factor, although hundreds of people from different institutions and branches of them were directly or indirectly involved, the structure of the collaboration was fairly transparent with tasks and responsibilities detailed for all relevant BBC and BM staff. A steering group of one project leader from BBC and BM led. Subsequent working groups with representatives from each organisation were installed (on the website, on the exhibition, on a local level). The BBC circumvented rigid structures and procedures of both organisations, allowing flexibility in the project development (Interview with BM, February 2012).

The Canvas Collection

Inspired by initiatives in the Netherlands and the UK (e.g. the BBC's *Summer Exhibition*), *De Canvascollectie* was based on a joint editorial and operational partnership with arts organisations and renowned contemporary art museums. The initiative originated at VRT's television channel, Canvas, which was putting culture back in the forefront of its programming and was looking for a project that would appeal to culturally-engaged audiences, but also stimulate interest among broader audiences to get more acquainted with the arts. A complementary driver for *De Canvascollectie* was strenuous criticism from the cultural sector demanding more relevant programming and creative co-operation from VRT. Various cultural and educational institutions were therefore involved in the project at a relatively early stage, to enlarge the basis for the project, and to provide infrastructure efficiency. The project received an additional 150.000 euros from the Flemish government, and funding from sponsorships (interview with VRT represenative, August 2010).

While the project was conceived as a cross-platform initiative, *De Canvascollectie* mainly revolved around a television programme (10 episodes) where amateur artists presented their work to a professional jury and competed for awards. The best works were presented in an exhibition, with jury, sponsor and public prizes granted to the winners. The project was renewed for a third series in 2012. With each series the scope and scale of the partnership enlarged. For the second series the Walloon PSB organisation, RTBF (for the French-speaking part of Belgium) joined the project, and for the third series the German language Belgian broadcaster, BRF, was added. The initiative to involve other partners came from the VRT and was motivated by potential benefits in scale and financial efficiency (interview with VRT representative, August 2010).

In the first series, 4,700 amateur artists presented more than 14,000 works of art. Selection weekends were organised at cultural venues all over Flanders. The project was picked up by the cultural sector in their promotional outlets. However, from the perspective of audience development, the direct benefits of the programme seem modest. The programme did not reach new audiences and showed a relatively low viewer share at an average of 3,4% (VRT 2008). The indirect benefits were better: the number of subscriptions to higher arts education increased, VRT got better acquainted with the culture sector, and the project proved beneficial for the Canvas brand (interview with VRT representative, August 2010; July 2010).

Despite serving as an example of good collaboration, the modest outcome and failure to provide an appealing project for audiences – at least in the first series – resulted from a struggle project leadership. The cultural sector and VRT did not set out from shared objectives and goals. Partly this lack of *mutuality* can be explained by the fact that the project grew as discussions took place, and partly because of the participants divergent underlying interests (interview VRT representative, August 2011). While the partners were keen on creative involvement, they were reluctant to financially contribute. As Canvas was the main financier, VRT claimed control over the project and the rights to the final copy of the broadcast.

VRT and the cultural sector were overlooking each others' core competencies and *distinctiveness*, and failed to produce a satisfactory agreement defining the tasks and responsibilities of each actor. Initially cultural players felt themselves merely involved as logistic partners due to their restricted input into the project, and so few were willing to actively participate in the project by providing logistic support for the organisation of events. The partners' commitment and mutual understanding has grown over the years, however, and the responsibilities of all participants, as well as the objectives and expectations are now much clearer (interview with VRT representative, August 2010).

In sum, *De Canvascollectie* shows how a lack of clear agreement and stipulated rules for the partnership structure, motives and interests hamper good collaboration. It furthermore shows that the success of partnerships and project outcome is not the same, despite the fact that both motives pursue public value.

Cinema.nl

Cinema.nl is the result of the Dutch broadcasting organisation, VPRO[3], teaming up with *De Volkskrant* newspaper to create an online platform for film. The project resulted from the consonant interests of two emerging digital media players to provide a new service for a similar target audience. Film is an important part of VPRO's (2011) cultural programming, and this venture helped VPRO gain momentum in repositioning itself as a PSM operator.

The website was launched in 2002. VPRO provided the name and handled development and hosting of the web platform, also delivering related radio and television content, audiovisual clips from festivals, and managing user interaction. All reviews came from *De Volkskrant*. Their contribution focused on reviews for film in cinema, on television and DVD, and provided news updates and coverage of film festivals in the Netherlands and abroad. The site was complemented by a newsletter and offered RSS feeds and comments for registered users. On radio, Cinema.nl had a broadcast programme. Since 2010 the web platform has provided a weekly film programme, *CinemaTV*, focusing on festival news, new releases and tips on television (De Volkskrant 2006).

VPRO and De Volkskrant together provided news updates on the Dutch documentary festival IDFA, where both operated as a sponsor in barter deals (interview with NPO representative, June 2011). The goal of the project was to provide reviews to broader audiences and to increase the impact and position of their respective brands. As such, both partners set out from *mutuality* in goals and shared interest, while maintaining *distinctiveness* through clearly demarcated tasks of each partner without editorial interference.

The project was honoured with the Pritchet prize for best broadcasting related multimedia site. By 2006 it reached 900.000 unique visitors monthly. In 2011 Cinema.nl reached 12.000 movie fans on daily basis. Both VPRO and De Volkskrant considered the partnership fruitful. The web platform is referred to as an example of a beneficial partnership project that is based on the combined strengths of two partners (VPRO 2011; interview NPO, June 2011; VPRO July 2011).

The success of the project and the intrinsic quality of the platform is strongly dependant on the collaboration where shared efforts with an interesting crossover between audiovisual competences and newspaper journalism. However, when *De Volkskrant* planned to include commercial services (ticket sales and ads) to increase the financial worth of the platform, a conflict of interest arose. These plans conflicted with existing media law, at which point both decided to end the partnership and steer their own respective courses (interview with NPO representative, June 2011; July 2011).

Opposing public and private logics resulted in divergent plans that, for one partner, conflicted with *legislative* provisions that ended the partnership after ten years.[4] In the Netherlands, the *legislative* leeway for players to co-operate with third parties is quite restricted (Commissariat for Media 2009). Interestingly, legislative provisions make no distinction between public and private players, but allow exceptions for culture, sports and media partnerships. Since

2008 increased efforts have been made by the government and the Commissariat for Media to facilitate partnerships and make existing regulation more transparent. This resulted in a clear separation between core tasks and additional tasks (*nevenactiviteiten*, allowing more co-operation when the costs of the initiative do not supersede revenue), a new public-private co-operation scheme, and most recently an experimentation period under which rules are less stringent (interview with media regulator, 2011). The provisions were pushed by broadcasters, cultural sector and private media partners, making government increasingly aware of the paradoxical policy of stimulating partnerships on one hand, and prohibiting the same ventures on the other (interview with broadcasting representative).

Both partners have pursued their interest in film on their own platforms.

Comparing the cases

The cases demonstrate a combination of public value motives from broadening and enhancing the PSM remit to increasing support and legitimacy for the PSM's position and operations. An underlying factor is the drive for efficiency as well, with a focus on increased scale by involving partners or by sharing costs and logistic operations (e.g. website development and maintenance, marketing costs, etc.). Direct motives and public value goals are hence often, but not necessarily always, intertwined.

Measuring the public value of the partnership project is complex and requires subjectivity. While the value of these projects is unmistakably connected with the inclusion of partners in the project – all three cases demonstrate that the project could not have been realised without external partners – measuring the specific contribution of value of these partnerships compared to a scenario without them is impossible. Secondly, while the public value that broadcasters were pursuing with these partnerships in direct terms (i.e. the short-term aims) can be modest, a partnership project can provide indirect benefits in the long run (enlarging consensus amongst partners, legitimising PSM, increasing the appreciation of culture by its public). Thirdly, the cases acknowledge that partnership success is not the same as the value of partnership projects. While failed projects can often be traced back to difficulties in co-operation, successful co-operation does not guarantee the success of the project. Variables including crossmedia embeddedness, theme and target groups, financial input, expertise, programming and promotion, viewers, ratings, etc. play a part in the success of projects. The cases therefore looked into the constituting enabling or restraining factors as described in the second part of this chapter.

Regarding *interdependence*, the cases demonstrate the importance of agreements and clearly spelled out tasks. The cases furthermore demonstrate the ad hoc and project-driven character of projects as much as the process-driven character of partnerships. An overarching strategic framework is crucial for avoiding fragmentation partnerships and networks.

While some public broadcasters may feel uncomfortable to burden a partnership project as early as the development stage with formal obligations, it appears a necessary precondition for the *distinctiveness* of both partners. At the BBC clear rules and a concise agreement was essential for success. Conflicts with VRT often resulted from a perceived risk of losing distinctiveness due to interference in each other's core tasks and expertise.

Safeguarding distinctiveness is a feature of *legislative* restrictions, the third constituing factor. Much of the regulation on partnerships centre around financial restrictions, guarading against favouritism rules on fair trading, transparency, choice of partners, financial contribution, and rules about promotion and commercial activities (e.g. Commissariat for the Media 2009; VRT & Flemish Government 2011). All of this creates the boundaries and establishes the scope of opportunity for partnership.

The fourth factor contributing to the success and value of partnership projects is *organisational structure*. This was considered in terms of the number of departments involved and the flexibility of project leaders and organisations (Sydow & Staber 2002). The VPRO case is fruitful here, as the bottom-up structure of the small organisation allows more intense ties with external allies, more informal contacts and lowers the threshold for PSM professionals and partners to explore new partnerships. But a lack of coherent motivations rendered the responsibilities between VRT and its partners' obscure. For the BBC, the organisational management undoubtedly weighs highest. Not only are there different departments involved in the public value partnerships (legal, editorial policy, radio or television branches, strategy and executives, compliance), they are also often physically dispersed. Organising a partnership therefore required a long investment in time, effort and personnel, and a necessity for continuous co-ordination between the various internal departments and project partners (interview with BBC strategist, February 2012). The coherent and transparent project structure avoided most organisational hazards.

As for *mutuality*, contrary to what might be assumed from a Digital commons perspective, PSM and cultural partners certainly pursue their own interests and power relations define the ways partnerships are set up, as well as the amount of mutual acknowledgement, effort, investment, and control within a partnership. For *Cinema.nl*, diverging logics with the private player obstructed the mutuality in the end. Both *HOTW* and *De Canvascollectie* grew out of a genuine interest to broaden the scope of culture and integrate content and expertise the PSM organisations could not have without involving partners. However, at VRT the motive for third-party involvement gradually shifted and partners were mainly involved to cover external costs and enlarge the scale and promotion of the project, rather than for their expertise (inteview with VRT representative, August 2010). Moreover, compared to the UK example, cultural institutions did not depart from the same footing as VRT. The cultural sector in Flanders is a web of dispersed, relatively solely operating artistic 'islands'. Institutions were not familiar with partnership strategies, let alone partnerships with the VRT and, conflicting interests stem from a problematic relation VRT had with the cultural sector until 2010 (Raats & Moons, 2012).

Conclusions: Making partnerships work

Based on a review of public value literature and analysis of three partnership initiatives, this chapter provides a resonably nuanced treatment of the role and position of PSM within a Digital commons, and demonstrates success factors for partnership strategies.

One the one hand, PVPs have proven to be essentially a matter of context. Factors are intertwined and vary depending the specific organisational, political, ideological and financial realities of the PSM organisation and its partners. As such, implementing best practices from one case does not guarantee success in another context.

On the other hand however, analysis reveals underyling factors that constitute the ways partnerships are organised, integrated and set-up, as well as the crucial role of the regulatory framework. Problems damage the possibilty for public value to result from partnership.

The public value pursued in PVPs rests on a series of interwining motives. Public value can directly pursued in the intrinsic quality of the service and the outcome intentions. Certainly efficiency is a characteristic pursuit, and the interests to strengthen legitimacy is similarly characteristic. From an ecosystem perspective, public value can also be indirectly achieved, as it is the result of a dialectical process between various players and PSM operators. Indirectly, these partnerships might for example enhance support for the PSM activities, or facilitate provision of services by other players that deliver public value (e.g. libraries, archives, education, etc.).

While an excellent partnership does not guarantee a project to achieve the value or quality it sets out to deliver, both are interlinked and failure of a project can often be traced back to the way in which partners collaborated, or to the way in which a partnership contract was drawn out, or even as early as defining the objectives of a partnership. As such, the findings suggest that when legitimation or efficiency are the sole aim of a project, collaboration within the project becomes difficult and burdensome, or risks to miss its target in terms of output, performance and reach. To prevent partnership becoming an end in itself, or something PSM experience as an obligation rather than benefit, public value partnerships should be explicitly tied to public remit objectives and success should be assessed in outcomes, not only output. The Flemish case, as have other examples (Raats 2014), has indicated that efficiency as a driver for public-public partnerships often results in the partnership becoming an end in itself. Additionally, for smaller broadcasters the financial contribution of external partners still seems to prevail over the public benefits the partnership might generate.

What remains to be answered is how and the extent to which partnerships enhance quality and create value for audiences. For our study this can only be surmised by indicators of the comparative involement of populations as audiences, contributors and users. Of course that is insufficient for a firm conclusion about the public value of partnerships. This needs to be addressed in future research.

Notes

1. In the Netherlands, collaboration between the broadcasters was heavily pushed by government as part of a large-scale efficiency operations on the one hand, and cooperation with cultural and other public institution was put forward as part of a significant downsizing of the budgets for culture (Raats, 2012).
2. All episodes can be streamed and downloaded via the project website: http://www.bbc.co.uk/ahistoryoftheworld/programme/
3. In the Netherlands, the public broadcasting system is comprised of a central overarching broadcasting structure NPO and various broadcasting organizations, gaining legitimacy from the nature of their services (news, culture, religious, etc.) and/or the number of public memberships. VPRO is one of these broadcasting organizations.
4. The Dutch media law prohibits forms of partnership where public broadcasters enrich third private parties, which would have been the case when Cinema.nl would sell tickets, include advertisements or cooperate with specific cinemas.

References

Alm, A. & Lowe, G.F. (2003) Outsourcing core competencies. In Lowe, G.F and Hujanen, T. (eds.) *Broadcasting & Convergence: New Articulations of the Public Service Remit*, RIPE@2003. Göteborg: Nordicom, pp. 223-235.

Aslama, M. (2010) Re-thinking PSM audiences: Diversity of participation for strategic considerations. In Lowe, G.F. (ed.) *The Public in Public Service Media, RIPE@2009*. Göteborg: Nordicom, pp. 9-35.

BBC (2004) *Building Public Value: Renewing BBC for a Digital World*. Retrieved at: downloads.bbc.co.uk/aboutthebbc/policies/.../bpv.pdf

BBC (2008) *Public Service Partnerships: Helping sustain UK PSB*. Retrieved at at: http://www.bbc.co.uk/aboutthebbc/insidethebbc/howwework/partnerships.html

BBC (2010d) *Statements of Programme Policy*, 2010/2011. London: BBC

BBC (2013a) *Editorial Guidelines*. London: BBC.

BBC (2013b) *Editorial Guidance*. London: BBC.

BBC (2013c) Partnerships. Arts and culture (online) Retrieved at: http://www.bbc.co.uk/about-thebbc/insidethebbc/howwework/partnerships/arts_and_culture.html (07.10.13)

BBC Press Office (2009) The BBC and British Museum announce A History of the World – a unique and unprecedented partnership focusing on world history for 2010. November 25.

BBC Trust (2008) BBC response to Ofcom's Second Public Service Broadcasting Review, Phase 1. London: BBC Trust.

Benington, J. & Moore, M.H. (2011) *Public Value: Theory and Practice*. London: Palgrave Macmillan.

Bovaird T. (2004) Public-private partnerships: From contested concepts to prevalent practice. *International Review of Administrative Sciences, 70*(2), pp. 199-215.

Brinkerhoff, D.W. & Brinkerhoff, J.M. (2011) Public-private partnerships: Perspectives on purposes, publicness and good governance. *Public Administration and Development, 31*(1), pp. 2-14.

Brown, C. & Goodwin, P. (2010) Constructing public service media at the BBC. In Lowe, G.F. (ed.) *The Public in Public Service Media*, RIPE@2009. Göteborg: Nordicom, pp. 119-132.

Clegg, S. (1989) *Frameworks of Power*. London: Sage.

Collins, R. (2010) From public service broadcasting to public service communication. In Lowe, G.F. (ed.) *The Public in Public Service Media*, RIPE@2009. Göteborg: Nordicom, pp. 53-69.

Collins, R. (2007) The BBC and public value. *Medien und Kommunikationswissenschaft*, 65(2), pp. 164-184.

Commissariat for Media (2009) Publiek-Private Samenwerking Brochure. Hilversum: Commisariat for Media.

De Volkskrant (2006) Cinema.nl begint filmprogramma. In: *De Volkskrant*, July 25.

Donders, K. & Raats, T. (2012) Analyzing national practices after European State aid control: are multi-stakeholder negotiations beneficial for public service broadcasting? *Media, Culture and Society*, 34(2), pp. 162-180.

Goring, H. (2011) A history of the world in 100 Objects. *Ceramics Monthly*, 59(5): pp. 24-25.

Hensher, P. (2010) Philip Hensher: The objects of my affection. In: The Independent, October 15.

Himmelstein, H. & Aslama M. (2003) From Service to Access. Re-conceiving Public Television's Role in the New Media Era. In Lowe, G.F., Hujanen, T. (eds.) *Broadcasting & Convergence: New Articulations of the Public Service Remit. RIPE@2003*. Göteborg: Nordicom, pp. 255-268.

Hoynes, W. (2003) Branding Public Service: the new PBS and the Privatization of Public Television. In: *Television & New Media*, 4(2), pp. 117-130.

Jackson, L. (2010) Harnessing collaborative innovation for the evolution of public service media. Paper presented for RIPE@2010 Conference, Londen UK, on 9th September.

Jakubowicz, K. (2008) Participation and partnership: a Copernican revolution to reengineer public service media for the 21st century. RIPE keynote presentation. Mainz, Germany on 9th October.

Karlsson, C. & Picard, R. G. (2011) *Media Clusters: Spatial Agglomeration and Content Capabilities*. Cheltenham: Edward Elgar.

Kennedy, M. (2010) "Radio 4's A History of the World in 100 Objects draws to a close". In: The Guardian, October 14.

Kettl, D.F. (1993) *Sharing power: Public governance and private markets*. Washington, DC: Brookings Institution.

Kraus, D. & Karmasin, M. (2012) Multistakeholderism in Media Management. In M. Glowacki & L. Jackson (eds.) *Creativity, Innovation and Interaction: Public Media Management Fit for the 21st Century*. London: Routledge.

Leurdijk, A. (2007) Public service media dilemas and regulation in a converging landscape. In Lowe, G.F. & Bardoel, J. (eds.) *From Public Service Broadcasting to Public Service Media*. Göteborg: Nordicom, pp. 71-86.

Lowe, G.F. (2010) Beyond Altruism. Why Public Participation in Public Service Media Matters. In: G.F. Lowe (ed.) *The Public in Public Service Media*, Ripe@2009. Göteborg: Nordicom, pp. 9-35.

Lund, A.B & Lowe, G.F. (2013) Current challenges to public broadcasting in the Nordic countries. In Carlsson, Ulla (ed.) *Public Service Media from a Nordic Horizon: Politics, Markets, Programming and Rules*. Göteborg: Nordicom, pp. 51-74.

Mjos, O.J. (2011) Marriage of convenience? Public service broadcasters' cross-national partnerships in factual television. *International Communication Gazette*, 73(3), pp. 181-197.

Murdock, G. (2005) Building the Digital Commons. Public Broadcasting in the Age of the Internet. In Lowe, G.F. & Jauert, P. (eds.) *Cultural Dilemmas in Public Service Broadcasting, Ripe@2005*. Göteborg: Nordicom, pp. 213-230.

Norbäck, M. (2010) Collaborative financing and production: Making public service content at SVT Sweden. In: Lowe, G.F. (ed.) *The Public in Public Service Media, RIPE@2009*. Göteborg: Nordicom, pp. 243-256.

NPO (2010) Concessiebeleidsplan 2010-2016. Hilversum: NPO.

Ofcom (2009) Ofcom's Second Public Service Broadcasting review. Putting viewers first. London: Ofcom.

O'Flynn, J. (2007) From New Public Management to Public Value: paradigmatic change and managerial implications. *Australian Journal of Public Administration*, 66(3), pp. 353-366.

Raats, T. (2014) 'And now for something completely different.' De rol en positie van de publieke omroep in een genetwerkte media- en maatschappelijke constellatie. Brussels: VUB, unpublished doctoral thesis.

Raats, T. (2012) Public Service Media and partnership practices. Matching public policy with broadcasting policy. *International Journal for Media and Cultural Politics*, 8(1), pp. 105-125.

Raats, T. & Moons, A. (2012) Het middenveld: de publieke omroep in een democratische samenleving. In Donders K., Van Den Bulck H. & Pauwels C. (eds.) *De VRT in de 21st eeuw: overbodige luxe of maatschappelijke meerwaarde*. Antwerp: University Press.

Rosenau, P.V. (ed.) (2000) *Public-Private Policy Partnerships*. Cambridge MA: MIT Press.

Severson, P. (2006) Public Service Broadcasting and the need for innovation through collaborative approach. Paper presented for RIPE@2006, Amsterdam Netherlands, 17th November.

Smith, R. (2003) *Focusing on public value: Something old and something new*. Victoria, Australia: Monash University.

Stoker, G. (2006) Public Value Management. A New Narrative for Networked Governance? *American Review of Public Administration*, 36(1), pp. 41-57.

Sydow, J. & Staber, U. (2002) The institutional Embeddedness of Project Networks: The case of content production in German Television. In: *Regional Studies*, 36(3), pp. 215-227.

Thompson, M. (2011) MacTaggart Lecture. Edinburgh: Edinburgh International Television Festival.

VPRO (2011) VPRO alleen door met Cinema.nl. Samenwerking stopt na tien jaar, June 8.

VRT & Flemish Government (2011) Management Contract 2011-2016. Retrieved at: *http://www.vrt. be/opdracht/de-beheersovereenkomst*.

VRT & Flemish Government (2006) Management Contract 2006-2010. Brussels: VRT.

VRT (2008; 2010) Evaluation Canvas Collection. Brussels: VRT.

YLE (2009) Kulttuurikonto. Cultural Fitness Programme (online) Retrieved at: http://kulttuurikunto.yle.fi/

The Authors

CHRISTIAN EDELVOLD BERG (Ph.D. 2013 Copenhagen Business School) is a post-doctoral research fellow at the Department for Business & Politics in the Copenhagen Business School. He is Senior Advisor at the Office for Media at the Danish Agency for Culture. Berg's research focuses on the relationship between state, market and civil society from a political economy perspective. He authored an article on Financing Public Service Broadcasting in the *Journal of Media Business Studies* (2012), and co-authored (with Lowe) an article about the financial situation of PSM in Europe in the *International Journal on Media Management* (2013). He contributed an article to the *International Communication Gazette* special issue on size in 2009, and has produced reports related to media markets for the Danish government.

PAUL CHADWICK (LL.B. Hons. 1998 University of Melbourne) is non-executive director of *Guardian Australia*, a digital-only operation of the London-based Guardian newspaper. Chadwick has worked as both a journalist and a lawyer and was the Director of Editorial Policies at the Australian Broadcasting Corporation from 2007-2012. Before that was Privacy Commissioner of the State of Victoria (2001-2006), lead drafter of the revised Australian Journalists' Association code of ethics, and is the author of books on media and on freedom of information law.

JESSICA CLARK (M.A. University of Chicago) conducts research on the transformation of independent and public journalism and is a consultant to producers and foundations seeking to create high-impact media. As the media strategist at AIR, she is currently focusing on Localore, a national initiative designed to build innovation capacity at public radio and TV stations across the country. She was a Media Policy Fellow at the New America Foundation from 2010-2012, where she collaborated on a series of reports, policy briefs and events on the information needs of communities. From 2007-mid 2011, Clark directed the *Future of Media Project* for American University's Center for Social Media, co-authoring the influential 2009 report *Public Media 2.0: Dynamic, Engaged Publics*, organising events such as the *Beyond Broadcast* conference. Clark has conducted related research on journalism policy and futures for the Open Society Foundations, Harvard's Berkman Center for Internet and Society, and the Corporation for Public Broadcasting and is co-author of *Beyond the Echo Chamber: Reshaping Politics Through Networked Progressive Media* (Free Press 2010).

KAREN DONDERS (Ph.D. 2010 Vrije Universiteit Brussel) is Professor of Policy Analysis and European Media Markets at the Vrije Universiteit Brussel in Belgium. She is a senior researcher at the Centre for Studies on Media Information and Telecommunication (iMinds-SMIT). Donders has published widely on public service media policies and strategies, among others in *Journal of Media Law, Media Culture and Society*, and *International Journal of Media and Cultural Politics*. Palgrave Macmillan published an updated version of her Ph.D., *Public Service Media and Policy in Europe*, in 2012. She recently co-edited with Caroline Pauwels and Jan Loisen the book titled *Private Television in Western Europe: Content, Markets and Policies* (2013 from Palgrave Macmillan). In 2011 Nordicom published a collection of essays on *Exporting the Public Value Test*, edited with Hallvard Moe.

PETER GOODWIN (Ph.D. 1999 University of Westminster) is the Director of Research of the Faculty of Media, Arts and Design at the University of Westminster in the UK. He is the author of *Television under the Tories: Broadcasting Policy 1979-1997*, and contributed work for the 2009 and 2011 RIPE readers.

MINNA ASLAMA HOROWITZ (Ph.D. 2008 University of Helsinki) is Assistant Professor at St. John's University and research fellow at Fordham University in the USA, and also teaches at the University of Helsinki. She has been active in international research for a decade and is conducting comparative work based on the Open Society Foundation's global *Mapping Digital Media* project. From 2008-2009, she served as Programme Officer in the Necessary Knowledge for a Democratic Public Sphere of the Social Science Research Council. Recent research includes new conceptualisations of media audiences and the concept of 'participation', public service media, health communication and social media, and media policy flows in the globalising media environment. She is especially interested in new forms of collaboration in relation to media justice and reform movements. She edited a book (with Philip Napoli) on scholar-activist collaborations in 2011: *Communications Research in Action. Scholar-Activist Collaborations for a Democratic Public Sphere* (Fordham University Press).

JONATHON HUTCHINSON (Ph.D. 2013, ARC Centre of Excellence for Creative Industries and Innovation, Queensland University of Technology) has recently completed his thesis investigating the role of user-generated content within the ABC. Hutchinson also worked at the ABC as the community manager of the UGC site, *ABC Pool* (2010-2013). Hutchinson has been published in the *Australian Journal of Communication, Media International Australia, M/C Journal and Platform*, and is the 2013 winner of the Australian and New Zealand Communications Association's Grant Noble Prize for Best Postgraduate Student Paper Award. He is currently co-editing (with Jean Burgess, Kathleen Kluen and Brady Robards) an international collection titled *Digital Media and the Creative Industries: Platforms, Politics and Participation* (Routledge, forthcoming).

GREGORY FERRELL LOWE (Ph.D. 1992 University of Texas at Austin) is Professor of Media Management at the University of Tampere in Finland. He is a founder and the Continuity Director of the RIPE initiative. Lowe previously worked as Senior Advisor for Corporate Strategy and Development at Yleisradio (1997-2007), the Finnish public service broadcasting company, and was Head of Yle Programme Development (2002-2005). Lowe has edited and co-edited the series of RIPE Readers published by Nordicom since 2003 (six with this volume), and recently co-edited with Christian S. Nissen the book titled *Small Among Nations: Television Broadcasting in Smaller Countries* (2011 from Nordicom). He serves as an editorial board member for the *International Journal on Media Management* and is currently Deputy President of the European Media Management Education Association (EMMA).

ANKER BRINK LUND (Ph.D. 1998 University of Roskilde) is Professor of Media Management at Copenhagen Business School. He is a founder of the CBS Center for Civil Society Studies. Lund previously worked as a Professor of Journalism Studies at the University of Southern Denmark (1999-2004), conducted the Danish Media Subsidy Audit (2006-2009) and coordinated a Cross-Scandinavian Study on Public Service Media (2004-2007). Among his recent publication in English are "Media System, Public Knowledge and Democracy: A Comparative Study." *The European Journal of Communication* 2009;24(1):5-26 (Co-Authors: James Curran, Shanto Iyengar and Inka Salovaara-Moring), Financing Public Service Broadcasting: A Comparative Perspective. *Journal of Media Business Studies* 2012;9(1):7-21 (Co-Author: Christian Edelvold Berg), and Currrent Challenges to Public Service Broadcasting in the Nordic Countries. In: Ulla Carlsson (ed): *Public Service Media. Politics, Markets,Programming and Users.* Nordicom, 2013:51-73 (Co-Author: Gregory Ferrell Lowe).

FIONA MARTIN (Ph.D. 2008 Southern Cross University) was the University of Sydney co-host for the RIPE@2012 conference. She lectures in Convergent and Online Media and has a background in public service broadcasting. She was a journalist and producer with the ABC's Radio National and Sydney 702 networks (1990-1996). Her research investigates digital transformations in PSM and online media industries, and she is published in *Virtual Nation,* (ed.) G. Goggin (2004), *Media and Communications in Australia,* (eds.) S. Cunningham and G. Turner (2008, 2nd edition), and *Histories of Public Service Broadcasting on the Web,* (eds.) N. Brügger and M. Burns (2012). She is currently undertaking two Australian Research Council Discovery projects, *Mediating the Conversation*, which investigates inclusive frameworks for managing public comments on news and opinion websites, and an international comparative study titled *Moving Media: New Policy Modes for Mobile Internet*, together with Prof. Gerard Goggin and Dr Tim Dwyer.

GEORGIE MCCLEAN, Dr, (Doctorate of Cultural Research, DCR, 2012 University of Western Sydney) is Manager of Strategy and Research at Screen Australia, Australia's primary screen sector funding agency. In this role she develops screen policy and manages research about Australian audiences and film, television, online and games production sectors. Prior to 2013, she was the Manager of Policy, Research and Community Engagement in the Strategy and Communications team at SBS. She has lived, studied and worked in Indonesia, Argentina and Japan. She has been published in the *International Journal of Communications, Media International Australia, Continuum: Journal of Media & Cultural Studies* and *the Global Media Journal* as well as a chapter in Jakubowicz, A & Ho, C (eds.) *For those who've come across the seas: Australian Multicultural Theory, Policy and Practice* (2013 for Australian Scholarly Press). She has executive produced programs for SBS television, including *Connecting Diversity* and *SBS CQ: Cultural Intelligence*.

HALLVARD MOE (Ph.D. 2009 University of Bergen) is Professor of Media Studies at the University of Bergen in Norway. He is co-author of three books, most recently one on methods for media studies (*Fagbokforlaget* 2013) and *The Media Welfare State: Nordic Media in the Digital Age* with Trine Syvertsen, Gunn Enli and Ole Mjøs (University of Michigan Press, forthcoming in 2014). Moe is also co-editor of collections on public sphere theory and of *Exporting the Public Value Test: The Regulation of Public Broadcasters' New Media Services Across Europe* with Karen Donders (Nordicom 2011). In 2013-2014, Moe is researching the online news provision of Norwegian public broadcaster NRK. Website: hm.uib.no.

CAROLINE PAUWELS (Ph.D. 1995 Vrije Universiteit Brussel) lectures on European and Flemish media policies as well as communication science and theory at the Vrije Universiteit Brussel. She was appointed Professor in the Department of Media and Communications in 1995 and currently heads the department. Pauwels is Director of the Centre for Studies on Media, Information and Telecommunication (SMIT), part of the interdisciplinary research centre iMinds, where she also leads the Digital Society department. Pauwels is a member of several media and culture-related boards, and currently acts as government commissioner for the Flemish public service broadcaster VRT. She has published widely in academic journals (including the *European Journal of Communication, Convergence*, the *International Journal of Media and Cultural Politics*) and edited various collections.

STOYAN RADOSLAVOV (M.A. 2010 Ruhr University Bochum) is a Ph.D. student at the Ruhr-University of Bochum, Germany. He graduated in media studies and social psychology in Bochum, Germany and Milan, Italy. In his Ph.D. project he examines media literacy promotion as a function of public service media. He is a member of the German Association for Communication Studies (DGPuK), founder and chairman of Daheim e.V. – a non-profit organization dedicated to the practical promotion of media literacy.

TIM RAATS (Ph.D. 2014 Vrije Universiteit Brussel) is a senior researcher at the Centre for Studies on Media, Information and Telecommunication (iMinds-SMIT) at the Vrije Universiteit Brussel, conducting research on audiovisual policy issues and media management challenges. He finalised his Ph.D. dissertation with a grant from the Fund for Scientific Research (FWO-Vlaanderen). The project analysed the role and position of PSM in a networked media ecology. He currently lectures political economy of the creative industries at the Vrije Universiteit Brussel. Raats has published in several edited collections and has peer reviewed articles in *Media, Culture & Society* and the *International Journal of Media and Cultural Politics*.

TOSHIYUKI SATO (B.A. 1973 Waseda University in Tokyo) is Special Controller, General Broadcasting Administration of NHK. He has been with NHK more than 40 years with posts in Bangkok, Manila, Seoul, Washington D.C. and Kuala Lumpur, as correspondent and bureau chief. He covered the falls of two dictators in Southeast Asia, Ferdinand Marcos (1986) and Suharto (1998). He was Chief-editor of International News (1999-2003 during the Afghan and Iraqi wars) and Director-General of NHK's International TV broadcasting service. Mr. Sato chaired the Asia-Pacific Broadcasting Union [ABU] News Group (93-03) and has been involved with ABU and PBI (Public Broadcasters International) and is often sent to work with public broadcasters in developing countries for capacity building (Egypt, South Sudan, Kosovo, and others). He lectures at the National Graduate Institute for Policy Studies in Tokyo (Media Training) and at NHK Cultural Centre.

JAMES SPIGELMAN AC QC is Chairman of the Australian Broadcasting Corporation (2012-) and a Director of the Board of the Lowy Institute for International Policy. From 1998 to 2011 he was Chief Justice and Lieutenant-Governor of New South Wales. From 1980 to 1998 he was a barrister and was appointed Queens Council in 1986. Between 1972 and 1976 he served as Senior Adviser and Principal Private Secretary to the Prime Minister of Australia and as Permanent Secretary of the Commonwealth Government's Department of the Media. Mr Spigelman has been a member of the Australian Law Reform Commission (1976-1979) as well as Chair and board member of a number of cultural and educational institutions. In 2013 he became a Non-Permanent Judge of the Court of Final Appeal of Hong Kong.

TAKANOBU TANAKA (Ph.D. 2009 Graduate School of International Development, Nagoya University) is Senior Researcher for the Broadcasting Culture Research Institute of NHK. Tanaka joined NHK as a news announcer and reporter in 1988. A broadcast journalist for nearly 25 years, Tanaka has covered natural and man-made disasters such as the earthquake in Kobe, Japan (1995), the 9.11 terrorist attacks in the U.S. (2001), and the Indian Ocean tsunami disaster (2004) in Indonesia, Thailand and Sri Lanka. At the time of the Great East Japan earthquake (2011), he was stationed in the Radio Broadcasting Centre at NHK headquarters and went to the disaster struck areas in Tohoku to provide coverage. He moved to BCRI in 2011. His main research themes include disaster broadcast and international co-operation and Public Service Media in Europe and Asia.

MICHAEL TRACEY (Ph.D. 1975 University of Leicester) is Professor in Journalism and Mass Communication at the University of Colorado at Boulder (since 1988). Earlier he was head of the London-based Broadcasting Research Unit and a Research Fellow at the University of Leicester's Centre for Mass Communication Research. Tracey has written eight books, including *A Variety of Lives; a Biography of Sir Hugh Greene* (1983, Bodley Head) and *The Decline and Fall of Public Service Broadcasting* (1998, Oxford University Press). Tracey has authored scores of articles on many aspects of media and communication, mainly on the history, condition and future of PSB. He is working on a biography of legendary BBC television executive, Donald Baversrock. Tracey has produced documentaries (with his friend and colleague David Mills) that have aired in the UK on Channel Four and ITV, in America on CBS, Court TV and A&E, and in other countries (about 20).

JOSEF TRAPPEL (Ph.D. 1986; Habilitation 2008) is Professor of Communication Policy and Media Economics at the University of Salzburg, Austria. He is Director of the Department for Communication Studies and Co-Director of the Center for Advanced Studies and Research in ICTs and Society (ICT&S). Before the current posting, he was the Head of IPMZ, the Centre for Knowledge Transfer and Applied Media Research at the Institute for Mass Communication and Media Research at the University of Zurich in Switzerland, and member of the Board of Directors of SwissGIS – the Swiss Centre for Studies on the Global Information Society. His scientific and research work concentrates on media and democracy, (digital) transformations in communication structures and their implications on society, national and international communication policy and media economics. Together with Werner A. Meier, he is the convener of the Euromedia Research Group.

HILDE VAN DEN BULCK (Ph.D. 2001 Katholieke Universiteit Leuven) is Full Professor of Communication Studies, Head of the Media Policy and Culture research group and Dean of the Faculty of Social and Political Sciences at the University of Antwerp. In 2014 she is also part time guest professor at the University of Bergen in Norway. Van den Bulck combines complementary expertise in the areas of media structures and policies with a focus on public service broadcasting, and of media culture and identities with a focus on celebrity culture. With regards to the former, she works on the (policy) history as well as on contemporary policy issues relating to public service broadcasting and its transition to public service media. She published on this topic in journals such as *Media, Culture and Society* (2001), *Convergence* (2008), *International Journal of Media and Cultural Politics* (with Hallvard Moe 2012) and *European Journal of Communication* (with Donders 2014), amongst others. She is vice-chair of the Communication Law and Policy section of ECREA and vice-president of NeFCA, the Netherlands-Flanders Communication Association.

Publications from Nordicom Regarding Public Service Media

Publications from RIPE

Regaining the Initiative for Public Service Media. RIPE@2011
Gregory Ferrell Lowe & Jeanette Steemers (eds) Nordicom, 2012, 203 p., ISBN 978-91-86523-33-6.

The Public in Public Service Media. RIPE@2009
Gregory Ferrell Lowe (ed.) Nordicom, 2010, 276 p., ISBN 978-91-978-91-86523-33-6.

From Public Service Broadcasting to Public Service Media. RIPE@2007
Gregory Ferrell Lowe & Jo Bardoel (eds) Nordicom, 2008, 259 p., ISBN 978-91-89471-53-5.

Cultural Dilemmas in Public Service Broadcasting. RIPE@2005
Gregory Ferrell Lowe & Per Jauert (eds) Nordicom, 2005, 330 p., ISBN 978-91-89471-32-6.

Broadcasting & Convergence. New Articulations of the Public Service Remit. RIPE@2003
Gregory Ferrell Lowe & Taisto Hujanen (eds) Nordicom, 2003, 335 p., ISBN 978-91-89471-18-0.
Available in PDF-format, free of charge, http://www.nordicom.gu.se/sites/default/files/publikationer-hela-pdf/81_ripe2003.pdf

A Nordic Public Service Media Map

A Nordic Public Service Media Map
Eva Harrie (compiled by) Nordicom, 2013, 90 p. (Nordic Public Service Media Map; 3), ISBN 978-91-86523-61-9.

Public Service Media from a Nordic Horizon. Politics, Markets. Programming and Users
Ulla Carlsson (ed.) Nordicom, 2013, 176 p. (Nordic Public Service Media Map; 2), ISBN 978-91-86523-60-2.

Public Service Media in the Nordic Countries – Facts & Figures
Eva Harrie (compiled by) Nordicom, 2012, 168 p. (Nordic Public Service Media Map; 1), ISBN 978-91-86523-37-4.

Other Publications

Swedish Broadcasting. Communicative Ethos, Genres and Institutional Change
Monika Djerf-Pierre & Mats Ekström (eds) Nordicom, 2013, 379 p., ISBN 978-91-86523-73-2.

Exporting the Public Value Test.
The Regulation of Public Broadcasters' New Media Services Across Europe
Karen Donders & Hallvard Moe (eds) Nordicom, 2011, 188 p. ISBN 978-91-86523-26-8.

Small Among Giants. Television Broadcasting in Smaller Countries'
Gregory Ferrell Lowe & Christian S. Nissen (eds) Nordicom, 2011, 231 p., ISBN 978-91-86523-16-9.

The Digital Public Sphere. Challenges for Media Policy
Jostein Gripsrud & Hallvard Moe (eds) 2010, 168 p., ISBN 978-91-86523-02-2.